FOOD MOBILITIES

CULINARIA

Food for Thought
Food for Pleasure
Food for Change

Series Editors

Jayeeta (Jo) Sharma (Toronto)
H. Rosi Song (Durham)
Robert Davidson (Toronto)

EDITED BY DANIEL E. BENDER
AND SIMONE CINOTTO

Food Mobilities

Making World Cuisines

UNIVERSITY OF TORONTO PRESS
Toronto Buffalo London

© University of Toronto Press 2024
Toronto Buffalo London
utorontopress.com

ISBN 978-1-4875-0902-6 (cloth)   ISBN 978-1-4875-3954-2 (EPUB)
ISBN 978-1-4875-2649-8 (paper)   ISBN 978-1-4875-3953-5 (PDF)

Library and Archives Canada Cataloguing in Publication

Title: Food mobilities : making world cuisines / edited by Daniel E. Bender
    and Simone Cinotto.
Names: Bender, Daniel E., editor. | Cinotto, Simone, editor.
Description: Series statement: Culinaria ; 1 | Includes bibliographical
    references and index.
Identifiers: Canadiana (print) 20230449344 | Canadiana
    (ebook) 20230449433 | ISBN 9781487509026 (cloth) |
    ISBN 9781487526498 (paper) | ISBN 9781487539535 (PDF) |
    ISBN 9781487539542 (EPUB)
Subjects: LCSH: Food – Case studies. | LCSH: Food habits – Case studies. |
    LCSH: Food consumption – Case studies. | LCSH: International cooking –
    Case studies. | LCSH: Globalization – Case studies. | LCGFT: Case studies.
Classification: LCC GN407 .F66 2024 | DDC 394.1/2–dc24

Cover design: Sandra Friesen
Cover and title page image: Yara Ferreira Clüver

We wish to acknowledge the land on which the University of Toronto
Press operates. This land is the traditional territory of the Wendat, the
Anishnaabeg, the Haudenosaunee, the Métis, and the Mississaugas of the
Credit First Nation.

University of Toronto Press acknowledges the financial support of the
Government of Canada, the Canada Council for the Arts, and the Ontario Arts
Council, an agency of the Government of Ontario, for its publishing activities.

Canada Council   Conseil des Arts
for the Arts   du Canada

ONTARIO ARTS COUNCIL
CONSEIL DES ARTS DE L'ONTARIO
an Ontario government agency
un organisme du gouvernement de l'Ontario

Funded by the   Financé par le
Government   gouvernement   Canada
of Canada   du Canada

Contents

Illustrations

FOOD MOBILITIES

Introduction: Mobility and the Making of World Cuisines

DANIEL E. BENDER AND SIMONE CINOTTO

Food Mobilities: Making World Cuisines places the entwined, historical mobility of peoples, plants and animals, food goods, and commodities at the centre of our understandings of the emergence of modern cuisines. The volume brings together food scholars using the conceptual and analytical frame of mobility studies. In its many forms, mobility has been the essential category of analysis in the study of food, at least since the publication of Sidney Mintz's landmark *Sweetness and Power: The Place of Sugar in Modern History*.[1] In his field-defining text, Mintz identified the multiple mobilities that, since the sixteenth century, transformed sugar: the global circulation of the commodity itself; the technologies and political formations that enabled its movement; the mobilization of labour, notably slaves; the movement of capital; the global mutations of taste; and the shifts in the social meanings of sugar across time and space. These entwined mobilities, Mintz demonstrated, remade sugar from a plant of Southeast Asian origin into an imperial commodity cultivated in Caribbean plantations that transformed human, animal, and botanical biodiversities across the globe.

In the quarter-century since Mintz published *Sweetness and Power*, food studies, as a multidisciplinary field, has both contributed to and depended on the study of diverse forms of mobility. Food studies scholars have powerfully demonstrated the ways the production and consumption of food is shaped by – and, in turn, shapes – the mobilities of humans, plants, animals, microorganisms, capital, and ideas. Key studies of food as it relates to migration, food and empire, food aid, food systems and commodity chains, culinary tourism, and even food nationalism all acknowledge overlapping mobilities.

Food is grounded in place through conceptualizations of cuisine, nation, region, climate, regulation, and terroir, but the development of the human diet over time depends on mobility. This recognition opens a dialogue between food studies and mobility studies, an approach that acknowledges that our world is on the move. Mobility is an omnipresent part of the experience of modernity, so much that immobility also needs to be conceptualized as a condition rather than as a given. Societies, cultures, and identities, including foodways and cuisines, must therefore be studied as mobile, in flux, and crossed by translocal connections.

This approach represents a departure in the social science and humanities that have often treated societies as static.[2] *Food Mobilities* accordingly connects themes and methods in the study of migration, food systems, and food globalization. Migration studies, when focused on food, has insisted on food insecurity as a motive for migration and has explored migrant foodways as the re-articulation of identities and economic opportunities within diasporas. Labour and slavery studies have chronicled the mobilization of peoples often for the production of food commodities. Within food studies, scholars have traced commodity chains and global food systems. Historically, if we scratch the surface of the claims of traditional cuisine and tangible cultural heritage, whether local, regional, or national, we find mobility. It took the agency and selective assessment of generations of mobile farmers, traders, cooks, and eaters to incorporate ingredients, even from long distances, in the material and symbolic landscapes of taste we call cuisines.

Change over time, the essays in this collection demonstrate, is crucial to the ways food studies contributes to and is informed by mobility studies. Rather than a compendium of approaches to applying the mobility paradigm to the study of food, *Food Mobilities* offers a specific focus on the making of world cuisines with broad methodological and chronological application. The essays in this volume illustrate how mobility is movement across space but grounded in time and systematized by varying social formations. The volume adds specificity to understanding how that mobility changes over time, partly through various disciplinary approaches (including from food history) that theorize the chronological. As well, *Food Mobilities* brings a historical lens to our understanding of mobility studies, a corrective, we believe, to a field that, as it diverged from migration studies, tended to shed the temporal. Mobility studies, as it relates to food, can privilege food chains over local identities and historical contingencies. This collection focuses especially on change over time in its relationship to culinary practice and tradition, social movements, and cross-cultural encounters.

Change over time helps us think, especially, about immobility and labour. Immobility is rarely conceptualized within mobility studies and labour is typically treated as an input, rather than central to the way communities negotiate an industrializing food system. This volume deliberately focuses on the bottom-up and on the experiences and movements of working people. The essays in *Food Mobilities*, as well, employ a chronological approach to highlight the sensory: eating, cooking, tasting, and provisioning practices. Taste, too – Mintz's work on sugar again demonstrates – has a lot to reveal about mobility.

Together, these essays chart change and progression, a concentration as clear in overtly historical essays, such as those by Bender, Cinotto, Diner, Ipsen, Mendiola-Garcia, Pilcher, Sharma, and Zanoni, as in the more contemporary ones such as those by El-Sayed and Spackman, Elton, Hull, Ray, Rousseau, and Vandebroek. This focus allows *Food Mobilities* to move towards the present, identifying the key factors that today and in the coming years will propel mobility, including climate change or global tourism. We conceptualize future circulations through a recognition of how mobilities are shaped, accelerated, experienced, and contested over time.

We begin, then, with a glass of vermouth and the mobilities that shape its flavours.

Food That Moves Us: Food Mobilities, the Body, and the Self

In 1869, when Federico Peliti was just twenty-five years old, he dreamed of working as a sculptor. At that point, his life remained firmly bound within the political borders of his native Piemonte in northern Italy. Over the next few decades, politics and empire drew Peliti away from Piemonte and away from the fine arts. During Italy's Risorgimento, the peninsula's era of reunification, he served in the calvary. After reunification, he moved to British colonial India, lured by employment as a pastry maker to the Viceroy.

However, the 1872 assassination of the British sub-regent delayed Peliti's spectacular rise from rural Italy anonymity to colonial prestige. Rather than returning to Europe, the Italian pastry maker remained in the British colony, where he eventually opened several successful restaurants, selling pastry and vermouth. He built a colonial restaurant chain, based on British imperial expectations of Continental foods as the mark of distinction and their growing reluctance to sample local foods. Thus, when the Prince of Wales visited Burma in 1891, Peliti prepared a banquet for the prince using food grown, produced, and processed in Italy and transported to India. The prince's foods travelled along commercial arteries of steamships, canals, and open oceans. These were the routes that carried seeds, wheat and other commodities, canned goods, bottled wines and spirits, and meats back and forth between European metropoles and their colonies. In India, Peliti manufactured his own signature vermouth from indigenous Italian grapes aromatized with Indian spices – a drink born from the mobilities of empire.[3]

Peliti's vermouth bottles a journey from the counters of the medieval pharmacy to the shelves of contemporary liquor stores. Vermouth began as a medicinal concoction of herbs and spices, some imported from afar. With mobile entrepreneurs like Peliti in the age of empire, it became a drink to enjoy with food. In a pastry shop in India, it represented a mark of leisure and a civilized way to digest the exotic tastes of the colony. This journey highlights the larger movement of food within the boundaries of edibility, into the body itself, and across political, social, and cultural spaces.

The human relationship to food is one of mobility. We grow it and move it. We collect it, transform ingredients into food through cooking, and, in the very last few centimetres of the food chain, we bring food towards us with hands, forks, or chopsticks. Nutritionally, food moves through the body. Our digestive system, from the mouth, down the esophagus and into the stomach, the intestines, and, finally, the rectum, is an infrastructure of highways and roads, channels, chutes, and conduits. There is an occasional regulator of traffic, such as the liver, the pancreas, and the kidneys. Congestion of the traffic, or clogged mobility, as in constipation, is a condition of the system that needs to be cured (sometimes with other food and sometimes with medicine, ingestible, but not always defined as food). Writ large, this model of nutrition also reads like a representation of an urban food system: food comes into the city – the urban body – and waste is removed.

Even the critical decision about ingesting or refusing to eat an item involves mobility. If we decide to consider something as food and choose to eat it, our body moves towards it. Refusal is expressed in the movement of our body away from it.[4] Ethnobotanists study how human groups, farmers and pastoralists, variably place different plants, animals, and minerals inside or outside the sphere of the edible. A bad weed to extirpate for some is foraged for food by others. These scholars suggest that human and non-human migration and intercultural exchange are fundamental to the creative search for the edible and the choice. The ingenious results they produce become part the making of cuisine.[5]

Early in the development of food studies, structuralist anthropologist Mary Douglas and materialist anthropologist Marvin Harris debated a foundational question: why we do not eat everything that is edible. The same fruit or part of the dead animal can be welcome food for some, but forbidden, religiously taboo, or disgusting to others in different places and times. In her *Purity and Danger* (1968), Douglas suggested that food taboos, such as the Jewish prohibition on pork, reflect underlying binary oppositions around definitions of the pure and the impure, the safe and the polluting. Food, argued Douglas, must be good to think before we move toward it and eat it.[6] In his *Good to Eat: Riddles of Food and Culture* (1985), Harris countered Douglas' view, arguing that it is the balance between the costs and benefits of the production of any single food in its environmental and social context that sanctions its edibility. Harris pointed out that pork was widely consumed in the Middle East when forests covered the westernmost sections of the Fertile Crescent, an ideal landscape for pigs that do not sweat and require shade and water. Climate change and desertification turned pig farming and pork consumption into excessively costly practices, and the pig – forced by deforestation and by domestication to roll in mud and its own feces in its pigsty to find solace from the heat – became an "abominable" animal for Judaism and Islam, two of the three monotheist religions born in the Middle East. For Harris, food needs to be good to eat before becoming good to think.[7]

While useful lenses on the mobility of nutrients in and out the sphere of edibility, Douglas' and Harris' different approaches to food choices are, in fact, both static. They do not account for exchange and spatial mobility. As well, they largely gloss over the fact that not all that enters the body is understood as food. Some comestibles are redefined culturally as medicine, not edible, but ingestible.[8] Others are intoxicants and stimulants, ingested for somatic, rather than nutritive, reasons.[9] As the case of Peliti's vermouth suggests, mobility links food industrialization, processing, transportation, and medical, nutritional knowledge, sometimes institutionalized into sciences. Histories of contact, exchange, and movement reveal trajectories that, in different times and places, define something as worth ingesting or delicious rather than abominable, disgusting, or dangerous.

Even our emotional relationship to food and cuisine evokes movement. We take seriously the "motion" embedded in "emotion." As Douglas and Harris implicitly agree, food sparks excitement, pride, nostalgia, happiness, trust, comfort, and disappointment. Because food enters powerfully in the creation of self from early socialization, starting with breastfeeding, it defines identity within families and broader imagined communities. Food expresses and represents individual and collective identities and politics. This might include, for example, national belonging or veganism.

Because of this convergence of emotional relationships to food and identification with and through different ingredients and recipes, food shapes our sense of affiliation and motivates us to act. It mobilizes us. A national taste for food can even precede the formation of the political nation-state or help forge communities in diasporas.[10] Mobile and nomadic people, in particular, experience food as a source and expression of belonging. In related ways, the omnivorous engagement with culinary diversities, often expressed as virtual tourism of cuisines, can be a source of distinction.[11] *Food Mobilities* incorporates notions of cultural identity, ethics, edibility, and religion into a discussion of mobility. Ideas about the symbolic, sensory, and ethical/religious approach to food are linked to the physical mobility of ingredients, producers, consumers, and knowledge.

A Safeway in Fairbanks: Infrastructures and Pathways of Food Mobilities

Food moves. There is a Safeway supermarket in Fairbanks, Alaska, about 300 kilometres from the Arctic Circle. That part of Alaska has a growing season measured in mere weeks. The Safeway, though, sells arborio rice from Italy, jasmine-scented long grain rice from Thailand, and basmati rice grown in Texas (and re-branded Texmati). In the seafood case, Alaskan wild salmon (flown daily in the summer from coastal rivers to inland Fairbanks), nestles alongside frozen shrimp from Thailand, Florida, or Vietnam. In a city that advertises its geographic isolation and cold climate to tourists, visitors can snap a family photograph posed next to the world's most northern jackfruit (for sale whole or in slices). Scholars might employ multiple methodologies to explain the food mobilities visible in a supermarket like this one. In an elegant study of commodity chains that supply fresh vegetables to European supermarkets, Susanne Freidberg reveals the exporters, importers, growers, and other agents that bring African-grown beans to French and English supermarkets in a matter of hours. Freidberg challenges a model of "diffusion" in which foodstuffs simply diffuse globally. Rather, she demonstrates, the fresh economy finds its roots and routes in older colonial and postcolonial resource-extraction economies.[12]

Eight minutes farther south from the Safeway along the Parks Highway is Lemongrass Thai restaurant, advertising "authentic Thai cuisine with Alaskan ingredients." The basil, beets, bok choy, broccoli, cabbage, zucchini, and so many more greens, the restaurant boasts, are grown – seasonally – in Alaska. Sockeye salmon is chopped and cooked with rice powder, shallots, mint, kaffir lime, and lemongrass.[13] Multiple mobilities account for Thai cuisine in Fairbanks, the popularity of the food for tourists and locals, and the labour, knowledge, and ingredients needed to support restaurants in a small, subarctic city. Take the case of Laong and Charlie Boonprasert. Laong owns the Thai House restaurant in Fairbanks which her late husband, Charlie, opened in 1989. Charlie migrated first to Alaska to work in a gold mine, but soon found employment serving in a Chinese restaurant. He dreamed of opening the city's first Thai restaurant. Though hesitant about the cold weather, Laong finally moved to Fairbanks. Other owners of Fairbanks' Thai restaurants, including those at Lemongrass Thai, began their careers working in the Thai House's kitchen.[14]

Gendered patterns of migration draw men like Charlie to Alaskan resource extraction industries, like gold mining or oil drilling. Similar patterns shaped older diasporas, specifically Chinese, and, today, Chinese restaurants in Alaska provide contemporary migrants with restaurant work in slack seasons and industry downturns. Long-distance global trade that has turned Anchorage into an airline, if not geographical, centre of the world, provides for the rapid movement of agricultural commodities, including that jackfruit. At the same time, the scale of Asian migration to Alaska, the popularity of Thai food throughout the state, and the value-assigned to "local" ingredients creates opportunities, especially for ethnic entrepreneurs, to produce the Thai basil that Lemongrass advertises as "seasonal Alaska grown vegetables." Understanding Thai cuisine in Alaska or subarctic jackfruit demands attention to what Valerie Imbruce calls "the social network of trade." Imbruce identifies webs of distribution, enabled by ties of cuisine, culture, and ethnicity, that provide a vast diversity of plants to New York City's Chinatown – or to a Fairbanks restaurant.[15] Culinary tourism, what Lucy Long defines as "exploring foods new to them as well as using food to explore new cultures and ways of being," has transformed both rural and urban Alaskan public dining.[16] Even as Alaska heavily promotes "local" food – and Lemongrass advertises its "Alaskan Curried Crab" – Fairbanks, by 2016, supported fourteen Thai restaurants. "The tours," noted a local tourist promoter, "they want to eat Thai food."[17]

Food moves because someone moves it, sometimes a larger-scale importer, sometimes an individual, saving seeds or carrying finished products. Far from diffusing locally or globally, the movement of food depends on labour (human, mechanical, and animal). Food mobility responds to desires that, in turn, spring from human mobility. Take the example of jackfruit, edible evidence of an Alaskan city that is being reshaped by migration. Though Fairbanks remains majority white (58 per cent) and American-born (92.4 per cent), immigrant populations are growing. People of self-identified Asian origin compose 5 per cent of

Fairbanks' population, almost equal the city's Native Alaskan popula-tion, and 54 per cent of foreign-born residents claim Asian origin.[18]

"Foods and culinary cultures," notes Elizabeth Zanoni, "do not simply diffuse or spread across the world, disconnected from mobile people."[19] Zanoni's concept of "migrant marketplaces," the "global commercial spaces defined by physical and imagined links between themselves and their traveling foods and culinary experiences," helps explain the remarkable transfer of Southeast Asian ingredients and cuisine to the subarctic. Thai food in Fairbanks is the result of the mobility of culinary knowledge, diasporic longings, social mobility, and infrastructures of transport and retail. Mobility produces world cuisines belonging to both real and imagined spaces. Lemongrass' claims to authenticity as northern Thai cuisine depend on the real migrant experience of "our chef Gor," who has "refined" his "authentic recipes with his own style which he has refined since 1996 when he first started up the restaurant in far-away Alaska." Belonging is, paradoxically, a question of mobility. As well, that authenticity is maintained by long-distance ties of migrant entrepreneurship; Lemongrass has another location in the night bazaar in Chiang Mai, Thailand, just behind a Burger King and McDonald's.

The Menu in Chiang Mai: Food Mobilities, Human Mobilities, and Immobilities

Mobility is good to think with at the McDonald's in Chiang Mai, a des-tination for tourists and labour migrants from rural areas. The global fast-food chain is located at the heart of the city's night market at a place where the local mobility of vegetables, fish, and meat joins the transnational circulation of industrially produced foods. McDonald's in Chiang Mai offers a tangible, quickly cooked example of the multiple mobilities that make world cuisines.

As James L. Watson reminds: "East Asian consumers have quietly, and in some cases, stubbornly transformed their neighborhood McDonald's into local institutions."[20] The same can be argued in Southeast Asia, as McDonald's has arrived and set up locations even in the heart of local areas of public dining, like the Chiang Mai night bazaar. Watson and his co-authors' insistence on understanding the relationship of place and the local to global fast food helps understand the multiple mobili-ties that bring a McDonald's to a Thai night market. They point to the food chains that enable the mass mobilization of ingredients and tech-nologies; the global transmission of tastes; the transformation of the exotic into the quotidian; the proliferation of food knowledge, includ-ing through digital media; and the very speed of eating itself. As well, they interrogate the relationship of fast food to other forms of mobile dining, including street stalls common in places like a night bazaar and urban market, and the relationship of corporate/fast foods to regional, national, and local cuisines. As Zanoni has noted, dishes, restaurants, and industries are transformed by the very fact of movement and the demands of local consumers. Ingredients from aboard merge with those available locally in the movement of recipes, sometimes as the informal sharing of knowledge or more formally in cookbooks or more recently, digitally.[21] In the night bazaar, cultural knowledge circulating globally about fast food links to more local understandings of street foods – a curious amalgam of mobile foods.

At the McDonald's in Chiang Mai, some offerings, such as the inevitable Big Mac, reflect the large-scale circulation of foods and recipes, and the knowledge around them that identify them as American. Others, like the Samurai Burger, suggest a more complex mobility of fast food. As well, customers can order McDonald's krapao gai grob – a basil fried chicken that is a staple Thai street food. Like Lemongrass Thai in Fairbanks, McDonald's in Chiang Mai reflects and caters to a mobile experience of dining for customers and cooking for employees. They together enforce corporeal, economic, and cultural encounters with global mobility, local ingredients, and regional cuisine, what Bell and Valentine describe as "movement and mixing."[22]

Krapao in a McDonald's in Chiang Mai and curried snow crab on the menu at Lemongrass in Fairbanks penetrate the dichotomy between fast food and cuisine. As Watson asks: "does the spread of fast food undermine the integrity of indigenous cuisines?"[23] Such a framing raises two key questions: first, is the "integrity" of cuisine understood by scholars, cooks, and diners by its economic, political, and cultural grounding in place? Second, is the notion of cuisine as "indigenous" a nod to the idea of cuisine as somehow "undermined" by certain kinds of mobilities? Moreover, Watson's use of the term "indigenous" (perhaps without intention) invites examination of the ways the very articulation of cuisine depended on both the expulsion and denigration of ingredients vital to Indigenous communities and the appropriation of their food-producing lands. In their encounter with settler colonialism, Native Alaskan communities, 15 per cent of the Alaska's population, have grappled with histories that turned edible animals from salmon to seals, the basis for local foodways, into global commodities. Missionaries and government agents together worked to substitute foods imported from the lower forty-eight states for subsistence food production, and, since World War II, Native Alaskans have struggled to defend the cultural and legal right to harvest migratory marine animals, including for food.[24]

Sarah Gibson notes that "food is good to think mobilities with," and, we argue, the reverse is true as well.[25] Mobilities are good to think food with, providing new understandings of the making of world cuisines. The point is not simply that food engages multiple mobilities, but, even more, that mobility around food is necessarily plural. We turn to mobilities to consider the emergence of cuisines, even if cuisines are rhetorically and politically grounded in articulations of national and regional belonging that frequently expelled the Indigenous. "Regional cuisines," noted Sidney Mintz, "contribute to the appearance of a national cuisine because ingredients, cooking methods, and dishes drawn from regional cuisines become the repertory of chefs who cook for persons whose knowledge, taste, and means transcend locality."[26] Arjun Appadurai further distinguishes cuisine from cooking (as the production of ingredients into something edible).[27] We extend that understanding to consider the ways the articulation of cuisine through place demarcates cultural, political, and social boundaries, even as it expresses, what Uma Narayan calls "personal and collective identities." Cuisine is the interplay of cooking methods and culturally and economically significant ingredients, produced in socially important sites of private and public dining. It is articulated in ways that engage discourses of belonging, including national, diasporic, ethnic, or regional, as well as exclusion. The "complicated and sometimes contradictory cultural meanings" that Narayan locates in the British "fabrication" of curry powder, speak even more broadly to the tension between lived experiences of multiple mobilities and the expression of cuisine.[28]

A McDonald's in Thailand and a Thai restaurant in Alaska are grounded, multiple places. Yet both assert claims to belonging. One offers fast food versions of local street foods, suggesting a locally comprehensible way of consuming foods of faraway origins. The other, by advertising Alaskan produce, highlights the locality of migrant food, yet ignores longer histories of Indigenous food production. Our goal here is not to locate a unitary formula to account for historic, contemporary, and global food mobility. Different cases, we argue, demand different methodologies. "Food traditions," notes Krishnendu Ray, "are as much a matter of movement and emplacement, as they are of roots."[29] Each of those concepts, from tradition to movement, have unique histories. Jeffrey Pilcher argues that the case of the taco, once unknown outside of Mexico, but, today, available virtually everywhere, "raises larger questions about the nature of globalization." It also raises specific questions, notably about "how foreigners think about Mexican food and how Mexicans understand their own national cuisine."[30] The story of tea, while equally a narrative about the globalization of food, follows a different trajectory. As Erika Rappaport notes, tea, as drink, drug, and commodity, calls attention to the ways the British Empire altered vast environments; mobilized millions of workers; and transformed taste through advertising, retail, and infrastructures of distribution. As well, as Jayeeta Sharma notes in this volume, the British Empire actively devalued local and Indigenous knowledge about tea and its production.[31] Tacos and tea each call attention to questions of nation, empire, infrastructure, environment, and labour, but their significance as mobile foods depends on the contingencies of their histories.

That attention to specificity is how we both engage with the mobility turn and refine it for food studies scholars. John Urry has argued that "the analysis of mobilities transforms social science," and while much the same can be said specifically about food studies, it is also true that the circulation of food commodities, plants, animals, resources, and labour have individually long been at the centre of this field.[32] The utility of the engagement with the "mobility turn" helps identify the overlapping, multiple mobilities that together make world cuisines. In a valuable parallel to what has been a focus of food scholarship, Urry insists on the centrality of social interaction. Culinary encounters need not be in person. "But," note Monika Büscher and Urry, "many connections with peoples and social groupings are not based upon propinquity."[33] The case of fast food in Chiang Mai produces very real encounters between locals and American tourists, and, as well, more virtual encounters between Thai and American consumers who realize, mid-bite, that they are eating similar foods in fairly similar outlets located continents apart. That moment, challenging for diners the spatial belonging of what they are eating, represents another aspect in the long association of eating and travel.

We argue here that food mobilities can be understood, necessarily as plural, as an amalgam of material, social, and imaginative mobility, what Urry calls "interdependent 'mobilities.'" The very real "corporeal travel" that includes migration, forced or coerced movement, and tourism, as well as the circulatory travel of someone like Peliti, joins the "physical movement of objects."[34] Mobility, too, includes "imaginative travel" and "virtual travel." An advertisement for tea aimed at the British drinker, for example, might evoke the faraway Indian tea garden. If an advertisement promotes particular fantasies about land and people, "communicative travel" demands attention to flows of and contests over food knowledge.[35] James Clifford, in shifting the focus of analysis from places to the routes linking them, identifies "travels and contacts" as "crucial sites for an unfinished modernity."[36] Cuisine, as something that incorporates the products of empire, traces the boundaries of inclusion and exclusion, and as an urgent political project linking cooking to spatial belonging, is one of those key sites of unfinished modernity.

Cooking Tomatoes: Food Mobilities, Biodiversity, Taste, and Nation

Another sip of Peliti's vermouth: wines from the Italian region of Piedmont travelled the rails and routes of colonial infrastructure all the way to a segregated eating establishment where Indian spices combined in a cultural alchemy to produce an Italian vermouth marketed to British colonial drinkers. By contrast, salmon, caught in the midst of their migration up Alaskan rivers, cleaned, prepped, and favoured with Alaskan-grown herbs and vegetables by migrant chefs remains Thai.

The making of world cuisines defines communities through claims to spatial belonging, while still drawing upon ingredients from afar. In the project of defining what is within and what is outside of cuisine, ingredients can be naturalized, like Indian spices that mark Piemontese wine as Italian vermouth. Other ingredients might be gathered locally but in the hands of migrant or otherwise racialized cooks remain outside of what Michelle King calls "food based ethno-nationalism."[37] Thus, as Lily Cho notes, food served in a Chinese restaurant in rural Canada might actually include fries and burgers and that restaurant might serve as a local gathering place. Yet both the foods and the restaurant remain firmly outside of any nascent Canadian claims to cuisine.[38] As King writes: "every cuisine is merely the claim of some people, from some region, which highlights their own food, while erasing, marginalizing, and misrepresenting culinary cultures of the margins and minorities."[39]

That recognition reflects both the instability of cuisine as an ethno-national project and the political need to define spatial claims in the face of the mobility of cooks, ingredients, recipes, and diners. We call attention to the "biodiversity of cuisine," as it might be termed. By this we mean: first, a very real biodiversity, that is, the particular set of ingredients that are incorporated within cuisine or rejected in the project of defining a cuisine. This project includes, of course, the compilation and publication of national cookbooks and, more recently, state-led campaigns that define national cuisine as "intangible cultural heritage."[40] Second, we locate a particular kind of taxonomy in which certain material items are given symbolic values as choice, edible, disgusting, medical, toxic, luxurious, and more. Third, we call attention to the patterns of movement through which ingredients are introduced and incorporated. These patterns represent, in effect, a re-localizing process of ingredients. Finally, we recognize that cuisines are made through a cultural use of, and a selective attack on, biodiversity. The processes of human mobility catalyze the movement of seeds, plants, animals, germs, and vectors, which, in turn, transform environments. Through culinary practices, farmers, artisans, vendors, cooks, and eaters reconcile the tension between the experience of exchange, trade, and movement, and claims to a taste of place that are integral not only to the articulation of cuisine but also to expressions of "terroir."[41]

A colonial vermouth is an aromatic example of the articulation of biodiversity crucial to the making of world cuisine. As a political project of both incorporation and exclusion, cuisine must make sense of food mobilities. Italian cuisine, specifically, reconciled realities of a vast diaspora and the trade and encounters it produced with claims to local, regional, and national belonging.

A relatively small territory, the narrow Italian peninsula extends from the northern half-moon crown of the Alps directly into the centre of the Mediterranean Sea, with Sicily at the latitude of Northern Africa. A densely populated, hilly land with few plains available for extensive crop agriculture, the Italian countryside impelled generations of farmers, in the face of pervasive hunger, to figure out how to process limited crops into a variety of preservable and transportable foodstuffs. The relationship between food and place is firmly established in Italian culture. Even classical Roman writers such as Virgil and Cicero extolled foods like ricotta cheese and prosciutto associated with particular places and peoples. Today, recipes like alla bolognese and alla napoletana evidence regional cuisines. However, ingredients like tomatoes, peppers, corn, potatoes, and most types of beans, reached Italy as part of the Columbian Exchange, and many others arrived from the Islamic world. Italy today boasts the highest number of local specialty foods recognized, patented, and labelled as Protected Denomination of Origin (PDO) by the European Union, since the introduction in 1992 of the law identifying Geographic Indication of Origin (PGI) foods.

Regionality and mobility coexist and the identification of food with place is articulated at the moment of its mobility. Though codified in law as local, the foods produced by Italian farmers' selection and hybridization of seeds, plants, and animal breeds, as well as their development of food processing actually produced foods well adapted to mobility within and beyond the Italian peninsula. As Alberto Capatti and Massimo Montanari have argued, Italian local specialty foods and culinary identities depended on networks of trade and exchange.[42] Take the case of Parmigiano: the eponymous cheese dusting pastas across Italy's vast diaspora was already a shared "Italian" taste long before Italy became a nation state. Once produced solely in a monastery in the plains between Parma and Reggio Emilia from the monks' own cows and for their own consumption, the cheese became inextricably entwined with the city of Parma only when it was distributed broadly.

The articulation of biodiversity within cuisine also valorizes some ingredients and their producers while explicitly excluding others. Postmodern and post-Marxist progressive food movements like Slow Food aim to protect Italian regional cuisines from corporate standardization. Such movements claim independent farmers as guardians of biodiversity. Yet in the 1930s, fascism also celebrated regional cuisines as part of its autarchic, racist, and imperialist project. Contemporary neonationalist right-wing populists have followed the Fascist model in representing cuisine as the purest expression of local cultures and landscapes. They cite cuisine as the tangible, edible evidence of how immigration, multiculturalism, and supranationalism threaten national sovereignty. Thus, in 2009, the right-wing administration of the Tuscan city of Lucca prohibited the opening of any restaurants within the walls of the old town that did not serve "traditional" local food, as a way to halt the "invasion" of immigrants' ethnic cuisines.[43]

Food Mobilities demonstrates that, contrary to xenophobic gastropopulists' propaganda, the process of food localization and the making of cuisine demands mobile peoples.[44] Today, Italian food and biodiversity can exist only because of the work of the thousands of international migrants from the Global South who harvest the grapes, pick the fruits and the tomatoes, butcher the pigs, and milk the cows from which Parmigiano Reggiano PDO cheese is made. Sikh migrants, for example, compose a large segment of the labour force of the Po Valley's dairy industry.[45]

Consider the tomato, a key part of the biodiversity of Italian cuisine. The tomato, South American in botanical origin, became by the nineteenth century a gustatory emblem of Italian cuisine. In 1548, in one of the first recorded appearances of tomato in Italy, the Florentine lord Cosimo de' Medici received a basket of the golden fruit (in Italian, pomodoro) directly from the New World. For most of the following two centuries, interest in the tomato remained confined to intellectual and professional elites: botanists describing a taxonomy of plants from the Americas; physicians locating the new plants' nutritional qualities within the humoral medicine of the time; and court chefs tentatively wondering what use to make of new ingredients. The tomato remained an ornamental plant until southern Italian farmers began cultivating tomatoes for harvest in the hottest weeks of the summer when little else could be grown. Such farmers turned to the tomato at a time when they were struggling with dramatic population growth and consequent Malthusian unsustainability of the local food system. Just as important, farmers discovered that tomato juice, when heated with fire and painstakingly stirred under the hot southern Italian sun, produced a preservable and transportable tomato paste (in Italian, conserva).[46]

The transatlantic Italian tomato demonstrates how foods are localized as they become mobile. Given the meanings assigned to ingredients within the biodiversity of cuisine, their consumption can also announce social mobility. The industrialization of the tomato through the mass production of canned products and the gastronomic innovations of saucing pasta and, slightly later, pizza were mutually reinforcing processes. By the turn of the twentieth century, Italian canned tomato products and manufactured semolina pasta, along with hard cheese and canned olive oil, composed an Italian food industry that found a mass market in the large Italian immigrant enclaves of cities like New York and Buenos Aires. This market as yet was non-existent in mostly rural and poor Italy. For such migrants, who rarely had enjoyed those foods at home, the opportunity to consume canned tomatoes and industrially manufactured pasta represented a significant sign of social mobility.[47]

Consumption of and knowledge about "ethnic cuisines," whether through travelling or eating out at "ethnic restaurants" – at the same time an act of actual and figurative mobility – are means of accumulating cultural and social capital for global middle-class eaters with disposable money and time.[48] Migrant entrepreneurs and workers, overrepresented in the global agro-food industry, depend for their social mobility upon their exclusive cultural and social capital, that is, their knowledge of desirable foods, markets, and tastes of their intended customers.

However, food mobilities can also be factors of downward social mobility. The extensive industrial farming of products, like the tomato, intended for a global commodities market, concentrates where the land is inexpensive, and labour is non-unionized. This concentration is often accompanied by land grabbing, desertification, climate change, and the coerced movement of Indigenous populations. Analyzing the global tomato in the age of deregulation reveals overlapping mobilities: corporate capital, which freely and swiftly moves financial resources, farming operations, labour, and distribution markets; and workers, forced to migrate over short and long distances.

Their labours are increasingly temporary, seasonal, disposable, feminized, and non-unionized.[49] The inequality compounded by corporate global agroindustry in the sites of food production, just as in places of food distribution and consumption, combined with its toxic impact on the environment and the impoverishment of biodiversity have motivated food-centred social movements. From the Black Panthers to Via Campesina to Slow Food, social movements promoting food security, food justice, and food sovereignty are often as mobile and concerned with the local and the global as the agroindustries they confront.[50] Contemporary movements build upon a heritage of food rebellions. E.P. Thompson noted that food riots tended to increase in number and intensity with the emergence of the modern state, because of the collapse of the "moral economies" in which lords and elites recognized an obligation to care for the starving populace in times of famines. Poor crowds expected to receive such emergency help. Modern mobs have been excited more because of the betrayal of elite's moral obligations than because of physical hunger.[51]

Both the French Revolution of 1798 and the Russian Revolution of 1917 started with enraged crowds demanding bread. In those and other occasions, women were at the forefront of the mobs, as the nature of the protest, so inherent to their publicly legitimated maternal role of nurturers to their children, allowed them to claim and occupy a public space and polity otherwise denied to them. In the context of today's dramatic crises of ideologies and traditional party politics, food as basic right and universal political language has become the issue of choice for contemporary social movements addressing questions of race, gender, class, and the environment in global perspective. The remarkably global legibility of such movements urges scholars of food mobilities to consider the pathways that food travels around the globe without sitting back and admiring the sheer ability to deliver, for example, fresh tuna to a landlocked sushi bar. It also demands that we recognize what is at stake, economically, socially, and environmentally.

Essays in Food Mobilities

Donna Gabaccia's opening essay puts food mobilities in a long and global historical perspective. The mobile, early hominids populating Africa 50,000 years ago consumed immobile plants until they needed to move on in search of new vegetable resources. As well, they followed animal herds. Between 30,000 and 3,000 years ago, this food-seeking mobility encouraged *homo sapiens* to spread to all continents. About 15,000 years ago, with the introduction of settled agriculture, more sedentary humans and travelling foods integrated nomadic hunting, gathering, and pastoralism. As part of this process, cities developed marketplaces for the exchange of mobile food. From its origins to the contemporary, food systems emerged out of the tension between mobile foods and localized food practices and ideas.

The chapters that follow this broad chronological intervention are organized in four sections, each addressing the connections between the intimate, emotional, entrepreneurial, and symbolic relations of mobility to systems of food politics, production, processing, exchange, and consumption.

"The Body and the Self" concentrates on the scale of the body and the mobilities of food toward, within, and away from the body. The essays in this section collectively conceptualize the mobile relationships people establish with the plants, animals, nutrients, and germs they ingest or refuse. Humans turn away from many foods, even if they are edible. Religion, science, state regulation, social norms, class, consumer culture, memory, and taste all advise us, and sometimes compel us, to move our mouth toward some nutrient in excitement, or away from it in disgust. Edibility, too, can be understood as mobility: the body moves towards some foods or away from it, sometimes in physical repulsion. Religious food taboos – or, in Foucauldian terms, power/knowledge – represent a powerful example of the authority that generates mobility of the body in relation to food.[52] In more secular ways, social media such as Instagram globally mobilize images of food to stimulate consumption and the satisfaction of bodily desires. At the same time, social media push diets and physical exercise to sculpt the kind of body valorized by consumer culture.[53] *Food Mobilities* defines the body and the self in relation to food as sites of pleasure, emotion, and well-being as well as resistance and inequality. Food moves us, provoking emotions ranging from hunger and longing to repugnance, fear, shame, nostalgia, love, and pride.

Within this section, Sara El-Sayed and Christy Spackman link culinary change, understood as bodily practice, in contemporary Egypt to state-led regulation and trade policy. In the name of combating mobile germs like avian influenza H5N1, the state regulated the poultry ordinary Egyptians could ingest, but with the goal of ensuring export markets. Authoritarian government regulations have undermined traditional husbandry. The state's "military-style sterilizing ideology" has mobilized the resistance of Egyptian farmers.

Signe Rousseau highlights how the rapid turnover of food fashions, diets, and tastes reproduces the flexible mobility of late capitalism. In examining the dietary narratives in social media, Rousseau argues that the "phygital" (physical+digital) ascent of foods like avocado and kale to the status of superfood reveals mobile food narratives that emphasize delivering nutritious foods to entitled consumers. The touristic approach that offered a tasteful way for privileged eaters to consume globalization, Rousseau concludes, faced a rude awakening with the COVID-19 global pandemic and its immobilizing effects.

Sarah Elton interrogates the corporeal and emotional relationships humans forge with edible plants. Plants move too. Diasporic communities in Toronto have resisted mass-produced food, reconnected to their food origins, and reclaimed their food sovereignty by mobilizing seeds and plants from their diasporic homes. Even in Canada's cold climate, migrant urban gardeners grow culturally significant vegetables and fruits, whose seeds they brought with them from South Asia or the Mediterranean.

"Infrastructures and Pathways" examines the roots and routes of food mobilities. Infrastructure, including farms, plantations, and feed-lots; processing plants; warehouses and stockyards; marketplaces and stock exchanges; railroads, container ships, and aircraft; trucks and cars; supermarkets, food stores, and restaurants, all connect different environments, often across vast distances. Infrastructure enables pathways that simultaneously transform biodiversity and diets. Embedded in histories that reach back to the ancient spice trade, food mobilities are fuelled by injections of capital and the reinvestment of profit, ushering in the various globalizations of food and taste. Modern states and Euro-American empires further extended the pathways of food provision and supply through the exploitation of other ecologies and poorer countries, populations, and labour.[54] Gastrodiplomacy, culinary tourism, and the export of processed food by national food industries and food multinationals represent more recent global pathways of food production, processing, exchange, distribution, and consumption. Yet the history of modern empires remains critical, not least for their legacies of inequalities and exploitations. These empires established pathways that, alongside ever-improving technologies of transport and preservation, accelerate the movement of fresh foods from plantations in post-colonial countries to the supermarket shelves of neo-imperial metropoles.[55]

In the first essay of this section, Simone Cinotto examines the Italian fascist project of demographic settler colonialism in Ethiopia. Beginning in 1935, this project called for the substitution of indigenous biodiversity and agricultural landscape with a crop economy designed to provide for Italy's food self-sufficiency. The most durable result of the Italian empire in Africa was the construction of an infrastructure of highways and roads intended for the shipment of fresh colonial food from East Africa to Italy. In fact, this infrastructure transported industrially produced, imported food from Italy for Italian settlers in East Africa. The Ethiopian armed resistance targeted this infrastructure, recognizing the importance of the food mobility network for the fascist colonial project.

On board Pan American World Airway's jet airliners, Elizabeth Zanoni theorizes a "taste of pace" that emerged in the 1960s. Meals consumed in flight "were literally the fastest fast food in the world," she notes. They entwined the rapid movement of people with a culinary infrastructure for the mass movement of meals. By the 1980s, with deregulation, airlines competed on price, not service. Meals that once linked modernity to food mobility became cheap, highly processed meals. Airline food mobilities nowadays revolve less around the glamour of physically fast food and more around the logistics of food processed in giant centralized facilities.

The construction of a transnational trade and food mobility network depends on the work of producers, traders, and tastemakers. In his history of southern Italian olive oil, Carl Ipsen notes that once a grease lubricating the machines of early northern European workshops in the eighteenth century, extra virgin olive oil is today a globally valued condiment redolent of the sunny Mediterranean. Ipsen links the circulation of consumer expertise and knowledge to the development of the infrastructure of ports, railroads, and roads that from an early age linked groves in Apulia and Sicily to global olive oil markets.

Jayeeta Sharma considers the botanical, medical, and commercial mobilities of tea, within and across empires, and its significance for social mobility. *Camellia sinensis* went from being a rare luxury in 700s China and Japan to a mass-traded commodity in twentieth-century Great Britain. Imperial infrastructure provided the pathways that transformed tea, but that transformation of both land and plant, cultivated resistance. Indigenous, nationalist, and diasporic anticolonial and postcolonial agriculture and cuisine have worked, with varying degrees of success, to reclaim tea. Foodie websites, newsletters, and social media have globalized local and Indigenous knowledge about wild, single-origin varieties of *Camellia assamica* once denied by the colonial-era enterprise.

"Mobilities and Immobilities" demonstrates how people on the move – migrants, merchants, traders, planters, explorers and plant hunters, labourers, soldiers, priests, professional cooks, domestic workers, travellers, and tourists – have actively promoted food change, transformed biodiversities, and accelerated the globalization of the modern age. This recognition challenges food-systems approaches that, too often, assume the diffusion of edible plants and animals, crops and foods. The essays in this section insist upon the agency of workers, vendors, cooks, and eaters, thus drawing analytical focus to labour, environment, and the state. As well, they introduce the key concept of immobility as a crucial way communities negotiate an industrializing food system. They do so by exploring the "last mile" of food provisioning, with examples ranging from Jewish neighbourhoods in early twentieth-century urban America, supermarkets in rural South Africa, and street vending in India during the contemporary COVID-19 pandemic.

Hasia Diner traces the culinary infrastructure of turn-of-the-twentieth-century Jewish American immigrant neighbourhoods. Religious norms and laws as well as rabbis helped regulate food circuits of production, trade, exchange, distribution, selling, and purchasing of ritual and everyday food items. Religious expression, Diner argues, played an outsized role in the shaping of city streets as sources for food vending and consumption aimed specifically at Jewish migrants. As well, it linked migrant foodways in specific urban settings to the culture, political, and economic life of the larger Jewish global diaspora.

Krishendu Ray examines the material, social, and cultural functions of urban markets, both for migrant street vendors and consumers, through the lens of the forced immobility of the COVID-19 pandemic. From Delhi and Bhubaneswar, India, to New York, United States, the "last mile" in the food system offers livelihoods to mobile workers who can make the most of their cultural and social capital to compensate for their meagre or non-existent financial capital. In turn, vendors provide culturally meaningful food to the urban poor. Yet even before COVID-19 lockdowns, capitalists, state officials, and urban planners have portrayed street food retail as an unhygienic obstacle to their preferred use of streets as corridors for automobility.

As Elizabeth Hull argues, in rural South Africa, food street vendors and itinerant traders still operate as "the veins and capillaries along which food is distributed." The resilience of the informal economy of street food preparation and selling that mobile vendors vitalize in "immobile" rural areas is even more striking given the significant share of poorer South Africans' food budget that comes in the form of relief grants that the state requires them to spend in supermarkets and fast-food restaurants.

"Biodiversity, Taste, and Nation" turns, finally, to the making of cuisines, demonstrating how symbolic, ethnic, gendered, ecological, and economic meanings attach to food. The representation of cuisine as luxury, national, or ethnic anchor food in place. Simultaneously, the demands of cuisine generate trade, consumption, distribution, and production. The essays in this section present the making cuisines as not only a logistical question of moving people, animals, plants, and commodities but also knowledge production about place, products, traditions, and medicine. In this perspective, national cuisines appear as taste communities shaped by different kinds of mobilities, from migration to tourism. This section also examines the relationship between diaspora and the Indigenous. Indigeneity, crucially, is not immobility. Foods, culturally and nutritionally crucial to Indigenous communities and cuisines, have circulated, including within the diasporas of Indigenous peoples. So, too, have national cuisines, in their articulation, for example, in cookbooks denied place to Indigenous foods and those who prepared them. Sandra Mendiola Garcia examines the re-localization of migrant foods into national cuisines. During the nineteenth century, Cornish migrants arrived in Mexican mines with pastes, half-moon-shaped pastries filled with meat, potatoes, turnips, and onions. At the turn of this century, as the mining industry in Real del Monte and Pachuca declined and jobs disappeared, this emblem of the local working-class culinary culture became a symbol of local identity and place as well as a tourist attraction. Pastes, once localized as a food specialty of the state of Hidalgo, became entrenched in middle-class tourist mobilities.

Tourist mobilities can be virtual. Cold War American home cooks, Daniel Bender argues, assumed the role of virtual tourists as they tentatively engaged with foods from the Global South. Bender evaluates the career of the cookbook writer and travel guidebook author Myra Waldo and the popular genre of around-the-world cookbooks. Waldo's *The Complete Round-the-World Cookbook*, published for Pan Am airlines in 1954, launched the idea of the consumption of exotic and ethnic food as central to the accumulation of cultural capital for the American middle class.

If home cooks mobilized recipes, and, later, ingredients from around the world as tourists, Jeffrey Pilcher, similarly, examines how the circulation of craft beer as a craft, product, and taste challenged distinctions between the global and the local. Producing transnational communities of taste, turn-of-the-twenty-first-century craft brewers claimed to re-establish the artisanal values lost with mass production. Through articulations about "craft," beer offered forms of social mobility through consumption as global consumers reimagined beer as an authentic product with unique cultural value.

Ina Vandebroek offers perspectives on biodiversity, mobility, and empire. Her chapter highlights how Caribbean cuisines and traditional medicines stemmed from the tension between the immobile geography of the Caribbean and the mobility of humans and plants. European empires accelerated that mobility through the formation of multi-ethnic colonial societies, the slave trade, and the global commodity exchange. In the Caribbean, Indigenous peoples, European colonists, and African slaves selected and manipulated available plants for their food and medical uses. Through cross-cultural practices, such plants became markers of local biodiversities, cuisines, cultures, and nations. Caribbean peoples in diaspora continue to mobilize the food and medical use of plants across historical and national boundaries, as they cross immigration and customs controls at the US, Canadian, or UK borders.

In 2019, we began the collaboration that produced this volume with travel, gathering on the campus of the University of Gastronomic Science in Pollenzo, Italy. We sampled Peliti's vermouth and thought with its spices. Since, then, as authors, collaborators, and, indeed, consumers, we all also faced the immobilizing effects of the COVID-19 pandemics. We finished our individual chapters in 2021, locked down in five different countries. In the midst of this immobility, the study of the mobility of our foods, our cuisines, seems all the more vital.

NOTES

1 Sidney W. Mintz, *Sweetness and Power: The Place of Sugar in Modern History* (New York: Penguin Books, 1985); see also: Donna R. Gabaccia, "Food, Mobility, and World History," in *The Oxford Handbook of Food History*, ed. Jeffrey M. Pilcher (New York: Oxford University Press, 2012), 305–23.
2 Mimi Sheller and John Urry, "The New Mobilities Paradigm," *Environment and Planning A: Economy and Space* 38, no. 2 (2006): 207–26; Tim Cresswell, "Mobilities I: Catching Up," *Progress in Human Geography* 35, no. 4 (2011): 550–8; Caren Kaplan, *Questions of Travel: Postmodern Discourses of Displacement* (Durham, NC: Duke University Press, 1996).
3 Federico Peliti, *Federico Peliti: Un fotografo piemontese in India al tempo della Regina Vittoria* [A Piemontese Photographer in India in Queen Victoria's Times] (Rome, Italy: Peliti Associati, 2002).
4 Sarah Gibson, "Food Mobilities: Traveling, Dwelling, and Eating Cultures," *Space and Culture* 10, no. 1 (2007): 4–21.
5 Michael J. Balick and Paul Alan Cox, *Plants, People, and Culture: The Science of Ethnobotany* (New York: W.H. Freeman, 1996).
6 Mary Douglas, *Purity and Danger: An Analysis of Concepts of Pollution and Taboo* (London, UK: Routledge and Kegan Paul, 1968).
7 Marvin Harris, *Good to Eat: Riddles of Food and Culture* (New York: Simon and Schuster, 1985).
8 Jaclyn Rohel, "Introduction: Genealogies of Edibility in Global Culture," *Global Food History* 3, no. 2 (2017): 105–10.
9 Wolfgang Schivelbusch, *Tastes of Paradise: A Social History of Spices, Stimulants, and Intoxicants* (New York: Pantheon Books, 1992).

10 Simone Cinotto, *The Italian American Table: Food, Family, and Community in New York City* (Urbana: University of Illinois Press, 2013); Jeffrey M. Pilcher, *Planet Taco: A Global History of Mexican Food* (New York: Oxford University Press, 2012); Krishnendu Ray, *The Migrant's Table: Meals and Memories in Bengali-American Households* (Philadelphia: Temple University Press, 2004); Purnima Mankekar, "India Shopping: Indian Grocery Stores and Transnational Configurations of Belonging," *Ethnos* 67, no. 1 (2002): 75–97.

11 Josée Johnston and Shyon Baumann, *Foodies: Democracy and Distinction in the Gourmet Foodscape* (New York: New York University, 2010).

12 Susanne Freidberg, *French Beans and Food Scares: Culture and Commerce in an Anxious Age* (New York: Oxford University Press, 2004).

13 https://www.lemongrassalaska.com/.

14 http://www.newsminer.com/features/sundays/becoming_alaskan /building-of-a-life-and-a-thai-restaurant-in-fairbanks/article_ed03661c -7567–11e5–89b2–6789870a78d8.html.

15 Valerie Imbruce, *From Farm to Canal Street: Chinatown's Alternative Food Network in the Global Marketplace* (Ithaca, NY: Cornell University Press, 2015).

16 Lucy Long, *Culinary Tourism* (Lexington: University of Kentucky Press, 2004), 1.

17 https://www.explorefairbanks.com/restaurants-and-shopping/food-and -drink/.

18 https://censusreporter.org/profiles/16000US0224230-fairbanks-ak/.

19 Elizabeth Zanoni, "Migrant Marketplaces: Globalizing Histories of Migrant Foodways," *Global Food History* 4, no. 1 (2018): 3.

20 James L. Watson, "Introduction: Transnationalism, Localization, and Fast Foods in East Asia," in *Golden Arches East: McDonald's in East Asia*, ed. James L. Watson (Palo Alto, CA: Stanford University Press, 2006), 6.

21 Zanoni, "Migrant Marketplaces."

22 David Bell and Gill Valentine, *Consuming Geographies: We Are Where We Eat* (New York: Routledge, 1997), 169.

23 Watson, "Introduction," 5–6.

24 Diane J. Purvis, *Ragged Coast, Rugged Coves: Labor, Culture, and Politics in Southeast Alaska Canneries* (Lincoln: University of Nebraska Press, 2021); Amanda Watch et al., "A Scoping Review of Traditional Food Security in Alaska," *International Journal of Circumpolar Health* 77 (January, 2018).

25 Gibson, "Food Mobilities."

26 Sidney W. Mintz, *Tasting Food, Tasting Freedom: Excursions into Eating, Culture, and the Past* (Boston: Beacon Press, 1996), 96.

27 Arjun Appadurai, "How to Make a National Cuisine: Cookbooks in Contemporary India," *Comparative Studies in Society and History* 30, no. 1 (1988): 3–24.

28 Uma Narayan, "Eating Cultures: Incorporation, Identity and Indian Food," *Social Identities* 1, no. 1 (1995): 63–86.

29 Krishnendu Ray, "Migration, Transnational Cuisines, and Invisible Ethnics," in *Food in Time and Place: The American Historical Association Companion to Food History*, ed. Paul Freedman, Joyce E. Chaplin, and Ken Albala (Berkeley: University of California Press, 2014), 209.

30 Pilcher, *Planet Taco*, 4–5.

31 Erika Rappaport, *A Thirst for Empire: How Tea Shaped the Modern World* (Princeton, NJ: Princeton University Press, 2017).

32 John Urry, *Mobilities* (Cambridge, UK: Polity Press, 2007), 44.

33 Monika Büscher and John Urry, "Mobile Methods and the Empirical," *European Journal of Social Theory* 12, no. 1 (2009): 101.

34 John Urry, "Mobility and Proximity," *Sociology* 36, no. 2 (2002): 255–74.

35 John Urry, "Moving on the Mobility Turn," in *Tracing Mobilities: Towards a Cosmopolitan Perspective*, ed. Weert Canzler, Vincent Kaufmann, and Sven Kesselring (Aldershot, UK: Ashgate, 2008), 13–14.

36 James Clifford, *Travel and Translation in the Late Twentieth Century* (Cambridge, MA: Harvard University Press, 1997), 2.

37 Michelle T. King, ed., *Culinary Nationalism in Asia* (New York: Bloomsbury, 2019), xi.

38 Lily Cho, *Eating Chinese: Culture on the Menu in Small Town Canada* (Toronto: University of Toronto Press, 2010).

39 King, *Culinary Nationalism in Asia*, x–xi.

40 Eric C. Rath, *Japan's Cuisines: Food, Place and Identity* (New York: Reaktion Books, 2016).

41 Amy B. Trubek, *The Taste of Place: A Cultural Journey into Terroir* (Berkeley: University of California Press, 2008).

42 Alberto Capatti and Massimo Montanari, *Italian Cuisine: History of a Culture* (New York: Columbia University Press, 2001).

43 Rachel Donadio, "A Walled City in Tuscany Clings to Its Ancient Menu," *New York Times*, 13 March 2009.

44 Mintz, *Tasting Food, Tasting Freedom*; Cinotto, *The Italian American Table*.

45 Elisabetta Povoledo, "In Italian Heartland, Indians Keep the Cheese Coming," *New York Times*, 7 September 2011.

46 David Gentilcore, "Taste and the Tomato in Italy: A Transatlantic History," *Food and History* 7, no. 1 (2009): 125–39.

47 Cinotto, *The Italian American Table*; Elizabeth Zanoni, *Migrant Marketplaces: Food and Italians in North and South America* (Urbana: University of Illinois Press, 2018).

48 Lisa Heldke, *Exotic Appetites: Ruminations of a Food Adventurer* (New York: Routledge, 2003).

49 Deborah Barndt, *Tangled Routes: Women, Work and Globalization on the Tomato Trail* (Lanham, MD: Rowman and Littlefield, 2002).

50 Warren Belasco, "Food and Social Movements," in *The Oxford Handbook of Food History*, 481–98; Eric Holt-Gimenez and Raj Patel, eds., *Food Rebellions! Crisis and the Hunger for Justice* (Oakland, CA: Food First, 2009); Alison Alkon and Julie Guthman, eds., *The New Food Activism: Opposition, Cooperation, and Collective Action* (Berkeley: University of California Press, 2017).

51 E.P. Thompson, "The Moral Economy of the English Crowd in the Eighteenth Century," *Past & Present* 50, no. 1 (1971): 76–136.

52 Michel Foucault, *Power/Knowledge: Selected Interviews and Other Writings, 1972–1977* (New York: Vintage, 1980).

53 Mike Featherstone, "The Body in Consumer Society," in *The Sociology and Politics of Health: A Reader*, ed. David Banks and Michael Purdy (New York: Routledge, 2001), 228–36.

54 Shane Hamilton, *Supermarket USA: Food and Power in the Cold War Farms Race* (New Haven, CT: Yale University Press, 2018).

55 Susanne Freidberg, *Fresh: A Perishable History* (Cambridge, MA: Belknap Press, 2010).

Mobility and Its Discontents: Movements of Foods and Peoples from the Palaeolithic to the Present

DONNA R. GABACCIA

That food moves can scarcely be questioned, but the significance of mobility in Food Studies – much like the significance of food in Mobility Studies – is little understood. Editors Daniel Bender and Simone Cinotto offer a working hypothesis for integrating the two – that the intersection of human mobility (including mobile humans' culinary cultures) and the movability of foods drive changes in food production, consumption, and taste. By offering a chronological, capacious perspective on their intersection, this chapter encourages readers to think in new ways about what many understand to be an industrial or global food system.

According to a United Nations definition, a food system is the "entire range of actors and their interlinked value-adding activities involved in the production, aggregation, processing, distribution, consumption and disposal of food products that originate from agriculture, forestry or fisheries, and parts of the broader economic, societal and natural environments in which they are embedded."[1] Food Studies scholarship offers structuralist and presentist analyses of a food system that consolidated around 1850, that rests on long-distance movements of food commodities that are mass produced in unsustainable ways for distant consumers, and that fosters culinary homogenization, inequalities, and environmental and nutritional degradation.

Even scholarly terminologies have histories: the terms food system and food regime were invented during debates over public feeding programs during famine crises associated with the British industrial revolution and twentieth-century international warfare.[2] Although used occasionally in the 1940s and again in the 1970s, both terms found a place in Food Studies scholarship in the early 2000s as discussion increasingly linked global climate change to threats of mass hunger.

A big history of entangled food and human mobilities across many millennia produces different insights than analyses focused on a single decade or century.[3] (In fact, the historians' tool of periodization – assigning start and end dates to an analysis – does much the same work as choice of a theoretical framework.)[4] This chapter's big history encourages an appreciation of the extremely diverse and variable cultural and economic dynamics of intersecting human and food mobilities, while revealing mobility as essential to the feeding of all human societies. It especially highlights the centrality of cities in the globalization of food. For five thousand years, cities have been hubs in the trade circuits where food and human mobilities intersected most obviously.[5] As sites of transit, cities have been places of culinary exchange, diversity, and innovation, linking local to global dynamics.

This chapter also engages with several perspectives developed within Mobility Studies. That field's attention to relations among movements of goods, people, and ideas unifies what Food Studies more often segments in studies of commodity chains, culinary cultures, and knowledge networks. In their 2006 article, John Urry and Mimi Sheller also urged scholars to acknowledge the relationship of mobility and immobility.[6] Over millennia, dynastic, city, imperial, and national states have often privileged food mobilities while restricting, forcing, or controlling human mobility. Today's industrial food system presents an excellent example. By demonstrating the newness of and changeability within this system, readers will be better able to imagine the intersecting human and food mobilities that hold the potential to transform it.

The Palaeolithic Era: Foraging and Mobility as a Way of Life

The Palaeolithic Era (once labelled the Stone Age) began roughly 2.5 million years ago and has been defined by the increased use of stone tools by the earliest humans; it ended about 15,000 years ago, when modern *homo sapiens* began to cultivate plants and grains. According to Patrick Manning, humans must be considered a mobile species, as their bipedalism constituted their most important evolutionary advantage in adapting to diverse environments as they populated the entire earth.[7] Human and food mobilities in the Palaeolithic Era were not so much interacting as coterminous. Across millennia, mobility has remained a foundation for human survival.

As bipedalism first extended hominids' territorial, food-seeking range within Africa, the earliest humans learned to survive by living in small, mobile foraging groups that collectively accomplished all food-related activities.[8] Some scholars today regard their foraging as the material base for the most equitable of known human societies. There was no sharp Palaeolithic division of productive labour and no sharp differentiation between producers and consumers.[9] All engaged to some degree in the shared activities of hunting, fishing, and gathering, and only small amounts of food were transported as humans moved about. Patterned, cyclical, and continuous movements through ecologically varied and vaguely delineated territories allowed foragers to assemble nutritionally complete diets. Fire and cooking allowed them to extract greater nutritional value from animal and plant foods. Foragers might follow the paths of the migratory animals they hunted but obtained most calories from plants that were rooted in place.

Foraging mobility persisted during the so-called Great Expansion – the migrations that globalized human life on earth. Beginning about 60–70,000 years ago and likely initiated during a period of climate and environmental change that threatened familiar African food supplies, *homo sapiens* travelled on foot and later with simple boats and rafts to colonize new territories in West Asia, Europe, South and Southeast Asia, outer and inner Eurasia, and Australia. By 15,000 years ago, they had settled the Americas; 1,500–3,500 years ago, they occupied smaller Pacific islands.[10] Human globalization produced a thinly populated foragers' world. Foragers mixed hunting and gathering in varied ways and developed increasingly diverse diets. In warmer and wetter climes, plants provided most calories, supplemented by occasional animal or fish foods; in colder and drier climes, hunted animal meat or fish more often dominated diets.[11]

By the end of the Palaeolithic Era, humans had developed the first culinary technologies – tools to cut, dig, kill, carry, pound, and store small quantities of foodstuffs.[12] Simple forms of art appeared, and suggested humans' fascination with animals. Language facilitated cross-generational but only intra-group transmission of knowledge of tool making and of food procurement. Scholars have found no evidence of Palaeolithic food exchanges across groups; at most, a few rare, highly valued objects (shells, stones) "trickled" from group to group.[13] Obviously, there were no Palaeolithic cities.

Sedentary Humans, Mobile Foods: Agrarian Societies

Human use of technology increasingly mobilized food during the Neolithic Era, while small groups of humans became sedentary. Beginning 10–15,000 years ago, the first web-like if still modest Neolithic food circuits developed: human cultivators of a few grains and vegetables settled more permanently in villages they shared with a growing list of smaller and larger domesticated animals. Foods, humans, and animals travelled short distances between fields and villages, but cultivators no longer ranged over large territories.

Although this process was once labelled as a Neolithic or Agrarian Revolution, scholars now know that humans instead engaged in millennia-long experiments in feeding themselves through ever-shifting combinations of gathering, hunting, managing wild plants, cultivation, and animal husbandry.[14] While experimenting, humans developed new tools and began to produce surpluses of grain and seeds for storage. Over millennia, agrarian villages developed in a number of particularly fertile and well-watered environments – first in the Fertile Crescent, the Yangtze and Yellow River Basins in China, and the New Guinea Highlands, then in Central Mexico, South America, Sub-Saharan Africa and North America. Humans likely began to understand their villages as homes, identified with cooking hearths and storage of locally cultivated, and appreciated grains and vegetables. Technological innovation facilitated the building of storage facilities, irrigation systems, grinding stones, ceramic (and later metal) vessels, allowing humans to extend and intensify cultivation and to process, store, and cook foods, through brewing, fermenting, drying, preserving, and baking. Taste and culinary knowledge remained largely local.

Scholars agree that cultivators' diets, typically based on a single stored grain supplemented by vegetables and (depending on location) meat from pig, chicken, cow, goat, sheep, guinea pig, fowl, eggs, and goat or sheep milk produced mixed results[15] Living in denser settlements with animals facilitated the spread of infectious diseases, producing higher death rates than among foragers. Divisions of village labour sharpened, differentiating the work of men and women, households of cultivators, herders and animal breeders, and artisans producing tools, houses, clothing, bread, and beer. Specialists produced surpluses to be stockpiled, distributed, and exchanged. Physical objects from excavated villages document new cosmological imaginaries and religious rituals as well as local inequalities in wealth and power.[16] Still, most villages and agrarian hinterlands remained surrounded by vast foraging territories.

Villages became sites of the earliest food exchanges, albeit on a small scale. Through exchange, neighbouring foragers had their first tastes of grain. Knowledge of cultivation, animal husbandry, and even distinctive tastes continued to trickle from village to village and from villagers to foragers[17] – although hunters living in harsh climates could not easily incorporate cultivation into their annual mobility cycle and few cultivated foods travelled far. Knowledge of cultivation, seeds, domesticated animals and culinary skills began to travel longer distances with the human migrations occurring toward the end of the Neolithic Era. Physical evidence from burial sites documents long-distance trade in ritual and decorative items and tools but little evidence of longer-distance trade in foodstuffs. Both humans and foods were mobile but both tracked each other within and across spatially limited territories.

Cities and New Mobilities (500–5,000 years ago)

The emergence of cities fundamentally changed human mobility and facilitated the first longer-distance culinary exchanges through trade. Beginning five thousand years ago, agrarian surpluses could support significant population increases and concentration, resulting in the consolidation of the first dynastic and urban states, some of which developed into expansive empires. Facilitating all these developments was a new and mobile way of life now labelled by scholars as nomadic pastoralism and based on transhumance and management of large herds of mobile animals. Especially in drier, colder, and more mountainous environments within Eurasia, the entanglement of agrarian and nomadic food producers established a material foundation that – modified over millennia by improved transportation and military technologies – gradually lengthened trade routes, connecting Eurasia and Africa. For the historian of food, the most salient aspect of early cities was their centrality in these new trade circuits, created by intersecting human and commodity mobilities. Although foodstuffs remained marginal in long-distance trade, foods that did travel began to transform urban culinary cultures.

Cities first developed in areas of settled agriculture in Mesopotamia, in south and west Asia and in China. By 2,500 years ago, central and South America and east and west Africa all claimed urban centres. Early cities were relatively small; their most important residents were newly powerful and wealthy religious and political elites, serviced by urban artisans and workers and provisioned by village cultivators.[18] The rulers of wealthy cities invested in sewers, roads, and grand buildings; the wealthiest urban residents demanded a wide array of commodities – cloth, clothing, baskets, pottery, metal utensils, and building materials. Specialized groups of merchants soon used new technologies (including wheeled carts) to transport commodities over greater distances, expanding the reach of urban markets. Luxurious court cuisines and the generous and varied diets of wealthy urban merchants increasingly incorporated foods transported from afar into the local surplus foods extracted from local cultivators, surpassing cultivators' monotonous grain-based diets so dramatically that scholars can identify the class backgrounds of the dead by analyzing their bones and teeth.[19]

Living beyond the reach of the new states, nomadic pastoralists had originated among village households that bred and herded animals.[20] Pastoralists soon managed enormous herds and travelled with them as green pasturage shifted seasonally from river valleys, to distant grassland plains or steppes and mountains (still sparsely inhabited by foragers). Pastoralists' diets reflected their mobile way of life: they consumed grilled and preserved meats as well as milk and fermented milk products but ate sparingly of cultivated vegetables and grains from urban markets. In central Asia, pastoralists became expert equestrians; horse meat, milk, and blood supplemented their diets. Continuing to hunt, pastoralists also developed considerable expertise with weaponry. Armed, mobile clans competed for pasturage and regularly raided others' herds; they also plundered cultivators' villages and riches stockpiled by urban elites.

While pastoralists and agrarians often disparaged each other's culinary choices and tastes, they traded extensively with each other. Scholars have identified a so-called secondary products revolution[21] occurring as herders used their vast herds not only to feed or clothe themselves but to produce surplus animals and animal products. Cultivators wanted plough animals; merchants wanted animals to haul trade goods on their backs or in carts; urban dwellers wanted milk, milk products, skins, wool, and felts to be transformed into meals, clothing and furniture, tools and storage vessels. Herders purchased grain and vegetables, metal tools, and tanned leather goods.

In short, city markets brought together pastoralists, hinterland cultivators, villagers, urban merchants, artisans, and political or religious elites. Initially, the new trade circuits were limited to Africa, Europe, and Asia. In the Americas, only the Andes saw a secondary products revolution emerge with llama herding.[22] In Northern Europe and Southeast Asia, furthermore, it was mobile seafaring, fishing, and fish-eating people – not pastoralists – who lived by raiding, plunder, and transport.[23] And beyond all these circuits lived surviving populations of foragers who still procured their own food in large parts of the world.

Although market exchanges symbiotically entwined agrarian and nomadic pastoralist modes of food production and cities became important sites where new food knowledge and tastes circulated, trade did not eliminate mistrust, fear, hostility, and conflict. Having mastered writing, city dwellers consistently portrayed themselves, their diets, and their tastes as "civilized," peaceful, and sedentary while disparaging pastoralists as illiterate, mobile, warlike, and "barbarian."[24] States regularly sought ways to demobilize those they labelled as barbarians: ancient China built walls to stop the incursions of raiding nomadic pastoralists; Roman cities, too, flourished behind powerful walls with tightly controlled gates where trade goods entered.

In sharply differentiating themselves from mobile barbarians, urbanites ignored or naturalized their own forms of mobility, especially trade, as unremarkable. In fact, no empire was ever sedentary. Cities depended for their food not only on the sedentarism of nearby cultivators but also on the mobility of the pastoralists.[25] Subject to persistent infectious disease, cities also required continuous admission of new residents.[26] Building grand religious and secular monuments required large gangs of labourers, usually coerced as slaves or as prisoners, to move and to work.[27] Expanding empires mobilized large armies. Merchants too were highly mobile, travelling to organize or oversee lengthening trade routes to far-off cities. In some places, they became seafarers or negotiated with so-called pirates for transport and safe passage of their trade goods. In AfroEurasia, merchants and pastoralists forged an extensive network of overland trade routes – the so-called Silk Roads – that ultimately connected China to western Asia and Europe.[28] Whether by land or by sea, a few merchants relocated permanently, creating what they called factories (and what scholars call diasporas) in port cities and trade oases.[29] Scholars have also traced a unique sea to mountaintop network of commerce in the Andes,[30] and identified routes of human runners and porters that stretched from central Mexico into the Mississippi Valley.[31]

The basic dynamics of globalization were established in this ancient world, but the mobility of commodities was more highly valued than human mobility. The expansion of land- and sea-based empires that developed and extended circuits among cities and their imperial hinterlands often rested on forced mobilizations of sedentary cultivators and slaves captured in inter-imperial wars. Ideas, agrarian knowledge, soldiers, commodities, diseases, seeds, plants, animals, and religious missionaries all travelled, with somewhat higher levels of human choice, over lengthening routes. Scholars have identified an "embryonic world system,"[32] first in the years between 500 BCE and 200 CE[33] and then in the eight interlocking trade circuits of the Mongol empires and Silk Roads.[34] Valerie Hansen has even posited the year 1000 as the date "when explorers connected the world – and globalization began."[35]

For Food Studies scholars, assertions of globalization through food mobility before 1500 fall somewhat flat, however. Certainly, plants, seeds, culinary knowledge, and some food commodities now travelled longer distances. Arab empires spread sugar, citrus fruits, bananas, mangos, spinach, and eggplants into the Mediterranean from Asia, while grapes and a few other Mediterranean cultivars travelled eastward, and watermelon and sorghum travelled by sea from Africa to India.[36] But only a few foodstuffs travelled as commodities. Within empires, all roads might lead to Rome or Beijing (both inland cities) but staples such as wheat, rice, dried fish, wine, or oil travelled mainly by sea. Under existing transportation technologies, grains, vegetables, meat, and fish were too heavy, too voluminous, and too perishable to travel far or in large quantities. Compact, lightweight, and expensive food commodities such as tea, spices, salt, and sugar travelled alongside Silk Road luxury goods such as silks and ceramics, while even the spice trade more often utilized sea routes and is by far the best documented and understood of early food commodity mobilities.[37] Even under these constraints, urban and court cuisines by 1500 had become culinary melting pots, incorporating ingredients and tastes from far away. But the globalizing tables of the wealthy contrasted ever more sharply with the still quite monotonous diet of those eating local foods. Although slavery existed as a form of coerced labour, it was not yet racialized; the sharpest culinary distinctions and inequalities differentiated forager and pastoralist from peasant and urban foodways, and within agrarian societies between the tastes and culinary cultures of peasant cultivators and urban elites. Cities had assumed their central place as hubs in the extending trade circuits through which both commodity and human mobilities pulsed. The material foundation for culinary globalization through entwined human and food mobilities through trade now existed. Still, transport technologies, celebrations of sedentarism as civilized, and hostility between agrarians and pastoralists limited food mobilities.

The Making of the Industrial, Global Food System

A global, industrial food system was constructed over the next 500 years through four temporally overlapping mobility transitions. Each transition rearranged the intersection of human and food mobilities and the balance of mobility and immobility. New empire- and nation-building and revolutionary technological changes especially transformed transportation and communication, while the rates of both food and human mobility increased. Still, the basic material foundation linking cities, hinterlands, and continents through trade circuits did not so much change during these four transitions as expand and contract.

Transition 1: The Early Modern Globalization of Food

The mobility of foods and humans expanded exponentially after 1500 although initially it was more coercion than choice that mobilized humans to facilitate the production and transport of new foodstuffs. In 1453, the expanding Ottoman Empire disrupted westward land-based trade routes, encouraging Europeans to find better sea routes to Asian spicelands. Improved sailing ship design and naval technologies enabled ambitious empire-building dynasts and merchants in China and Europe to invest in long-distance voyages, finally linking all continents. The so-called Columbian Exchange developed along sea routes circumnavigating Africa and linking AfroEurasia to the Americas via Atlantic and Pacific Oceans. Empire builders may have regarded newly encountered American, African, and Asian foragers as barbarians and their foods as attractively exotic, but an emerging ideology of race soon justified their annihilation or coercion through slavery as labourers for the cultivation of food production and transport. Culturally diverse crews of migrant seamen, explorers, empire builders, enslaved Africans, indentured servants, prisoners, and missionaries quickly brought American corn, beans, pumpkins, potatoes, turkeys, and tomatoes to Europe, Africa, and Asia, while sugar, chickens, pigs, bees, diverse fruits, spices, yams, okra, wheat, rice, and other seeds and grains departed from AfroEurasia for the Americas.[38]

Capital invested in new trade routes originated in cities, as did most European and Asian seamen, ships captains, merchants, and imperial administrators in the corporate British and Dutch East Indies companies. While the largest cities in 1700 were still older imperial centres (Istanbul, Beijing, Cairo, Vijayangar), Columbian Exchange circuits moved mainly through newer, smaller port cities. Some were metropoles of global sea empires (London, Paris, Amsterdam, Seville); others were colonial cities (Batavia, Manila, Capetown, Boston, Montreal, Lima, and Havana) or coastal entrepôts for collecting conquered peoples and managing new territories within increasingly global empires. Both global metropoles and colonial cities functioned as ports for the loading, unloading, transport, and distribution of seeds, plants, germs, animals, enslaved labourers, and other workers and settlers.[39]

The most immediate impacts occurred in rural hinterlands. The old system of agrarian and pastoralist food production could not easily be replicated. In the Americas – where as many as 90 per cent of Indigenous peoples died – imported sheep denuded the countryside, transforming local environments as European missionaries forced native labourers to cultivate wheat, wine, and other European foodstuffs and animals with limited success. The naturalization of European horses instead empowered some Native hunters to become raiders on their agrarian neighbours and to hunt bison (etc.) for European fur traders. The Navajo did become pastoralists, herding European sheep but without becoming completely nomadic purveyors of surplus wool or meat.[40]

Culinary transformation now extended well beyond urban or court elites. Around the world, even relatively humble cultivators considered the possibility of tasting exotic new foods and incorporating them into their own food repertoire. Corn (maize) and tomatoes found enthusiastic reception in some parts of West Africa while European peasants outside Italy and Spain reacted with initial scepticism. Since Indigenous American women and their culinary knowledge (of nixtamalization of corn, e.g.) rarely travelled, corn-eating Europeans soon suffered from pellagra. During famines, hungry cultivators in China and Africa quickly welcomed American potatoes while those in India and northern Europe resisted them for centuries.[41] Human mobility also shaped hinterland culinary dynamics. Unable to provision themselves as they moved inland, hungry colonizers with their enslaved or indentured workers had especially powerful incentives to eat local foods, regardless of how unusual they may have tasted.

Early experiments in the industrialization of food production and the creation of food commodities began in colonized hinterlands within racially oppressive labour systems. In the Caribbean and Brazil, enslaved Africans cultivated and processed sugar cane for export, not only on a vast scale but so intensively they had to eat imported food commodities such as salt codfish, dried beef, salt pork, and rice. A by-product of sugar refining, molasses, was distilled locally into rum or exported for distillation and sale in colonial and metropole cities.[42] (Sailors and seamen also received rum as part of their wages.) The fishing banks of the northern Atlantic – exploited already for five hundred years by Vikings – attracted new investors, merchant ship captains, and seasonal seamen wage workers from Europe. Some produced pickled or wet salt cod on shipboard, while others dried lightly salted cod on seasonal, coastal fishing wharves for transport and sale in Europe and the Caribbean.[43] Elsewhere, China expanded tea cultivation as Dutch traders in Batavia opened European and American markets; like cod, dried, rolled, and fermented red or black (but not green) tea exports could survive long sea voyages.[44]

Changes in the production and circulation of foods that have been understood as mercantilist became first steps toward the industrialization of a few foods. Mercantilists imagined empires as competing for global trade by enhancing their own exports while importing little or no food or resources from beyond colonial borders.[45] Mercantilist policies toward mobilities were thus paradoxical. Demand for plantation and ship labour encouraged Europeans to force Africans and prisoners from their own homelands to move while imposing draconian restraints on them where they worked as food producers. Mercantilists also restricted where and with whom merchants could trade. Their prohibitions against the entry of foreign ships or foreign commodities (including, eventually, enslaved humans) into colonial ports; their requirements that plants, animals, and foodstuffs enter through a single metropole port; their levies of taxes, tariffs, and licences, and stamps on ships and mobile commodities all generated heated resistance.

Thus, the globalization of foods generated its own backlash. Piracy – essentially illicit trade – burgeoned, as did the numbers of run away, enslaved labourers. Movements to abolish slavery developed in the eighteenth century. Nationalist revolutions around the Atlantic between 1770 and 1830 typically rejected imperial and mercantilist restrictions, unravelling colonial trade circuits by abolishing slavery and indenture without always questioning their racialized and class-based foundations.

Food Studies scholars have not yet devoted attention to culinary dynamics in this era's global cities, but culinary hybridization certainly occurred.[46] The vast majority of European and Asian migrants in colonial cities were male;[47] they knew how to eat and might have preferred familiar foods but rarely knew how to cultivate, process, or cook them. Men depended on enslaved men and women and male and female local or Indigenous migrants to provision and prepare their foods. Returning home, male migrants proved poor conduits for new foods and tastes. Urban elites adopted some new foods – refined sugar, milled chocolate, distilled rum, and dried or fermented teas and fish. Elaborate sugar sculptures graced aristocratic banquet tables, and sweetened hot chocolate drinks redefined urban refinement. But metropole elites also stigmatized the urban poor as consumers of colonial products, through recurring portraits of sailors and workers drunk on rum. Some evidence also suggests it was hinterland peasant cultivators who first experimented with foods from the colonies.[48]

Transition 2: Creating a Worldwide Industrial Food System

Globalization began anew around 1850 after almost a century of anti-colonial struggles and inter-imperial warfare. For the next century, freer migrations (usually called the proletarian mass migrations) and new technologies applied to food production and processing changed diets worldwide. Cities prospered and proliferated as trade hubs: only 3 per cent of the world's population lived in urban areas in 1800; by 1920 the proportion was 14 per cent. Cities provided capital and remained hubs for railroads, steamships, and ports. With vast, new human migrations and growing international trade in staple foodstuffs and commodities, cities became ever more important sites of culinary exchange and transformation. Industrialization of food production changed how rural grain and animal surpluses travelled while continuing to depend on migrant human labour. Fears of mobile humans generally outstripped fears of circulating foodstuffs, and no one yet used terms such as global food supply chains, let alone a global food system.

The expansion of cultivation further marginalized the world's remaining foragers and pastoralists during this era, often through racialized discourses focused on their inadequate diets and intelligence. Expanding corporations in Europe and North America drove investment and trade, seeking profit at every step along lengthening food commodity chains and vertically integrating to connect farming, transport, and wholesale/retail enterprises. European migrants hoping to remain family farmers as settler colonialists further pushed racialized, indigenous foragers to the margins and repopulated grasslands and other hinterlands in Australia, Canada, Russia, Manchuria, South Africa, the United States, Argentina, and Brazil. But even with growing use of chemical fertilizers and irrigation, they could not compete with large new and specialized and corporate corn and wheat farms or with colonial plantations of rice, tea, sugar coffee, and chocolate – both developed to produce food for export. Corporate experiments with hybridization created crops adaptable to mechanized cultivation; large-scale farms and plantations imported and used chemical fertilizers, mechanized equipment, and seasonal, often foreign, waged labourers while blending grains from many farms in huge storage silos. Observers called such operations "factories in the fields" and compared their degradation of soils to pollution created by urban factories. Elsewhere, citrus, grapes, and other fruits and vegetables such as potatoes became the basis for other specialized trade-oriented farming monocultures. Once an adjunct to family farming, the pasturing of cattle and sheep also became huge corporate enterprises employing gangs of seasonal, migrant, often foreign-born labour; the production for sale of pigs, chickens, and eggs also became more specialized and larger scale.[49]

Railroads transported mass-produced grains, meat, and dry foodstuffs to urban consumers and to centralized, urban, food-processing sites; cattle drives delivered huge herds of animals to urban slaughterhouses. City dwellers complained of their stench. With the invention of refrigeration, meat packing too became concentrated in a few large cities. Bottling, canning, or pasteurizing milk, beer, and wine also facilitated longer-distance travel of liquid and alcoholic foodstuffs. Canning, preserving, and marketing of processed fruits and vegetables became big business, as exemplified by the H.J. Heinz Corporation. By the twentieth century nation-wide chain grocery stores marketed foods to urban consumers with little knowledge of the origins of their home-cooked meals.

Food commodity chains soon reached beyond to far-off port cities. US farmers exported grain to Asia and Europe; Argentina and New Zealand became important exporters of meat to the urban industrial workers of Great Britain. Many American nations explicitly developed policies to expand food exports. Although food-processing corporations such as Heinz sought foreign markets for their canned and bottled processed foods, their experiments remained modest when compared with the enormous power of the world's first international grain traders (today's Archer Daniels Midland, Bunge, Cargill, and Louis Dreyfus) and meat exporters.

However smoky or smelly, cities again became important sites of cross-cultural culinary hybridization and innovation. Studies of American immigration especially emphasize changes in the foodways of immigrants and natives but innovative culinary hybrids also developed in colonial cities as empire builders and colonial cooks adjusted their eating habits to each other and carried culinary innovations back to metropoles and hinterlands.[50] Scholars have identified Atlantic marketplaces where migrants organized transnational trades (e.g., canned tomatoes and olive oil linking Naples and Buenos Aires) and found ways to sell imported foods to native consumers.[51] To lower prices and expand urban markets, migrant businessmen invested in import substitution through agricultural and processing enterprises that made and exported Italian-style cheeses from Milwaukee and Buenos Aires and raised and canned Chinese vegetables in California, Cuba, or Southeast Asia. Migrants operated grocery stores, cafes, and restaurants that introduced curry to London and Capetown, and German-style lager beer to all the British colonies of the world. (The most successful migrant food businesses were eventually purchased by large food processing corporations and produced as canned spaghetti or chop suey vegetables, unsettling a food's associations with a particular nationality.)[52]

Around the world, imperial leaders and national governments wrestled with the opportunities and dangers posed by an increasingly international marketplace for staple foodstuffs and processed commodities.[53] In colonies and post-colonial nations alike, nationalism could literally colour culinary knowledge in racialized terms, producing culinary food fights as cookbook compilers included or rejected foreign or corporate influences to create ostensibly pure, national cuisines. Heated debates raged over the imposition of restrictive tariffs on sugar, meat, and wheat and restrictions on human migrants but were advocated as protectives of national interests. Nationalists worried about the purity of imported, processed foods. Nation states increasingly implemented inspection systems aimed at excluding invasive species, contaminated foodstuffs and migrants understood as racially inferior.[54] Globalization had again produced a backlash determined to unravel the era's entanglement of human and food mobilities.

Transition 3: A Retreat from Globalization?

In the middle years of the twentieth century, international warfare and a global depression succeeded in reducing both human and food mobilities. Despite growing rejection of racialized ideologies as scientifically false, many nation states worldwide restricted human migrations in the years between 1920 and 1940. During the 1930s, most countries in the world also imposed high, protective tariffs on a wide array of foods. Nevertheless, "Our World In Data" illustrates both the rise, decline, and subsequent return of the financial, trade, and migration circuits after 1970.

Economic historians have noted a general retreat from globalization in the twentieth century;[55] Italy provides one case study. In Italy, Mussolini came to power determined to break the human and food mobilities he believed had undermined national strength. He sought to introduce autarky (economic food sovereignty) through a program he called the battle for grain, together with prohibition of emigration. As Italy increased grain production and placed tariffs on grain imports, suffering increased: rural families lost access to the migrant remittances that had purchased improved diets for peasants; the price of grain rose, driving rural dwellers into Italy's cities and intensifying urban hunger.[56] In response, Mussolini proposed that Italians abandon pasta to achieve self-sufficiency. No scholar has ever found such food policies to be successful. On the contrary, pursuit of food sovereignty sharpened rural/urban conflicts, undermining national unity, with urban Italians convinced (against all evidence) that peasants ate well while they starved.

One nation's experiment with food sovereignty could not destroy global circuits of food trade or human migrations – depression and war did that. But culinary nationalism was far more common and popular.[57] And while restriction, authoritarian nationalism, trade wars, and anti-imperial nationalist movements all contributed to the twentieth century's international conflicts and warfare, the alliance of nation states that emerged victorious from depression and war in 1945 seemed determined to re-establish the foundation for continued culinary globalization. It created international organizations – think of the United Nations and its FAO and the World Trade Organization – that increasingly posited free trade as a foundation for postwar peace and prosperity while leaving nation states free to restrict human migrations.

Transition 4: A Global Food System?

The globalization of the late twentieth century – which began around 1970 – replicated some patterns of earlier periods of global integration. Foraging disappeared as a way of life, persisting only as a hobby in some wealthy nations. Cities re-assumed their significance as hubs in global circuits. The mobility of tourist and business travellers soared, but people hoping to move abroad more permanently (estimated at 15 per cent of global populations) still faced high obstacles and national restrictions; only 3.4 per cent of the world's population now lives outside their countries of birth. Culinary knowledge circulated more easily with new media and communication technologies. New concerns about industrialized food production's impact on climate, environment, and human health revived worries about food purity, especially with the onset of new discussions about global warming and global climate change in the 1990s and early 2000s. Still, even critics of the current food system acknowledged declining rates of world hunger (from 35 per cent in 1970 to 13 per cent).

Since the 1970s, observers have argued that multinational, vertically integrated food business monopolies constitute the new empires that drive food mobilities. Nation states committed to the postwar geopolitical strategy of free trade and increasingly also to neoliberal economic theory, have either abandoned efforts to regulate corporations or have struggled unsuccessfully to do so. The same nation states that supported free trade often dismantled anti-monopoly regulations of food production (e.g., the use of chemical fertilizers) and agricultural inspections, removing oversight and allowing corporate transformation of many public goods (seed hybridization, water, even photosynthesis) into private, patentable corporate property – a breathtaking transformation of nature into private property. Transnational grocery businesses have become largely self-regulating, with customer choice rather than government agencies assessing the safety of their brands. These same corporations have extended monoculture internationally through green revolutions, expanded cultivations of a dwindling list of oil, feed, grain, and plant crops (still raised with heavy inputs of chemical fertilizers and insecticides) and developed snack or so-called junk foods specifically to absorb surplus products of monoculture such as palm oil or corn glucose.[58]

Nevertheless, food mobilities are arguably relatively less important today than they were a century ago. True, corporations such as Nestlé, Anheuser-Busch InBev, Kraft, Coca-Cola, Pernod-Ricard, McDonalds, Kroger, Costco, Walmart, PepsiCo, and Mondelez appear on lists of the largest of global multinational corporations. Some specialize in the production and retailing of bottled beverages (including beer, water, sweet drinks), sparking concern about the proliferation of plastic waste. Others manufacture easily transportable snack foods of limited nutritional value. The new, international salience of groceries and fast food retailers are however more the product of managerial innovations (McDonaldization; Walmartization)[59] than of restored or increasing international trade in meat or grain. Even McDonalds uses foodstuffs from and offers tastes appropriate for local and national markets. Grain trading companies and meatpacking companies – once purveyors of staple foodstuffs and still employers of large migrant populations, along with the migrants who work in restaurant and food service positions – no longer dominate international food mobility as they did a century ago.

Today's food system is increasingly industrialized but its globalization is easily exaggerated. Food commodities travel to a wider array of destinations than in the past but they travel via older transport systems (sea, highway, rail), not by air. The recent containerization of global shipping and worldwide innovation in port facilities was not driven by international food trade. The twelve agro-food corporations on lists of the most powerful one hundred corporations are seriously outnumbered by oil, energy, and finance companies. Food commodities represent only about 6 per cent of globally traded exports (1.1 trillion of 18 trillion dollar value in 2014). Collectively, all exported food commodities equal less than a third of the value of exported cars alone. Miscellaneous drinks and snack foods together generate the greatest value (525.2 billion), with grains trailing at 242 billion and meat and meat products at only 188 billion. Even the UN's FAO reports on the persistence and impact of restrictions on food trade.[60] The average diet of today's humans is not dominated by internationally traded foods. And the percentage of people working in agriculture has dropped from almost 45 to under 30 per cent since 1990. Still, critics of industrialized food production have convincingly demonstrated the environmental and climatic costs, even when such foods are transported and traded within national markets.

Most food commodities still pass through cities and their closely allied suburbs as do most of the world's international migrants, refugees, tourists, and business travellers. Overall, the number and size of global cities have increased. The deindustrialization of Western and northern global cities has relieved residents of pollution generated by the processing of foodstuffs by shifting those costs, along with many others, to global cities elsewhere. Although most global cities remain transportation hubs, their wealth now comes more from circulating finance capital than from entangled food and human mobilities. As global cities have increasingly concentrated wealth, modest labour migrants, refugees, and migrant professional workers live not in global cities but in "ethnoburbs," peripheral slums, and provincial cities.

Despite the declining relative importance of food trade and human mobility, long-standing urban culinary dynamics have nevertheless intensified. Everywhere, migrants continue to initiate and operate restaurants and grocery stores that provide urban consumers with alternatives to corporate fast foods and that generate culinary hybrids as migrant and native consumers experiment with new tastes and culinary traditions, preparing kimchi, burritos, or falafel in surprising new ways.[61]

New culinary dynamics are also evident. Protests have emerged against racialized culinary appropriation, when financially successful and usually white restaurateurs popularize the foods of cultures of migrants for wealthy diners or educated hipsters. Such restaurateurs and their consumers have often learned migrant culinary practices not from migrants but through tourism, international study, or media. As new cosmopolitans, residents of global cities abjure corporate, globalized, and fast foods as tasteless and environmentally unsustainable, and they demand local, authentic, organic, or so-called slow foods provided by artisanal producers using older techniques of farming and animal husbandry. Such consumer preferences seem to invert older food mobilities by raising once-disparaged foods of poor peoples to prestige status, encouraging some so-called "foodies"[62] to explore foodstuffs in migrant groceries and retailers. Many more prefer to purchase from the high-end downtown restaurants accused of appropriation or from local, boutique truck farmers – who both depend heavily on low-wage migrant labour. Critiques of the industrial food systems by cosmopolitan urbanites have also generated an impressive array of new dietary philosophies that circulate unattached from human mobility through new media – "clean" or "slow" eating, a return to an imagined "paleo" diet. Rejection on ethical, environmental, or nutritional grounds of the consumption of meat (vegetarianism) or all animal products (veganism) has also proliferated in global cities.

In ethno-burbs, the suburban peripheries of global cities, and rural areas or Indigenous populations, culinary dynamics generate quite different political mobilizations against industrial and globalizing foods. Critiques of culinary hybridization in global cities manifests as defence of the purity of traditional, local, or national foodways imagined as fixed, unchanging, and immobile, as in recent UNESCO designations of cuisines as a form of intangible cultural heritage. Marginalized, colonized, and racialized groups are particularly likely to formulate a defence of culinary localism around the concept of food sovereignty and to emphasize control over food supplies through local initiative, traditional forms of culinary knowledge, and the expansion of community-based subsistence hunting, gardening, animal husbandry, and foraging. By problematizing the distance foods travel, arguments for food often focus on the threats of environmental degradation, global climate change, and species extinction. Like elite critics of the industrial food system, their formulations posit the power of large food corporations as enemies of community health. In some analyses, nation states seem dispensable, irrelevant, or part of the problem, rather than offering regulatory solutions to low agricultural incomes, high food prices, unsustainable farming techniques, or unhealthy diets. In other rural areas, consumers defend traditional culinary cultures based on earlier corporate fast foods as exemplars of national foodways (as touted in 2019, for example, when an American president offered visiting athletes a celebratory banquet of fast foods). Given the diversity of culinary dynamics developing within and beyond global cities, it should be no surprise that there is still little agreement about what new food systems might replace the current one, let alone about how best to achieve change.

Conclusion

University courses on big history usually begin with the cosmological Big Bang, and carry reminders of the fragility and belated appearance on earth of human beings. They enable us to imagine the possibility of species extinction and declining populations, which many fear as the inevitable outcome of global climate change. This chapter instead offers a big history of the entwining of food and human mobilities over several dozen millennia; it allows readers so inclined to do so to begin to imagine alternatives to the current food system. This food system is a product of human actions taken in piecemeal fashion over five millennia. It can and should be picked apart, uncovering several quite different eras of globalization (of human populations, of foodstuffs, of human labour, of food commodities), outlining diverse forms of backlash against globalization, and documenting significant alterations in the relationship and relative importance of food and human mobilities, even within the past 150 years.

For those more interested in the future than the past, a big history of humanity and food brings to the present moment an awareness of the amazing diversity of ways that human and food mobilities have repeatedly intersected to feed human populations. And it especially complicates our understanding of the benefits of culinary localism. Palaeolithic foraging provided an excellent example of how small and – as best we can tell – equitable human societies ate quite well without extensive cultivation, processing, storage, or tools. Still, in today's world of roughly 7.8 billion, scholars estimate that foraging as a mobile way of life would, under current environmental and climatic conditions, support a worldwide population of only 10 million.

A big history shows further that the relatively short travels of both cultivated grains and animal foods during the Neolithic and early world of agrarian cultivators and nomadic pastoralists generated considerable inequality and inequities, and did so long before the racialization of such differences, the industrialization of food production, or the Columbian Exchange globalization. Local food and human mobility circuits supported high levels of expropriation of surplus foodstuffs, with levels of inequality in access to food that were at least as high, if not higher, than those seen today. Levels of malnutrition and ill health were almost certainly very high, since populations increased far more slowly before 1500 than they did after the Columbian Exchange. More recently, too, as the cautionary case of Italy suggests, efforts to restrict food and human mobilities and to encourage local or national food sovereignty emerged in tandem with xenophobia and racism, rather than undermining either.

Finally, a big history points to continuities as well as to diversity, fluidity, and change. Mobility of humans and/or foods has been foundational to human culinary culture in every known society and in every time period. Mobility is likely to remain central in the future. Furthermore, so continuous has been the place and functions of cities in the entanglement of human and food mobilities for 5000 years that it is difficult to imagine them disappearing in the face of even a radically altered food system, an altered climate, or reduced human populations. Cities have repeatedly proved themselves flexible and adaptable; they thrived when food supply chains were still short and local. And it has been in cities where human and food mobilities intersected most obviously, producing culinary mixing, blending, innovation, and contestation that have been common for millennia.

The question for the future is not whether but how food and human mobilities and the current global and industrial food system will change in the years ahead. Five hundred years ago investors and empires had to force, coerce, and enslave humans to move long distances to labour in food production. Today, millions who wish to move cannot do so, largely because of national restrictions on human mobility. Even though nation states have for seventy years diminished trade restrictions, international food trade has not returned to the central place it occupied in the nineteenth century. Today, communication technologies and tourism are as likely to mobilize culinary knowledge, tastes, and hybridization as is human migration or consumption of internationally traded foods.

Industrial production for local and national consumers – not international food trade – is likely the largest generator of environmentally harmful consequences. Nevertheless, the recent viral pandemic produced a cascade of critiques of the vulnerability of long-distance food commodity chains, and in the United Kingdom, Brexit's limits on trade with Europe have turned millions of eyes nervously toward supermarket shelves for further signs of disruption. Even if the arc of culinary dynamics is now bending still further away from globalism and toward localism, the central question posed by Bender and Cinotto about the origins of the industrial system in unique entanglements of human and food mobilities must be understood. Otherwise further restrictions on food and human mobilities will be unable to avoid poisoning positive demands for culinary change with the xenophobia and racism so amply illustrated by big history.

NOTES

1 U.N. Food and Agricultural Organization, "Sustainable Food Systems: Concept and Framework," http://www.fao.org/3/ca2079en/CA2079EN .pdf.

2 Great Britain, House of Commons, *Parliamentary Papers* Vol. 33 (1848): 37, a discussion of Ireland; Margaret Meade, "Food and Feeding in Occupied Territory," *Public Opinion Quarterly* 7, no. 4 (1943): 618–28.

3 A recent introduction to the big history project is David Christian, *Origin Story: A Big History of Everything* (New York: Little, Brown, Spark, 2018). Applying this approach to Food Studies are Jeffrey Pilcher, *Food in World*

History, 2nd ed. (New York: Routledge, 2017), and Linda Civitello, *Cuisine and Culture*, 3rd ed. (Hoboken, NJ: John Wiley and Sons, 2011). See also Gabaccia, "Food, Mobility, and World History," in *The Oxford Handbook of Food History*, ed. Jeffrey M. Pilcher (Oxford: Oxford University Press, 2012), 305–23.

4 Donna R. Gabaccia, "Time and Temporality in Migration Studies," in *Migration Theory: Talking across Disciplines*, ed. Caroline B. Brettell and James F. Hollifield (New York: Routledge, 2015), 37–65.

5 Greg Clark, *Global Cities, a Short History* (Washington, DC: Brookings Institutions Press, 2016). Histories focused on food and cities include Alberto Capatti and Massino Montanari, *Italian Cuisine, a Cultural History* (New York: Columbia University Press, 2003); Michael Freeman, "Sung," in *Food in Chinese Culture: Anthropological and Historical Perspectives*, ed. K.C. Chang (New Haven: Yale University Press, 1977), 141–76.

6 Mimi Sheller and John Urry, "The New Mobilities Paradigm," *Environment and Planning* 38, no. 2 (2006): 207–26; Bryan S. Turner, "The Enclave Society: Towards a Sociology of Immobility," *European Journal of Social Theory* 10, no. 2 (2007): 287–304.

7 Patrick Manning, *A History of the Humanity: The Evolution of the Human System* (Cambridge: Cambridge University Press, 2020), see esp. ch. 2–4.

8 Ashley K. Lemke, ed., *Foraging in the Past: Archaeological Studies of Hunter-Gatherer Diversity* (Boulder: University Press of Colorado, 2018).

9 Katheleen Stirling, "Man the Hunter, Woman the Gatherer? The Impact of Gender Studies on Hunter-Gatherer Research (A Retrospective)," in *The Oxford Handbook of the Archaeology and Anthropology of Hunter Gatherers*, ed. Vicki Cummings, Peter Jordan, and Marek Zvelebil (Oxford: Oxford University Press, 2014), 151–75.

10 Brenna M. Henn, L.L. Cavalli-Sforza, and Marcus W. Feldman, "The Great Human Expansion," *Proceedings of the National Academy of Sciences* 109, no. 44 (2012): 17758–64.

11 See e.g. for inner Eurasia, David Christian, "Inner Eurasia as a Unit of World History," *Journal of World History* 5, no. 2 (1994): 173–211.

12 Ofer Bar-Yosef, "The Upper Paleolithic Revolution," *Annual Review of Anthropology* 31 (2002): 363–93.

13 Malcolm C. Webb, "Exchange Networks: Prehistory," *Annual Review of Anthropology* 3 (1974): 357–83, esp. 361.

14 Roger Lewin, "A Revolution of Ideas in Agricultural Origins," *Science* 240 (20 May 1988): 984–6; Peter Bellwood, *First Farmers: The Origins of Agricultural Societies* (Malden, MA: Blackwell, 2005).

15 Peter S. Ungar, "The Neolithic Revolution," in *Evolution's Bite: A Story of Teeth, Diet, and Human Origins* (Princeton: Princeton University Press, 2017).

16 T. Douglas Price, "Social Inequality at the Origin of Agriculture," in *Foundations of Social Inequality*, ed. T. Douglas Price and Gary M. Feinman (New York: Springer Publishing, 2014), 129–51.

17 Webb, "Exchange Networks," 361.

18 George L. Cowgill, "Origins and Development of Urbanism: Archaeological Perspectives," *Annual Review of Anthropology* 33 (October 2004): 525–49.

19 Brenna Hassett, *Built on Bones: 15,000 Years of Urban Life and Death* (London: Bloomsbury Sigma Press, 2017).

20 Fred Scholz and Gunther Schlee, "Nomads and Nomadism in History," in *International Encyclopedia of the Social & Behavioral Sciences*, 2nd ed., ed. James D. Wright (Amsterdam: Elsevier, 2015), 838–43; David Christian, *A History of Russia, Central Asia, and Mongolia, 1: Inner Eurasia from Prehistory to the Mongol Empire* (Malden, MA: Blackwell, 1998).

21 Andrew Sherratt, "Plough and Pastoralism: Aspects of the Secondary Products Revolution," in *Pattern of the Past: Studies in Honour of David Clarke*, ed. Ian Hodder, Glynn Isaac, and Norman Hammond (Cambridge: Cambridge University Press, 1981), 261–305.

22 David Christian, *This Fleeting World, A Short History of Humanity* (Great Barrington, MA: Berkshire Publishers, 2008), 3.

23 A.D. Blue, "Piracy on the China Coast," *Journal of the Hong Kong Branch of the Royal Asiatic Society* 5 (1965): 69.

24 Randolph B. Ford, *Rome, China and the Barbarians: Ethnographic Traditions and the Transformation of Empires* (Cambridge: Cambridge University Press, 2020).

25 Heidi M. Sherman, "Hinterland," in *Encyclopedia of World Geography*, ed. R.W. McColl (New York: Infobase, Facts on File, 2005), 414–15.

26 William McNeill, "Cities and Their Consequences," *The American Interest* 2, no. 4 (2007): 5–12.

27 Monica Smith, *Cities: The First 6000 Years* (New York: Viking, 2020).

28 David Christian, "Silk Roads or Steppe Roads? The Silk Roads in World History," *Journal of World History* 11, no. 1 (Spring 2000): 1–26. See also Valerie Hansen, *The Silk Road: A New History* (Oxford: Oxford University Press, 2012).

29 Phil Curtin, *Cross-Cultural Trade in World History* (Cambridge: Cambridge University Press, 2014), chs. 4–6.

30 Pilcher, *Food in World History*, ch. 2.

31 Valerie Hansen, *The Year 1000: When Explorers Connected the World – And Globalization Began* (New York: Scribner, 2020), 64–5.

32 Christian, "Inner Eurasia," 194. Immanuel Wallerstein, *The Modern World System: Capitalist Agriculture and the Origins of the European World Economy in the Sixteenth Century* (New York: Academic Press, 1974).

33 William McNeill, *The Rise of the West: A History of the Human Community* (Chicago: University of Chicago Press, 1991), 295.

34 Janet L. Abu-Lughod, *Before European Hegemony: The World System A.D. 1250–1350* (New York: Oxford University Press).

35 Hansen, *The Year 1000*, 2.

36 Pilcher, *Food in World History*, chapter 2.

37 M.N. Pearson, ed., *Spices in the Indian Ocean World* (Abingdon: Routledge, 1996).

38 Alfred W. Crosby, *The Columbian Exchange: Biological and Cultural Consequences of 1492* (Westport, CT: Greenwood, 1972).

39 Carola Hein, "Port Cities" *The Oxford Handbook of Cities in World History*, ed. Peter Clark (Oxford: Oxford University Press, 2013).

40 Marsha Weisiger, "The Origins of Navajo Pastoralism," *Journal of the Southwest* 46, no. 2 (2004): 253–82.

41 Rebecca Earle, *Feeding the People: The Politics of the Potato* (Cambridge: Cambridge University Press, 2020); Sucheta Mazumdar, "The Impact of New World Food Crops on the Diet and Economy of China and India, ca. 1600–1900," in *Food in Global History*, ed. Raymond Grew (Boulder, CO: Westview Press, 1999), 58–78; James C. McCann, *Maize and Grace: Africa's Encounter with a New World Crop, 1500–2000* (Cambridge, MA: Harvard University Press, 2005).

42 Sydney Mintz, *Sweetness and Power: The Place of Sugar in Modern History* (New York: Viking, 1985).

43 John F. Richards, *The Unending Frontier: An Environmental History of the Early Modern World* (Berkeley: University of California Press, 2003), ch. 15.

44 Peter C. Perdue, "Nature and Power: China and the Wider World," *Social Science History* 37, no. 3 (2013): 373–91.

45 Jeff Shanz, "Mercantilism," in *The Business of Food: Encyclopedia of the Food and Drink Industries*, ed. Gary J. Allen and Ken Albala (Westport, CT: ABC-CLIO, 2007), 262–4.

46 Pilcher, *Food in History*, ch. 3.

47 Katharine Donato and Donna Gabaccia, *Gender and International Migration: From the Slavery Era to the Global Age* (New York: Russell Sage Foundation, 2015).

48 David Gentilcore, *Pomodoro! A History of the Tomato in Italy* (New York: Columbia University Press, 2010).

49 Pilcher, *Food in History*, ch. 6.

50 Hasia R. Diner, *Hungering for America: Italian, Irish and Jewish Foodways in the Age of Migration* (Cambridge, MA: Harvard University Press, 2001);

Gabaccia, *We Are What We Eat: Ethnic Food and the Making of Americans* (Cambridge, MA: Harvard University Press, 1998).

51 Elizabeth Zanoni, *Migrant Marketplaces: Food and Italians in North and South America* (Urbana: University of Illinois Press, 2018).

52 Pilcher, "Global Migrant Foodways," in *Cambridge History of Global Migrations*, ed. Donna Gabaccia, vol. 2 (Cambridge and New York: Cambridge University Press, 2023).

53 Pilcher, *Food in History*, ch. 8.

54 Harvey Levenstein, *Fear of Food: A History of Why We Worry about What We Eat* (Chicago: University of Chicago Press, 2012).

55 Sebastian Conrad and Dominic Sachsenmaier, eds., *Competing Visions of World Order: Global Moments and Movements, 1880s–1930s* (Basingstoke, UK: Palgrave MacMillan, 2007).

56 Carol Helstosky, "Fascist Food Politics: Mussolini's Policy of Alimentary Sovereignty," *Journal of Modern Italian Studies* 9, no. 1 (2004): 1–26.

57 Pilcher, *Food in History*, ch. 7.

58 For a brief overview, see Fabio Parasecoli, *Food* (Boston: MIT Press, 2019).

59 George Ritzer, *The McDonaldization of Society: An Investigation into the Changing Character of Contemporary Social Life* (Thousand Oaks, CA: Pine Forge Press, 1993); "The Wal-Martization of America," *New York Times* 15 November 2003.

60 Jennifer Clapp, "Food Security and International Trade: Unpacking Disputed Narratives," 2014–15, http://www.fao.org/3/i5160e/i5160e.pdf.

61 Pilcher, "Global Migrant Foodways."

62 Josée Johnston and Shyon Baumann, *Foodies: Democracy and Distinction in the Gourmet Foodscape* (New York: Routledge, 2009).

PART ONE
The Body and the Self

1 Mobility of Food and Ideas in Egypt: Between Sterilization and Inoculation

SARA EL-SAYED AND CHRISTY SPACKMAN

Egypt sits at the intersection of three continents. Since the first century, cookbooks have documented the flow of foods and ideas related to food along major trade routes.[1] The beginning of the twentieth century witnessed the spread of a particular idea, Pasteurian "germ theory," through Egypt. In the framing of "germ theory" diseases moved between colonies, and colonial rulers implemented hygienic standards as a benchmark of good governance.[2] These concepts still reverberate throughout Egyptian society, due in large part to the value attributed to trade circuits by Egyptian policymakers. As policymakers adopted Western ideas about food safety and maintaining biosecurity as a form of securing the state against economic and political woes, they increasingly distinguished between food products and production practices in ways that changed what is considered safe and unsafe.[3] The Egyptian government's efforts to eradicate disease extend beyond efforts to control microbial life. They have attempted to control the mobility of microbes, animals, and people by creating impermeable barriers.[4] Policymakers' ideas about types of foods and production practices, too, are infectious. These attitudes hinder the mobility of foods and ideas, despite the overlapping and intertwined nature of food mobility in the early twenty-first century.

This chapter examines the tension that exists between the Egyptian state and its sterilizing and militarized approach and a subset of the population that is pushing back against such a rigid system. This sterilizing approach has been indirectly imported to Egypt through US aid to various developing countries. We follow the contested case of late twentieth- and early twenty-first-century chicken raising practices in northern Egypt. We examine how efforts spearheaded by the Egyptian government to promote entrance into the global food market conceptualized traditional poultry husbandry practices as threatening to modernization. This conceptualization turned to one of contamination when mobile germs, specifically Avian influenza H5N1, quickly spread throughout Egypt. The state apparatus responded with what we define as a military-style sterilizing ideology.[5] We see securitization framed by state-led efforts to oust infectious ideas and practices as a form of sterilization.[6] While this discourse of securitization most often appears in militarized counter terrorism efforts, food, too, has long been subjected to the scrutinizing gaze of states in the effort to maintain the food supply's biosecurity while responding to increased global trade infrastructures. Sterilization is a process that marks distinct moments of purposeful intervention in the mobility of microbial life. As such, we find it useful for framing and thinking about government intervention into food systems to remove not only microbial life seen as contaminating, but also ideas.

Government efforts to intentionally eliminate ideas set off a counter movement. In this movement, young activists inspired by the 2011 Arab Spring drew on and mobilized external ideas about food sovereignty to "inoculate" against the government's sterilizing moves. To analyze these events, we draw together scholarship examining the effects of mobility of foods, ideas, technologies, goods, people, and non-humans. The "new mobilities" paradigm demonstrates how increased globalization through transport and communication technology have increased "liquidity" among people, things, and locales.[7] In this conceptualization terrains are not spatially fixed and static geographies but rather are characterized by fluid movement of people, images, and information across regions.[8] While acknowledging the increase in connectivity and empowerment in some cases, the new mobilities paradigm posits that mobility can create social, economic, and political exclusion.[9] This liquidity of information, people, and goods is not without consequence: Skeggs argues that "mobility is a resource to which not everyone has an equal relationship."[10]

Twenty-first-century Egypt provides a powerful case for examining how the liquidity of information about food and food-oriented technologies expands understanding of previous mobilities theories that conceptualized mobility between static "terrains."[29] In this case, information about food and food-oriented technologies moved even as people did not. Food activists in Egypt accessed this information through an increasingly globalized and interconnected media in an effort to upend neoliberal government policies. These policies, created under the umbrella of a liberal open market, facilitated top-down, autocratic control of food production. They did so by increasing safety regulations, a move that prioritizes securitization over other forms of life.[11] The sterilizing nature of these "modernizing" policies, purposefully implemented through a militarized approach that is forceful and top-down, carries the potential to eliminate traditional modes of food production by prioritizing corporations over smallholders.[12] In the process, they confine the flow of ideas while attempting to control and police people and, in this case, poultry.

This chapter draws on literature about government attempts to encourage certain forms of life (e.g., biopolitics),[13] geography, and food studies to build a framework that highlights how mobilities of foods and ideas weave together with biopolitical concerns. We contextualize this framework through Egypt's political situation before and after the 2011 revolts, showcasing how the state's top-down approach relies on securitization and sterilization of ideas, especially as it relates to raising poultry. We explore how Egyptian food activists worked to inoculate against this top-down sterilization, to "live with the disease,"[14] by borrowing and modifying ideas from exogenous alternative food movements. Through participant observation data collected over the course of six years, we explore the "inoculating" work of reintroducing the native *Begawi* chicken into poultry-raising households by the Egyptian social enterprise Nawaya. In using the word inoculation, we are thinking of the practice of adding microbes to a culture to promote desired growth such as fermentation, and the practice of vaccination – giving an attenuated dose of a pathogen to induce immunity. This contrasts with sterilization, which we understand as the effort to completely remove a contaminating substance or idea. By introducing the Begawi chicken, activists sought to protect against the state's sterilizing efforts, enacting an inoculation through education and market building that countered the push to eradicate small-scale poultry raising. Nawaya's work exemplifies how in a globalized world, the liquidity (i.e., free flow) of food and ideas between different people around the globe carries distinct political power even in the face of sterilizing impulses, and does so by providing small, counter-inoculations, of animals, microbes, and values into the food system.

Monoculture and Monopolitics

The Egyptian government began adopting neoliberal policies, privatizing government programs, and minimizing regulatory oversight to promote a capitalist market economy under President Anwar Sadat's Open-Door *Infitah* policy in the 1970s. These efforts continued in the 1980s with President Hosney Mubarak's collaboration with the United States Agency for International Development (USAID) and

International Financial Institutions (IFIs), such as the World Bank, to implement policies promoting additional market liberalization. These included agri-business support for capital-intensive, commodity-driven agriculture models.[15] This, in turn, consolidated previously state-owned food industries to a handful of banks and private equity firms such as Unilever or Concord.[16] The mobility of ideas favouring a free market economy and the reduction of government meant that the neoliberalization of Egyptian policy resituated Egypt's economy from a more diversified economy built on indigenous and traditional practices, to a commodity-driven one run by a handful of banks such as EFG-Hermes and Citadel-Capital.[17]

We see a sterilizing ideology undergirding these recent efforts to liberalize Egypt's food economy. In using the word sterilize, we refer to the complete removal of microbial life through purposeful human intervention. Sterilization does not just remove microbial life; when implemented in public health or medical practice, it can protect economies by preventing disease spread. We follow scholars such as Hinchliffe and Ward in seeing efforts to secure the state against outside influences as being in tension and working in parallel with efforts to ensure the biosecurity of individual bodies within the state.[18] Biosecurity refers to the idea that states can protect economic security and sovereignty by putting in place measures to manage the movement of agricultural pests, diseases, and other biological threats across and within their borders through actions such as border controls, inspections, and quarantines.[19] "Security in this view," Hinchliffe and Ward note, "depends on technologies of sorting, categorizing, and importantly allowing some things and people to circulate while rendering others as detainees or bodies to be ex-communicated."[20] Biosecurity is thus translated as restricting the mobility of certain foods and ideas, based on what is considered secure and free from microbes and contamination.

In agriculture, the Egyptian state's adoption of a sterilizing ideology began in the 1970s with the Open Door policy *and* support from USAID advisers.[21] As the government enacted policies supported by large investments in the agricultural sector, it pushed for a commodity-driven approach aimed at increasing exports.[22] These policies favoured intensive large-scale industrial farms informed by US-based models of farming[23] and sought to reclaim desert lands for agriculture. Unlike traditionally farmed areas, which often exist in the Nile valley and delta, state officials saw large agri-business in desert spaces as offering the potential for controlling and sanitizing agricultural practices.[24] These changes in the 1970s resulted in abandonment of the traditional Egyptian diet primarily composed of vegetarian foods, dairy, and grains, in favour of a more Westernized diet.[25] Scholars link this change in diet with higher rates of obesity and chronic diseases like diabetes.[26]

In the 1980s, the government began sidelining small-scale farms as insufficiently competitive due to their inefficiency and inability to meet global standards.[27] Land tenure reforms in 1992 furthered this, raising rent from 7 to 22 times the land tax and pushing small-scale farmers to the economic and geographical margins. Incentives such as the promise of ensured produce sales, encouraged small-scale farmers towards food production practices valued by international financial agencies.[28] Farmers found themselves pushed and pulled into Egypt's new food regime by these policies. We see this as the beginning of the Egyptian government's efforts to sterilize agricultural processes, in the sense of systematically removing processes and practices seen as contaminating the food system.

Sanitary and Phytosanitary Standards

Sterilizing efforts reflect Egyptian politicians' desire to participate in the world food market. Policies framed as protective or as caring for the population prioritize global-facing business over local success. They reflect the inherent power of circulation, whereby mobility and control over mobility reinforce power.[29] During Mubarak's era, collaborations between the Ministry of Health and Agriculture and corporations not only pushed for a reimagining of farming practices, they also started campaigns to promote adoption of Western-informed food safety practices. These campaigns pushed the Egyptian population towards the wide-scale adoption of industrially produced packaged products. For example, in the 1980s, the Ministry of Agriculture began a media campaign to prevent vendors from selling milk. These vendors traditionally brought fresh, unpasteurized milk from farms into urban areas in large stainless-steel containers for distribution to people's homes. Instead, by means of public–private partnerships, the government promoted hygienically packaged milk to control both the origin and "safety" of the product.[30] Such efforts represent "harmonizing" moves intended to ensure that Egypt meets the production standards of a global market.[31] Global ideas about food safety, embedded in sterilizing policies funded by IFIs, and pushed by a government that is willing to exert its power, eroded local food traditions and sovereignty.

The consequences of these policy changes in Egyptian food production and consumption particularly affected women's livelihoods. Rural women play a key role in local food systems; they have traditionally been responsible for the household's health and nutrition. For example, rural women will wash their hands before and after handling animals or produce, a basic practice in maintaining hygiene. However, new policies and infrastructural constraints have pushed women away from their traditional roles in food production. While many of the younger generations appreciate moving away from traditional roles, they also regret the concomitant loss of their food culture. Policies discouraging the production of traditional foods, many of which the state and urban inhabitants understand as neither nutritional nor hygienic, have meant a systematic erosion of rural agricultural practices. This is especially true of the poultry sector, where women have been central raisers for centuries.

History of Chicken Production Practices

Poultry production is economically, socially, and culturally important in Egypt. Industrial poultry began in 1964 with the establishment of the National General Poultry Company (GPC), a state-owned entity that subsidized poultry sales at cooperative shops. Prior to 1964, backyard and village producers produced the majority of eggs and poultry meat. Today, poultry production practices are aimed at immobilizing microbes and contaminants, and are categorized into one of four sectors, based on how much they actively control microbes: (1) an industrial, integrated system with high-level biosecurity that produces commercially marketed products, primarily aimed at a local market until the 2017 rise in chicken exportation; (2) mid-scale corporate poultry operations for local consumption with moderate to high biosecurity that maintain strict borderlines between poultry and other wildlife; such birds are marketed to local supermarkets; (3) commercial production characterized by minimal biosecurity; birds are sold in live bird markets; (4) village-level, backyard production, often raised on rooftops, typically with no biosecurity measures in place. The animals are often native breeds, and the products are consumed domestically or sold at a live market.[32] The industrial sector is now composed of five corporations, due to a wave of consolidations that took place between 2000 and 2003.[33] The mid-scale corporate and commercial production sectors make up 75 per cent of all broiler productions in Egypt. Meanwhile, village and backyard producers find themselves increasingly excluded from the production ecosystem.[34]

Since the mid-1960s, the state has pushed for an open market that produces poultry at an industrial scale. This was further reinforced in the 1990s. During this time, agri-business actors and bureaucrats at the Ministry of Agriculture full-heartedly embraced Pasteurian "germ theory" and the importance of biosecurity in an attempt to control microbial mobility. The policies resulting from this attempt to control microbial mobility explicitly support the first three sectors and impose implicit barriers for the fourth. As a result, producers in the fourth sector have been steadily pushed to the margins. This is unfortunate, as the fourth sector produces poultry for the majority of poor people, is a main income stream for rural women, and is the only sector raising native birds.

From the establishment of GPC in 1964 to the 1990s, the Egyptian government focused its political and legislative support on promoting the growth of industrialized poultry production. This included a ban on poultry importation, first introduced in the 1980s and fully implemented by 1997, with the aim of encouraging commercial domestic production.[35] In 1988, the government removed feed subsidies that existed for private companies. Sale of the state-owned GPC to the private sector was accompanied by reduced regulations on industrial zones, and decreased subsidies for agricultural exports, to further incentivize industrial and mid-scale corporate sectors.[36] These policies were successful: In the 1990s the growth of poultry industry rose at an average of 8.7 per cent per year; in the early 2000s mergers consolidated poultry companies into large multinationals.[37] Policies promoting industrialization and corporatization of the poultry sector enacted a sterilizing process with the aim of entering the global market. These efforts succeeded: Egypt joined the WTO in 1995.[38]

Arrival of Avian influenza: Biosecurity and Sterilization

Use of market-driven policies to sterilize Egypt's food production modes is especially apparent in the government's treatment of H5N1, avian influenza. The first cases of H5N1 appeared in Egypt in February 2006, initially appearing in twenty-one of twenty-eight governorates – a governorate is a local region with an administrative body run by a governor. Government officials reported the first cases of human transferral less than a month later.[39] Since then, Egypt has experienced minor and major outbreaks, which have affected backyard and industrial poultry production. Epidemiological work attributed initial outbreaks of H5N1 to traditional backyard production, which subsequently spread to mid-scale commercial producers.

The state responded to H5N1 by encouraging the creation of large-scale poultry facilities capable of implementing high biosecurity measures in reclaimed desert lands. During the crisis, Prime Minister Ahmed Nazif stated, "The world is moving towards big farms because they can be controlled under veterinarian supervision ... The time has come to get rid of the idea of breeding chickens on the roofs of houses."[40] This viewpoint showed up in increased importation of frozen chickens, and implementation of strict culling mandates for hundreds of backyard and cottage chicken production operations.[41] The Ministry of Agriculture attributed disease spread to backyard producers' lack of appropriate biosecurity measures. Practices highlighted as suspect included letting animals roam freely, not wearing appropriate gear, and not following standardized disinfection protocols.[42] These practices, opponents argued, allowed microbes free mobility. In response, the government engaged in globally accepted disease prevention measures, and adopted sanitary (human and animal) and phytosanitary (plant) standards codified by the WTO,[43] with the hope of controlling microbial mobility. This meant controlling healthy animals, their feeds, and spatially separating slaughtering and meat storage, in contrast to traditional approaches. Acts such as these created what theorist Bruno Latour refers to as "immutable mobiles."[44] In other words, policymakers tried to control and hold stable that which is constantly mobile, namely germs, using methods that ensured certain producers retained access to a global trading market while protecting national security.

Egyptian officials were not alone in this. Border inspections and import regulations posit food mobility as a constant threat to state security. For example, UK regulators responded in 2001 to the foot and mouth disease outbreak by implementing stricter measures, such as culling entire herds.[45] Egypt adopted a similar, best-standards approach to address the outbreak of avian flu in poultry, enacting what geographers term a "material ordering" of the world.[46] This ordering prioritizes one pathway forward – the ability to enter into global markets – by ordering avian life over the lives of poultry raisers. In the process, biosecurity practices act as sanitization efforts that ignore the role smallholder chicken production plays in Egypt's local, rural economies, as well as the fact that poultry raising is a main source of income for rural women.[47] In so doing, the state created border controls that included new means of surveillance and, ironically, excluded the backyard poultry producers and their so-called risky chickens, located within the state's borders, from full participation in the economy.[48] Evidence that H5N1 can be contagious to humans gave the government an even stronger incentive to prioritize large agribusinesses.[49] Culling birds and focusing support on industrial chicken production allowed the state to sidestep the more laborious work of partnering with small-scale producers to develop solutions that preserved rural economies.

Regulators and policymakers during the H5N1 understood backyard and rooftop poultry raisers and small-scale farmers as failing to keep up to date with modern food production practices. Policymakers viewed small-scale farmers as traditional, uneducated, with erratic behaviours, and thus as unwanted partners in responding to the epidemic. The state instead confiscated chicken coops, culled more than 40 million backyard/cottage birds in villages,[50] and temporarily closed live bird markets as well as the slaughtering of birds in small-scale village slaughterhouses.[51] Extension officers and veterinarians at the Ministry of Agriculture did not try to educate the raisers or implement vaccination programs as they had done for larger producers, nor did they focus on finding ways to "live with the disease."[52] Yet many of the standard interventions – mass vaccinations, animal efforts, and poultry importation – failed to eradicate H5N1. Over subsequent years, pathogen transmission remained high, with a major outbreak in 2014.[53] Despite attempts to eliminate the virus through vaccination programs, culling of backyard production, and closing down live markets, the virus remained. This has been observed elsewhere, such as with ostrich raising in South Africa, where strict biosecurity measures didn't result in an eradication of the disease, but rather meant the disease returned with a higher virulence.[54] Similarly, Egyptian government-driven attempts to sterilize poultry and manage the disease produced stronger virulence of H5N1 virus and increased microbial resistance in animals,[55] while almost completely eradicating backyard production. This top-down securitization approach can be seen in other sectors of managing food, such as handling food shortages, and has set the stage for creating a culture focused on immobilizing ideas and foods.

Mobilizing Foods and Mobile Ideas

Egyptian politicians sought simultaneously to increase mobility of Egyptian-produced foodstuffs outside of Egypt while decreasing the movement of political ideas into Egypt. Although the two may seem separate, themes of contamination and sterilization reveal their connections. Egypt's food system has depended on imports since the 1980s to bolster its extensive food subsidy program. The subsidy program that began in the 1940s today has expanded to offer over 100 commodity foods, known as *Tamween*.[56] In 2007, global food prices spiked. According to Egypt's Central Agency for Public Mobilization and Statistics, half of Egypt's population is poor or near poor; the number of people qualifying for *Tamween* in 2015–16 reached 60 million.[57] *Tamween* provided staples in an effort to support food-insecure inhabitants. The program's focus on staples, and dependence on imported wheat, strained bakeries. As bread prices spiked, people could no longer afford to meet their basic food needs. Despite the Egyptian proverb that "nobody sleeps hungry and nobody dies of hunger,"[58] reality proved more dire. Lack of access to affordable food contributed to escalating tensions between Egyptians and their government.[59]

Food shortages coupled with foreign ideas about regime change threatened the Egyptian power structure. Tensions that arose during the financial crisis culminated in protests, fuelled by the success of similar efforts in Tunisia.[60] Mobilized via Facebook and Twitter, in early January 2011, activists called on Egyptians to protest police brutality and change the government's status quo.[61] Social media's ability to give ideas mobility provided people with means to oppose the government and state-run media in previously unprecedented ways; Egyptian protests have remained minimal since passage of the Emergency Law of 1981, which extended police power, suspended constitutional rights, and allowed censorship.[62] In this context, members of the government and state media treated the ideas circulating through social media as contaminating. Dubbed *Talawth Fekry* (Polluting Ideas), officials claimed protests organized by groups such as the *Setta Ebril* (April Six) movement through social media were spearheaded by youth who had been influenced by ideas made mobile through Western media. For fear of the social media influence, the government shut down communication, cutting cellular phone connection for five days, and blocking social media on 29 January.[63]

The shutdown of non-official communication channels by Mubarak's government and its media apparatus sought to protect the government from contaminating ideas about issues of justice, freedom, and bread. Bread, an important aspect of daily life, became a symbol of oppression, symbolized by long lines of people fighting to get their quota of subsidized bread (figure 1.1).[64] Despite laws that allegedly encourage freedom of speech, the emergency law put in place during the revolt overturned any semblance of freedom.[65] In September 2011, a few days after the government extended the use of the emergency law against entities accused of spreading rumours, security forces raided the news offices of Al Jazeera *Mubasher Misr* and barred their broadcast for allegedly not having a permit.[66] Such tactics sought to sterilize messages seen as contaminating the state's ability to control people's thinking and actions.

The 2011 revolts resulted in a surge of food activism backed by the slogan "Bread, Freedom, and Social Justice." Activists worked to imagine a more inclusive, diversified food system rooted in self-sufficient wheat production and focused on small-scale farmers and their land tenures. These

Figure 1.1 Frustrated people, lining up daily at local bakeries to receive their daily quotas of subsidized bread. Image by Nawaya.[67]

activists aimed to counter the Egyptian state's "sterilizing" approach that sought to remove "polluting" ideas by working to enable the mobility of new ideas about justice and food production into Egypt's food system. Beyond the initial mobilization by social media to take to the streets,[68] the following years saw ideas circulated first through social media translated into physical manifestations, such as workshops and comedy shows that discussed diverse issues, including food. Through these efforts activists worked to expand how Egyptians at all levels defined the food system. They sought to valorize Egypt's geography and history of incorporating multiple foods and ideas within its culture.[69] In other words, activists sought what Carlo Petrini refers to as "virtuous globalization": an embrace of diversity through globalization, where ideas and foods are traded, reinvented, and re-localized by those normally excluded by market monopolies.[70]

For example, young Egyptians, including author El-Sayed, began collaborating with independent farmers' unions to promote agrarian reforms after 2011. These unions had unsuccessfully battled with the government for land rights since the 1950s. Together, activists and independent farmers' unions drew on ideas made mobile via social media. They borrowed approaches from movements such as La Via Campesina, an international peasant movement founded by small and mid-scale producers from Latin America in 1993.[71,72] Although statistics are difficult to verify in Egypt's non-transparent climate, the Cairo-based Sons of the Soil Land Centre reported that from 2009 to 2010 there were 180 sit-ins, 132 demonstrations, and six strikes in rural areas. Police arrested more than 3,000 farmers and their supporters; more than 2,500 were injured, and 400 died.[73] In Egypt's sterilizing system, farmers' unions' demands were opposed by parliament and the Ministry of Agriculture. This is because small-scale farmers are seen by the state as non-modern and harmful to Egyptian progress, an understanding extended to the public through state-controlled media.[74] Combating the sterilizing efforts of government crackdowns and state-controlled media called for a different approach, one that drew on the liquidity of ideas to mobilize alternative approaches to food production.

Liquid Ideas

The period around the Arab Spring saw a number of grassroots organizations in Egypt begin working to valorize traditional foods and production practices. Here we focus on one such organization, Nawaya. Co-founded by El-Sayed in 2011, Nawaya is a grassroots social enterprise that aims to improve livelihoods in Egyptian farming communities. Nawaya was inspired by ideas from the Slow Food movement about food sovereignty and agro-biodiversity. The group understands agriculture as the backbone of Egypt's past and present. It argues that agricultural reforms and state policies seek to sterilize Egyptian food production, and in the process erase key aspects of Egypt's identity. Nawaya's core members are urbanites with strong networks to education, funding, and markets. They partnered with ten small-scale producers in the peri-urban area of Badrashin in the Giza governorate who shared a willingness to innovate to improve the food system. Together, Nawaya's founders, activists, and farmers sought to build and strengthen relationships between rural and peri-urban farmers and urban eaters in greater Cairo. In the process, they enabled a new set of ideas to flow into the food system from outside of Egypt.

In Arabic, *Nawaya* means seed. The term also connotes good intentions. Nawaya was created to spread the seeds of ideas from organizations such as Slow Food that focus on food sovereignty, thus facilitating the mobility of ideas to seed a return to and reinvention of traditional and indigenous Egyptian products. Nawaya tackled issues of food and social justice by providing training to small-scale producers in the techniques necessary to bring back and commercialize traditional foods, thereby enabling a liquidity of knowledge through various means. This training inoculated producers against the negative impacts of biosecurity efforts to eradicate H5N1, as well as the larger sterilizing rhetoric that devalued backyard production. The good intention at the heart of Slow Food, adapted by Nawaya, was to provide sustainable livelihoods and new means of income for farmers. This, the founders posited, would offer producers marginalized by the land reforms – and accompany "sterilizing" concepts of what "good" agriculture looked like – the opportunity to carve out new ways of living and production that sustained reinvented rural, smallholder life. Nawaya imported ideas to valorize the farmers' traditional forms of living and translate those ideas into emergent farming and food production systems. These systems, Nawaya argued, would reflect cultural traditions while ensuring viability in Egypt's market economy. Nawaya sought this by creating alliances with organizations, such as Slow Food and Access Agriculture (a group that develops farmer-to-farmer educational videos). These alliances facilitated a global flow of ideas and people to and from Egypt. Through these alliances Egyptians learned from the lived experiences of other people in other places, inoculating themselves against the state's sterilizing rhetoric with a more expansive and mobile conception of what a biologically secure agriculture could look like. The mission and day-to-day interventions for Nawaya's founders focused on the ability of food producers to reclaim their lost identity, and of Egyptians to reclaim their disappearing food heritage.

Nawaya's seeding effort sought to redefine and valorize Egypt's food biodiversity.[75] Food biodiversity refers to a variety of indigenous products based on climatic adaptations as well as methods of processing and transforming them. However, members of Nawaya struggled to assess what constituted Egyptian food. This struggle was due in part to Egypt's historic and geographical position as a crossroads where different cultures met. Nawaya's members needed to determine which foods made economic, political, and strategic sense to reintroduce and reinvent. Poultry emerged as one clear traditional and culturally valued product. Visit a rural home and as a sign of generosity the hosts will welcome you by slaughtering and grilling a chicken; it is considered more valuable to offer a protein dish to a visitor than a simple vegetarian one. However, as seen above, the Egyptian government's attitudes towards home-produced poultry drastically shifted with the onset of avian influenza and subsequent sterilizing efforts like culling, interrupting this traditional mode of hospitality. In 2013, Nawaya began introducing *Begawi* chickens to small-scale producers and the public. In reintroducing a native poultry breed, Nawaya sought to mobilize the idea that small-scale and backyard producers can raise a safe product.

Begawi chickens have existed in Egypt for more than 3,000 years. Used primarily for egg production, producers globally breed *Begawi* chickens in conjunction with other breeds to produce a hardier, tastier, more disease-resistant egg. However, as Nawaya tried to support the return of this indigenous breed, concerns about H5N1, and its contagiousness to humans, threatened efforts to bring *Begawi* chickens back into Egyptian food production. The question became how to "live with the disease."[76] Nawaya responded by creating its own safety measures to promote the development of cottage (or backyard) industries in peri-urban regions in Egypt's north. Nawaya's leaders embraced geographers' claims that microorganisms, flora, and fauna will flow and cannot be contained within borders. In this they adopted ideas about a more expansive concept of building immunity,[77] drawing on ideas about food safety and animal husbandry from Slow Food projects in rural Italy. They also collaborated with a consultant from the Integrated Poultry project in Fayoum,[78] who had been working both on researching the breed, as well as documenting the husbandry practices of rural women. Since 1983, the Integrated Poultry project has focused on raising indigenous pure breeds of *Begawi* and Fayoumi chickens.[79] These ideas and know-how included changing the perceptions that poultry raising is hazardous, finding ways to create increased immunity. Adopted practices included selecting hardier breeds, changing poultry handling practices, using alternative natural feeding programs, training on some vaccination and safety protocols, and, most critically, devising new specifications for chicken coops.

To succeed in Egypt's sterilizing environment, Nawaya needed to inoculate ideas of good hygiene practices. Chicken coops proved a critical passage point for the effort to allow producers to continue breeding their own chickens. Traditionally, cottage poultry is rarely raised in coops. Rather, producers allow animals to roam on rooftops and through streets. This sometimes results in interaction with wild animals. However, new legal restrictions on poultry production required poultry to be limited in contact with each other and humans, and imposed sanitary measures that threatened to undermine smallholder producers' ability to continue their own poultry raising efforts. To address these legal concerns, Nawaya worked with producers in the form of collaborative workshops to develop standards guiding cottage poultry raising. These standards deviated from industrial-scale biosecurity measures. Members tested these measures with an initial group before encouraging widespread adoption. Measures included limiting the numbers of chickens per coop, identifying types of feeds used, setting in place vaccination schedules, egg handling and packaging protocols, and separating sick animals from healthy. In order to ensure

Figure 1.2   Informal chicken houses (left image) with little ventilation, proper food, water, and hatchery, and improved Nawaya coops (right image) with ventilation, hygienic feeders and waterers, and appropriate space for chicken raising. Images by Nawaya.

implementation, a new configuration emerged: one person was selected from within the community to do random visits to ensure avian and human safety (figure 1.2). These efforts provided a means for backyard raisers to deal with diseases through culturally relevant safety protocols built on ideas mobilized from external and internal sources as to how humans, animals, and disease can coexist.

Nawaya's efforts to create spaces where cottage industry production could thrive contrasted with the Egyptian government's preferred approach: eliminating cottage industries through time-intensive education and inspection requirements. Instead, the government chose to maintain safety standards by facilitating production through larger farms capable of hiring veterinarians that monitor vaccine protocols, and by trading with international companies for frozen meats.[80] The trend towards stricter biosecurity protocols did not originate in Egypt. Rather, these ideas entered Egypt via international scientific networks largely unconcerned with the impact of biosecurity protocols on the lives of poor or geographically marginalized producers. In contrast, Nawaya explored the most inclusive ways to safely raise poultry. Laura Tabet, Nawaya co-founder, and project manager for the traditional poultry project, went on training tours in rural Italy to learn from others in the Slow Food network. By connecting with Slow Food, Nawaya increased the mobility of ideas; this enabled the Nawaya project to nominate the *Begawi* chicken as a Slow Food Presidia.[81] Inoculating Egyptian practices with Italian ideas required on-the-ground contextualization and adaptation, given the differences of raising chickens in the Italian countryside and on Egypt's rooftops. Therefore, Nawaya organized a hybrid biosecurity approach in which animals needed to be kept in chicken coops and given vaccines, while also roaming freely for a period of time during the day. These efforts were coupled with awareness-raising programs for consumers on the significance of consuming local breeds to encourage growth of this cottage industry.

The twinned effort of educating people about traditional foods while also pushing for legislative change permitted an expansion of approved cottage industries. To take advantage of this, Nawaya members and a multi-generational group of women from the peri-urban area of Saqqara[82] began exploring how they could mobilize the idea of *Baladi* food. *Baladi* is home-bred food; the word literally means "from the country."[83] This was part of the effort to expand ideas about what food should and could look like in Egypt by bringing more people into the "Baladi" space. Group members explored how to use *Begawi* eggs produced by Nawaya farmers with inadequate market reach. After iterations, the group adopted the idea of making homemade pasta. While for outsiders this may seem strange, pasta making in Egypt is widespread across small villages; women often get pasta machines as a wedding gift. Pasta's presence reflects Egyptian comfort in adapting and adopting foods and techniques that have circulated across its borders. The decision to make pasta from *Begawi* eggs in the face of Egypt's sterilizing agricultural policies resulted in another form of food mobility: one that embraced Egyptian food as capable of encountering foods and ideas from elsewhere and transforming them into something capable of engaging with current political and economic needs. This product exemplified the value of food mobility, both in terms of ideas and finding ways of reinventing a traditional product and adding value to it, as well as mobility in terms of the fusion that Egypt has experienced over its history.

Conclusion

The ideas made mobile by food activists like those involved with Nawaya centred on concepts of heritage and food sovereignty. Activists understood from their contact with organizations like Slow Food and la Via Campesina that enabling the adoption or return to more sustainable food production practices was central to creating a just food system. This shows up in the language activists successfully proposed by a food sovereignty working group into article 79 of the 2014 constitutional amendment. The new language declared that "the State shall also ensure sustainable food sovereignty and maintain agricultural biological diversity and types of local plants in order to safeguard the rights of future generations."[84] By incorporating the broad concept of food sovereignty, the

Constitutional Assembly adopted internationally informed ideas about the value of smallholder farming. Unfortunately, the amendment did not significantly alter policies that marginalize smallholders. It remains evident that previously adopted neoliberal policies and large companies' interests are still central to contemporary policy.

Grassroots organizations including independent farmers, researchers working on rights-based legislation, and small social enterprises, work to ensure a more inclusive, diverse, and economically viable road to opening up Egypt's food system. Nawaya, with its *Begawi* chicken project sought to align with virtuous globalization, linking old traditions and native breeds with innovative ideas. The poultry project was a trial of the arduous work needed to be able to live with disease while partnering with small-scale producers to preserve rural economies. This created a new niche, one capable of reinvigorating smallholder poultry production in a manner that also enabled the safety of the producers and consumers.

The mobility of ideas, like the mobility of microbes, is shaped by politics.[85] As such, it too is understood by governments as amenable to sterilizing techniques. The Egyptian government took the role of this sterilizing body, acting to remove contaminants with the intention of bringing Egypt to the global marketplace. This, however, was met with internal food activist movements and demonstrates that the liquidity of ideas can flow in multiple directions. Food sovereignty movements have drawn on mobile ideas to alter the current government structures. In Egypt, this process has been both top-down, in terms of constitution and policies, and sparked by the 2011 revolts that introduced or inoculated concepts of food sovereignty into Egypt's sterilizing approach to food production, as well as bottom-up, at the community level, where a handful of small-farmer projects are carving new spaces for Egypt's food system. Movement of ideas via various innovations, such as the internet and mobile technologies, influenced activists as they drew from Slow Food and other food sovereignty movements. Despite these mobilities, the Egyptian state continued to sterilize ideas and foods. The move to create more expansive spaces for the concept of Egyptian food laid the foundation for a diversity of food production practices. These include devising more flexible cottage industry regulations, reinventing traditional foods to access new markets and valorize heritage products, and finding new technologies to give small-scale farmers access to knowledge and know-how. We anticipate that as ideas continue to flow, those working to change Egypt's food system will have an increasingly powerful array of tools at hand, as well as a wealth of knowledge to similarly send along to others seeking to institute change.

NOTES

1 Hala N. Barakat, "We Are What We Eat, We Were What We Ate," in *Cairo Papers in Social Science*, ed. Malak Rouchdy and Iman A Hamdy (Cairo: Cairo Papers In Social Science, 2016), 7–23.

2 M. Harrison, "War, Epidemics and Empire: British Military Government in the Middle East, 1914–1918," *Journal of the Society for Army Historical Research* (2018): 1–25.

3 Marion W. Dixon, "Biosecurity and the Multiplication of Crises in the Egyptian Agri-Food Industry," *Geoforum* 61 (2015): 90–100.

4 Steve Hinchliffe, *Geographies of Nature* (London: Sage, 2007).

5 Hinchliffe, *Geographies*.

6 Steve Hinchliffe et al., "Biosecurity and the Topologies of Infected Life: From Borderlines to Borderlands," *Transaction of the Institute of British Geographers* 38, no. 4 (2013): 531–43.

7 Mimi Sheller and John Urry, "The New Mobilities Paradigm," *Environment and Planning A* 38, no. 2 (2006): 210.

8 Zygmunt Bauman, *Liquid Modernity* (Cambridge: Polity Press, 2000); Sheller and Urry, "New Mobilities Paradigm."

9 Stephen Graham and Simon Marvin, *Splintering Urbanism: Networked Infrastructures, Technological Mobilities and the Urban Condition* (Hove, UK: Psychology Press, 2001).

10 Beverley Skeggs, *Class, Self, Culture* (London: Routledge, 2004), 49; Yasmine M. Ahmed and Reem Saad, "Interview with Shahenda Maklad," *Review of African Political Economy* 38, no. 127 (2011): 159–67.

11 Steve Hinchliffe and Kim J. Ward, "Geographies of Folded Life: How Immunity Reframes Biosecurity," *Geoforum* 53 (2014): 136–44.

12 Hinchliffe, *Geographies*.

13 Bruce Braun, "Biopolitics and the Molecularization of Life," *Cultural Geographies* 14, no. 1 (2007): 6–28.

14 Hinchliffe, *Geographies*; Charles Mather and Amy Marshall, "Living with Disease? Biosecurity and Avian Influenza in Ostriches," *Agriculture and Human Values* 28, no. 2 (2011): 153–65.

15 Ray Bush, "Politics, Power and Poverty: Twenty Years of Agricultural Reform and Market Liberalisation in Egypt," *Market-Led Agrarian Reform: Trajectories and Contestations* 28, no. 8 (2007): 1599–1615.

16 Marion W. Dixon, "The Land Grab, Finance Capital, and Food Regime Restructuring: The Case of Egypt," *Review of African Political Economy* 41, no. 140 (2014): 232–48.

17 Dixon, "The Land Grab."

18 Hinchliffe and Ward, "Geographies of Folded Life."

19 FAO, *Biosecurity for Highly Pathogenic Avian Influenza, Organization*, 2008, https://doi.org/10.1046/j.1365-2869.1997.00023.x; Mather and Marshall, "Living with Disease? Biosecurity and Avian Influenza in Ostriches."

20 Hinchliffe and Ward, "Geographies of Folded Life," 137.

21 Bush, "Politics, Power and Poverty."

22 Dixon, "The Land Grab."

23 Bush, "Politics, Power and Poverty."

24 Dixon, "Biosecurity."

25 Habiba Hassan-Wassef, "Food Habits of the Egyptians: Newly Emerging Trends," *Eastern Mediterranean Health Journal* 10, no. 6 (2004): 1–18.

26 Marion W. Dixon, "Food and Crisis in Egypt: Corporate Food and Class Inequalities," *Thimar* no. 184 (2017).

27 Marion W. Dixon, "Plastics and Agriculture in the Desert Frontier," *Comparative Studies of South Asia, Africa and the Middle East* 37, no. 1 (2017): 86–102

28 Saker El Nur, "Challenges of Food Sovereignty in the Arab World (Egypt as a Model تحديات السيادة الغذائية في العالم العربي (مصر نموزجا)," *Alternative Economy Series* سلسلة الاقتصاد البديل, 2017, http://www.socialjusticeportal.org/wp-content/uploads/2017/11/تحديات-السيادة-الغذائية-في-العالم-العربي-مصر-نموذجا.pdf; Hassan-Wassef, "Food Habits of the Egyptians."

29 Sheller and Urry, "The New Mobilities"; Skeggs, *Class, Self, Culture*.

30 Marion W. Dixon, *The Making of the Corporate Agri-Food System in Egypt* (Ithaca, NY: Cornell University Press, 2013); "Juhayna Food Industries: EFG-Hermes Buy Rating," EFG-Hermes, 2010, http://mec.biz/term/uploads/JUFO_29-07-2010.pdf%0AEgypt.; Dixon, "Biosecurity."

31 Dixon, "Biosecurity."

32 I. ElMasry et al., "Avian Influenza H5N1 Surveillance and Its Dynamics in Poultry in Live Bird Markets, Egypt," *Transboundary and Emerging Diseases* 64, no. 3 (2017): 805–14; Farid A. Hosny, "Poultry Sector Country Review," *Food and Agriculture Organization of the United Nations* 147 (2008): 25–7; FAO, "Poultry Sector Country Review: Egypt. Food and Agriculture Organization of the United Nations," 2006, ftp://ftp.fao.org/docrep/fao/011/ai355e/ai355e00.pdf.

33 Dixon, "The Land Grab."

34 Hosny, "Poultry Sector."

35 Hosny, "Poultry Sector."

36 Dixon, "Biosecurity."

37 Hosny, "Poultry Sector."

38 Dixon, "Biosecurity and the Multiplication of Crises in the Egyptian Agri-Food Industry."

39 F.O. Fasina, V.I. Ifende, and A.A. Ajibade, "Avian Influenza A(H5N1) in Humans: Lessons from Egypt," *Surveillance and Outbreak Reports* 15, no. 4 (2010).

40 Against the Grain, "The Top-Down Global Response to Bird Flu," *Against The Grain* (Barcelona, 2006), 2.

41 Dixon, "Biosecurity."

42 F.O. Fasina et al., "The Cost-Benefit of Biosecurity Measures on Infectious Diseases in the Egyptian Household Poultry," *Preventive Veterinary Medicine* 103, nos. 2/3 (2012): 178–91; ElMasry et al., "Avian Influenza."

43 Jamie Gallagher and Aideen McKevitt, "Laws and Regulations of Traditional Foods: Past, Present and Future," in *Traditional Foods: History, Preparation, Processing and Safety*, ed. Mohammed Al-Khusaibi, Nasser Al-Habsi, and Mohammad Shafiur Rahman (Berlin: Springer, 2019), 239–71.

44 Bruno Latour, "Drawing Things Together," in *Representation in Scientific Practice*, ed. M. Lynch and S. Woolgar (Cambridge, MA: MIT Press, 1990), 19–68.

45 Law and Mol, "Globalisation."

46 Law and Mol., "Globalisation."

47 Habib Ayeb and Reem Saad, "Gender, Poverty, and Agro-Biodiversity Conservation in Rural Egypt and Tunisia," *Agrarian Transformation in the Arab World: Persistent and Emerging Challenges* 32, no. 2 (2009): 129–55.

48 Hinchliffe and Ward, "Geographies of Folded Life," 137.

49 Dixon, "Biosecurity."

50 Hosny, "Poultry Sector Country Review"; Dixon, "Biosecurity"; FAO, *Biosecurity for Highly Pathogenic Avian Influenza*.

51 Dixon, "Biosecurity."

52 Hinchliffe, *Geographies*; Mather and Marshall, "Living with Disease? Biosecurity and Avian Influenza in Ostriches."

53 Dixon "Biosecurity"; ElMasry et al., "Avian Influenza H5N1 Surveillance and Its Dynamics in Poultry in Live Bird Markets, Egypt."

54 Mather and Marshall, "Living with Disease?"

55 Adèle Mennerat et al., "Intensive Farming: Evolutionary Implications for Parasites and Pathogens," *Evolutionary Biology* 37, no. 2 (2010): 59–67.

56 Moustafa Abdalla and Sherine Al-Shawarby, "The Tamween Food Subsidy System in Egypt Evolution and Recent Implementation Reforms," in *The 1.5 Billion People Question: Food, Vouchers, or Cash Transfers?* ed. Ugo Gentilini, Harold Alderman, Ruslan Yemtsov (Washington, DC: World Bank, 2017), 107–50. The *Tamween* program includes subsidies for five loaves of *Baladi* bread per person/day or 10 kg per individual/month; ration cards give a monthly allowance of 15LE ($1) per person/month.

57 Tamween Subsidies, CAPMAS, https://www.capmas.gov.eg/HomePage .aspx.

58 Chris McGreal, "Egypt: Bread Shortages, Hunger and Unrest," *The Guardian*, 26 May 2008.

59 Dixon, "Plastics and Agriculture in the Desert Frontier"; Nahed Eltantawy and Julie B Wiest, "The Arab Spring: Social Media in the Egyptian Revolution: Reconsidering Resource Mobilization Theory," *International Journal of Communication* 5 (2011): 18.

60 Eltantawy and Wiest, "The Arab Spring | Social Media in the Egyptian Revolution."

61 Serajul I. Bhuiyan, "Social Media and Its Effectiveness in the Political Reform Movement in Egypt," *Middle East Media Educator* 1, no. 1 (2011): 14–20.

62 Bhuiyan; Eltantawy and Wiest, "The Arab Spring | Social Media in the Egyptian Revolution."

63 Bhuiyan, "Social Media and Its Effectiveness in the Political Reform Movement in Egypt."

64 Habib Ayeb and Ray Bush, "Small Farmer Uprisings and Rural Neglect in Egypt and Tunisia," *Middle East Report* 272, no. 44 (2014): 9.

65 Abdalla and Al-Shawarby, "The Tamween."

66 Abdalla and Al-Shawarby, "The Tamween."

67 Peter Heba Saleh, "Egypt's Loan Conditions Leave Poor on the Bread Line," *Financial Times*, 5 May 2017, https://www.ft.com/content/77e6649e-3017-11e7-9555-23ef563ecf9a.

68 Eltantawy and Wiest, "The Arab Spring | Social Media in the Egyptian Revolution."

69 Barakat, "We Are What We Eat"; Hassan-Wassef, "Food Habits of the Egyptians: Newly Emerging Trends."

70 Stephen Schneider, "Good, Clean, Fair: The Rhetoric of the Slow Food Movement," *National Council of Teachers of English* 70, no. 4 (2008): 384–402; Adrian Peace, "Terra Madre 2006: Political Theater and Ritual Rhetoric in the Slow Food Movement," *Gastronmica* 8, no. 2 (2008): 31–9.

71 La Via Campesina pioneered concepts of food sovereignty encoded in 2007 in the Nyéléni declaration. Defining an international agenda for food sovereignty developed by the international steering committee of the International Forum for Food Sovereignty. Food sovereignty was defined as: "the right of people to healthy and culturally appropriate food produced through ecologically sound and sustainable methods, and their right to define their own food and agriculture systems." Peter Rosset, "Food Sovereignty: Global Rallying Cry of Farmer Movements," *Food First* 9, no. 4 (2003): 1; "Nyéléni 2007 Forum for Food Sovereignty," *Nyeleni*, 2007.

72 "Nyéléni 2007 Forum for Food Sovereignty."

73 Ayeb and Bush, "Small Farmer Uprisings and Rural Neglect in Egypt and Tunisia."

74 Ayeb and Bush, "Farmers and Farming."

75 Sara Pozzi and Sara El Sayed, "Where Is Our Baladi Food?," in *The Food Question in the Middle East*, ed. Malak S. Rouchdy and Iman A. Hamdy (Cairo: American University in Cairo Press, 2017), 45–60.

76 Mather and Marshall, "Living with Disease?"

77 Hinchliffe, "Biosecurity"; Hinchliffe and Ward, "Geographies of Folded Life"; John Law, "Disaster in Agriculture: Or Food and Mouth Mobilities," *Environment and Planning A* 38, no. 2 (2006): 227–39.

78 The region of Fayoum is well known within Egypt and to poultry experts around the world for its poultry production.

79 Sarah Salah and Michele Abd El-Aal, الدواجن التكاملى: مخزن السلالات المحلية والمستنبطة Integrated Poultry – Storage Facility for Local and Mixed Breeds," *ElWatan News*, 2018.

80 Dixon, "The Making of the Corporate Agri-Food System in Egypt."

81 Slow Food Presidium is a type of organization that sustains quality production at risk of extinction, protects unique regions and ecosystems, recovers traditional processing methods, and safeguards native breeds and local plant varieties. www.fondazioneslowfood.com/.

82 Pozzi and El-Sayed, "Where Is Our Baladi Food?"

83 Ayeb and Saad, "Gender, Poverty, and Agro-Biodiversity Conservation."

84 El Nur, "Challenges of Food Sovereignty in the Arab World (Egypt as a Model)" 5 تحديات السيادة الغذلئية في العالم العربي :مصر نموزجا.

85 Braun, "Biopolitics."

2 Let's Get Phygital: Food Representations on the Move

SIGNE ROUSSEAU

This chapter recognizes that while the challenges and opportunities resulting from the mobilities of globalization relate most obviously to the concrete logistics of building food security for communities in flux, they can also profoundly affect the less quantifiable issue of how *ideas* about food are represented and consumed in a world increasingly characterized by a hybrid experience between the "virtual" and "IRL" (In Real Life). This fluidity between the digital and the physical was captured in the 2018 portmanteau "phygital" – somewhat regrettably for those of us who grew up with the ear-worm chorus "let's get physical, physical" from Olivia Newton-John's 1981 aerobics smash hit "Physical" – coined to describe how some brands already were, and most *should* be, going forward: by prioritizing a consumer experience more closely aligned with how a growing number of people spend their time moving seamlessly between off- and online worlds.[1] In that scenario, a commodity is not simply the end product of a value chain that involves, for example, the processes of transforming an avocado from an exotic fruit into a globally accessible – and affordable – staple, all of which depend on the intricacies and infrastructures of trade, transportation, politics, and economics, which to a large degree inform the study of "mobility." It is also the process by which an avocado can be apotheosized into a celebrity in its own right, thanks to its place on trendy brunch menus (typically "smashed" on artisanal sourdough), its virtues as a hair- or facemask extolled by someone "famous for being famous," or by being chosen as the tattoo du jour of another cultural icon.

None of this would be possible without arguably the most powerful – and mobilizing – tools of all: digital platforms for generating and capturing attention. So, while an exhaustive narrative of mobility of an avocado likely includes a dark journey in a container on a ship, train, or truck operated by largely anonymous bodies, that story is not the focus of this chapter, because it is not the one we can typically *see*, crucial though it is. Yet the stories about avocados and kale related here – as just two examples of foods with notable semantic fluidity beyond their dictionary definitions – are about movement, and attention, and the extent to which digital representations of food are key examples of the "mobility turn" that rejects a view of culture and society as *immobile*: the physical and digital spaces we inhabit are indeed not static units, and as long as technology provides opportunities to roam, explore, create value, and assign meaning – even without being physically on the move – they likely never will be.

BC (Before Coronavirus)

For the physical part of the "phygital" equation, it bears noting that the specific mobility of globalization is not a new phenomenon. The migration of people and (in the context of this volume) edible commodities is a dynamic that has been on the move, so to speak, at least since the centuries-old exploits of the Roman Empire to conquer new territories. Yet we can, following economist Tim Harford, isolate an early (BC) version of "modern" globalization as contingent on a series of technological and industrial developments in the last few decades that have accelerated the "trade of goods and services; migration of people; the exchange of technical knowledge; 'foreign direct investment,' or building or buying factories and companies abroad; and cross-border investments in financial assets like shares and bonds."[2] But the modern *experience* of these changes is perhaps best summarized by Harford's observation that "the most visible manifestation of the world's increasing economic interdependence is the availability of foreign products in familiar settings."[3] Nowhere does this ring truer than in the world of food, both in terms of finding products from Thailand in a supermarket in Alaska, and of being able to virtually follow every meal a friend enjoys on a vacation to Thailand from the increasingly familiar (but always moving) "place" of one's mobile device.

   With the advent of the internet generally, and social media in particular,[4] there is a lot more happening, and possibly at stake, than moving money and goods around the world. One early example of the "phygital" included clothing stores featuring "smart" fitting rooms equipped with digital platforms through which shoppers could request assistance rather than having to get dressed and physically collect different sizes or items (or find an employee to do so for them).[5] In China, Kentucky Fried Chicken (KFC) introduced in-store smart screens in 2016 that use facial recognition and AI technology to personalize offers, and to facilitate easy online payment. The prospect of this particular direction can arguably be as chilling as it is convenient (it is not difficult to conceive of repeat visits to KFC affecting a Chinese citizen's "social credit" score with the result of effectively "de-mobilizing" them).[6]

In this chapter, however, I want to focus on a slightly different manifestation of this (relatively) new "phygital" world in relation to food; namely, how technological developments facilitate the mobilization of *ideas* about food in and through the physical and digital spaces we occupy and operate in, often with the result that the *material* significance of the food in question (its nutritional value and contribution to a varied diet, but also issues related to trade and availability, food security, environmental sustainability, and, crucially, price) is often overshadowed by the cultural capital generated by its *representation*. Put simply, Instagram-favoured foods like avocado and kale can demonstrate more than just the movement and availability of goods thanks to globalization and physical mobility. Examining these examples through the broader theoretical lenses of attention economics and media studies, they reveal narratives of economic, racial, and gendered privilege and inequality, and ultimately the inherent flux and volatility of a "mobilized" world; even if that world – and the extent to which so many of us had come to take its dynamism for granted – would be thrown into sharp relief by the global pandemic that began in 2019.

Fruits and Vegetables: The A-Listers

In 2019, the BBC's *The Food Chain* podcast (which "examines the business, science and cultural significance of food, and what it takes to put food on your plate") dedicated an episode to exploring how and why fruits and vegetables "get famous"; specifically, "Who's behind all the noise – savvy farmers, slick marketeers, or health campaigners?" and "who really wins when one vegetable becomes a star?"[7] As an opening gambit to the episode, these questions immediately set up a playing field that notably undermines the possibility of *knowledge*-based agency on the part of the consumers who would likely be key contributors to the "noise" set in motion by either farmers, marketeers, and/or health campaigners and subsequently shared by followers on various social media platforms.[8] Instead, the suggestion is that any "virality" achieved about the benefits of, say, avocados or kale (the key A-Listers we'll return to shortly) is a trickle-down effect of consumers being *told* so, rather than having the confidence or expertise to *know* so – in other words, simply falling for the proverbial hype.

With reference to açaí berries and chia seeds from South America as further recent examples of fruits and vegetables that make it to the A-List in terms of virtual fame, Jessica Lawyer – a "food values" researcher from the University of Adelaide interviewed on the program – noted that in addition to the visual aesthetic that stylized images of these foods can provide on social media platforms like Instagram, and the existence of *some* evidence confirming their nutritional benefits (albeit often from research conducted and/or financed by an "interested party"), the "history of traditional or indigenous use of that food – the exotic allure – definitely adds a lot of elements to the modern consumer, [who is] drawn to the novel and the exotic."[9]

Here, then, is an implication that values associated with "traditional," "indigenous," and "exotic" are somehow antithetical – or at least unfamiliar – to the core base of consumers who participate in apotheosizing a particular foodstuff (typically) via social media platforms. This perspective is, of course, an unrealistically broad brush with which to characterize a group of consumers who, in the case of the no-longer-so-humble avocado, are quite literally dispersed all over the world, meaning that avocados cannot realistically be considered "exotic" to everyone who enjoys eating and/or photographing them. Indeed, as *The Food Chain* podcast outlines, since first tasted some 10,000 years ago, the avocado has travelled to every continent in the world, but with demand particularly spiking in the last decade; so much so that the phrase "avocado hand" is now recognized by medical professionals as a description of increasingly common injuries resulting from cutting the fruit open;[10] and an Australian property developer quoted on the show claimed that millennials would probably be able to afford real estate if they were not spending so much money on avocado toast.

Why the Avocado?

Scientifically or nutritionally speaking, neither avocados nor kale (the other vegetal "A-Lister" to be discussed shortly) are special. Much more plausible, then, is the influence of social media, and the cultural capital that comes with being associated with one of Instagram's most popular hashtags (#avocado had approximately 10.7 million posts on the platform by March 2020, 11.7 million by the end of that year, and close to 13 million by the end of 2021). Avocados are also the fruit that Miley Cyrus chose to add to her tattoo collection in 2015, and which Kim Kardashian apparently uses as a hair mask. The Chinese market alone has grown from virtually nil consumption in 2012 to 50,000 tonnes in 2018, and is expected to grow further, not least thanks to the efforts of the World Avocado Organization (WAO), which spent $65 million promoting the fruit in the United States in 2018. WAO's CEO told the host of *The Food Chain* that, as an organization that promotes avocados "generically" (rather than pushing one specific brand), they "have a lot of free riders, [but] that's the spirit of the avocado; it's a very democratic fruit [...] it appeals to everyone."[11]

Yet the brunching millennials who have helped to put avocado toast on the Instagram map, and who may or may not also use it on their hair, Kardashian-style, remain at odds with negative environmental consequences thanks to the water intensity of its production and the high carbon footprint generated by its transportation.[12] Here are where the economics of attention come into play, combined with the unique capacity of the internet to encourage "filter bubbles."[13] Closely related to what psychologists and behavioural economists term "confirmation bias" (whereby people choose to pay attention to whatever confirms rather than challenges existing beliefs and opinions), filter bubbles describe how we often choose to pay attention to what suits us best, and to ignore (or at least pay less careful attention to) the rest.[14] Unsurprisingly, this can fuel both cognitive biases and significant semiotic mobility. The example of the avocado is well summarized by two headlines published by the UK tabloid *The Express* at the time of Kate Middleton's and Meghan Markle's respective pregnancies: the first, in 2017, read "Kate's morning sickness cure? Prince William gifted with an avocado for pregnant Duchess," while two years later, a headline read "Meghan Markle's beloved avocado linked to human rights abuse and drought, millennial shame."[15]

That is not to say that something cannot be "beloved," useful for morning sickness, *and* linked to human rights abuses or environmental concerns. As researcher Jessica Lawyer adds in relation to "famous" food, while there can be "economic benefits in the region where the food is produced [there are] also opportunities for exploitation of land rights, and of people, [...] of indigenous cultural property, or intellectual property."[16] But the opportunities available to frame a situation, idea, or object in a way that effactually *mis*represents its context, or encourages a particular (often biased) view of its subject are all too commonly exploited by public voices in both the food media world and beyond, particularly in a digital landscape largely constructed as a competition for limited attention. In this context, it would not be absurd to question whether a celebrity like Miley Cyrus could be guilty of "cultural appropriation" for having an image of an avocado tattooed on her arm, as she did – and shared with millions of followers on Instagram – in 2015. (In another nod to the fruit's semiotic mobility, it was later reported that she chose to have the avocado covered by a rose in 2019.)[17] (See figure 2.1.)

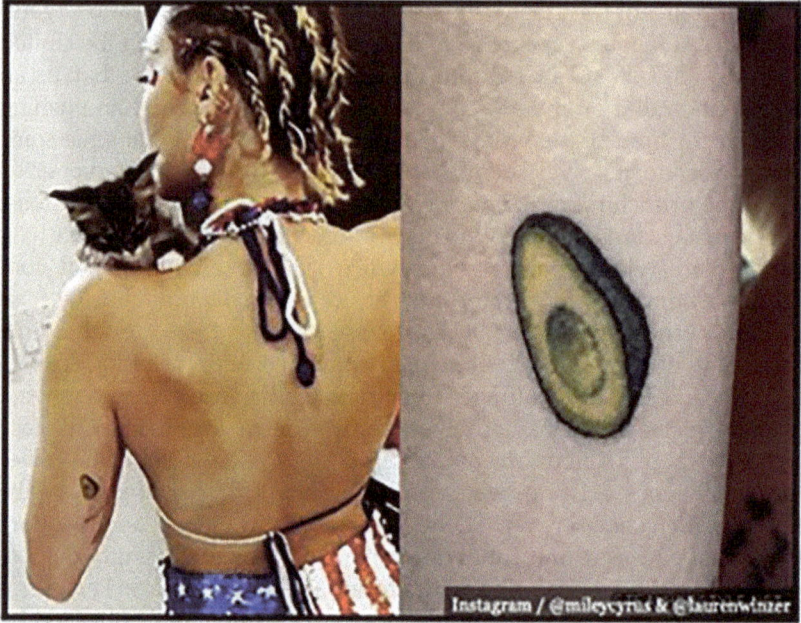

Figure 2.1 Miley Cyrus' avocado tattoo, shared on Instagram on 4 July 2015. As of March 2023, @mileycyrus had 199 million followers on that platform. https://stealherstyle.net/tattoo/136877/.

Eat More Kale (and Probably Less Pho, if You're White)

It should, of course, be absurd to consider a tattoo of a fruit a form of cultural appropriation. How could it be? Without venturing too deeply into a topic to which many people have already devoted thousands of words on paper and minutes of airtime,[18] suffice it to underscore that cultural appropriation – particularly in the food world – is a highly divisive notion because it challenges permission when it comes to (expressing) taste and expertise regarding a particular cuisine. In the context of this volume, its complexities relate directly to questions of food mobilities, and more specifically to this chapter's focus on "phygital" exchanges. Most controversies stem from specifically *digital* representations of foods and/or dishes with culturally specific histories – a (perceived, at least) mediated manipulation of the "correct" *physical* manifestation of a particular food that is understood to undermine a set of cultural values related to taste and cuisine by way of *unauthorized* mobility.

As such, charges of cultural appropriation are fundamentally centred on notions of authority: who has the "right" to say, do, cook, or show. The Pho in the heading for this section refers to a video published (and summarily unpublished, following an immediate online backlash) by *Bon Appétit* in which Tyler Akin, a white, American chef and restaurant owner, explained "how you should be eating Pho."[19] The (now-defunct) blog *Intersectional Analyst*'s post on the story does well to summarize the general sentiment of those who were quick to lay the charge of cultural appropriation:

> The backlash, in my opinion, was justified: that a white chef should be considered an authority on how food from other cultures is consumed is both absurd and worthy of outrage. But the reality is, Akin is far from being the first chef to tell racialized folks how to eat their food.
>
> For instance, simply take a glance at a few critically acclaimed chefs/food writers and their online biographies, and you'll learn that Fuchsia Dunlop, Nina Simonds, and Carolyn Phillips (among many others) have all made a career out of specializing in Chinese cuisine, despite their whiteness. You don't need to read closely to quickly learn that they love calling themselves *authorities* on the food of others. According to her website, Nina Simonds is "one of the country's top authorities on Asian cooking." Fuchsia Dunlop tops Nina – her website includes a quote saying that she is "a *world* authority on Chinese cooking."[20]

The central dynamic here is clearly one of ownership based primarily on ethnicity (rather than, say, immersion in a particular culture), which is to say a blatant refusal of the possibility of authority and/or expertise as something that can be earned rather than simply granted by heritage. In this narrative, representing foods (or worse, versions of foods typically considered to be bastardized)[21] external to one's indigenous cultural idiom is an offence rather than a marketing opportunity, corporate or otherwise, or most sympathetically, flattery. These examples also suggest that cooked dishes – and particularly those associated with a national identity, and therefore easier to justify as having an "exotic" appeal to anyone not from that specific country or region – elicit a far stronger emotional response to any unauthorized attention than would an avocado or bunch of kale.

To be sure, kale tells its own story of empowerment rather than disenfranchisement that has little to do with what it provides on the nutritional balance sheet (considerable, but not significantly so when compared to fifteen other vegetables found to be more nutritious in a 2015 study).[22] While cultivated around the globe for at least 2,000 years, kale

Figure 2.2 As an example of the cultural cachet of a leafy green, singer Beyonce famously wore a sweatshirt with the world "KALE" in the video for her 2014 song "7/11". https://www.shape.com/celebrities/celebrity-photos/beyonce-confirms-kale-here-stay.

farms in the United States more than doubled between 2007 and 2012. The reason for the initial spike in demand remains shrouded in some mystery,[23] but Vermont-based T-shirt artist Robert Muller-Moore (who now goes by "Bo the Eat More Kale guy") claims some stake in the boom after being asked to make T-shirts for kale growers selling the leafy green at farmers' markets as early as 2001. Interviewed on *The Food Chain*, Muller-Moore explained he came up with a simple "Eat More Kale" slogan for the T-shirts, which apparently sold so well that others soon took to replicating the design and selling copycat versions online. In an effort to safeguard his intellectual property rights, Muller-Moore applied in 2011 to trademark the slogan, only to be issued with a Cease and Desist notice from fast food restaurant chain Chick-fil-A, who deemed the phrase "too confusingly similar" to their own "Eat Mor Chikin" motto. A three-year legal battle followed, during which "Bo" claimed to do ten years' worth of business, correlating with the "meteoritic rise of kale." He was awarded the trademark the day after Chick-fil-A's founder died in 2014 (also the year Beyoncé famously wore a sweatshirt emblazoned with the word "Kale" [figure 2.2]). Asked in conclusion if "kale […] is the symbol of the underdog […] it's transcended food – it represents something else?" Bo eagerly replied, "You nailed it […] you're exactly right. To so many people, it did become a symbol of standing up for what you believe is right."[24] Such, apparently, is the mobilizing power of narrative over nutrition when it comes to food.

Childish Who?

As a final example of the fluidity of meanings attached to foods, in April 2019, sports apparel brand adidas posted a series of clips on YouTube entitled "Donald Glover Presents." Also starring actress-comedian Mo'Nique, the protagonist-presenter is the actor-musician otherwise known by the stage name Childish Gambino (and the DJ handle mcDJ). Adidas described the collaboration with Glover as:

> [T]he fruits of a creative relationship that began in September 2018. […] With a focus on the personal narrative that worn-in sneakers can hold, and the wealth of experiences they bear, the collection is inspired by subtle imperfections. "Rich is a concept," said Donald Glover. "With this project, I wanted to encourage people to think about how their stories can be told on their feet. Value isn't quantified by what you wear, rather the experiences from them. And you make the decision on what works for you, you live through your own lens. The partnership for me is about being able to exemplify what doing your own thing truly looks and feels like."[25]

One segment, simply titled "Avocado," begins with the camera panning up from the floor, where we see the sneaker-clad feet (the only moment anything related to the sports brand is apparent) of a person wearing a beekeeper's suit, scraping honey from a beehive. Mo'Nique (also in a beekeeper's outfit, but without the headgear) walks into the frame:

MO'NIQUE: "This does not look like sourwood honey – it's too dark. What does it say on the side?"

GLOVER: (whose face has not yet been revealed), after looking on the side of the box: "Uhm … Avocado."

MO'NIQUE: (in an irritated tone): "Avo…, that's avocado *blossom* honey. Pour that down the drain!"

GLOVER: "Wha-at? Why?"

MO'NIQUE: (curtly): "Because. That's why!"[26]

Mo'Nique then walks away mumbling under her breath, but audibly enough to hear her describing him as a "damn fool, asking all these questions." The clip ends with Glover taking off his mask with an incredulous look on his face, and doing a mock salute behind her back. The screen fades to black, and the adidas logo appears.

This clip, like the others in the series ("Polenta" and "Timber" are two other titles), is a profoundly strange thing to behold, and to understand in terms of its presumed function as an advertisement for a product that is hardly featured and therefore easy to miss in the actual segment. Yet it is also telling of the cultural capital of a fruit that is marshalled by advertisers here not for any of its material significance – and not even as part of narrative that provides a compelling example of "doing your own thing," as Glover describes the series. Why avocado? "Because. That's why."

Like kale, the avocado has become a symbol – a nod to a shared mentality, rather than materiality, which works to validate its deployment in contexts that evidently do not need to make sense. It can be used to advertise sports apparel, or to signal trendiness by having its likeness permanently etched on human skin (without any acknowledgment of the irony of immortalizing a trend). As long as restaurants that prioritize some of the problems with the physical reality of producing avocados over their digital "cool" factor are avoided, everyone can have their avocado and eat it too.

DC (During Coronavirus)

For now, that is. This chapter has so far focused on the mobility of food representations in a globalized world largely defined by the physical and digital freedoms to move, experience, interpret, and reinterpret. Avocados can signal creativity; kale stands up for your rights. They can also be enjoyed as they are – by those who can afford them, and quite possibly in ignorance of the labour and environmental processes that have facilitated their mobility from plant to plate. Yet as this book goes to press, the previously "normal" fluidity between the physical and the digital we knew in 2019 has been abruptly punctuated by various states of fear, panic, and lack of mobility across the world due to a virus with unspeakable mobility. COVID-19 has journeyed farther, and faster, than even the most seasoned of travellers in such a short space of time; its estimated total physical volume in November 2020, having infected approximately 53 million people around the globe in one calendar year, was only slightly larger than a teaspoon.[27] From March 2020 (and later in the year due to widespread "second waves"), entire countries entered emergency "lockdowns" (closed borders; heavily restricted personal and commercial transactions), and communities exhorted to observe "social distancing," a concept and practice deeply at odds with the movement of people and commodities that characterizes modern globalization, and more specifically, the global food systems we have all come to rely on.

Every day, already exhausted attention spans faced a flood of stories with more bad news: an increase in the number of confirmed cases and fatalities; of supermarkets running out of food and other essentials; of restaurants and bars forced to shutter and lay off their staff; of unkind, unnecessary, irrational conduct like xenophobic attacks on Chinese restaurants (the first cases were detected in China, leading to some media representations of the virus as ethnically distinct); of unintended poor choices that no one could have predicted – KFC's long-standing "finger-lickin' good" slogan was transformed, practically overnight, from connoting comfort food to the worst possible descriptor of a desirable food product once consumers everywhere were cautioned to avoid touching their faces to prevent transmittal of the virus.

But there were also surprising stories of kindness, charity, and creativity, which signal a whole new kind of mobility: landlords asking shuttered restaurants to pay their employees instead of paying rent; quarantined Italians and Spaniards serenading one another from their balconies; celebrity chefs like Massimo Bottura and Michael Symon taking to Instagram to offer lessons on cooking with limited ingredients. As Julia Moskin and Kim Severson detailed in the *New York Times*, there emerged a veritable sense of World War II, when

> Americans tended victory gardens,[28] needing both fresh food and a sense of participating in a national cause. In the last few days [of March 2020], Ms Hysmith ["a doctoral candidate at the University of North Carolina studying food history"] said, a similar urge has set in: Diners are using apps to order from the favorite local restaurants in an effort to save them, knowing that places without financial safety may never reopen.[29]

This perspective echoes that of German journalist Joel Dullroy, who argues that "the only welcome victim of coronavirus will be the myth of the 'entitled millennial.' Let us hear no more accusations of individualism, selfishness and over-avocado-eating from older generations. Many baby boomers now owe their lives to the selflessness of the young."[30]

Conclusion

The prospect of limited physical movement in the foreseeable future – at least the freedom to move on the scale that we as global citizens have enjoyed for the last several decades – may of necessity prioritize what the editors of this volume refer to as "imaginative" or "virtual" travel, or a precedence of the digital over the physical. Indeed, it was such a priority that fuelled the development of the meal-replacement product Soylent™ by software engineer Rob Rhinehart in 2013, for whom cooking and eating were unwelcome interruptions to his working day (the homepage on Soylent's early website simply asked the question "What if you never had to worry about food again?"). For people who enjoy thinking about food – and who have the privilege of not having to worry about having enough of it – Soylent unsurprisingly seemed to pose the threat of "social dissolution"[31] by removing the rituals of cooking and eating together. One journalist (among many at the time) tried the product and reached the following conclusion:

> Reducing food to a powder that can be mixed and drunk undermines millennia of evolution and culture and removes one of the fundamental differences between humans and other animals, even other hominids. We *homo sapiens* actually cook, and a significant part of our culture comes from that cooking and the rituals surrounding the preparation and consumption of food.
>
> These are absolutely valid points – *if one is arguing for or against the total replacement of "normal" food with Soylent.* But not every meal needs to be a festive life-affirming display of cultural pageantry where we march from kitchen to table bearing the carefully plated masterpieces of locally sourced delicacies while hidden speakers blare the "Circle of Life" song from the *Lion King.*[32]

These comments are not included here as encouragement for anyone to consider substituting "real" food with Soylent (or any other meal replacement), but rather because they speak to the centrality of traditions of preparing and sharing – even as these evolve and mobilize – when it comes to eating. As we have witnessed the world slowing down its physical pace, we have also been offered a prescient reminder that food cannot stop: we will continue to need it for sustenance, and we will likely continue to assign more than nutritional value to what we eat. But there is perhaps a greater likelihood that we will need Instagram and other digital platforms more than ever – at least for time being – to share it with others.

NOTES

1 Harshavrdhan Chauhan, "The New Retail Journey: From Omnichannel to Phygital," *SMBStory,* 31 October 2018.

2 Tim Harford, *The Undercover Economist* (London: Abacus, 2006), 214.

3 Harford, *Undercover Economist*, 205.

4 For an early discussion of the role of social media in relation to food, see Signe Rousseau, *Food and Social Media* (Lanham, MD: Altamira, 2012).

5 Although online shopping has grown exponentially in recent years, research suggests that most shoppers prefer the physicality of trying on clothes and shoes in particular, which online retailers like Amazon typically acknowledge through return and exchange policies at no additional cost to shoppers, but these naturally include the potential inconvenience of having to wait several days for a replacement. Successful examples of stores with smart fitting rooms include Ralph Lauren's Polo store on New York's Fifth Avenue, which in addition to allowing shoppers to request assistance, provide a range of lighting options to simulate different environments, and interactive mirrors that can offer recommendations based on a shopper's preferences. Rustam Tagiev, "Smart Fitting Rooms: How They Work and Why Stores Need Them," *Facelet*, 5 December 2017.

6 China's social credit system (reminiscent of a "real life" vision explored in one episode of the famously dystopian TV series *Black Mirror*) essentially ranks citizens across all areas of life (shopping, banking, traffic behaviour, to name a few), with the possible result of "bad" behaviour leading to being blacklisted from, for example, getting a bank loan or buying a plane ticket. Nicole Kobie, "The Complicated Truth about China's Social Credit System," *Wired*, 7 June 2019.

7 BBC, "When Foods Get Famous," *The Food Chain*, 3 March 2019, https://www.bbc.co.uk/programmes/w3cswpnx.

8 This aligns with a key principle of "Socialnomics." Eric Qualman, *Socialnomics: How Social Media Transforms the Way We Live and Do Business* (Hoboken, NJ: Wiley, 2009), which describes the growing importance of social media to commercial transactions, namely that "You can't just say it. You have to get the people to say it to each other."

9 BBC, "When Foods Get Famous."

10 Dianne De Guzman, "'Avocado Hand' Is Sending People to the ER because People Don't Know How to Cut Their Fruit," *SFGate*, 11 May 2017.

11 Some have, however, evidently taken the versatility of the fruit a little too far, like when Virgin Trains introduced an "Avocard" in the UK in March 2018. The offer was that 26–30-year-olds could claim a discounted ticket on presentation of an avocado. Social media responses from the age group in question called the deal a "condescending marketing stunt." Sophie Williams, "Virgin Trains Avocado Offer Infuriates Millennials," *Evening Standard*, 14 March 2018.

12 In 2019, a number of UK cafés announced that they would no longer include avocado on their menus due to concerns over the high carbon

footprint involved in importing the fruit from South America, where "forests are being thinned out to make way for avocado plantations," production "places pressure on local water supplies," and an unprecedented contemporary demand has "pushed up prices to the point where there are even reports of Mexican drug cartels controlling lucrative exports." Sabrina Barr, "Avocados Banned from Trendy Cafes over Environmental Concerns," *The Independent*, 2 December 2018.

13 Eli Pariser, *The Filter Bubble: How the New Personalised Web Is Changing What We Read and How We Think* (New York: Penguin Books, 2012).

14 For an extended discussion of Attention Economics and its implications for food media, see Signe Rousseau, *Food Media: Celebrity Chefs and the Politics of Everyday Interference* (London: Berg, 2012), 13–22.

15 A charitable reading of these headlines might infer that new information had come to light about the avocado industry in the time between them, yet these examples were included in a collection of headlines from various tabloids covering the two duchesses in similar situations; the series intended to demonstrate a clear media bias against Meghan Markle. Ellie Hall, "Here Are 20 Headlines Comparing Meghan Markle to Kate Middleton That May Show Why She and Prince Harry Are Cutting Off Royal Reporters," *BuzzFeed*, 13 January 2020.

16 BBC, "When Foods Get Famous."

17 See https://www.dailymail.co.uk/tvshowbiz/article-7600895/Miley -Cyrus-gets-tattoo-week-covers-avocado-ink-tricep.html.

18 See, for example, Ash Sarkar, "Why We Need to Pause before Claiming Cultural Appropriation," *The Guardian*, 29 April 2019; Vanessa Friedman, "Dior and the Line between Cultural Appreciation and Cultural Appropriation," *New York Times*, 30 April 2019.

19 In September 2020, *Bon Appétit* was the subject of further controversy when erstwhile editor-in-chief Adam Rapaport resigned from his post after a 2004 photograph depicting him and his wife posing as Puerto Rican "resurfaced" on Twitter and was widely viewed as an example of systemic racism in the organizational structure of the magazine. Kim Severson, "Bon Appétit Editor Adam Rapoport Resigns," *New York Times*, 20 September 2020.

20 Lorraine Chuen, "Food, Race, and Power: Who Gets to Be an Authority on 'Ethnic' Cuisines?" *Intersectional Analyst*, 8 January 2017.

21 To name just one chef who cannot seem to stay out of trouble in this context, Jamie Oliver has reportedly upset various entire countries – and a whole continent – for his interpretations of national dishes, including Ghana, "Africans Reject Jamie's Jollof Rice Recipe," *BBC*, 20 October 2014; Jamaica, "Jamie Oliver's 'Jerk Rice' Accused of Cultural Appropriation," *BBC*, 21 August 2018; and Spain, "Jamie Oliver's Paella Blasted by Spaniards over Inclusion of Chorizo," *The Independent*, 5 October 2016.

22 As related on *Food Chain* by Anna Taylor of the UK's Food Foundation.

23 Some sleuthing by Eve Turow of the blog *Mind Body Green* suggests it was the work of a consultant named Oberon Sinclair, apparently hired by the (fictional) American Kale Association to "make kale cool." Eve Turow, "The Strange Mystery of Who Made Kale Famous ... and Why," *Mind Body Green*, n.d.

24 At the time of writing, Muller-Moore's online site (https://www .eatmorekale.com/) was recently up and running again – "with new products being added daily" – after having had to temporarily shut down in early 2020.

25 "Donald Glover and Adidas Originals Officially Launch Donald Glover Presents," *Adidas*, 18 April 2019.

26 Available at https://www.youtube.com/watch?v=0PGURvZuwVU.

27 Tony Winterburn, "The Entire World's COVID Could Almost Fit on a Teaspoon," *Euro Weekly*, 15 November 2020.

28 Victory gardens were also established in the UK, Canada, Australia, and Germany during World War II.

29 Julia Moskin and Kim Severson, "Food, a Basic Pleasure, Is Suddenly Fraught," *New York Times*, 17 March 2020.

30 Joel Dullroy, "Opinion: Coronavirus Has Killed the Entitled Millennial," *Deutsche Welle*, 19 March 2020.

31 Signe Rousseau, "Food and Entertainment," in *Routledge History of American Foodways*, ed. Michael Wise and Jennifer Wallach (New York: Routledge, 2016), 379.

32 Lee Hutchinson, "The Psychology of Soylent and the Prison of First-World Choices," *Ars Technica*, 3 September 2017.

3 People–Plant Mobilities: Growing Bitter Melon and Bottle Gourd in Toronto

SARAH ELTON

On a late-summer morning, I visited an allotment garden in Toronto with Kamal, a gardener and a participant in my study. The sun was still low in the sky and the plants cast long, cool shadows. The allotment is one of several run by the city and is sought after by gardeners who, for the most part, have cultural ties to other regions of the globe. For less than $100 a season, gardeners can rent a patch of earth from the municipality to tend for the summer. The gardeners typically plant intensively, squeezing in many plants that are so important to them. The gardeners grew hyacinth bean – known as lablab to Bengalis in the allotment or bonavist to some Caribbean gardeners – with its bushy leaves and purple flowers. Bitter melon, a more delicate vine with yellow-white flowers, was so fragrant that I could smell it from more than a metre away. In the sunniest spots, people had sown heat-loving plants like eggplant, tomatoes, chilli peppers, as well as sweet potatoes and jute – the latter two plants both grown for their edible leaves. I had been to this garden on several occasions to meet Kamal, but that day he took me to see something I had never noticed before. We walked around to the back row of the allotment where one of his friends had a plot. The friend wasn't there. As we approached, it didn't look like much was there beyond a handmade, metre-high structure – a trellis platform – that was covered with what appeared to be squash leaves. Kamal bent down and beckoned for me to have a look beneath the platform. I peered under the canopy. Sunlight filtered through the leaves, casting a green hue. It took a moment for my eyes to adjust. Then I saw the bottle gourds – gourd after gourd hanging down from the trellis.

Bottle gourd – *Lagenaria siceraria* – is a beloved vegetable in South Asia. It's called lokhi in Hindi, lau in Bengali, dudhi in Gujurati, and is known by other names in other languages. Bottle gourd is a warm-weather plant that can fruit continuously in the subcontinent.

In Toronto, a gardener must save and plant seeds every year to grow it. Bottle gourd likes the sun. The vines of some fast-growing varieties can rapidly turn sunlight, carbon dioxide, and water into plant material and spread quickly across a trellis. When a vine is established, the plant fruits and the gourds grow large – some varieties can reach up to four or five kilos a piece. Kamal, too, grows bottle gourd. Even though bottle gourd is a heat-loving plant from the southern hemisphere, it does very well in Toronto. In 2018, Kamal grew more than 100 gourds on his plot. But it is not straightforward to grow this plant that originates in a warmer climatic zone than Toronto's. Gardeners must start their seeds indoors in early spring and then transplant the seedlings to the garden when the risk of frost has passed. Also, the white flowers of the bottle gourd open only around sunset. In Bangladesh, insects come out at night and pollinate the female flowers with the pollen from the male flower. What Kamal discovered after he immigrated to Canada from Bangladesh, was that the nighttime conditions here do not include insects flying around pollinating the bottle gourd flowers and ensuring consistent fruiting. This is only one of the reasons it is harder to grow bottle gourd in Toronto than it is in Bangladesh.

But mobile plants and mobile people often adapt to new circumstances. Kamal is an agronomist, practises plant breeding in his leisure time, and brings a wealth of knowledge to the garden. Part of learning to grow food in Toronto involved realizing that he needed to hand fertilize the bottle gourd flowers to ensure his ample northern harvest. He learned tricks to help increase the plant's yields, like touching the male to female flowers to pollinate. Then he spread word among some gardeners in the allotment, who told others how to grow better bottle gourd in Toronto. "Everyone in Jonesville knows that you have to hand pollinate now!," he told me. In the Jonesville Allotment garden, the bottle gourd is mobile. It has moved around the globe, accompanying those who value it as a food source, and, like them, has changed and adapted to this new place.

I identify and define people–plant mobilities in Toronto gardens: these are interspecies relationships defined by migration and life in the diaspora. People–plant mobilities are multispecies partnerships between people and food-producing plants that span climatic zones and are informed and shaped by histories of colonialism. Through my study of gardeners in Toronto and their food-producing plants, I have found that people–plant mobilities are adaptive, innovative, and characterized by partnership and exchange. It is these relationships that I will describe in this chapter, with a view to deepening understanding of the human–plant relationship among immigrant gardeners. This view of the people and plants sheds light on their entwined mobilities. For the most part in food studies, as in many fields in the social sciences and humanities, a condition called "plant blindness" has pervaded.[1]

This condition is widespread in North American society and keeps people from seeing the fundamental role that plants play in supporting human life and well-being. It is an ignorance of the intimate relationship between people and plants. We rely on Kingdom Plantae to produce oxygen to breathe, to cleanse water systems, to produce food to eat. Plants of all kinds create materials that become our clothes and our dwellings, cast shade to cool our bodies and homes. Plants create energy to fuel our machines and to produce heat to warm us and cook our food – including the dead plants of past geological eras, turned fossil fuel, that have stoked the global economy for centuries. It is plants, too, that are interdependent with all other life – biodiversity – on planet earth, from charismatic megafauna, such as elephants and moose, to pollinators and the microbiota. These are beings with which we humans too are connected. In this way, every aspect of human life and well-being is dependent upon plants. The tally does not include the pleasure that plants of all kinds provide. Plants are nice to look at in gardens, on window sills, in bouquets, and in vistas. They provide not only food but also flavour. What is pesto without basil? Kebob without garlic and chillies? Plants have always been silent partners to humans, on migrations, during colonization, and in economic systems of trade and exchange.[2] Part of plant blindness is not recognizing plants as being constant travelling partners to mobile humans. A plant turn in the social sciences and humanities is characterized by Myers as the recent rise in interest in plants by both academic and popular writers.[3] The plant turn brings flora of all sorts (including fungi)[4] into focus, and makes way for thinking about how the biophysical materiality of this life form is bound up with sociopolitical and economic forces as well as culture (see Sheridan[5] for an example). This chapter adds to an evolving understanding of human–plant relationships in the context of urban food production and migration while also contributing to an understanding of food mobilities. A scholarly gaze cast to the garden draws attention to an aspect of food procurement that is often overlooked in food systems studies. It also offers insight into the importance to newcomers to Toronto of the role of plants in their lives.

Research has demonstrated how the growing practices of people like the gardeners in this study – captured by the umbrella term urban agriculture – contribute substantively to food security in cities around the world.[6] City plants have fed people when long-distance mobile food systems have failed, such as during World War I in Britain when, as described by Barthel, Parker, and Ernston, urban spaces such as parks and sports fields were turned into gardens to replace food supplies cut off by Germany.[7] The potential for urban food production is found to remain strong even in the context of today's globalized food system with its steady stream of fresh produce from afar that is always available in the seasonless supermarket. In Toronto, it is estimated that the city could meet 10 per cent of its produce demands by scaling up urban agriculture, specifically commercial operations.[8] Urban agriculture has also been recognized in the scholarly literature as being particularly important for immigrant growers in maintaining a supply of culturally important foods in American cities, as I will explore further in this chapter.[9] No matter where people move, they take not only plants, but their gardening practices with them too.

Yet the practice of growing food is contested. The importance of gardening is often challenged by those who view it more as a leisure activity. The result has been that urban agriculture is seen frequently as a fringe hobby by policymakers, who have the power to decide how much urban space to allocate to gardening. In Toronto in 1999, the Food Policy Council published a report that concluded that the municipal government should support urban agriculture as part of building a resilient food system. It called for protecting urban agricultural lands and creating an urban agriculture commission to make agroecosystem planning part of city planning. More than twenty years later, no such commission exists, and initially during the COVID-19 pandemic, community and allotment gardens on public land were closed along with parks facilities to enforce physical distancing policy. The closure was met with outcry from community groups who make the connection between these growing spaces and food security, especially for the city's low-income growers and equity-seeking groups. Only after intense lobbying did the government allow gardens to open – weeks after gardeners would normally have started working their soil. The municipality's and province's initial decision to close the gardens exemplified the prevailing ideas in the public sphere that vegetable gardening is leisure, that foods flow into the city from agricultural areas, and that vegetables do not need to be grown by citizens in the city. It was an example of plant blindness, an ignorance of the key role that plants play in maintaining various aspects of human health and well-being. In these ways the practice of growing food for oneself, in a small city plot, not only is a personal act but also has larger significance as it is a reminder of the important role that growing food plays in urban life. For people who have migrated to a distant city, growing food takes on yet more meanings.

People–Plant Relationships in the City

Researchers across disciplines including sociology, public health, geography, and food studies, have examined from many angles the diversity of growing that takes place in cities, in backyards, allotment and community gardens, apartment balcony pots, as well as in commercial operations and non-profit community organization projects. Read in sum, this area of research demonstrates that these diverse ways of producing food are common to cities in both the Global North and the South. In cities in the Global South, urban agriculture plays a key role in food security and income support. It is often an informal sector of the economy, in which food is produced and sold in the city in commercial spaces such as small urban farms and dairies, and it is integral to the functioning of low-income communities in particular.[10] In the Global North, urban agriculture provides food to city dwellers, supports biodiversity, and provides other health benefits including exercise, connection with community members, and democratic involvement.[11] It is not a politically neutral activity – urban agriculture is bound up in questions of food access, gentrification, and debates about who has the right to the city.

Research into urban agriculture's importance to new immigrants deepens an understanding of how and why foods travel with migrants as they shift from one place to the next.[12] Migrants express their culture through the choices of plants they cultivate in their gardens[13] – what Wekerle, citing Nabhan, describes as "culture-specific land management practices."[14] These are the ways that people express their culture and make meaning through the choice of plants they sow and the ways that they tend to them in diasporic landscapes. In the case of Vietnamese market gardeners in New Orleans in the early 1990s, Airriess and Clawson found that growing crops like taro, ginger, and cassava provided people the opportunity to practise their traditional foodways, with the gardens acting as a symbol of their identities.[15] For Hmong gardeners in California, the act of growing food allowed for people who grew up in agrarian communities in Vietnam, and who felt minimized by society as elderly immigrants, to experience the self-worth of contributing to their families.[16] Importantly, Corlett et al. note that the migrant's garden is the physical manifestation of the new roots an immigrant puts down in a new country.

The plants referenced in these studies are described as accessories to culture, things that people who are mobile grow and eat, allowing them to express who they are. The Vietnamese market gardeners, described by Airriess and Clawson, grow plants typical of Vietnamese cuisines such as taro and bitter cucumber.[17] They write "the recreation of a garden landscape reminiscent of rural Vietnam represents a familiar past environment in the tangible present." The garden as described is a mobile landscape, transplanted from Vietnam to the United States. The actual plants that make up these landscapes are key to being able to recreate familiar agriculture and make cultural mobility possible. In a study of Toronto gardens, the Sri Lankan and Caribbean gardeners who participated in the research grew cabbage, tomatoes, peppers, as well as jute and sweet potato spinach. These plants, observed Baker, spoke to "the gardeners' cultural backgrounds and culinary preferences."[18] Clarke and Jenerette surveyed the plants in community gardens in Los Angeles and also found that there is a correlation between ethnicity and plant species. They attribute the high biodiversity in these gardens to the culture of the gardeners who plant them, in combination with their management techniques, income, and the size of the gardens.[19] Graham and Connell compare the gardens of Greek and Vietnamese immigrants in Australia to determine what kinds of plants each group tended to grow and to consider the reasons for these choices. They found that one of the two primary influences on plants grown by these two groups was culture. The plants provided a connection to tradition and a way to pass this on to the next generation. Also, by growing what they refer to as Australian plants, immigrant gardeners begin to incorporate the flora of their adopted country in their gardens and identities.[20] It is clear that culture plays a significant role in determining what gets put in the soil. Plants from elsewhere, grown in the diaspora, put down their roots along with the gardeners.

The Garden Research

I spent the growing season of 2018 conducting a mixed methods study of humans and plants in the Toronto area. The larger purpose of my study was to investigate the relationship between humans and non-human nature in the context of health and food systems. I surveyed 103 gardeners about their growing practices, conducted twenty-three semi-structured interviews with people who grow food-producing plants and also spent time in gardens doing participant observation of people and plants.[21] The gardeners whom I interviewed were purposively selected for the diversity of their countries of origin: six participants were born in Canada with seventeen born in other countries. The participants belonged to different socio-economic categories and age groups; however, most gardeners were more than fifty years old. Their gardens also were different with some tending to their plants on private land, while others grew food on public land like community gardens and in municipal allotment plots. I recruited a diverse group of participants in order to identify commonalities across different social groups, as well as to investigate questions of power and politics.[22] Despite their disparate personal stories, there was one commonality that stood out: all gardeners described an intimate relationship with plants. As Brenda, a ninety-two-year old gardener said to me with fervour one-day: "I love plants." Another day, a younger man, with whom I gardened while conducting participant observation, said to me: "I like plants … You know, guys like plants too." All the gardeners in the study cared for, respected, and marvelled at plants. For the immigrant gardeners, the plants that were mobile like them – such as the bottle gourd – were particularly special.

One cluster of gardeners that emerged was in the Jonesville allotment garden – the same garden I visited with Kamal. This allotment is the third largest on city property, with 160 individual plots leased annually to the public to grow food.[23] Jonesville is located on an unnoteworthy strip of land, sandwiched between a hydro corridor, which is a channel of land reserved for hydro towers, and a side street that feeds traffic onto a busy arterial road. The Jonesville allotment stood out for its industrial, suburban feel unlike the other allotments I visited for the study that were nestled in a picture-perfect park or at the edge of a conservation area near the shore of Lake Ontario. The nearby arterial road meant the constant noise of loud traffic, including from what often felt like a steady stream of heavy trucks. It was also different from the other city allotments I visited in that gardeners had erected homemade fences between the plots, with gates that locked in the produce. This indicated to me the high value placed by gardeners on the foods they grew. And, unlike the other allotment gardens, the majority of growers appeared to be people with deep roots to other countries, migrants from the Global South who were growing plants from the diaspora. The questions I asked about mobility and food surfaced partway through the project when I noted differences between gardens that could be attributed to stories of migration. It was these gardeners, partnered with their plants to maintain their foodways in the diaspora, who became one of the foci in my study.

Critical qualitative research has underlined the importance of a researcher's reflexivity – the process of considering one's subjectivity.[24] I, too, have had a life-long and intimate relationship with plants and the other living things in the garden.[25] To the field, I brought this plant knowledge and world view. I learned to think this way from my father, who lives with non-humans of all sorts as his friends and companions, including plants. He learned to grow plants from his mother and fills his house with orange, lemon, and fig trees, among many other plants, and has always conducted his own botanical experiments, like growing ginger, avocado, and persimmon from what would have otherwise been food waste. He taught me as a child to identify trees and plants, both domestic and wild, and showed me all the free snacks available to eat when we walked in the forest, field, or ravine. My parents still tend a large food garden on private land that they have owned for decades. This learned awareness of plants fundamentally shaped my research project in that it allowed me to easily recognize the importance of the plants, not just as objects but also as subjects and even participants in the research. In many cases, this plant knowledge helped me as a Canadian-born white woman of European descent to connect with the gardeners whose life stories as immigrants were very different from mine and who inhabit a different Toronto than I do. I live in an upper-middle-class neighbourhood in the downtown where there is homogeneity of socio-economic status and most people I encounter speak English and have been living in Toronto a long time. In contrast, many of the gardeners in this study were more recent newcomers not only to Toronto but also to Canada. The reasons that brought them to this country ranged from war to economic challenges to a desire for different opportunities and an appetite for adventure. Our lived experiences may have been different but we could talk plant.

Further, my work as a food scholar is informed by the decade I spent working as a food journalist in the city, reporting frequently on foodways in diasporas. At the time of the 2016 Census, 46 per cent of the Toronto population were immigrants, 27 per cent of them having immigrated before 2001.[26] These numbers do not include the children of immigrants who often maintain the cultural food practices that their families value, nor does this number speak to the Indigenous peoples in the city who maintain non-Eurocentric foodways. My time as a journalist, interviewing people such as home cooks and restaurateurs, shop owners, produce suppliers, and many others, provided me with an in-depth and experiential understanding of the role that food plays for people who are newcomers to Toronto as well as for longer-term residents who practise foodways in the diaspora. This immersion also allowed me to witness first-hand how diasporic foodways shape the "culinary infrastructure" of this city, from inner-suburb strip malls, to downtown take-out, to markets, supermarkets, community caterers – and, gardens too.[27]

People–Plant Mobilities

People–plant mobilities are the multispecies partnerships between gardeners and their plants that I witnessed at the Jonesville allotment in Toronto. These partnerships are the enactments of the mobilities of empire described by Bender and Cinotto in this book. They describe food mobilities as the "local and global circulation of food, ingredients, cooks, commodities, labour, and knowledge." When it comes to gardening plants to eat, this global circulation involves the plants themselves and their seeds as well as gardening expertise required to produce the gardens as diasporic landscapes. The gardens of migrants to Toronto in this study come to be as a result of the movement of people and plants, largely from the Global South to the Global North. What is being made in the gardens of Jonesville is not incidental as one can trace the path of the bottle gourd and other culturally important vegetables to Toronto along the routes of empire. The gardeners in my study who grow food in the diaspora are largely from the British Commonwealth – Bangladesh, Sri Lanka, St. Vincent. They arrive in Toronto, another Commonwealth city in a settler colonial state that, as of recently, has in many cases welcomed newcomers. Their garden neighbours include people from other countries colonized by Europeans and Americans, such as Ethiopia, Vietnam, and the Philippines. Interestingly, the productive backyard of the Ethiopian gardeners in my study reminded me of the elaborate Italian gardens that have been characteristic of downtown neighbourhoods in Toronto, with their fig trees and robust tomato plants and rows of arugula and basil.

These gardeners work side by side to create culturally meaningful spaces tinged by what could be an example of what Bender and Cinotto call "diasporic longings." The cultural allegiances of gardeners were apparent in the gardens. After a few weeks of doing fieldwork in the summer of 2018, I began to be able to "read" the gardens I visited. I could often tell which cuisine a gardener practised based on the plants growing in their beds. Bengali gardens typically had small-leafed green and magenta amaranth plants – lal shak – growing early in the season and then hyacinth beans and tall-stem amaranth plants with large, bright magenta flowers that bloomed later in the summer. Vietnamese gardens were notable for their herbs, like the fragrant Perilla, and in Filipino gardens I saw sweet potato leaves, hyacinth beans, and bitter melon. My method of cultural identification was validated by the gardeners I spent time with, including that day at Jonesville when Kamal took me to see the bottle gourds. After we visited his friend's plot, we strolled around the allotment and he made observations. "That is a Bengali grower. That is a Filipino," he said. "This one here belongs to a 'Canadian.'" This term "Canadian" is often used by newcomers to Canada to describe a white person who appears to be of European descent. I have observed that typically the people who use this term, who are newcomers to Canada, do not intend to imply that they are not Canadian. During interviews and surveys for the study, many newer immigrants expressed a pride in their own Canadian citizenship. So, when Kamal observed that the "Canadian" gardens at the Jonesville allotment tended to be cared for differently, he implied that these gardeners were longer-term residents of this country and that they had a different relationship to the land than he did. These gardens were not as intensively planted as the other plots. Flowers took up space along with plants that did not produce a lot of food per square metre, such as strawberries. Kamal said that he didn't see those people come to the garden very often. These gardens stood in contrast to the highly productive and intensively planted spaces of the diasporic gardens where plants grew even on the outside of the garden fences, sprouting into the public pathways. Kamal told me that these slow encroachments on the communal paths between the plots were at risk of being mown by maintenance workers. This intensive planting, oftentimes bursting out from the confines of the individual plots, gave the impression that the gardeners were trying to squeeze in as many plants as was possible to maximize food production. This practice, along with the locks on the fences, signalled the perceived value of the plants.

The plants chosen for these gardens were culturally meaningful to the gardeners and important to different recipes. Bottle gourd, hyacinth bean, and leafy greens like amaranth, Indian and Malabar spinach that grows from a thick vine-like stem, are key ingredients in the cuisines of people from Bangladesh. Kamal described how hyacinth bean cooked with fish and greens are simmered with particular spices. Bitter melon, tomato, and eggplant, were favoured by people from South Asia but also ingredients used in the cuisines of different gardeners. Hyacinthe bean, as well as jute, and chilli peppers, were grown often by Filipino gardeners in the allotment. Not only were the plants themselves specific to the gardeners' different cultures but also the way they used the various parts of the plants depended on cuisine and were mobile too. For example, the zucchini, which are commonly grown in Toronto for their fruit, provided some Bangladeshi gardens with leafy greens. The broad-faced leaves of the zucchini plant (and other squashes too) were relished by a few participants in the study who chopped them well and cooked them with spices. Whereas some Bangladeshi growers ate the zucchini leaves, they did not eat the chilli or bitter melon leaves that

Nori, a woman originally from the Philippines, told me she cooks with fish, as she was taught to do before she moved to Canada. The edibility of different parts of the same plant depended on cultural practices that appeared to have migrated along with the gardeners.

It is important to note that the Toronto gardens where bottle gourd and hyacinth bean thrive are not recreations of something that existed back home. Rather, the characteristics of the gardens in Jonesville were a response to life in Toronto. I found that there are many reasons specific to circumstances in the city that explain why the gardeners in the study invest so much time and effort in producing food that they could buy at the store. In Toronto today, there are many supermarkets and grocers that cater to a diversity of cuisines. While the major supermarket chains might still feature the so-called ethnic aisle, a concentration of products representative of non-European food cultures, this is a relic of a time when European and British food culture dominated in Toronto. In 2018, many supermarkets and groceries stores sold a steady supply of culturally meaningful vegetables like bottle gourd and bitter melon. Some of the vegetables sold were even fresh, as opposed to canned or frozen, flown in from distant farms in Asia, shipped from the Caribbean or trucked in from the United States. Thus, in theory, the gardeners could go to the supermarket and buy the same vegetables that they grow in their gardens. But many of the participants explained that they could not afford this imported food. As one gardener, Shathee said: "A lot of the vegetables that grow in Bangladesh, when they brought it here, it is very expensive. So, I cannot buy that. [...] So I brought seeds and plant in here and I can preserve it for the whole year. I have a small plot but I am very happy that I have got it." Even if the sought-after produce is for sale, it does not mean it is necessarily available to those who want it.

The gardeners also described the quality of these air-freighted foods as being poor since long distance shipping lengthens the time between harvest and consumption. As one gardener named Nazmul observed of his community's desire to grow their own vegetables: "It's not the same taste [at the supermarket]. So they grow their own." Food is ultra-mobile in the global food system that can speedily fly fresh beans and squashes from distant farms, in the cargo hold of passenger planes, over thousands of kilometres before they rot. The technology of the system, fast and refrigerating, has made this kind of food mobility possible, as Freidberg observes.[28] Conversely, the mobility of the plants in the study and the gardeners too is more durable and slow-moving. It is a long-term, interspecies relationship that is maintained from growing season to growing season in the diaspora. This global circulation of people and plants that has taken place over decades and even generations, that is shaped by histories of empire and connects Toronto with the Global South, have created another kind of mobility. And these people–plant mobilities are adaptive, innovative, and founded in partnership and exchange.

Adaptive and Innovative

It is not easy to take plants from a warm region and transplant them to northerly Toronto. To start, the plants cannot grow outside in the winter – and even the fall and spring can be problematic. Many food plants are annuals, cannot survive over the winter, and must be replanted every year. Also, a cool spring and fall present challenges – soil temperature can impede seed germination and frost can obliterate cold-intolerant plants. For example, a late frost can damage plants in the spring and an early fall frost can cut a growing season short. Even farmers of crops conventionally grown in Ontario wrestle with the seasons. Some apple orchards in Ontario employ fans to push warm air down on the trees on particularly cold spring nights to protect their blossoms from frost damage. Farmers can lose their tomatoes and peppers to a sudden September cold snap. The growing season for warm-weather plants is shorter here than in warmer climates and plants do not have the same length of time to grow, blossom, and fruit. For this reason, gardeners have many informal rules about when to put which vegetable in the soil. For plants like Indian spinach, hyacinth bean, bottle gourd, and bitter melon, which are heat-loving and originate at more southern latitudes, the risk is particularly high because unlike more cold-tolerant plants such as kale, they have little resilience to cool temperatures.

Because growing food-producing plants from warm-weather regions is complicated in Toronto, both the gardeners and the plants are adaptive and innovative. The gardeners described to me the challenges. For example, okra will not fruit well if the night temperature drops too much, and jute requires high humidity. While daytime temperatures in Toronto can easily rise to over 30 degrees Celsius in July, and the city is notoriously humid in the summer, it is not guaranteed that nights will be warm nor that the humidity will be sufficient for jute. So gardeners come up with a work around. One woman placed a bowl of water beside her jute plant to generate the humidity it needed. Kamal has developed a growing system in his garden that takes advantage of Toronto's latitude to maximize space and to grow foods in a way he would not be able to in Bangladesh. His system involves planting Indian spinach in the shade of the bottle gourds, an unorthodox choice. But he explained that spinach can grow in the diffuse sunlight beneath the gourds because the period of daylight is longer in Canada. "We need 6 hours [of sunlight to grow the spinach], but we get 14 hours [of sunlight in the Canadian summer]. So the spinach grows in shade of bottle gourd." In so doing, this ingenious system adapts southern hemisphere plants to the northern hemisphere. Also, the gardeners in the study have adapted to a shorter growing season by starting some varieties of seedlings indoors and transplanting them to their plots. This has long been a practice in Canada for anyone growing plants such as tomatoes and eggplants and it works for bottle gourd too. Also, numerous gardeners told me they grow warm-weather plants inside, all year round. One grower who came to Canada from Bangladesh described the trellis he had built in his apartment where Indian spinach grows like a vine across the ceiling. Another grower who came to Canada from Sri Lanka told me that she grows cilantro in the winter as well as jasmine flowers. These are the techniques employed to extend the growing season beyond what the climate would permit. I note that the gardeners volunteered only their success stories, not mentioning the crops that they chose not to plant because it would not be possible, despite their ingenuity, to grow those foods, such as mango (one needs two mango trees to produce fruit).

The genetic material of the plants, too, must adapt to the new environment. The plants change as they adapt to the growing conditions in Toronto. That is, plants with the traits that allow them to grow more quickly and fruit sooner are preferred by gardeners who save seeds. "The character of the plants are changing because of the climate," said Kamal. He is breeding a winter variety of Bangladeshi bean that blossoms and produces beans in the cooler season in Bangladesh, in the hope that this variety will produce well in the shorter Toronto growing season. By collecting and saving seeds from the food-producing plants from year to year, the gardeners believe that their plants are adapting to the micro-climates of their gardens, expressing the genes that will aid them most in their own reproduction. In these ways both people and plants adapt to Toronto, and demonstrate that this adaptation is a necessary part of successful mobility.

Relationships of Partnership and Exchange

Spending time with the gardeners allowed me to see how food mobilities are dependent upon relationships of partnership and exchange, both between humans as well as between species. To start, the plants are active participants in exchange. The way the gardeners came to possess the seeds they require to produce the food they so value, is the product of interspecies partnership and the generosity of plants. Many seeds are saved from one year to the next. Saved seeds help to ensure that the plants they value can be sowed again and again, year after year. This is a low-cost source of plant genetic material – though it is not free of cost. For most plants, such as beans, if you choose to save seeds, you must forgo the food. Seeds and food are often two of the same – we eat the seed that would grow into a bean plant if you were to sow it. The saving of seeds from year to year makes for a deep relationship with the food plants that stretches over twelve months. The relationship begins early, in the season when seeds are sown and the cotyledon first pokes through the soil, then continues into the summer when plants need to be watered and protected from pests and weeds. It extends through flowering and fruiting and the harvest of food and seeds. Then seeds need to be dried and kept safe over the winter – different seeds require different treatment – before they are sown again.

A number of the gardeners I interviewed, as well as 73 of the 103 respondents to the survey I conducted, said they saved their seeds from year to year. There are late winter and early spring community seed exchange events organized to facilitate trading between gardeners, as well as seed libraries where people can access free seeds. Forty-nine of the respondents picked up seeds at a seed-saving exchange. Other people buy seedlings that have been grown in greenhouses; however, seedlings are far more expensive than seeds – especially when compared with seeds that are saved or traded. I attended a seed-saving exchange with Kamal that he helped to organize. He and other senior members of his community provided extension information in Bangla to an audience of several dozen. At the end of the meeting, organizers distributed hundreds of seeds that Kamal himself had grown and saved the previous year. The event offered a way for global knowledge and plant DNA to circulate locally.

These systems are necessary to support food mobilities. Even if the funds to purchase seeds were unlimited, the varieties of food plants that immigrant gardeners want are largely unavailable in Canada. I surveyed the 2018 seed catalogues of ten Canadian seed companies, including a company specializing in Asian vegetables, to assess the availability of the top eight most common food plants valued by the immigrant growers.[29] While some seeds were for sale in Canada – for example, amaranth was sold by five of the ten companies, with perilla and bottle gourd sold by four of them – the genetic material for the culturally meaningful foods was less easy to access than seeds for plants familiar to foodways from Europe and the Americas. Another way I was told by respondents that gardeners acquire seeds for the food they wish to grow involved bringing them into Canada unofficially. "I saved the seeds from back home. Then I share with my friends," one gardener told me. Some reported asking friends, returning to the home country for a visit, to retrieve seeds. It is not permitted to bring seeds with you when you cross into Canada, without acquiring a certificate of declaration for the Canadian Food Inspection Agency (CFIA Government of Canada, 2012). The cross-border informal seed networks exist because, the gardeners told me, seeds are less expensive in other countries and more available than in Canada.

Another characteristic of the food mobilities is their dependence on relationships between the gardeners and their communities. The food that they grow is often shared. The respondents to my survey overwhelmingly described giving food to friends and family, and the gardeners I interviewed did the same. A man named Nazmul described how good he felt to give away the bottle gourds he grew. He knew he could have sold them as they are so prized in his community, but he explained that he enjoyed the social reward of giving them away. Kamal's experiences echoed this. He described how happy his friends are when he brings a bottle gourd as a present, as opposed to a run-of-the-mill host gift. A couple, of which the husband learned to grow food at school in Ethiopia as a young person, described how cultivating food in their impressive backyard garden allowed him and his wife to share the organic vegetables they valued so much with their close friends. The woman of the family told me: "We have actually another Ethiopian family who grew up here when we first came to Canada and raised our children together. They are part of our family. They have children and grandchildren so we give them a lot [of food] for their children so they can have organic food. [...] And it is nice to share. What is the point of having something if you don't share it? Sharing is part of enjoyment in life." The sharing of the food provided external affirmation for the hard work of maintaining these foodways.

Conclusion

Donna Gabaccia observes that "when people of different foodways come together, they will peek into each other's kitchens and want to try some."[30] Gabaccia explores how, in the United States, migrations transform foodways, explaining the ways in which American foodways have changed over time and the reasons for the shift. This same phenomenon takes place in the gardens. Numerous gardeners told me that oftentimes, exchange was cross-cultural. A Bangladeshi grower observed that the Vietnamese gardener in a neighbouring plot was now growing some of the vegetables she calls Bangladeshi. Another gardener told me that she uses kale, a vegetable she associates with European cuisine, instead of the Bangladeshi greens in her recipes. They described how some vegetable plants, and recipes too, are adopted into one cuisine from another in these diasporic encounters. Gabaccia observes that foodways change in a fundamental way. Immigrants introduce new flavours and recipes to the places where they settle. Some of these techniques and tastes are taken up by their neighbours; others are not. But in sum, she writes, this mixing typifies the American diet.

Considering Gabaccia's analysis in the context of food gardens in Toronto sheds light on the longer-term implications of this food mobility. The research, while providing insight into the nature of food mobilities in Toronto gardens and among immigrant growers, also raises questions. Do these foods grown by immigrants in the garden become intergenerationally meaningful? Will gardens in Jonesville continue to be identifiable by cuisine, or will Gabaccia's mixing mean that within a certain period of time these landscapes of diaspora will be completely altered? Some questions will only be able to be answered with the passing of time. Will hyacinth bean find itself into salads in vegan cafés? Can bottle gourd be substituted for sweet potato in the tempura of a bento box lunch? Or perhaps these plants are playing a cultural role for first-generation immigrants only, and possibly their children and grandchildren too. Scholars might dig deeper in the garden to investigate the relationships between biodiversity and cultural diversity, piecing together the depth of meaning that comes from human–plant relationships.

The chapter started with bottle gourds and ends with bottle gourds. Lokhi, lau, or bottle gourd is a special food in Canada. One of the participants described to me how he gains status in his community for being someone who grows such produce and shares it with others. People are willing to buy Toronto-grown bottle gourd for $20 a fruit if they can find someone to sell them one. However, mostly they are given away – like Kamal who gifts them to friends when he goes for dinner. I came to see the bottle gourd as a symbol of people–plant mobilities. Their success here as fruiting vines is dependent entirely on adaptation, innovation, and partnership. The seeds come from elsewhere but adapt to the Toronto environment as gardeners save the seeds from year to year. To fruit in this city, the people must partner with the plants and carry out the pollination. Then the gourd grows. It is harvested and shared among people who taste its history but relish this food in its adapted form, here in Toronto.

NOTES

1 James Wandersee and Elisabeth E. Schussler, "Toward a Theory of Plant Blindness," *Plant Science Bulletin* 47, no. 1 (2001): 2–9.
2 Sarah Besky and Jonathan Padwe, "Placing Plants in Territory," *Environment and Society* 7, no. 1 (2016): 9.
3 Sophie Chao, "Seed Care in the Palm Oil Sector," *Environmental Humanities* 10, no. 2 (2018): 421–46; Ruth Goldstein, "Ethnobotanies of Refusal: Methodologies in Respecting Plant(Ed)-Human Resistance," *Anthropology Today* 35, no. 2 (2019): 18–22. Natasha Myers, "Conversations on Plant Sensing: Notes from the Field," *NatureCulture* 3 (2015): 35–66.
4 Anna Tsing, "Unruly Edges: Mushrooms as Companion Species," *Environmental Humanities* 1, no. 1 (2012): 141–54.
5 Michael Sheridan, "Boundary Plants, the Social Production of Space, and Vegetative Agency in Agrarian Societies," *Environment and Society* 7, no. 1 (2016): 29–49.
6 M.A. Altieri and C.I. Nicholls, "Agroecología Urbana: Diseño de Granjas Urbanas Ricas En Biodiversidad, Productivas y Resilientes," *Agro Sur* 46, no. 2 (2018): 49–60.
7 Stephan Barthel, John Parker, and Henrik Ernstson, "Food and Green Space in Cities: A Resilience Lens on Gardens and Urban Environmental Movements," *Urban Studies* 52, no. 7 (2015): 1321–38.
8 Rod MacRae et al., "Could Toronto Provide 10 Per Cent of Its Fresh Vegetable Requirements from within Its Own Boundaries? Part II, Policy Supports and Program Design," *Journal of Agriculture, Food Systems, and Community Development* 2, no. 2 (2012): 147–69.
9 Christopher A. Airriess and David L. Clawson, "Vietnamese Market Gardens in New Orleans," *Geographical Review* 84, no. 1 (1994): 16–31.
10 Sarah Elton, *Consumed: Food for a Finite Planet* (Chicago: University of Chicago Press, 2013).
11 Pierre Paul Audate et al., "Scoping Review of the Impacts of Urban Agriculture on the Determinants of Health," *BMC Public Health* 19, no. 1 (2019): 672; Robin Kortright and Sarah Wakefield, "Edible Backyards: A Qualitative Study of Household Food Growing and Its Contributions to Food Security," *Agriculture and Human Values* 28, no. 1 (2011): 39–53; Charles Z. Levkoe, "Towards a Transformative Food Politics," *Local Environment* 6, no. 7 (2011): 687–705; Nathan McClintock, "Cultivating (a) Sustainability Capital: Urban Agriculture, Ecogentrification, and the Uneven Valorization of Social Reproduction," *Annals of the American Association of Geographers* 108, no. 2 (2018): 579–90; Laura J. Shillington, "Right to Food, Right to the City: Household Urban Agriculture, and Socionatural Metabolism in Managua, Nicaragua,"

Geoforum 44 (2013): 103–11; Lorraine Weller Clarke and G. Darrel Jenerette, "Biodiversity and Direct Ecosystem Service Regulation in the Community Gardens of Los Angeles, CA," *Landscape Ecology* 30, no. 4 (2015): 637–53.

12 G.R. Wekerle, "Multicultural Gardens: Changing the Landscape of the City," in *Proceedings of the International Symposium: Urban Agriculture and Horticulture: The Linkage with Urban Planning*, ed. H. Hofiann and K. Mathey (Berlin: Humboldt University of Berlin and TRALOG), 2; Sonia Graham and John Connell, "Nurturing Relationships: The Gardens of Greek and Vietnamese Migrants in Marrickville, Sydney," *Australian Geographer* 37, no. 3 (2006): 375–93.

13 Lauren E. Baker, "Tending Cultural Landscapes and Food Citizenship in Toronto's Community Gardens," *Geographical Review* 94, no. 3 (2004): 305–25.

14 Wekerle, "Multicultural Gardens: Changing the Landscape of the City."

15 Airriess and Clawson, "Vietnamese Market Gardens in New Orleans."

16 Jan L. Corlett, Ellen A. Dean, and Louis E. Grivetti, "Hmong Gardens: Botanical Diversity in an Urban Setting," *Economic Botany* 57, no. 3 (2003): 365–79.

17 Airriess and Clawson, "Vietnamese Market Gardens in New Orleans," 16–31.

18 Baker, "Tending Cultural Landscapes and Food Citizenship in Toronto's Community Gardens," 319.

19 Weller Clarke and Jenerette, "Biodiversity and Direct Ecosystem Service Regulation in the Community Gardens of Los Angeles, CA," 648.

20 Graham and Connell, "Nurturing Relationships: The Gardens of Greek and Vietnamese Migrants in Marrickville, Sydney," 390–2.

21 Sarah Elton, "A Posthumanist Study of Health and the Food System: Vegetal Politics in Toronto Urban Gardens in the Anthropocene," MA thesis, University of Toronto, 2019.

22 My study included investigation into "vegetal politics," the notion that plants are political actors in various social settings.

23 City of Toronto, "Allotment Gardens," reference material, City of Toronto, 17 November 2017.

24 Kate Caelli, Lynne Ray, and Judy Mill, "'Clear as Mud': Toward Greater Clarity in Generic Qualitative Research," *International Journal of Qualitative Methods* 2, no. 2 (2003): 1–13.

25 Elton, "A Posthumanist Study of Health and the Food System."

26 Statistics Canada Government of Canada, "Focus on Geography Series, 2016 Census, Census Metropolitan Area of Toronto," 2016.

27 Jeffrey M. Pilcher, "Culinary Infrastructure: How Facilities and Technologies Create Value and Meaning around Food," *Global Food History* 2, no. 2 (2016): 105–31.
28 Susanne Freidberg, *Fresh: A Perishable History* (Cambridge, MA: Belknap Press, 2010).
29 I determined the eight most commonly grown and culturally meaningful plants in the gardens of my study through my own observations. They were in alphabetical order of their English names: amaranth, bitter melon, bottle gourd, eddo, hyacinth bean, jute, perilla, taro.
30 Donna R. Gabaccia, *We Are What We Eat: Ethnic Food and the Making of Americans* (Cambridge, MA: Harvard University Press, 2009).

PART TWO

Infrastructures and Pathways

4 Gastrofascism in the Empire: Settler Colonialism and Food Mobility in Italian East Africa, 1935–1941

SIMONE CINOTTO

Food appeared to be in motion everywhere across Italian Ethiopia. In Addis Ababa, noted one Italian observer: "Caravans of trucks come through bumping on the road, wreaking havoc to the scared herds of cows. The columns of colonial troops snake around not to step on cultivated plots, picturesque processions of people, of animals, of things, of mules that disappear under the heterogeneous loads of weapons, ammunitions, bunches of chickens, pans, and pots, and their following of bleating goats, and jars of beer, mead, and tea."[1] Food on the move could be felt in the senses, with its look, sound, smell, and taste of sweat, of dirt, of diesel, of ingredients. "The organization was a mess, believe me," an Italian soldier remembered. "The trucks loaded with baking flour came down from Asmara and along the way the Abyssinians would attack them. Then, when they stopped to fill up, some of the gas would overflow and soaked the flour. When you ate that bread, you would taste the flavour of gas [laughs]."[2]

This chapter explores the politics of food, migration, and race that Fascist Italy implemented in Ethiopia between 1935 and 1941. That politics produced a circulation of foodstuffs, food meanings, and food practices in Italian East Africa – the empire created by the Second Italo-Ethiopian War and ended by World War II.

In its first section, the chapter describes the fascist project of transforming Ethiopia into "Italy's granary," in order to feed an expanding population of Italians. This granary aimed to help the fascist nation join the world's great powers. The plan, deployed as part of the last and most modern war of aggression in the European Scramble for Africa, sought to achieve autarchy, that is, food self-sufficiency for Italy. The Italian scheme for "demographic colonization" focused on the transplant of plant and animal breeding biotechnologies alongside Italian settlers to Ethiopia. Experimental model settlements would replace Ethiopian bio- and cultural diversity with Italian agriculture, husbandry, and civilization. The fascist project for mass colonization socially constructed Ethiopians as racially inferior. In turn, the racialization of Ethiopians denigrated Ethiopian agriculture as primitive and inadequate, despite its modernization by emperors Menelik II and Haile Selassie.

The second section examines the modern road and highway infrastructure that Italians built in Ethiopia. This infrastructure enabled the transportation of food and other colonial goods to feed the projected millions of Italian settlers to East Africa. The fascist regime believed that these same mobile networks would deliver fresh colonial food to the metropole and colonial crops to global markets. In fact, the transport system that Italians actually built in Ethiopia performed the opposite function. It distributed food imported from the metropole to the same Italian settlers who were supposed to guarantee autarchy. Colonial food self-sufficiency in the East African Empire stuttered and failed. In the end, Italian settlers – most of them lived in cities and worked in construction, transportation, and trade, rather than farming – enjoyed ample imported food, from pasta and flour to bottled water and tins of canned food. Paradoxically, such industrial food from home served as the most concrete sign of the social mobility promised by their migration to Africa.

The final section of the chapter suggests that the Ethiopian Resistance, which emerged after the end of the Italo-Ethiopian War, was just as aware as Italians themselves of the critical importance of the mobile colonial food system. Crushing Italian food security became the Ethiopian Resistance's principal objective. At the start of World War II, Ethiopian partisans, including many women, joined forces with British colonial troops invading Italian East Africa from Kenya and Sudan and rapidly defeated the Italian occupation armies. For Italian settlers, the collapse of their mobile system of food provisioning reflected both the failure of the fascist project of demographic colonization and the power of anti-colonial forces.

Italian East Africa remains an understudied example of food imperialism. Modern Euro-American empires constructed a global market for food. This market was based on the specialization of different colonies in the production of commodities aimed at consumers in imperial capitals. They integrated local food markets under the multinational capitalist umbrella, deterritorialized the world's diet, and made the mobilization of food, via transport and processing technology, essential to the functioning of the imperial system.[3] As Karl Marx would have put it, all that was solid about food melted into air. Fascisms of the 1930s and 1940s exaggerated the modernity of earlier imperialism into supermodern thinking and operating about global food.[4] Fascists made the goal of autarchy central to their ideology of nativism, racism, and imperialism.[5] Comprehensive policies included the Battle for Grain (1924), the reconversion of Italian agriculture toward the extensive production of wheat at the expense of other crops and meat, and Integral Land Reclamation (1928), a vast campaign of relocation of peasant families to create new farmlands. State-supported research in high-yield, pest-resistant, hybrid grain varieties even anticipated the postwar Green Revolution.[6] The conquest of Ethiopia extended such domestic food policies.

The same technology Italian armies applied to the war of aggression and occupation of Ethiopia was employed to create the Italian "empire of food" in East Africa. In propaganda movies, images of Italian tanks faded into those of tractors digging into Ethiopian agricultural lands.[7] The fascist project violently substituted Ethiopian farmers with Italian settlers and Ethiopian aboriginal agriculture with an industrial, mobile food system. It was colonization by biopolitical conquest. As Emperor Haile Selassie testified in front of the League of Nations, "[during the Italo-Ethiopian War] the Italian command followed the procedure which it is now my duty to denounce to the world. Special sprayers were installed on board aircrafts so that they could vaporize, over vast areas of territory, a fine, death-dealing rain. Soldiers, women, children, cattle, rivers, lakes and pastures were drenched continually with this deadly rain. In order to kill off systematically all living creatures, in order to more surely to poison waters and pastures, the Italian command made its aircraft pass over and over again."[8] In January 1936, frustrated by the enemy's resistance, Mussolini considered starting a "total biological war" against Ethiopia. His son Vittorio Mussolini, who served as an aviator, enjoyed burning "entire villages and fields of sorghum" to the ground from the sky.[9]

Italian food imperialism in East Africa, 1935–1941, illustrates the discourses, practices, and consequences of gastrofascism. Gastrofascism was the political complex of food nativism, state-sanctioned food sovereignty, and demographic agrarian colonialism. This story considers the dynamics of colonial food encounters for colonized people, their strategies of resistance to colonization, and the available practices of food decolonization. Although the duration of Italian occupation was short, Ethiopians experienced Italian colonialism as a violent interruption of the relationship between their bodies and their lands, the "highest form of alienation," according to Frantz Fanon.[10] Thus, for Ethiopians, the process of decolonization had to include the armed repossession of the land as well as the reclamation of pre-colonial and anti-colonial agricultural and culinary practices, cultures, and spaces. The ultimately failed

Italian colonization of Ethiopia was the product of the convergence of many mobilities that propelled foods, practices, and meanings across space and time.

Fascist Bio-Economies in Italian East Africa: Mass Colonization as Transplantation of Seeds, Rural Knowledges, and Farmers

After the occupation of Addis Ababa, on 5 May 1936, Italian colonial authorities concentrated immediately on food production and agricultural resources. The Ministry of Italian Africa and fascist leader Alessandro Lessona spelled out the resources of interest for Italian colonialism in Ethiopia: "Meat, milk, coffee, oil seeds, and grains. In the Empire, we will find these and other raw materials, or the opportunity to massively produce them."[11]

Italy mobilized an enormous amount of money and intellectual energy in the project of rural colonization of Ethiopia, before, during, and after the invasion. This mobilization was even more comprehensive than other previous cases of European colonialism in Africa. The Agricultural Institute for Italian Africa (AIIA) in Florence produced an expansive taxonomy of potential imperial food provision and rallied botanists, zootechnicians, and rural technologists. They studied tropical landscapes in order to accelerate the transfer to Ethiopia of agro-technologies such as hybrid wheat seeds, prophylactic vaccination for cattle, and selected livestock semen. In 1938 and 1939, AIIA transported to Ethiopia "over three-hundred specimen of cereal seeds, including whole and durum wheat, corn, sorghum, beer and common barley, rice, oat, and rye; over one-hundred specimen of leguminous plants, including beans, peas, chickpeas, fava beans, etc.; about one-hundred potato and manioc seeds and seedlings and sugary plants like sugar cane and red beets, greens, and fruits; another one-hundred oil plants like peanut, flax, soy, sesame, sunflower, etc."[12] The journal the Institute published, *Agricoltura Coloniale,* was just one of many journals disseminating knowledge about the Ethiopian environment, biodiversity, and human landscape and how to extract value in the form of foodstuffs. Politics and science merged in publications like *Africa Italiana,* the journal of the Fascist Institute for Italian Africa (figure 4.1). From its pages, the noted fascist anthropologist Lidio Cipriani described the racial inferiority of Ethiopian populations as a legitimate foundation for Italian colonial exploitation. "Research conducted for more than a decade," Cipriani claimed, "prove that natural biological causes prevent all African peoples from even beginning to develop an agriculture satisfying anything more than their basic necessities."[13]

Figure 4.1 The fascist plan for demographic settler colonialism in East Africa aimed at redirecting Italian surplus labour from international emigration to the newly conquered empire. In the fascist biopower project, Italian migrant farmers should have plowed the Ethiopian soil to extract the food to feed an expanding Italian population, which, through numbers, would have transformed Italy into an international superpower. Fascism mobilized Italian scientists into providing an ultramodern and rational approach to the colonial effort and producing a massive literature supporting and documenting imperial plans. *Africa Italiana* was the organ of the Fascist Institute for Italian Africa. Collection of the author.

Such settler colonialist plans considered Ethiopians a disappearing presence on the landscape or a source of cheap manpower to be put to work on occasion.[14] Italian colonization planners refrained from dealing with the complex Abyssinian *gäbbar* system of tenures, implementing their agrarian innovations mostly on confiscated imperial land to the exclusion of Ethiopian-owned plots. This guaranteed that the technologies brought from Italy firmly remained in Italian hands: "There was a large tract of land that was the property of Empress Manan around Qaliti," recalled an Oromo farmer. "Italians used tractors to farm large areas of land. They did use a very effective fertilizer, but they never gave it to the local people. There was a special Italian wheat that gave a good yield. They brought fallow and virgin lands into cultivation."[15]

Italian colonization plans merged botany and medicine, creating a parallel between the adaptation of vegetable species to the "transplant" of human organisms to new environments – notably white men's bodies in tropical regions they were set to colonize.[16] Italians' geopolitical imagination about the new colony in the Horn of Africa was ambivalent, as historian David Forgacs noted: "at once a part or extension of the nation and a place of otherness and difference; a place where the colonizing people claim to take possession but which [was] already occupied by indigenous inhabitants who greatly outnumber them."[17] The Italian masculine frontier fantasy, where barbarism and wilderness reigned, and the promise of sexual conquest over the bodies of native women lingered, had to be balanced with the fantasy of Ethiopia as another region of Italy. Thus, references to the Italian landscape were applied to Ethiopia and its food production. Such a geographical and botanical imaginary lured Italian farmers to Ethiopia with the promise of familiar environments and crops.[18] In his travel account of the early developments of Italian Empire in Ethiopia, fascist journalist Ciro Poggiali described a settlement that had been a Selassie's estate by evoking the landscape of Umbria: "The Negus' villa has become a magnificent farm that from the top of the hill dominates an immense checkerboard of fields, where wheat, sorghum, millet, chickpeas, fava beans, and peas grow marvelously. The colony extends on a soil rich in humus and water on to Addis Aläm, which stands on top of a hill, of which there are many between Perugia and Assisi."[19]

Mussolini disparaged British-style plantation and trade colonialisms as generating wealth only for a few capitalists. For him, mass settler colonialism should include a strategy of "total valorization" of the East African Empire under the direction of the state. Thus, the Ministry of Italian Africa envisioned three types of settlements: demographic settlements of *Enti Regionali di Colonizzazione* (Provincial Colonization

Agencies) under the control of the Fascist Party; settlements of the *Opera Nazionale Combattenti* (National Veteran Association), which assigned small plots to demobilized soldiers; and capitalist agro-industrial farms receiving land and operating concessions from the state and employing local labour. Plots for veterans, reflecting the idealization of the classical Roman farmer-soldier, turned Italian farmers into paramilitary settlers.[20]

The settlements of *Enti Regionali* represented the most genuine realization of Mussolini's demographic colonization in Ethiopia. Lessona crafted the original plan to transfer entire communities of farmers from specific areas of Italy to comparable rural environs in Ethiopia. Plans for state capital support imagined the transportation of settlers based on a racial evaluation of Italians that were deemed to acclimatize best to Ethiopia. The Ministry trusted Apulia, Romagna, Veneto, and Sicily to offer a wide availability of prospective colonists who "owned moral virtues such as thriftiness, temperance, spirit of sacrifice; preferably a family ready to migrate; and a proved fascist faith."[21] *Enti Regionali* received acreage in what were supposed to be prime farmlands. Chercher highlands in the Harar Governorate were selected to host the settlement of *Ente Puglia* because of the climate, a sparse and mostly pacified local population, access to the Addis Ababa-Harar road and the Addis Ababa-Djibouti railroad, and the presence of various cultivations – "wheat, barley, oats, maize, teff, durra, chickpeas, beans, peas, lentils, peppers, onions, garlic, and tomatoes, as well as coffee [and] bananas" – which suggested the fertility of the location. The settlement was renamed Bari of Ethiopia after Apulia's principal city. A group of 105 settlers left the port of Brindisi on 17 January 1938 amid a crowd waving Italian flags and imperial anthems blaring from speakers. The first settlers built a few small farmhouses using local construction material, stones and lime, and featuring their own ovens and wells. *Ente Puglia* had been able to obtain some 1,700 acres of cultivable land and fifteen tractors. On 10 February 1939, fourteen women and seventy-five children arrived in Bari of Ethiopia to join their husbands and fathers (figure 4.2).[22]

Upon visiting in 1938, the Inspector of the Fascist Party to East Africa, Davide Fossa, utilized the geo-emotional rhetoric assimilating Ethiopian and Italian landscapes. He reported that in Chercher "it feels like living on Murge [the highlands of Apulia]. In these gorgeous fields of life and human labor, Italian colonization is in full swing." The spectacle of modernity was as much a display of power as an edifying tale for Ethiopians: "The tractor, which arrived here with the first pioneers, takes off the ground and becomes alive, as if an ineffable force propels it. The shining and powerful machine cuts the earth, folds it, turns it."[23]

Figure 4.2 Families of the Ente Colonizzazione Puglia [Apulia Provincial Colonization Agency] in Wacho, Chercher, Harar, Ethiopia. The plan for the transplantation of peasants from their community in Italy to a similar farming landscape in Ethiopia was the most ideologically charged part of the fascist plan for mass settler colonialism in East Africa. The women in the photo below wear the Fascist Party uniform. Collection of the author.

Reality, though, was much less rosy. The total acres sown in Chercher declined from 1,700 in 1938 to 640 in 1940. Settlers managed to grow only two "minor" cereals such as durra and maize, alongside smaller quantities of wheat, barley, teff, and potatoes. Of the 105 original settlers, 42 were repatriated in the first two years for various misdemeanours or their "ineptitude." In a letter to Italy intercepted by censors, one farmer lamented: "I have moved my family to Bari of Ethiopia for fifteen months now and still not a single agricultural tool nor the cattle, mules, cows they promised they would have given to us have been provided ... We are treated like slaves in the very place where our beloved Duce ended slavery [Ethiopia]."[24] By 1940, only ninety-two Italians lived in the settlement.[25]

Why was Italian rural colonization of Ethiopia so unsuccessful in achieving goals of autarchy? The fascist bio-political plan was probably too ambitious to fulfil. Despite propaganda, environmental conditions were very difficult for European farmers in a diverse tropical country like Ethiopia. The transfer of rural technologies was considerable. In 1941, nineteen agricultural experimentation offices, twenty nurseries, two zootechnical stations, and twenty-two livestock insemination stations had been established across Italian East Africa. But even so, they were not up to the challenge of transforming Ethiopian soil into farmlands for Italians' favourite crops. Italian farmers' last wheat harvest in Ethiopia in 1940 was, in fact, the most disastrous after an invasion of grasshoppers and an infection of cereal rusts. The transplantation of the hybrid wheat varieties that were the pride of Italian applied genetics, *Mentana* and *Quaderna*, proved disappointing.[26]

As well, Italians remained ill-informed about Ethiopia's societal organization. They were unprepared to enter in a cooperative relationship with rural Ethiopians. Settlers found it difficult to secure available land and native labour. Abyssinian farmers lacked any significant incentive to provide their labour in support of the imperialists' agricultural goals of mass production. Such farmers equated working the land for wages to slavery, and resisted proletarianization. Few even trusted Italian lire, a paper currency.[27] The imperialist war of aggression also fostered Ethiopian armed resistance, which made life in remote settlements uninviting for migrant Italian farmers. Italians generally managed to control towns and the main roads by patrolling settlements and convoys. Yet just a few miles from these relatively safe havens they were constantly under threat from Ethiopian guerrillas. As a consequence, farmhouses had to be "built close together in military strategic positions, with surrounding walls and defensive works."[28]

Italian peasants settling in Ethiopia quickly recognized the false promises of land ownership. They were supposed to repay with twenty-five-year mortgages the *Ente*'s initial concession of land, tools, and housing, while promising to grow the crops the *Ente* wanted. As an old colonial officer confessed to a colleague who had recently arrived from Italy: The farmer, "who came to Africa because he was starving, who was disoriented in a foreign environment, lacking the skills to cultivate the land profitably and deal with natives, realizes that he faces years and years of hard work and scarcity; the land is hard to plow, it has not been plowed for centuries, perhaps it has never been plowed. At the same time, he sees other Italians getting rich with a little shop, a small business of any kind, with little effort. The consequence is that he is demoralized, unhappy, and at the first opportunity he leaves."[29]

Most importantly, as political propaganda demanded results immediately after the war for conquest, Italian decision makers disastrously began mass settlement before the completion of an effectual infrastructure of food logistics. This failure to coordinate food mobility and production doomed Italian rural colonization even before World War II terminated Mussolini's "place in the sun." The fascist plan for demographic colonization in every part of Ethiopia required a mobility system that could transport migrants to their settlements and crops to ports on the Red Sea and the Gulf of Aden (figure 4.3). The construction of roads, bridges, and overpasses across Ethiopia involved hundreds of firms, dozens of civil engineers, and thousands of workers. Such construction, however, diverted a large share of financial and labour resources from agriculture.[30] In contrast to farmers, Italian migrant construction workers typically spoke of their satisfaction with the job opportunity in Ethiopia that imperial mobility offered them in terms of the ample access to Italian foods: "The first time I went to Africa, they sent us to work on the Massawa-Asmara road. It was so hot that we just couldn't stand it. Yet we ate so well. There was rice, cheese, pasta, and fruits of many kinds that they brought us down from the highland. At noon, we would cook eggs by placing them on the sand under the sun."[31] The truck drivers carrying food to Italian settlements, forts, and colonial cities, were also paid wages many times higher than they would have received in Italy. A source for the fascist secret police worried about truck drivers' changing lifestyle as potentially revolutionary: "We have seen truckers that in the Fatherland would drink a glass of wine costing forty cents, drinking champagne for a hundred lire a bottle here."[32] The acute need for labour in construction also gave Ethiopian workers an edge in obtaining lucrative contracts in the trade, inclusive of good food rations.[33] In short, the better wages and labour conditions that the building of the road infrastructure provided Italian and Ethiopian workers crippled exactly what it was supposed to serve: white colonist settlement, the formation of a disposable Ethiopian wage labour force, rural development, and an international export crop trade.

Implementing Fascist Food Sovereignty in Italian East Africa: The Mobile Lives of Italian Foodstuffs in Ethiopia

Food imported from Italy signified social mobility for Italians in Ethiopia. In fact, imported canned, packaged, and bottled foods were a novelty for the many colonial migrants of rural origins. In Italy, they would have rarely had access to such industrially processed food. Through mobile packaged food, settlers created much of their sense of home in Africa while denying Ethiopian modernity and asserting Ethiopians' racial inferiority. Despite plans for importing food *to* Italy, imported food *from* Italy was the largest article in the colonial food system. Enormous amounts of food imports were mobilized via oceans, roads, and railroads as part of the fascist project of linking Ethiopia into Greater Italy.

That came at a high cost. After 1935, Italian ships to Italian East Africa represented a 20 per cent of the total tonnage passing through the Suez Canal. Such ships accounted for 25 per cent of Great Britain's revenue from the canal. The deficient development of farming in Ethiopia was reflected in the unbalanced trade between Italy and Italian East Africa. Bananas and pineapples from Somalia accounted for 50 per cent of total colonial exports to the metropole in 1936. The value of Italian East African exports to Italy grew from 61 million lire in 1934 to 246 million in 1937. After that, they plummeted to 137 in 1938. This represented a meagre 1.5 per cent of Italian total international imports. Coffee, Ethiopia's most valuable export crop, was the most notable fiasco. Much to the embarrassment of the Italian government, coffee exports actually declined below levels achieved under the Negus administration.[34] At the same time, exports from Italy to Italian East Africa rose from 71 million lire in 1934 to more than 2,100 million in 1937 – more than 20 per cent of total Italian exports. Most of these exports were food: wheat flour and semolina, pasta, salt, sugar, cheese, cured meats, canned vegetables and meat, olive oil, dried and candied fruit, wine, spirits, and mineral water.[35] Notably, such exports included grains, which fascism had declared the staples of the new Italian nation, and which Italians regarded as the foundations of their diet. In 1937 alone, Italian East Africa imported 127,003 tons of wheat flour and semolina and 14,122 tons of durum wheat pasta from Italy.[36]

Figure 4.3 The construction of an ambitious infrastructure of mobility connecting the Mediterranean Sea to the Indian Ocean for the transportation of foods and other colonial goods was at the centre of the geopolitical and bioeconomic project of fascist Italy and its empire. In this ad for the logistics and insurance company Lloyd Triestino, the bodies of colonized women are both presented as promise of sexual conquest for Italian men and incorporated in the system as means of transportation of the booty in food that came with the conquest of Ethiopia. AOI is the acronym of Africa Orientale Italiana [Italian East Africa]. Illustration by Gino Boccasile, 1937. Collection of the author.

Whatever its inefficiencies, fascist politics of taste guided the implementation of an imperial system of food distribution focused not only on the quantity but also on the cultural appropriateness of the food destined for Italian soldiers, workers, and settlers. The Fascist Authority for Production and Labour in Italian East Africa declared that Italian workers in Ethiopia should receive a full 6,500 calories a day, broken down into 2 pounds of bread, 10 ounces of rice, 10 ounces of pasta, 9 ounces of meat, 7 ounces of potatoes, 3.5 ounces of beans, 1.75 ounces of Parmesan cheese, 1.75 ounces of olive oil, 1.75 ounces of sugar, 0.8 ounces of coffee, and half a quart of wine.[37]

As a case in point, the Authority considered wine less as a working-class vice consumed for the purpose of intoxication and reducing labour efficiency than as an important provider of caloric content, a popular medium of conviviality, and a pleasure that met workers' taste and style of commensality: "All our workers are used to drinking wine on a daily basis, and here [in Ethiopia], because of the heat and the harder work they perform, they need it even more. Wine needs to be part of the daily rations because it has been proven that, while it represents a toxic substance for those conducting a sedentary life, for manual workers it is a complete food, generating energy and strength for the body." Mobile Italians, in fact, expected to drink wine in Ethiopia. Even the occasional lack of wine elicited protests: "One Easter we had just a spoonful of wine to drink," complained a Venetian soldier.[38] An Italian colonial administration officer reported the ubiquity of wine imports: "The flask of Chianti is on every table, red, white, ice-cold. Wine never stops flowing, and natives learned to love it, a lot, too. Our national winemaking industry will easily find a very large market in the Empire, and will solve all its problems, even if wine, at these temperatures, hazes the brains already dazed by the heat."[39] Soldiers' mass consumption of alcohol fuelled atrocities, from mass rape to indiscriminate massacres, during and after the Italo-Ethiopian War.[40] Though the fascist regime promoted thriftiness and sobriety at home, the colonial mobilities of wine demonstrate how the imperial food system accommodated Italian migrant tastes. It sustained their working and murdering bodies, rather than reshaping them.

In his study of the ruins of Italian military sites in Ethiopia, archaeologist Alfredo González-Ruibal was amazed at variety of bottles and tin cans he found even in most remote of garrisons. The detritus was evidence of the "enormous logistical effort [that] had to be made to bring supplies to this isolated outpost."[41] Even Ethiopian and Eritrean soldiers, enlisted in the Italian colonial army, must have been supplied with European food imports. He concluded that the only possible rationale behind Italians' investment in food mobility was to "civilize" the natives. Ethiopians ate the food of the masters, served on the lily white European plates and cups that González-Ruibal also recovered. In this way, Italians sought to display the racial and technological superiority of their foodways and taste. But the vast effort put into the construction of a supply chain that delivered Italian canned food and wine to Italian soldiers on the imperial frontier also had reflexive reasons. Food sovereignty for the Italian nation at home and in the empire remained the ideological justification for the entire demographic imperial project. Only by delivering on that promise even in the outposts of the empire could the regime bind Italian citizen-eaters to colonialism.

Bottled mineral water was among the most extensively imported Italian goods (figure 4.4). "[C]rate after crate of wine flasks, liquors, and bottled mineral water seemed to be the goods that Italian Ethiopia desired most ardently," Poggiali noted.[42] A rarity in Italy, consumed on occasion by the sick, babies, and elderly in middle-class urban families, bottled water was an everyday drink in Ethiopia. To settlers, bottled water represented a modern and portable antidote to the perils of African food. Even working men, bent on saving as much as they could from their African migration experience, drank mineral water: "A bottle of mineral water could cost up to two lire, but as I had intestinal pains, sometimes I needed to eat out at a restaurant if I wanted to have something decent. For a soup or pasta dish and a bottle of mineral water I could spend up to six lire."[43] As a portable liquid from a spring somewhere in Italy, mineral water was also one of the most characteristic forms of nostalgic consumption for Italians in East Africa.

Canned foods also suggested the global dimensions of the circulatory food mobilities that crisscrossed colonial Ethiopia. Tin cans from Italy and elsewhere entered East Africa through Massawa, Djibouti, or Mogadishu and travelled to the Ethiopian heartland by truck or train. "Among the many ironies of Italian East Africa is the provisioning of our soldiers and settlers with canned milk and butter from Holland," Poggiali explained.[44] A young colonial administration officer from Rome deployed to a remote settlement in southwestern Ethiopia wrote to his father to describe his purchase of a box of Swiss sterilized milk.[45] In Italy, mass industrial production of canned vegetables began in the 1860s when Francesco Cirio introduced his "method" of preservation. Canned beef followed by the end of the century. As late as the 1930s, though, canned food remained expensive in Italy, a modern commodity enjoyed by the urban middle-class.[46] Rural women, although encouraged to preserve food at home as their patriotic contribution to the national mission for food self-sufficiency, had little use for industrial

Figure 4.4 Ad for L'Acqua dell'Impero [Mineral Water of the Empire]. Contradicting the fascist-mandated strive for autarchy (food self-sufficiency) of the empire, bottled mineral water imported from Italy was immensely popular among Italian settlers to Ethiopia. Acqua dell'Impero was a colonial-autarkic effort at producing mineral water from local springs in Eritrea for distribution across Italian East Africa. From *Autarchia Alimentare*. Collection of the author.

brand canned or packaged food despite its much-advertised convenience. Similarly, working-class women in cities continued to buy all
their groceries at open markets or in grocery shops in bulk.[47] It was only
in 1929 that Colonel Ettore Chiarizia patented canned meals of beef, min-
estrone soup, and pasta with chickpeas for the Italian army. Although
the taste of *chiarizia* was disputable at best, the ration was ready to warm
up and eat. The cans were light and easier to open, perfect for the motor-
ized and airborne Italian troops that invaded Ethiopia in 1935.

The modern Italian consumer of canned foods was born in the process of settlement to Ethiopia. "We, soldiers and civilians, eat [canned
beef] every day, because in a country that we found absolutely deprived
of any vegetables that met our taste (hence the fantastic magnitude of
our imports of canned vegetables) it has turned out to be the most nutritious and inexpensive food," witnessed Poggiali.[48] Italian soldiers and
settlers to Ethiopia actually learned to crave imported canned food
products through transnational politics of food security, taste, and nostalgia. Through a diet of industrial food, they subscribed to ideas about
food sovereignty that extended from the motherland to the colonies.

The quintessential impersonal commodity the food industry delivers in
innumerable identical exemplars, canned food in Ethiopia reverted to the
status of a good with use value, exchange value, and emotional value. It
could be bartered or exchanged as a gift, thus reflecting the giver and the
receiver's subjectivities. More than fifty years after the events, an Italian
soldier remembered a particular can of soup as the catalyzer of a web of
relationships across space and time:

> I had a friend, now he's dead, he was a truck driver, and while our bat-
> talion was marching, he drove by and saw our platoon [named after the
> place in Italy where they both came from]: 'That's the Intra Batallion, there
> must be Bolongaro among them, he's my age, got drafted with me.' Some-
> body heard that someone was looking for me, we found each other, we
> hugged. He gave me a can of chiarizia, the canned soup of the military.
> So, I had this can in my backpack, always, I carried it with me for miles,
> everywhere. I thought: 'This, this can, I'm going to eat it when I'm really
> starving, and I can't stand it no more.' One-day I was indeed starving,
> then, I was with four or five friends, I said: 'Come on, let's open it.' It was a
> half-a-pound can, we mixed it with water in the mess tin, we heated it and
> added the biscuit. The biscuit swelled as it soaked inside the soup, and we
> had our meal together, happily.[49]

For this soldier and his comrades in arms, cooking was the cultural
work that revived the peripatetic canned soup to the state of a meaningful food making taste and commensality. To migrant cooks and eaters,

the cans and their labels told stories and described landscapes of the imaginary, enticed memories, and reproduced familiar gastronomies.

The circulating tin can became a vital element of the material culture of the "empire of food." Even emptied of their nutritious contents, cans provided a sense of belonging. Tin cans were often beautified by images and logos, from smiling young peasant women and landscapes to coats of arms and flowers. They were also sturdy enough that settlers often used empty cans as construction material, containers, and decoration. "After a while we got some real iron furniture, but in the early times all our furniture consisted of two chairs, a folding table, and two small beds supported by tomato cans in place of their legs," recalled a colonial civil officer who had settled in Gondar with his wife.[50] Italians sometimes claimed that they traded empty tin cans with the populations of southwestern Ethiopia, where contacts with Europeans had been minimal. Yet Ethiopians described the use of the empty can as evidence of distress caused by colonial power. Many Ethiopians, young men at the time, remembered standing outside bars and restaurants they weren't allowed to patronize. They were served their food and drink in rusty food cans, instead of the cups, glasses, and plates reserved for Italians: "Even if at work we rubbed elbows with Italians, we weren't allowed into public spaces like bars or restaurants. They served us from a little window on the side, in a tomato can."[51] It was a routine dehumanizing practice of consumption aimed at creating racial borders: when emptied of its original food contents, the can became a tool for Italians to relegate Ethiopians to the realm of the sub-human or animal. An army photographer immortalized some Italian soldiers in the act of extracting the severed head of Abyssinian dejazmach Hailu Kebede from a Lazzaroni cookies metal box (figure 4.5). In the photographs, the Italian soldier holding the cookie can is smiling while displaying the detached head to two officers.[52] The contrast between the memory of delicious cookies made by a fancy brand like Lazzaroni, redolent of family holiday dinners, and the celebration of the mutilation of the body of a feared enemy cannot be any more violent. But the imperial life of canned food accommodated such seeming contradictions. *Lazzaroni* in Italian means "petty street criminals," or "evil persons," its etymology deriving from the Spanish word for "lepers," which foreign rulers of Naples disparagingly called all plebeians of the city in the seventeenth century. In Ethiopia, the imperialist hegemony of violence endorsed "bad guys" to act out their cruel self and butcher the natives. Even the memory of Italian occupation of Ethiopia sometimes survived in empty tin cans of cookies, chocolate powder, or tomatoes refilled with photographs, letters, and memories.

Figure 4.5 Kerem, northern Ethiopia, 24 September 1937. Italian soldiers present to their officers the severed head of the captured Ethiopian Resistance leader Hailu Kebede in a box of imported Lazzaroni cookies. Photo by Angelo Dolfo. Collection of the author.

Along with bottled drinks and canned foods, wheat bread and pasta represented the supermodern mobilization of food demanded by plans for the mass colonization of Italian East Africa. With the Battle for Grain, fascism cast wheat bread and pasta as foundations of the national diet and as key symbols of *Italianità*. However, at home, these two foods were more idealized than actually consumed. Peasants still resorted to black bread made with coarse flour or, in northern Italy, to cornmeal polenta. Durum wheat pasta, which requires an industrial process to manufacture, was mostly unattainable for rural Italians except on special occasions. The chance to eat white bread and pasta every day was one of the most convincing promises that Ethiopia had to offer to prospective migrant settlers. "The trip was very nice. And there were those white bread rolls that were so good," reported one Italian settler about his journey across the Mediterranean to Africa. "Then, there was always pasta, which wouldn't make you seasick and throw up."[53] The colonial regime cast these essential "Mediterranean foods" as a necessity for the imperial food system. Fascist science even identified Ethiopia as the world's ancestral cradle of grain cultivation. Yet, in practice, the settler market required imports and long-distance motor transportation of wheat flour and pasta. Even Ethiopian agriculture, which anyway had typically privileged teff, durra, and barley over wheat, often turned towards an underground market.

Ethiopian Resistance, War, and the Demise of Italian Mobile Food System in East Africa

The great prize Italians put on their colonial food system as a vital instrument for making Ethiopia Italian did not go unnoticed by the Ethiopian armed resistance.[54] Italians linked their ability to patrol the land and capacity to repress the "rebels" to the size of their food stockpiles. In April 1937, the colonial government, wary of a possible siege of Addis Ababa, realized that the city had supplies of pasta for only thirty-six days. Anticipating partisan attacks, colonial officials sought to increase pasta stockpiles to last for 175 days. Military camps and schools were ordered to grow their own food in emergency gardens.[55] Pressed by the prospect of military vulnerability caused by scarce provisions, Italians finally began to look to Ethiopian agriculture to increase their food security. The colonial administration encouraged share-cropping contracts between Italian and Ethiopian farmers and created administrative units in charge of "native agriculture." Such units promoted the production of wheat in Ethiopian farms through supplies of seeds and tools. But this shift in policy came too late. Italians' racism, landgrabbing practices, and forced requisitions hindered any long-term collaboration. The theft of grains, cattle, and food by fascists was so widespread that it become a recurring theme in Ethiopian postwar literature.[56] Mussolini's decree that ordered that by 1 July 1938 Ethiopia had to be self-sufficient in wheat exacerbated tensions. Even the Duce privately knew Ethiopia would struggle to produce just one-third of the grain needed to satisfy the demands of the Italian army and of settlers.[57]

According to Tekalign Wolde-Mariam, a historian of Addis Ababa's urban food system, Ethiopian "patriots were well aware of the connection between wheat production and Italian military security." Interviews that Wolde-Mariam conducted in 1990 suggest that the Ethiopian Resistance sought to convince Abyssinian farmers not to collaborate with the Italian wheat campaign. They spread rumours that the improved wheat varieties Italians supplied them "would bring about impotence in men and sterility in women." Given the history of Italians' use of biological warfare weapons, as well as their strategy of biological imperialism aimed at replacing local agriculture with genetically developed European crops, the story seemed plausible. Wolde-Mariam's sources argued that the Ethiopian partisans' propaganda succeeded in preventing the expansion of wheat cropping in the area to the south and west of Addis Ababa.[58]

Ethiopian guerillas also regularly attacked food transport trucks. "I applied to work as a truck driver carrying food supplies for the army," an Italian truck driver recalled. "They sent me to Abyssinia, at May-chew, on the road to Gondar. My job was to bring food provisions to the men building bridges on the Mareb River. But it was so dangerous to drive in that area, there were many rebels, we were all scared to death."[59] Another worker building Italian forts remembered that Ethiopian partisans cut supply lines. "Then we were supplied with flour and other essential food items from airplanes, without parachutes, so much of the food got lost."[60] The Italian East African system of food distribution and logistics was not only complex but also frail.

Some Ethiopian women participated in the resistance as fighting soldiers, while others served as messengers and spies, with the goal of starving the Italian enemy. Others played key roles in feeding partisans. They carried utensils and pots, fetched water, chopped wood, foraged for wild plants, grinded grains, and prepared teff injera, doro wat, tej, and tella.[61]

Paradoxically, the technological and logistical innovation of the Italian colonial food system was most apparent in the darkest hour of Italian East Africa. In 1941, British colonial troops invaded Ethiopia and the Ethiopian Resistance joined them to defeat Italian occupation forces. While their military equipment and petrol supplies for tanks and vehicles were inferior to those of the British armed forces, Italians could boast better food provisions. Pier Marcello Masotti, an Italian colonial officer deployed to Dembi Dollo in southwestern Ethiopia reported that "according to British sources, Italian military warehouses at the warfront in Italian East Africa operations were fully supplied of what the British considered unnecessary luxuries, from champagne to bottled mineral water, I believe for the use of our senior officers. Dembi Dollo was not an exception. I must admit that the British, South African, and various other African colonial soldiers I met looked emaciated and seemed to have poorer food supplies than we did."[62] The Nigerian troops that occupied Mogadishu on 25 February 1941, were shocked to find the booty the Italians had left behind, "enough food and drink to keep ten thousand men well-nourished for seven to eight months."[63]

Figure 4.6 Bar Impero in Addis Ababa, 1938. Cafes, bars, and restaurants, which represented the terminals of the complex system of food mobility and distribution Italians implemented in Ethiopia, were racially segregated. Collection of the author.

British colonial forces advancing into Italian East Africa ended the Italian empire and shattered fascist dreams of mass settler colonialism. Italian settlers expressed their sense of defeat in the tangible collapse of a colonial food system that had created their sense of rootedness in Africa (figure 4.6). Masotti recalled that, when the Italian contingent in Dembi Dollo was eventually evacuated to Addis Ababa, "our impression [of the capital] was strange. We realized that the last months in Dembi Dollo had not been as plentiful as before and the eighteen days of marching had made us even thinner. The other Italians we met in the city looked fat and well-fed. In the stores there were all sorts of good things, from wine to Parmesan cheese to pasta, albeit the latter made in Addis Ababa. All delicacies we realized we had forgotten about. And we were mad about our own [army's] naivete at not defending a city fully stocked with all sorts of good foods."[64] Ironically, because of the disruption of international trade with Italy, the food autarchy that had been the primary ideological reason for Italy to invade Ethiopia became a necessity for Italians in Ethiopia at the fall of the empire. In Italian Ethiopia, rationing began even before Italy entered World War II. As early as September

1939, the butcher shops in Addis Ababa were closed on Tuesdays and Fridays, and restaurants could not serve meat on these same days, "for the protection of the animal populations."[65] During the tense summer of 1940, in Addis Ababa, the embattled regime introduced food stamps. Rationing for olive oil and sugar began on 13 June. On 1 July, it extended to bread, pasta, wheat flour, and rice. To settlers, the "empire of food" increasingly felt like a failure, as their letters seized by censors suggested: "In Harar you can't find anything to eat, you can only buy with food stamps and life is hard"; "I'm sick of this life, they charge you four lire for a glass of wine, food is bad, and a construction worker who works every day still cannot make enough to eat"; "If it goes on like this we will starve. There's no wine, no butter, I don't remember anymore what cheese is. These are the sacrifices of Africa."[66] Setters' sense of loss concretely gained a material, gustatory dimension. With the collapse of the imperial infrastructure of food distribution, scarcity became the dominating fact of everyday life in Italian Ethiopia.

Conclusion

Empire is not just a political organization aimed at ruling over diverse populations and lands. Nor is it simply a system of images and meanings. Empire is also a network of conduits that connects distant places to each other. This network circulates material cultures through ports and by roads. In its biopolitical frenzy, fascist imperialism in East Africa aimed at creating a colonial space for the circulation of bodies, crops, and agricultural technologies, as well as foods and culinary practices. This circulation ultimately intended to support demographic expansion. The fascist model of mass colonization between 1935 and 1941 centred on the transplant of life from the Italian motherland to the new colony of Ethiopia. Demographic settler colonialism aimed to create a homogeneous and continuous imperial farmland space. Within this plan, fascists regarded Ethiopians, Ethiopian agriculture, and Ethiopian foods as inherently inferior. The most noted legacy of the supermodern and technologically advanced Italian aggression and occupation of Ethiopia is the construction of a road infrastructure. These roads were vital to a system of food transport and distribution aimed at guaranteeing food sovereignty to Italian settlers. However, this ambitious project of logistics and mobility required so many resources that it actually undermined the plan for mass colonization. Ethiopians grasped the vital importance of the mobile colonial food system and made its destruction the core of their anti-colonial struggle. In this way, the fascist project for mass colonization, imperialist technology transfer, and destruction of Ethiopian bio- and cultural diversity actually sowed the seeds of its own demise.

NOTES

1 Ciro Poggiali, *Albori dell'Impero: L'Etiopia come è e come sarà* (Milan: Treves, 1938), 198.
2 Pierino Bertinotti, in Filippo Colombara, *Raccontare l'impero: Una storia orale della conquista d'Etiopia (1935–1941)* (Milan: Mimesis, 2019), unnumbered.
3 Jayeeta Sharma, "Food and Empire," *The Oxford Handbook of Food History*, ed. Jeffrey M. Pilcher (New York: Oxford University Press, 2012), 241–57.
4 Tiago Saraiva, *Fascist Pigs: Technoscientific Organisms and the History of Fascism* (Cambridge, MA: MIT Press, 2016).
5 Patrick Bernhard, "Hitler's Africa in the East: Italian Colonialism as a Model for German Planning in Eastern Europe," *Journal of Contemporary History* 51, no. 1 (2016): 61–90.
6 Carol Helstosky, "Fascist Food Politics: Mussolini's Policy of Alimentary Sovereignty," *Journal of Modern Italian Studies* 9, no. 1 (2004): 1–26.
7 Ruth Ben-Ghiat, *Fascist Modernities* (Berkeley: University of California Press, 2004), 132.
8 Haile Selassie, "Appeal to the League of Nations," 30 June 1936.
9 Angelo Del Boca, *Italiani brava gente?* (Vicenza: Neri Pozza, 2011), 203, 205, 197.
10 Frantz Fanon, *The Wretched of the Earth* (New York: Grove Press, 2004), 44, 135.
11 Alessandro Lessona, *L'Africa italiana nel primo anno dell'Impero* (Rome: Edizioni della Rassegna Economica dell'Africa Italiana, 1937), 18.
12 Ministero degli Affari Esteri, *L'opera di avvaloramento agricolo e zootecnico in Eritrea, in Somalia e in Etiopia* (Rome: Soc. Abete, 1970), 369.
13 Lidio Cipriani, "La decadenza razziale delle genti negre e la necessità di una protezione degli Etiopici," *Africa Italiana* 3, no. 1 (1940): 21.
14 Haile M. Larebo, *The Building of an Empire: Italian Land Policy and Practice in Ethiopia* (New York: Oxford University Press, 1994).
15 James McCann, *People of the Plow: An Agricultural History of Ethiopia, 1800–1990* (Madison, WI: University of Wisconsin Press, 1995), 211.
16 Costanza Bonelli, *Clima, razza, colonizzazione: Nascita e sviluppo della medicina tropicale in Italia* (PhD diss., Università di Roma Sapienza, 2019).
17 David Forgacs, *Italy's Margins: Social Exclusion and Nation Formation since 1861* (New York: Cambridge University Press, 2014), 87.
18 Alberto Sbacchi, "Italian Colonization in Ethiopia: Plans and Projects, 1936–1941," *Africa* 32, no. 4 (1977): 34.
19 Poggiali, *Albori dell'Impero*, 193.
20 Davide Fossa, *Lavoro italiano nell'Impero* (Milan: Mondadori, 1938), 472–90.

21 Gian Luca Podestà, "Il lavoro in Africa Orientale Italiana (1935–1939),"
    in *Il lavoro come fattore produttivo e come risorsa nella storia economica
    italiana*, ed. Mario Taccolini and Sergio Zaninelli (Milan: Vita e Pensiero,
    2002), 141.

22 Richard Pankhurst, "A Page of Ethiopian History: Italian Settlement Plans
    during the Fascist Occupation of 1936–41," *Ethiopia Observer* 13, no. 2
    (1970): 150–2.

23 Fossa, *Lavoro italiano nell'Impero*, 494, 492.

24 Emanuele Ertola, *L'Impero immaginario: I coloni italiani in Etiopia, 1936–1941*
    (PhD diss., Università di Firenze, 2014), 75–6.

25 Alberto Sbacchi, *Ethiopia Under Mussolini: Fascism and the Colonial
    Experience* (London: Zed Books, 1985), 107–14.

26 Angelo Del Boca, *Gli italiani in Africa Orientale*, vol. 3: *La caduta dell'Impero*
    (Milan: Mondadori, 2014), 210.

27 Richard Pankhurst, "Italian and Native Labour during the Italian Fascist
    Occupation of Ethiopia, 1935–41," *Ghana Social Science Journal* 2, no. 2
    (1972): 42–73.

28 Sbacchi, *Ethiopia under Mussolini*, 97.

29 Francesco Pierotti, *Vita in Etiopia, 1940–41* (Bologna: Cappelli, 1959), 36.

30 Guardia di Finanza, "Relazione sull'attività della R. Guardia di Finanza
    dell'Impero durante l'esercizio finanziario 1938–39," *Bollettino d'Archivio* 1,
    no. 1 (2005): 1–130.

31 S.P., in Irma Taddia, *La memoria dell'Impero: Autobiografie d'Africa Orientale*
    (Bari: Lacaita, 1988), 124–5.

32 Ertola, *L'Impero immaginario*, 205.

33 M. Guidotti and R. Guibellini, "Il problema dei salari della mano d'opera
    di colore nel periodo pre- e postbellico," *Agricoltura Coloniale* 30, no. 12
    (1936): 441–50.

34 Ernesto Massi, "Economia dell'Africa Italiana," *Rivista Internazionale di
    Scienze Sociali* 11, no. 3 (1940): 437.

35 Richard Pankhurst, "A Chapter in Ethiopia's Commercial History:
    Developments during the Fascist Occupation of Ethiopia, 1936–1941,"
    Ethiopia Observer 14, no. 1 (1971): 47–67.

36 Adriana Sciubba, "Il Commercio dell'Italia con l'AOI," *Rassegna Sociale
    dell'Africa Italiana* 3, no. 1 (1940): 57–62; Sbacchi, *Ethiopia under Mussolini*,
    99–100.

37 "Il lavoro e l'assistenza sociale," *Annnali dell'Africa Italiana* 3, no. 2 (1940):
    1067.

38 Colombara, *Raccontare l'impero*, unnumbered.

39 Pierotti, *Vita in Etiopia*, 17.

40 Ian Campbell, *The Addis Ababa Massacre: Italy's National Shame* (New York:
    Oxford University Press, 2017), 132, 157, 199.

41 Alfredo Gonzales-Ruibal, "Fascist Colonialism: The Archaeology of Italian Outposts in Western Ethiopia (1936–41)," *International Journal of Historical Archaeology* 37 no. 4 (2010): 566.

42 Poggiali, *Albori dell'Impero*, 163.

43 E.P., in Taddia, *La memoria dell'Impero*, 82.

44 Poggiali, *Albori dell'Impero*, 217.

45 Vincenzo Ambrosio, *Tre anni fra i Galla e i Sidama, 1937–1940: Lettere di un funzionario coloniale e testimonianze della sua morte sul campo* (Rome: Signorelli, 1942), 75.

46 Alberto Capatti and Massimo Montanari, *Italian Cuisine: History of a Culture* (New York: Columbia University Press, 2001), 252–7; Vittorio Daniele and Nicola Ostuni, "The Madeleine Effect: Italian Emigration and Exports of Preserved Tomatoes (1897–1933)," *Rivista di Storia Economica* 27, no. 2 (2011): 243–66.

47 Perry Wilson, "Cooking the Patriotic Omelette: Women and the Italian Fascist Ruralization Campaign," *European History Quarterly* 27, no. 4 (1993): 531–47.

48 Poggiali, *Albori dell'Impero*, 215.

49 Francesco Bolongaro, in Colombara, *Raccontare l'impero*, unnumbered.

50 Pier Marcello Masotti, *Ricordi d'Etiopia di un funzionario coloniale* (Milan: Pan, 1981), 72.

51 Dicodimos Tesfamikel, in Alessandro Volterra, *Sudditi Coloniali Ascari Eritrei, 1935–1941* (Milan: Angeli, 2005), 143.

52 Adolfo Mignemi, *Lo sguardo e l'immagine: La fotografia come documento storico* (Turin: Bollati Boringhieri, 2003), ill. inset, photographs 13–17; Forgacs, *Italy's Margins*, 120–2.

53 Egidio Antonioli, in Colombara, *Raccontare l'impero*, unnumbered.

54 Bahru Zewde, *History of Modern Ethiopia, 1855–1974* (Athens: Ohio University Press, 2002), 165, 171.

55 Sbacchi, *Ethiopia under Mussolini*, 100–2.

56 Richard Pankhurst, "L'occupazione fascista nella letteratura etiopica," *Studi Piacentini* 13 (1993): 135–48.

57 Sbacchi, *Ethiopia under Mussolini*, 100.

58 Tekalign Wolde-Mariam, *A City and Its Hinterlands: The Political Economy of Land Tenure, Agriculture, and Food Supply for Addis Ababa, Ethiopia (1887–1974)* (PhD diss., Boston University, 1995), 229.

59 O.G., in Taddia, *La memoria dell'Impero*, 138.

60 A.F., in Taddia, *La memoria dell'Impero*, 132.

61 Minale Adugna, "Women and Warfare in Ethiopia: A Case Study of Their Role during the Campaign of Adwa, 1895–96, and the Italo-Ethiopian War, 1935–41," *Organization for Social Science Research in Eastern and Southern Africa: Gender Issues Research Report Series* 13 (2001): 31–5.

62 Masotti, *Ricordi d'Etiopia*, 192.
63 Anthony Mockler, *Haile Selassie's War: The Italian-Ethiopian Campaign, 1935–1941* (New York: Random House, 1984), 364.
64 Masotti, *Ricordi d'Etiopia*, 214.
65 Ertola, *L'impero immaginario*, 46.
66 Ertola, *L'Impero immaginario*, 212.

5 The Fastest Fast Food in the World: Airplane Cuisine and the "Taste of Pace"

ELIZABETH ZANONI

In 1966, Roger Grosjean, Executive Chef at Pan American World Airway's flight kitchen at New York's John F. Kennedy airport, reflected with heady confidence on the airline's ability to keep up with the shorter transatlantic flight times anticipated by advances in aviation engineering: "If we can feed Bermuda and Nassau passengers a five-course meal within two hours, why not a supersonic jet to Europe, taking approximately the same time?"[1] By the time Grosjean had accepted his position with Pan American World Airways (Pan Am), he had a culinary pedigree for pioneering in what had arguably become the world's fastest and most widely distributed cuisine. After his culinary training in France, Grosjean had prepared meals in some of the best hotels and restaurants across Europe, including the famous Maxim's restaurant in Paris. During World War II, he supervised the French Foreign Legion kitchen in Algeria and afterwards, ran NATO's kitchen in Paris. Before arriving in Kennedy's Flight Kitchen in Hanger 14, Grosjean had, one Pan Am press release gloated, "literally cooked his way around the world, three and a half times."[2]

At Pan Am, the meals prepared by Grosjean travelled even further, with more regularity, and at much swifter speeds. These meals eaten at 40,000 feet were literally the fastest "fast food" in the world. Between the first forkful and last morsel of steak or dinner roll, the passenger and the meal had travelled hundreds of miles. These intertwined, rapid movements of people and food helped create what I call a *taste of pace*, a taste characterized by real and imagined speed and the culinary infrastructures that facilitated or frustrated it.[3] Airplane meals, as one of many foods consumed on the go, illuminates how taste captures and responds to the joined mobilities of eaters and food. As this chapter demonstrates, food and people on the move, together, combined to create an inflight cuisine that both capitalized on and was challenged by the actual and perceived pace of consumers and their meals.

This chapter articulates taste of pace as a paradigm for studying how the linked and hurried mobilities of food and people made possible by modern transportation and food technologies have influenced global food cultures. It utilizes airplane food, and in particular the meals imagined, assembled, and served by Pan Am in the postwar years, as a case study for considering how the tied travels of people and food produced taste based on positive and gendered concepts of speed, distance, technology, and modernity. This taste came to be defined mainly by male airline executives, food scientists, and other experts concerned with altitude, air pressure, dryness, noise, and vibration.[4] These positive connotations of modernity and cosmopolitanism associated with airplane meals also came to characterize the passengers who ate them, conceived mainly as jet-setting businessmen who consumed a global smorgasbord of food and the female flight attendants who served them. Conversely, taste of pace obscured, minimized, and maligned the labour and expertise of the mostly female commissary workers who made the meals and the flight attendants aloft who served them; the merged mobilities of airplane food and its eaters generated inequalities based on a gendered hierarchy that continues to haunt the airline and fast-food industries today. The taste of pace also complements and sits in tension with *terroir*, the term food studies scholars have employed to describe the "taste of place" in crops, food, and beverages, such as wine and cheese, whose flavour characteristics reflect local environmental (soil, region, climate, animal breed, etc.) and social-cultural (culinary traditions, identities, values, etc.) properties.[5] Taste of pace, instead, recognizes that mobility also fosters links between taste, technology, and local environments. Despite the ways in which inflight cuisines evoked ideas of "placelessness" or "everywhere-ness," a taste of nowhere and everywhere simultaneously, the linked movements of people and food depended on fixed, on-the-ground infrastructures – airport kitchens, freezing and reheating machinery, and broader developments within the food industry – that sometimes thwarted airlines' attempts to capitalize on pace.

Theorizing the Taste of Pace

The joined mobilities of people and food and their consequences for global cuisines are best tackled by combining the insights of scholars interested in migrating people with those interested in migrating commodities. Food historians have produced a vast literature on the history of industrialization that gave birth to "fast foods," especially in postwar North America but slowly, and not without opposition, in nations worldwide. In this literature, the "fast" in fast foods has referred mainly to changes in production and manufacturing technologies that allowed processed foods with long shelf lives to be made quickly, in mass quantities, and by unskilled labourers.[6] And while scholars have also studied the fast-paced, modern lifestyles such foods represented and sustained, rarely have they reflected with intentionality on the actual *pace* of both the foods and the people who eat them. Situating the real simultaneous movements of foods and eaters at the centre of our investigation promises to offer new insights into the history of food industrialization and globalization.

Today food moves faster than ever before, and over vast distances, a phenomenon that scholars interested in commodity chains have shown became central to food industrialization and the formation of national and global cuisines centuries ago. The expansion of global networks of food producers, packagers, shippers, and shoppers, this literature has shown, has had myriad political, cultural, and environmental consequences for our modern food systems that have benefited some (usually wealthy eaters in Western countries) at the expense of others (often poor labourers in food exporting countries of the Global South).[7] And yet, this critical historical work on global commodity chains tends to render the consumer motionless at a fixed place at the end of an inequitable web of moving ingredients. In these studies, food moves to the consumer, who is assumed to be a static recipient of a cup of coffee, a box of cornflakes, a hamburger, a banana – items that have moved hundreds of thousands of miles.

Whereas historians of food industrialization have concentrated especially on mobile foods, migration and mobility scholars have until recently focused predominately on mobile people. They have placed those mobilities at the centre of world history to show how the voluntary and forced movements of people across space and time – hunters and gathers, enslaved people, labourers, colonists, merchants, tourists, to name a few – were integral to histories of imperialism, slavery, global capitalism, nation-building, and a range of both conservative and radical social, cultural, and political movements.[8] While these studies have importantly conceived of human mobility, historically and today, as a common, rather than extraordinary, part of everyday life, they have concentrated predominately on human movements, with less attention to the objects and commodities, including foodstuff, that accompanied travelling people. More recently, migration historians have offered important models for investigating the role human mobilities have played in producing conceptions of taste. Scholars interested in migration and foodways have shown how mobile people carried ingredients and culinary traditions across oceans and continents.[9]

The consideration of both food and people puts these historians in conversation with an interdisciplinary group of social scientists who have embraced the "mobility turn." Mobility scholars consider relationships between different categories of people on the move, between various sites, vehicles, and scales of mobility, but also between moving people, capital, ideas and technologies, while also recognizing barriers, including power relations of gender, race, and class, to these connected movements.[10] This chapter offers a methodological intervention into mobility studies by locating "pace" at the centre of exploring the multiple, connected facets of mobilities – both real and imagined – that go into making taste. It borrows from migration and commodity chain research to offer an expanded paradigm for thinking about how people move food, how food moves people, and how together these joined mobilities shape global foodways and cuisines.

The meals consumed inflight are far from the first to be characterized by the pace of both the food and their eaters. Whenever and however people travelled they transported and consumed raw, processed, and prepared foods, whether on foot, on horseback, or in horse-drawn carriages, automobiles, trains, sailboats, and steamships. These modes of transportation and the act of travel itself created tastes that were informed by the pace of consumers. The mobility of airplane passengers, therefore, despite their relative elite status in years after World War II, connects them to mobile diners who came before them, both humble and affluent.[11] Even while the types of meals eaten on steamships and in railroad dining cars resembled those consumed aloft in the postwar era, innovations in aircraft design during and after the war accelerated the pace of travel and eating for airplane diners, offering new hurdles and opportunities for taste makers tasked with feeding travellers at lightning speeds.[12]

Wolfgang Schivelbusch argues that already by the nineteenth century rail travel had produced radically new facets of everyday life as they related to time, space, and social relations, experiences that taught passengers what it meant to be a modern industrial subject in a capitalist society.[13] Airline passengers, therefore, had been primed to accept mechanized speed and the new system of thinking and behaviour it introduced. However, unlike food served on the earth's surface, the meals served aloft faced conditions unique to eating in cramped, pressured cabins, at high attitudes, and at speeds that most nineteenth-century railroad travellers could not have imagined, making airplane food an excellent case study for thinking about how eating on the go relied on and inspired new relationships between taste and technology. And in this realm, Pan Am played a trailblazing role: even while the types of meals served by Pan Am would come to echo those served by other domestic and global airlines, Pan Am was the first to serve meals aloft in 1929 and the first to serve frozen entrees; unlike many of its competitors, Pan Am produced their own meals throughout most of the 1950s and 1960s, rather than contract out to catering services as its competitors did; and finally, as the nation's only international carrier until the end of World War II, and after the war, the leading international carrier until deregulation in 1978, Pan Am bore the lion's share of figuring out how to serve food on flights that spanned long distances, flight times, and time zones.[14]

Pan Am and the Taste of Pace

A 1946 article in the *New York World-Telegram* lauded changes in food technologies that allowed Europe- and Africa-bound air travellers to enjoy meals while "flashing through at 300 miles an hour." In just fifteen minutes, these meals, stored in a dry ice container on board, went from "frozen so hard it bends a fork" to "piping hot" with the help of new ovens installed in the pressurized cabins of Pan Am's Lockheed Constellation Clippers. Evoking words and concepts that would come to characterize the taste of pace, the article heralded a cuisine that increasing numbers of eaters around the world experienced in the postwar years as air travel skyrocketed.[15] It was a taste shaped by the thrill of transcending time and space at breakneck speeds and the challenges such movements posed for airplane meal producers, marketers, and eaters.

Before World War II, most passengers aboard Pan Am's "flying clipper ships" ate their meals at restaurants and hotels on the ground during refuelling and overnight stops; by the 1930s, Pan Am pursers began purchasing food from local restaurants or caterers, bringing these meals on board for passengers to eat en route.[16] But the taste of pace as it came to define airplane food by mid-century depended, above all, on the speed with which it was made, served, and consumed. That speed required specific machinery, technologies, distribution networks, and approaches to labour productivity, best exemplified in the flight kitchens established by Pan Am starting in the mid-1930s. By World War II, the airline had established flight kitchens at key Pan Am hubs in the U.S. and abroad, in cities ranging from

Seattle, San Francisco, New York, Port of Spain, Berlin, Rome, Honolulu, and Bangkok.

By 1960s, Pan Am's "ultra-modern kitchens" (figure 5.1) featured trays of food moving along electric conveyor belts as commissary workers filled single-portion trays with meal items.[17] In the background, male chefs in towering, authoritative *toques blanches* hovered over large roasts. The kitchen was a well-lit, spotless laboratory, stocked with stainless-steel equipment – trays, refrigerators, ovens, work surfaces, and a variety of pots, pans, and colanders. Reflecting the way in which male "experts" at the helm of Pan Am food service constructed a taste of pace based on gendered relationships between mobile food and people, flight kitchens exhibited a division of labour in which "expert" male culinary professionals held higher-paying, skilled positions of chef, lead cook, saucier, and butcher, while female commissary workers performed lower-paying work assembling, cleaning, and organizing as kitchen helpers, "pantrywomen," and dishwashers.[18]

While Pan Am flight kitchens sported production technologies employed in other industries for which food needed to be prepared quickly, cheaply, and in bulk – large hotels and restaurants, and especially corporate food businesses selling products to grocery stores – two technologies in particular produced the actual and imagined "speed" unique to airplane cuisine: freezing and reheating technologies.[19] Innovations in refrigeration combined with transportation advances during the late nineteenth and early twentieth centuries radically altered commodity chains, ideas about "freshness," and consumers' relationship to foods and nature. And yet, the frozen food industry was still in its infancy in the immediate postwar years.[20] Issues of time and distance distinctive to inflight meal experiences, however, made frozen foods ideal for the burgeoning commercial airline industry, and Pan Am employed speed – both actual and imagined – to link freezing and reheating food technologies to desirable understandings of modernity as it related to taste.

By the end of the war, hot meals served aloft were usually almost fully pre-cooked at one of Pan Am's flight kitchens and then either poured into thermos jugs – where they would continue cooking on the flight until served – or packed into dry ice and reheated on board with steam tables powered by airplane engines. Other meals were 100 per cent cooked and served hot almost immediately after departure.[21] During the war inventor W.L. Maxson of the W.L. Maxson Corporation developed the Whirlwind oven, an electric convection oven that held and heated trays of cold or frozen meals, meals produced by Maxson first for the U.S. Naval Air Transport Service during the war. Together, Pan Am and Maxson developed pre-cooked frozen meals, called Maxson

Figure 5.1 A circa 1960 photograph of commissary workers in one of Pan
American World Airway's flight kitchens. Photo of Pan Am Flight Kitchen
(n.d., circa 1960), Box 1, Folder 1 193 16: Food Service, 1944–1985 (2 of 2),
Sub-Series 7: Passenger Service, 1941–1985, PA Records, Pan American World
Airways, Inc. Records, University of Miami Special Collections, Otto G.
Richter Library, University of Miami, Coral Gables, FL. Courtesy of Special
Collections, University of Miami Libraries, Coral Gables, Florida.

Sky Plates, which were originally prepared at Maxson Queens Village
plant in Queens, New York. By 1945, Pan Am food consultants supervised all Maxson Sky Plates according to the airline's specifications.[22]
Early Sky Plates contained an animal protein, such as sirloin steak, ham,
or roast turkey, along with starches and vegetables like baby lima beans
and potato casseroles.[23]

The pre-cooked meals produced by Pan Am were not just frozen,
they were "flash" frozen, a speed of freeze discussed and extolled by

Pan Am. "All foods are cooked separately to just the right point, then placed on a specially designed plate and flash frozen at 20 degrees below zero," explained journalist Jean Kilbourne in a 1946 article for *New Horizons*, a Pan Am publication. The frozen meals were stored in low-temperature refrigerators and sent to Pan Am flight kitchens at key airports around the world, where they could be stored for several months before being loaded onto planes for use.[24] One 1966 Pan Am press release bragged about the airline's "revolutionary blast freeze system, which freezes prepared food within four hours, retaining all of the original fresh flavor and color."[25]

Airplane cuisine relied on the pace at which food was not only frozen but also unfrozen. In the mid-1940s, Pan Am hired Maxson to help redesign the galley sections of their newest Clipper fleet of Lockheed Constellations to accommodate Maxson's Whirlwind ovens as well as space for food storage containers, liquor, electric urns, ice boxes, and sinks.[26] Maxson's ovens with "high speed" fans quickly thawed and finished cooking the meals (see figure 5.2) once aboard. After being reheated in the air, flight attendants added other elements – appetizers, salads, and desserts – made before departure at a Pan Am flight kitchen. Subsequent improvements to inflight heating – more efficient, larger (yet lightweight) and faster ovens – allowed Pan Am to turn to pre-cooked frozen meals as its main source for feeding passengers aloft by the 1950s. As with freezing, Pan Am extolled the "high speed" reheating technologies involved in airplane cuisine as central to inflight dining. One press release noted that the new ovens "defrost and produce twelve piping-hot, home-style meals every 15 minutes that have all the goodness and flavor of choice meats and garden-fresh vegetables."[27]

By the late 1950s, improved infrared ovens with quartz panels below the oven's electric coils took only seventeen minutes to rise to 700 degrees. At this fast pace and with these roomier ovens Pan Am boasted that sixteen steaks were "cooked to perfection all at once."[28] A 1968 Pan Am press release boasted, "kitchens aboard a jetliner are not like others one is likely to meet anywhere else" because they were equipped with "high-speed, infra-red ovens" into which went foods as diverse as pancakes, eggs, and the flambéed cherries and liqueur sauce for Cherries Jubilee.[29]

In 1954, Pan Am entered into a formal partnership with Maxim's, the upscale Parisian bistro, who would supply most of Pan Am's frozen meals.[30] The airline played up its links to Maxim's at every occasion. It placed the restaurant's name on inflight menus along with their logo, "Good Food Is the Basis for True Happiness," a quote from Auguste Escoffier, the French chef credited with popularizing a modern, simpler version of traditional French cooking.[31] By the mid-1950s,

Figure 5.2 Flight attendant heating Maxson Sky Plates in a Whirlwind Oven in Kitchen Galley (n.d., circa 1950), Box 1, Folder 1 193 16: Food Service, 1944–1985 (2 of 2), Sub-Series 7: Passenger Service, 1941–1985, PA Records., Pan American World Airways, Inc. Records, University of Miami Special Collections, Otto G. Richter Library, University of Miami, Coral Gables, FL. Courtesy of Special Collections, University of Miami Libraries, Coral Gables, Florida.

Pan Am began supplying Maxim's not only with specific instructions regarding serving size and packaging, but also with the raw ingredients used to make meals in their kitchens, showing how the airline mobilized its transportation infrastructure to move the foods they desired to production centres.[32] A 1958 Pan Am brochure read, "Maxim's of Paris prepares 1,500 meals a day for Pan Am. Choicest fresh vegetables, best-fed meats, finest fruits, freshest dairy products are rushed to Maxim kitchens."[33]

When Pan Am finally got into the frozen food business itself – opening its first frozen food facility in New York in 1950, its second in San Francisco in 1960, and its third in Tokyo in 1965 – the company maintained the prestigious link to the famed eatery; it employed Maxim's trained chefs like Grosjean to oversee its flight kitchens and used recipes from the restaurant.[34] By 1970, one of these three frozen food kitchens supplied 91 per cent of all frozen meals served on Pan Am flights; they were sent on Pan Am cargo planes to Pan Am stations across the globe where they would be stored until loaded onto departing flights.[35]

Freezing and heating capacities did not alone create the taste of pace. Pan Am kitchens teemed with a diverse profusion of state-of-the art equipment. The company promoted flight kitchens as culinary laboratories where "time saving" machines, techniques, recipes, and processes related to food service were invented, tested, and perfected under the guidance of expert food authorities. At Pan Am's frozen food facility at Kennedy Airport, "everything is automatic, electric and conveyor belts are a common sight, not to overlook the big electric kettles and ovens and other mechanical delights."[36] The kitchen included a giant walk-in refrigerator – the largest in the world, Pan Am claimed.[37] By 1966, Pan Am praised its IBM computer that, after having been fed data on passenger numbers and supplies, spit out cards detailing the exact amount of ingredients and cutlery needed for every type of meal service – from first-class to economy – on every flight. The airline commended the computer as "invaluable in speeding up work and supplying the information on what is needed on the flight. It means accuracy and satisfied passengers."[38]

According to Chef Grosjean, even traditional French cuisine was improved by the pace of preparation these food technologies allowed. "American mechanics are the best thing to come along for French cooking," he pronounced, explaining how centuries-old French recipes were actually improved by modern American kitchen appliances.[39] With the help of engineers at a research and development centre in St. Louis, Grosjean even invented his own culinary tools, including an "ideal broiler" for steaks and veal chops and a blade for splitting lobsters, which he called the "Guillotine Roger." His ideal broiler produced 140,000 pieces of broiled steak and veal chops each month. It also saved Pan Am close to $1,000 daily in operation costs, especially in the form of labour, since it required only two operators to oversee the preparation of 12,000 filets a day, whereas before, twelve workers had been needed.[40] And yet, this celebration of cooking equipment, executive chefs, and quality ingredients rendered invisible the Pan Am commissary workers – cooks, sauciers, kitchen helpers, "pantrymen/women," etc. – who prepared and assembled the meals.[41] Individual labourers generated the mobility upon which the taste of pace depended. However, Pan Am fanfare instead insinuated that "ultra-modern, stainless steel, and always sparkling" flight kitchens, machines, and appliances did the important work.[42]

The association of the taste of pace with modern machinery, classically trained male chefs, and Maxim's not only obscured the labour done by commissary workers, especially female labourers holding low-paying positions, but it also served to alleviate the public's lingering concerns over the edibility, safety, quality, and nutritional value of frozen meals.[43] Pan Am worried about whether travellers would warm up to the frozen meals heated and served aloft. Pan Am Service Manager Ken Parratt, in a 1950 company memo wrote, "It is unfortunate that in the early days of development, frozen food got a poor reputation." He blamed that poor standing on the new frozen TV dinner, another postwar invention, whose producers did not care enough about quality. He hoped the tie-in with Maxim's would ease consumers' qualms about frozen food: "This restaurant had demonstrated to a number of gourmets that it is not possible to distinguish between their pre-cooked frozen food and their fresh kitchen prepared servings."[44] Pan Am worked hard to distance its meals from TV dinners. Henry Johnson, supervisor of San Francisco's frozen food facility commented, "It's important to realize these aren't like TV dinners. All of the food is fresh when it is cooked and then quick-frozen. Most commercial pre-packaged foods have gone through two or more freezing cycles before being delivered to supermarkets."[45]

Indeed, it was the speed of freeze that differentiated Pan Am meals from other frozen food items. Flash freezing, the airline assured customers, maintained, not compromised, taste. Unlike other frozen food businesses, Pan Am told travellers in a 1952 brochure, the company used "an entirely new and wonderful method of food service" in which during the cooking, chefs "test for taste, and at just the right moment, when it's perfectly done and the flavour is best, the food is quick-frozen."[46] Flash freezing allowed the airline to offer meals that were not only modern but also gourmet because fast-paced cooling gave the company access to the best foods year-round. "Pan Am follows the season, buying food when it is plentiful, at its best and at the lowest cost." Perhaps more accurately, Pan Am dominated the seasons, by freeing itself from the time- and place-specific cycles of the natural world. "The best lobster is available from Maine in May and June, so Pan Am buys and prepares large quantities which can be served in the months ahead. The best steak comes from the United States. Beef also is brought in England, France, pork in Germany and veal in Italy."[47] The tastes forged aloft depended on dominating local food environments globally and collapsing time and distance with speedy freezing techniques, making the entire world Pan Am's food market.

At every opportunity, Pan Am emphasized speed and movement in production processes that churned out meals fit for the modern, travelling epicures of the postwar era. Publicity inspired images of constant food mobility in and around flight kitchens; by the mid 1960s, Pan Am frozen food facilities contained new conveyor belt systems – one for cooking, another for freezing, and a third for loading finished frozen meals onto airplanes. A conveyor belt in San Francisco carried steaks "along an endless belt and sears them on all sides by flame." In another part of the kitchen a "conveyor belt freezing system using liquid nitrogen is expected to speed up the freezing process and improve quality," cutting freeze time from three hours to just twenty-five minutes, saving costs, increasing output, and preserving taste. Once finished, a new type of container and method loaded meals into airplane galleys using a "thin layer of air" to push meals onto the plane; the system allowed airplane meals to "roll on this blanket of air without friction ... and just float into the plane."[48] This constant movement enabled kitchens to run "day and night" year-round and produce the mass quantities of meals required to meet growing numbers of travellers. In 1966, commissary workers at Kennedy's Hanger 14 roasted 10,000 chickens, prepared 6,000 portions of rice pilaf, and broiled some 4,000 filet mignons daily.[49] In 1971, San Francisco's frozen food operation produced 450,000 first-class entrées and 4,500,000 economy entrées that used 3,200,000 portions of vegetables and starches, and 50,000 lbs. of different types of roasts.[50]

The intensity of both temporal change and vertical and horizontal movement, and of the mobility of both food and eaters, generated the taste of pace characterizing airplane food and distinguished it from similar industrialized foods. But these joined and rushed mobilities also threatened to destroy it, especially for an airline like Pan Am, who operated flights with "long legs and few stopovers in between" as the U.S.'s main international carrier until the late 1970s.[51] The makers, servers, and consumers of inflight cuisine navigated multiple temporal scales simultaneously: the length of the flight itself; the duration of meal service; and the "hop-scotching through time zones," amounted to a dizzying array of intertwined time- and space-related challenges.[52] In 1967, Parrott wondered, in ways that foreshowed the then expanding airport restaurant industry, "Should passengers be fed on the ground and planes scheduled to depart and arrive between meal periods? Should they be fed in-flight? Because time differences are shattered in transcontinental and trans-oceanic jet flights, both approaches will be necessary."[53]

These temporal and geographical obstacles were best met through frozen meals, especially for a company like Pan Am, whose routes spanned the globe and who served more passengers every year in the postwar decades. Technological advances in freezing and reheating and in automated production gave Pan Am the ability to maximize output while minimizing labour costs. Frozen food permitted the airline to standardize their meal service in ways that made it easier and more predictable for both passengers and flight personnel while still enabling Pan Am to change its menu easily for variety, especially since freezing meant nearly year-round access to seasonal foods. They also cut down on waste since unused frozen meals could be salvaged for future flights. They were portable, easily shipped on Pan Am airplanes, and delivered to flight kitchens around the world.

By the mid 1960s, Pan Am's three frozen food kitchens in New York, San Francisco, and Tokyo became the major nodes linking Pan Am's far-flung culinary pathways. From these locations, Pan Am meals were literally scattered throughout the world and eaten by passengers on flights leaving from cities across the globe. For example, Pan Am sent frozen meals made in New York to its stations in Bermuda, Glasgow, Brussels, Istanbul, Ankara, Dakar, and Teheran; it ferried those made in San Francisco to Shannon, Fairbanks, Sydney, Manila, and Los Angeles; and meals produced in Tokyo made their way to Honolulu, Hong Kong, and Guam.[54] In sum, given the company's complex and global culinary infrastructure – in which ingredients were sourced from locations around the world, in which different flight route segments offered different menus at different times (breakfast, lunch, and dinner), and in which finished meals were shipped to Pan Am stations across the world – frozen food was the obvious choice.[55]

Taste of pace, as defined by Pan Am, was in essence "expert" food, the result of partnerships between business, the military, and research institutes. In this, the industrialized meals offered to air travellers in the postwar years both encouraged and built upon similar partnerships that had long facilitated the industrialization of food in the U.S.[56] Pan

Am had a long-standing relationship with the military both directly – Pan Am served as the unofficial carrier of the U.S. government, ferrying mail and military personnel and supplies before and during World War II – and indirectly, through lucrative government contracts with airline companies such as Lockheed, Boeing, and Douglas.[57] In the 1940s, Pan Am engineers and mechanics, for example, worked with Douglas Aircraft Company to design a kitchen galley in the airline's fleet of DC-3 Clippers capable of handling, transporting, and storing larger quantities of food.[58]

Pan Am experts influenced the taste of pace not only in aviation design but also in food production itself. It was equally the stuff of scientists, airplane mechanics, logistical specialists, military liaisons, and others concerned with efficiency, profitability, aeronautics, and flavour. The airline employed food scientists "whose extensive studies have determined the foods to serve aloft" according to one Pan Am press release.[59] Their research affected the ways in which meals were made, packaged, frozen, reheated, transported, promoted, handled in flight, and, ultimately, received by consumers. Altitude, dryness, and weight restrictions posed the most serious problems. Low humidity at high altitudes affected the consistency of foods, cooking and reheating time, and human senses like smell integral to the physiology of taste.[60]

By the end of the 1960s, Pan Am food consultants experimenting with substitute ingredients discovered, for example, that arrowroot was better than baking power for maintaining the texture and lightness of food at high altitudes.[61] Experts also preoccupied themselves with the bulkiness of airplane meals. Given strict tonnage restrictions, there was nothing like weight to suppress the taste of pace. Pan Am's C.C. Snowdon, Passenger Service Manager, commented on frozen meals being so compact, "that they save about 65 pounds over the old method of storing meals in thermoses, thus allowing plenty of space for between-meal snacks and 'seconds.'"[62] The airline also studied packaging, portion size, and service. By 1969, "to speed up the output" of food production in the kitchen, Pan Am had turned to pre-cut portions of meats and other foods.[63] That same year the company ran a "time and motion study" to find out how long it took the cabin crew to pre-heat ovens, set up trays, cook the food, and serve the meals to passengers.[64]

The taste of pace, as studied and presented by experts, was largely the preserve of men. In publicity Pan Am completely ignored the contributions of commissary workers in Pan Am flight kitchens, many of them women. Furthermore, peppered throughout airline records, training guides, and press releases were not-so-subtle denunciations of the food skills of female flight attendants, denunciations that justified the instruction they received. "Alas," a Pan Am press release lamented about "girls" arriving at Pan Am's International Stewardess College in Miami, opened in 1965, "not many arrivals at the college appear to know their way around a kitchen, and … a few have failed to recognize the can opener."[65] Another press release noted that the gourmet meals served aloft "do not happen by chance nor are the lovely stewardesses responsible for cooking them. They simply put the finishing touch to a meal, created and cooked weeks ago" using Maxim's recipes at flight kitchens overseen by trained chefs.[66]

Flight attendants were no food authorities, Pan Am proclaimed. "We do not try to teach the girls to be chefs," College Supervisor Robert Nichols. Instead, they were instructed in proper food handling and reheating; they did not cook, but rather they "reconstituted the food through reheating."[67] While "reconstitution" meshed with the language of scientific modernity underpinning the taste of pace, it belittled the actual labour involved in food service by mainly female flight attendants. Even experienced women home cooks on the ground would struggle to master the taste of pace in their own kitchens. Since cooking on a jetliner was so reliant on fast-paced equipment, machinery, and experts, Pan Am's cooking techniques were "not as useful to the earth-bound housewife."[68]

Pan Am built the taste of pace not only on fast-moving, gourmet meals but also on the fast-moving consumers who consumed them aloft, tying favourable and luxurious associations of speed, modernity, and cosmopolitanism to travellers' identities. Unlike the housewife mentioned above, jet-setting airline eaters, depicted in Pan Am publicity as almost exclusively male, were not "earthbound." "Jet travellers are not only globe-trotters," Pan Am noted, "but also international gourmets."[69] By the mid-1950s, most of Pan Am's food offerings were versions of high-class French fare, and this was further enforced through the airline's association with Maxim's and by its menus, most of which were in French. By the early 1960s, Pan Am had expanded its menu to include meal items from the many culinary traditions of the nations that Pan Am serviced. The airline served the Brazilian meat, bean, and rice dish *feijoada* and Argentine *puchero de gallina*, a vegetable and chicken stew on flights to these two Latin American destinations. New Zealand chowder made from the local toheroa clams and Japanese Teriyaki skewered meat awaited passengers flying across the Pacific, and Pan Am offered fried rice and sweet and sour pork on route to Hong Kong. Wine included selections not only from France, but from Germany, California, Portugal, and Chile; cheeses came from France, Denmark, England, Italy, Switzerland, and Holland.[70] In 1969, Pan Am introduced its new "Pan Am Intercontinental Cuisine" emphasizing "food from the international marketplace," that gave passengers a sampling of "foods from around the world." The transition from French-oriented meals was done "to meet the ever-changing complexion and cross-section of passengers" said Harold L. Graham, Pan Am's Vice President of Service.[71]

While Pan Am devalued flight attendants' food skills, they made use of their diverse backgrounds and mobility to link food consumption aloft to a sexy, modern global cosmopolitanism. These "round-the-world girls" were "infinitely varied," bragged Pan Am, since they represented some fifty-seven nationalities from six different continents. "Unlike a jetliner, she has no prototype," Pan Am concluded.[72] Describing flight attendants as the "original Go-Go girls" seemed particularly apt, given the quick speed of food service and number of destinations to which she travelled. "She's a Pan American World stewardess, and her flight path takes her to six continents and all the seven seas, far below the equator and over the North Pole."[73] Pan Am, like other airlines, capitalized on the sex appeal of attendants, while exploiting racialized stereotypes about the femininity and sexuality of women from certain ethnic backgrounds in order to project itself as inclusive and cosmopolitan.[74]

Pan Am invited male passengers to consume an international smorgasbord of both food and the women who served it. "An imaginative passenger can turn any flight into a round-the-world trip by getting acquainted with the cabin crew," Pan Am trumpeted. "He can debate the merits of vintage Clos de Mouche with a Mademoiselle from Paris or wangle the formula for pisco sour from a Senorita from Quito ... All know the lure of faraway places and a working schedule that keeps them hop-scotching across time zones."[75] Pan Am executives fixed on modern machinery and gourmet foods invented, perfected, and controlled by male experts, but they also treated flight attendants as part of the airplane's culinary infrastructure to be studied and controlled by men. While Pan Am experts depicted flight attendants as devoid of expertise as food producers, they valued them for embodying and performing glamour, which involved concealing the enormous amount of labour, including food work, involved in flight service as skills and behaviours that came naturally to flight attendants as women.[76]

Pan Am emphasized that their meals, the female flight attendants who served them, and the passengers who enjoyed them were from everywhere – representing a global sampling of people, cultures, and nations – and nowhere – suspended in space, hovering between, over, and above national borders and oceans. Through its food, the airline produced and capitalized on a taste based both on *terroir* and its very

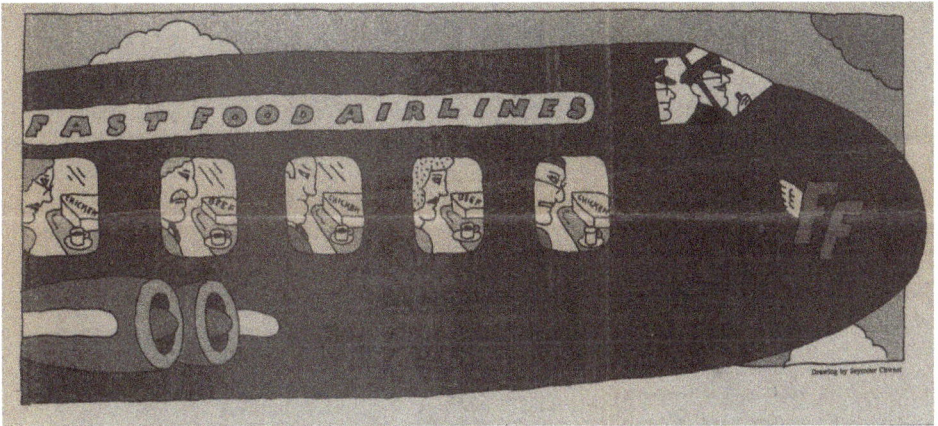

Figure 5.3 Seymour Chwast for the *New York Times*, 1985 in Marian Burros, "Airline Meals: Are They All the Same?" *New York Times*, 12 June 1985, Box 1, Folder 1 193 16: Food Service, 1944–1985 (2 of 2), Sub-Series 7: Passenger Service, 1941–1985, PA Records., Pan American World Airways, Inc. Records, University of Miami Special Collections, Otto G. Richter Library, University of Miami, Coral Gables, FL. Courtesy of Seymour Chwast and Special Collections, University of Miami Libraries, Coral Gables, Florida.

opposite, on both "roots" and "routes" to borrow anthropologist James Clifford's terminology.[77] Pan Am offered distinctive tastes of place, providing "meals native to various areas of the world," to give passengers "food he is likely to encounter in the particular part of the world in which he is travelling."[78] These tastes evoked singular origins, places, and cultures, even while they were stripped from the broader national culinary traditions of which they were a part.[79] But these dishes were simultaneously transformed through mobilities and speed into nowhere, into vague "faraway places." "*Somewhere* over the Atlantic, someone is popping a Danish shrimp into his lucky mouth," a 1970 article on Pan Am's new Intercontinental Cuisine began. "*Somewhere* in Germany, a gourmet is selecting his raw cut of beef to be cooked just the way he likes it best. *Somewhere* in Ireland, a fellow is downing a cup of Irish coffee."[80] The taste of pace embodied in airplane food, therefore, represents the contradictions between the universal and particular, between the local and the global, explored by scholars' work on the history of food globalization.[81]

Conclusion

"Some of the finest restaurants in the world are not on earth, but literally thousands of feet up in the air aboard the big jets," a 1966 Pan Am press release began. In these flying restaurants, passengers enjoyed "gourmet meals" made by Pan Am in flight kitchens overseen by Maxim's chefs.[82] Fast forward just twenty years. In June of 1985, graphic designer and artist Seymour Chwast drew a cartoon to accompany an article by Marian Burros for the *New York Times* on the poor quality of meals served aloft (see figure 5.3). The illustration shows airline passengers on "Fast Food Airlines" looking down with disdain at their boxed meal trays labelled either chicken or beef.[83] Her article opened with a story about a flight attendant who, after telling passengers about their three entrée choices, added, "Please don't be upset if your first choice is not available. They all taste the same anyway." By the 1980s, the fastest fast food in the world – once linked to modernity and cosmopolitanism – had turned into simply fast food, a cuisine instead associated with processed, bland, standardized, cheap fare. Burros wrote that airplane meals, "the food you love to hate," had "become synonymous with unimaginative, precooked, assembly-line fare." "In short," Burros concluded, airplane food had become "a midair version of a poor TV dinner."[84]

For as hard as Pan Am tried to disassociate the taste of pace it helped create in the immediate postwar decades from the emerging frozen and fast foods found in supermarkets and restaurants, the airline, and others who followed Pan Am's example by turning to frozen meals, could not sustain the prestige associated with eating high-tech, modern, and international meals at 40,000 feet.[85] The increased competition that came with airline deregulation in the late 1970s, the democratization of airline travel it encouraged, rising production and transportation costs, and the continued postwar development and popularity of fast foods challenged Pan Am's hold on images of mobile dining. Furthermore, much to Pan Am's chagrin, numerous regulatory and physical roadblocks rooted in particular places slowed down the taste of pace and the culinary infrastructures that allowed for it: government regulations regarding food safety and passenger security; national and international regulatory agencies such as the Civil Aeronautics Board and the International Airline Transport Association; and labour agitation among commissary workers at Pan Am flight kitchens.

But Chwast's cartoon suggests something beyond the public's falling estimation of the quality of airplane food. Instead, it points to pace – both real and symbolic – as a powerful force in generating the tastes that have come to characterize much of our modern, industrialized food system. It reveals how the joined movements of food and people through space and time posed both opportunities and problems for corporations, chefs, food experts, and consumers in the postwar era. It also suggests that airplane food mobilities depended on the exploitation and denigration of workers, mainly female food workers and flight attendants, situated in hierarchies of gender, sexuality, race, and class. And finally, Pan Am's transnationally expansive culinary infrastructure, the complex commodity chains it supported, and its use of food to showcase the everywhere-ness and nowhere-ness of Pan Am and its passengers, illustrates how pace, just as much as place, became central to articulations of cuisines.

NOTES

* The author wishes to acknowledge Daniel Bender and Simone Cinotto for their helpful feedback, as well as Donna Gabaccia, Megan Nutzman, Timothy Orr, John Weber, Brett Bebber, Nicholas Abbott, Elizabeth Fretwell, and Marvin Chiles for comments on earlier chapter drafts.

1 "Special Services Department," Pan Am Press Release (hereafter PA PR), 1966, Box 1, Folder 1 193 16: Food Service, 1944–1985 (1 of 2), Series: Technical Operations, Sub-Series 7: Passenger Service, 1941–1985 (hereafter TO PS), Pan American World Airways, Inc. Records, University of Miami Special Collections, Otto G. Richter Library, University of Miami, Coral Gables, FL (hereafter PA Records).

2 "Food Philosophy," PA PR, 1966, Box 1, Folder 1 193 16: Food Service, 1944–1985 (1 of 2), TO PS, PA Records.

3 Jeffrey M. Pilcher, "Culinary Infrastructures: How Facilities and Technologies Create Value and Meaning around the World," *Global Food History* 2, no. 2 (2016): 105–31.

4 Paul Freedman, *Food: The History of Taste* (Berkeley: University of California Press, 2007).

5 Amy Trubek, *The Taste of Place: A Cultural Journey into Terroir* (Berkeley: University of California Press, 2008); Thomas Parker, *Tasting French Terroir* (Berkeley: University of California Press, 2015).

6 Eric Schlosser, *Fast Food Nation: The Dark Side of the All-American Meal* (New York: Perennial, 2001); James L. Watson, *Golden Arches East: McDonald's in East Asia* (Stanford: Stanford University Press, 1997); Harvey A. Levenstein, *Revolution at the Table: The Transformation of the American Diet* (New York: Oxford University Press, 1988).

7 Examples include Richard R. Wilk, ed., *Fast Food/Slow Food: The Cultural Economy of the Global Food System* (Lanham, MD: Altamira Press, 2006);

Warren Belasco and Roger Horowitz, eds., *Food Chains: From Farmyard to Shopping Cart* (Philadelphia: University of Pennsylvania Press, 2009); Susanne Freidberg, *French Beans and Food Scares: Culture and Commerce in an Anxious Age* (New York: Oxford University Press, 2004).

 8 A good place to start is Dirk Hoerder, *Cultures in Contact: World Migrations in the Second Millennium* (Durham, NC: Duke University Press, 2002).

 9 For a review of this literature see Elizabeth Zanoni, "Migrant Marketplaces: Globalizing Histories of Migrant Foodways," *Global Food History* 4, no. 1 (2018): 3–21.

10 For an overview see Mimi Sheller and John Urry, "The New Mobilities Paradigm," *Environment and Planning A* 38 (2006): 207–26.

11 Jeri Quinzio, *Food on the Rails: The Golden Age of Railroad Dining* (Lanham, MD: Rowman & Littlefield, 2016); Simon Spalding, *Food at Sea: Shipboard Cuisine from Ancient to Modern Times* (Lanham, MD: Rowman & Littlefield, 2016).

12 Richard Foss, *Food in the Air and Space: The Surprising History of Food and Drink in the Skies* (Lanham, MD: Rowman & Littlefield, 2014); Jeremy R. Kinney, *Airplanes: The Life Story of a Technology* (Baltimore: Johns Hopkins University Press, 2009).

13 Wolfgang Schivelbusch, *The Railway Journey: The Industrialization of Time and Space in the Nineteenth Century* (Oakland: University of California Press, 2014).

14 Foss, *Food in the Air and Space*, 36–3, 105–6.

15 "Hot Meals 4 Miles Up; Here's How," *New York World-Telegram*, 6 April 1946, Box 1, Folder 2 399 12: Meals Aloft, 1946, TO PS, PA Records.

16 Foss, *Food in the Air and Space*, 37.

17 "Gourmet Meals for a Dieter," PA PR, 1966, Box 1, Folder 1 193 16: Food Service, 1944–1985 (1 of 2), TO PS, PA Records.

18 On the masculinization of public and professional culinary work see Priscilla Parkhurst Ferguson, *Accounting for Taste: The Triumph of French Cuisine* (Chicago: University of Chicago Press, 2004), 141–7.

19 See for example Tracey Deutsch, *Building a Housewife's Paradise: Gender, Politics, and American Grocery Stores in the Twentieth Century* (Chapel Hill: University of North Carolina Press, 2010); Roger Horowitz, *Putting Meat on the American Table: Taste, Technology, Transformation* (Baltimore: Johns Hopkins University Press, 2005).

20 William Cronon, *Nature's Metropolis: Chicago and the Great West* (New York: W.W. Norton, 1991); Susanne Freidberg, *Fresh: A Perishable History* (Cambridge, MA: Harvard University Press, 2010).

21 Ann Whyte, "The Way We Were … The Early Pursers – Chief Cooks, Bottlewashers and Inflight Typists" (July/August 1986) Box 1, Folder 1 193 16: Food Service, 1944–1985 (1 of 2), TO PS, PA Records.

22 Foss, *Food in the Air and Space*, 61; Jean Kilbourne, "Clipper Kitchens," *New Horizons*, April–June 1946, Box 1, Folder 1 193 16: Food Service, 1944–1985 (1 of 2), TO PS, PA Records; Whyte, "The Way We Were."

23 No title, PA PR, Box 1, Folder 2 399 12: Meals Aloft, 1946, TO PS, PA Records.

24 Kilbourne, "Clipper Kitchens."

25 "American Mechanization and French Cuisine," PA PR, 1966, Box 1, Folder 1 193 16: Food Service, 1944–1985 (1 of 2), TO PS, PA Records.

26 Kilbourne, "Clipper Kitchens."

27 No Title, PA PR; Whyte, "The Way We Were ... The Early Pursers."

28 Whyte, "The Way We Were ... The Early Pursers."

29 "'Write Me at Cloud Nine' Says Pan Am College Grad," Pan Am Press Release, circa 1968 or 1969, Box 2, Folder 1 392 21: Training: Stewardess College, 1965–1968 Lease, 1965–1969, Series 13: Technical Operations, 1919–1991, Sub-series 9: Training and Education (hereafter TO TE), PA Records.

30 PAA Frozen Meal Kitchens, Box 24, Folder 2 362 7: Commissary Report, 1970 (folder 2 of 2), LR LN, PA Records.

31 Pan Am Menu, n.d., Folder 2 362 8: Commissary Report, 1967, Box 25, LR LN, PA Records. See also Pan Am brochure, "You, Too, Can Be a World Traveler by Jet Clipper," n.d. (circa 1960), Box 1: Printed Materials, Folder 5 of 15, Series 17, Printed Materials, 1929–1991, Other, Sub-Series 1: Brochures and Booklets, 1930–1986 (hereafter PM BB), PA Records.

32 Memo from Ken Parratt to Reg. Traffic/Serv. Supts., May 17, 1951, Box 1, Folder 2 215 9: Passenger Handling: Meals and Sales, 1950–1951 (hereafter PH), Box 1, TO PS, Pan Am Records.

33 Pan American World Airways System, *A Story of People, Opportunities and Service* (1958), Box 1: Printed Materials, Folder 7 of 15, PM BB, PA Records.

34 PAA Frozen Meal Kitchens, Box 24, Folder 2 362 7: Commissary Report, 1970 (folder 2 of 2), LR LN, PA Records.

35 PAA Frozen Meal Kitchens, PAA Flight Kitchens, Box 24, Folder 2 362 7 Commissary Report (folder 2 of 2), Series 7: Labor Relations, Sub-Series 1: Labor Negotiations, 1928–1991 (hereafter LR LN), PA Records.

36 "American Mechanization and French Cuisine."

37 "Behind the Scenes," PA PR, 1966, Box 1, Folder 1 193 16: Food Service, 1944–1985 (1 of 2), TO PS, PA Records.

38 "Filing the Trays Electronically," PA PR, 1966, Box 1, Folder 1 193 16: Food Service, 1944–1985 (1 of 2), TO PS, PA Records.

39 "American Mechanization and French Cuisine."

40 "The Inventive Chef," PA PR, 1966, Box 1, Folder 1 193 16: Food Service, 1944–1985 (1 of 2), TO PS, PA Records.

41 Pan American World Airways System, *A Story of People, Opportunities and Service*.
42 "Behind the Scenes."
43 Freidberg, *Fresh*; Laura Shapiro, *Something from the Oven: Reinventing Dinner in 1950s America* (New York: Penguin Books, 2004), 5–24.
44 Memo from Ken Parratt to Regional Traffic/Sales, October 17, 1950, Box 1, Folder 2 215 9: PH, TO PS, PA Records.
45 Lindsey, "Dining Aloft … Golden Gate Style."
46 "It's a Pan Am World," Pan Am Pamphlet 1952, Box 1: Printed Materials, Folder 7 of 15, PM BB, PA Records.
47 "Stewardess Training Features Preparation of Gourmet Food," PA PR, December 7, 1965, Box 2, Folder 1 392 21: Training: Stewardess College, 1965–1968 Lease 1965–1969, TO TE, PA Records.
48 Linsey, "Dining Aloft … Golden Gate Style."
49 "Behind the Scenes."
50 "Station Hi-Lite: San Francisco Frozen Food Kitchen," *Pan Am News Catering Services*, Issue 5 (ca. 1972), Box 48, Series: Printed Materials, Subseries: Periodicals, PA Records.
51 "Hot Food Served in Pan Am Clippers," PA PR, Box 1, Folder 2 399 19: Passenger Service, 1941–1944, TO PS, PA Records.
52 "Round-the-World Girl Defies All Description," PA PR, 1968.
53 Philip J. Parrott, "Airline Food Service," *The Cornell H.R.A. Quarterly* (1967): 91.
54 Memo from Ken Parratt to Regional Traffic//Sales Manager, October 17, 1950; Report of Frozen Food and Industrial Feeding Task Force, Box 24, Folder 2 362 7 Commissary Report (folder 2 of 2), LR LN, PA Records.
55 Memo from Ken Parratt to Reg. Traffic/Service Superintendents, May 11, 1951, Box 1, Folder 2 215 9: PH, TO PS, PA Records.
56 Levenstein, *Revolution at the Table*.
57 On the relationship between Pan Am and the U.S. government see Jennifer Van Vleck, *Empire of the Air: Aviation and the American Ascendancy* (Cambridge, MA: Harvard University Press, 2013); Robert van der Linden, *Airlines and Air Mail: The Post Office and the Birth of the Commercial Aviation Industry* (Lexington: University Press of Kentucky, 2002).
58 "Hot Food Served in Pan Am Clippers."
59 No title, PA PR.
60 Foss, *Food in the Air and Space*, 66, 74–6.
61 Lindsey, "Dining Aloft … Golden Gate Style."
62 No Title, Pan Am Press Release.
63 Lindsey, "Dining Aloft … Golden Gate Style."
64 Memorandum from Service Manager Ken Parratt to Reg. Traffic/Service Superintendents, May 17, 1951, Box 1, Folder 2 215 9: PH, TO PS, PA Records.

65 "Pan Am Stewardess Is by Design," Pan Am Press Release, 1966, Box 2, Folder 1 392 21 Training: Stewardess College, 1965–1968 Lease, 1965–1969, TO TE, PA Records.

66 "Behind the Scenes."

67 "Stewardess Training Features Preparation of Gourmet Food."

68 "'Write Me at Cloud Nine'." Attempts to divorce the taste of pace from earthbound housewives seems particularly odd given the way in which food companies and advertising pressured women to cook quickly and save time in the kitchen by using new industrialized foods and kitchen technologies. Shapiro, *Something from the Oven*. Furthermore, while Pan Am delegitimized female expertise in airplane cuisine, the company simultaneously reached out to female homecooks by publishing cookbooks. See Daniel Bender's chapter in this volume.

69 "International Food Fare on Jets," PA PR, 1966, Box 1, Folder 1 193 16: Food Service, 1944–1985 (1 of 2), TO PS, PA Records.

70 "International Food Fare on Jets."

71 "Pan Am International Cuisine," PA PR, 1969, Box 2, Folder 1 111 4: Boeing B-747, 1969 (1 of 2), Series 2: Aircraft, 1919–1992, Sub-Series 6: 747, 1932–1989, PA Records.

72 "Round-the-World Girl Defies All Description," PA PR, 1968, Box 2, Folder 1 392 21: Training: Stewardess College, 1965–1968 Lease, 1965–1969, TO TE, PA Records.

73 "Write Me at Cloud Nine.'"

74 Christine Yano, *Airborne Dreams: 'Nisei' Stewardesses and Pan American World Airways* (Durham, NC: Duke University Press, 2019).

75 "Round-the-World Girl Defies All Description."

76 Kathleen Barry, *Femininity in Flight: A History of Flight Attendants* (Durham, NC: Duke University Press, 2007), 1–10.

77 James Clifford, *Routes: Travel and Translation in the Late Twentieth Century* (Cambridge, MA: Harvard University Press, 1997).

78 "Specialty Holiday and Religious Meals," *Pan Am Training Manual*, n.d., 130, Box 14, Folder 127: Flight Service, Training, Series 1, World Wings International, Inc. Records, University of Miami Special Collections, Otto G. Richter Library, University of Miami, Coral Gables, FL

79 On culinary displacement and replacement within the context of world cookbooks see Daniel Bender's contribution to this volume.

80 Bill Dreslin, "Here's Some Great, and High-Flying, Eating," *The Clipper*, 8 June 1970, Box 1, Folder 1 193 16: Food Service, 1944–1985 (1 of 2), TO PS, PA Records. The emphasis is mine.

81 Trubek, *The Taste of Place*; Pilcher, *Planet Taco*; Richard Wilk, *Home Cooking in the Global Village: Caribbean Food from Buccaneers to Ecotourists* (New York: Berg, 2006).

82 "Behind the Scenes."
83 Marian Burros, "Airline Meals: Are They All the Same?," *New York Times* 12 June 1985, Box 1, Folder 1 193 16: Food Service, 1944–1985 (1 of 2), TO PS, PA Records.
84 Burros, "Airline Meals."
85 "Airline Food Bill Tops $700 Million; Carriers Served 236 Million Meals in 1970," *TWA* (August 1971) Box 1, Folder 1 193 16: Food Service, 1944–1985 (1 of 2), PS, TO PA Records.

6 From Cloth Oil to Extra Virgin: Italian Olive Oil before the Invention of the Mediterranean Diet

CARL IPSEN

The mobilities paradigm that informs this volume derives from the dramatic increase in the mobility of people and things over the past half-century or so and arose in response to a perceived sedentarism in the social sciences dealing with present-day phenomena in this age of rapid change. Arguably, history has long concentrated on mobility – of people, armies, goods, and ideas.[1] This chapter looks specifically at the transformation of a millennial product, perhaps the quintessential Mediterranean foodstuff, over the past few centuries. That transformation involved men, women, and children toiling in the southern Italian countryside and started a process that involved traders, merchants, industries, and consumers in a trade of ever-expanding global scope. It is a story moreover tied up with the history of human migration and one during which both the meaning and uses of olive oil evolved over time.

The olive tree itself is bound by place. It was first domesticated from wild oleaster in the Middle East more or less contemporaneously with the invention of agriculture and spread from there throughout the Mediterranean; but not beyond as it could thrive neither in the colder north nor the tropical south. Only in the late modern period did the olive find its way, following colonial conquest and the expansion of European populations, to the "Mediterranean" climates of Argentina, Australia, California, South Africa, and elsewhere. Despite that geographic specificity, or rather because of it, the fruit of the olive tree and, more importantly, the marvellous elixir pressed from that fruit, has long been an item of international trade. In this piece, we look first at the Kingdom of Naples, the most important global producer of oil in the eighteenth and nineteenth centuries. Oil produced in the rural hinterlands of Puglia and Calabria travelled to the bustling capital city – Naples only lost its status as the third most populous city in Europe in the early nineteenth century – but also to ports throughout the Mediterranean and beyond: to Britain and the North and Baltic Seas.[2] Accompanying that trade were of course a host of international sailors, merchants, and modes of transport. Nor did oil serve a single and unchanging purpose. It was the staple fat of the southern Italian diet, but the international trade explored here responded initially and primarily to oil's industrial applications, as a lubricant, as fuel for lamps, and for the production of soap. So, oil moved not only in place and time but also in function.

Italian olive cultivation and oil production expanded throughout the eighteenth and nineteenth centuries, even as other centres of production, most significantly Spain, grew in importance; meanwhile the demand for industrial oil declined as cheaper seed oil substitutes became available. As a food, olive oil from the south and centre of Italy followed the foodways of the late nineteenth- and early twentieth-century Italian diaspora as masses of Italians migrated to other parts of Europe and to North and South America. Yet for all that movement and the global expansion of an olive oil network, still in the 1950s the consumption of comestible oil was largely restricted to its Mediterranean home and to those diasporic communities. As we shall see, while the British may have experimented with olive oil as food as early as the eighteenth century, a culinary pioneer like Elizabeth David – her *Italian Food* came out in 1954 – still had difficulty finding oil in her native Britain at that later date. Only in the late twentieth century did this once humble product – compare it with other dietary staples of the European popular classes like rye flour or dried fish – develop into the most celebrated of fats. Today, of course, extra virgin olive oil is universally acclaimed. So, while seed oils fill the deep fryers of fast-food restaurants the world over and contribute to our global health crisis, and animal fats – many fear – clog arteries and are shunned by vegetarians, only olive oil is everywhere praised for its salutary qualities. There is hardly a television chef who doesn't pour generous quantities of the elixir in the preparation of this dish or that. Extra virgin olive oil has even earned the immediately recognizable (and even pronounceable) acronym of EVOO. Just as pressed oil floats to the top of the separation tanks, so this staple of peasants over time has flowed upward through the social hierarchy.

This chapter traces the history of olive oil, primarily in Italy, as it moved in time, space, and function from the eighteenth century to 1960, when an Italian law introduced the appellation *extra virgin* to the culinary lexicon. Olive trees have shaped and defined the countryside of southern Italy for centuries, indeed millennia. In our period, they generated a mobility that started with rural wage labourers, often women, gathering olives from fall to spring. Over a shoulder or on the back of a mule, sacks of the collected fruit were transported to the thousands of olive mills scattered throughout the kingdom where men and beasts sweated over crushers and presses that extracted the oil. Much oil was consumed locally, among that same labouring class, but some travelled by way of an ever more cosmopolitan network that engaged multinational traders in ports like Gallipoli and Naples, feeding and lighting the capital city but also supplying French, British, Russian, and other manufacturers of wool and other products. Over time, that international network evolved, expanding across oceans and shifting from serving mostly industrial purposes to transporting mostly comestible oils. The story told here ends, not so long ago, when olive oil was still principally a food of the poor and of migrants but was poised, rebaptized as extra virgin, to conquer palates and chefs around the world as the centrepiece of what came to be called the "Mediterranean Diet."

Gallipoli Oil

The eighteenth century marks a crucial turning point in the millennial history of olive oil. Demand and production had increased steadily from the late Middle Ages, but our period saw dramatic increases as a vigorous mobile trade came literally to lubricate the wheels of European commerce. At that time, the leading producer of olive oil in the world was southern Italy, in parts of which extensive monocultures had been cultivated since at least the sixteenth century.[3] Southern Italy at that time meant the Kingdom of Naples, a territory that occupied the Italian peninsula south and east of Rome plus Sicily (see figure 6.1). And that kingdom's most important export was olive oil: large quantities left the ports of Puglia and to a lesser extent Calabria for Naples and destinations throughout the Mediterranean and northern Europe.

According to Vincenzo Ricchioni, fascist-era agronomist, politician, and sometime historian, in the eighteenth century the Kingdom of Naples satisfied the *entirety* of the world market for oil.[4] Nor is the eighteenth century an arbitrary starting point. To begin with, that century saw significant expansion of olive groves in the kingdom. The monarch (Charles, 1734–59, subsequently Charles III of Spain) sought to expand Neapolitan agriculture by exempting the farming of previously uncultivated terrain from taxation for twenty years, and he offered a special forty-year exemption for new olive groves.[5] Meanwhile, demand for oil generated a trade between the kingdom and other European states, from Austria to France to Great Britain to Scandinavia and Russia, that grew over the course of the century. Policy and economic opportunity conspired to effect what Piero Bevilacqua has described as an

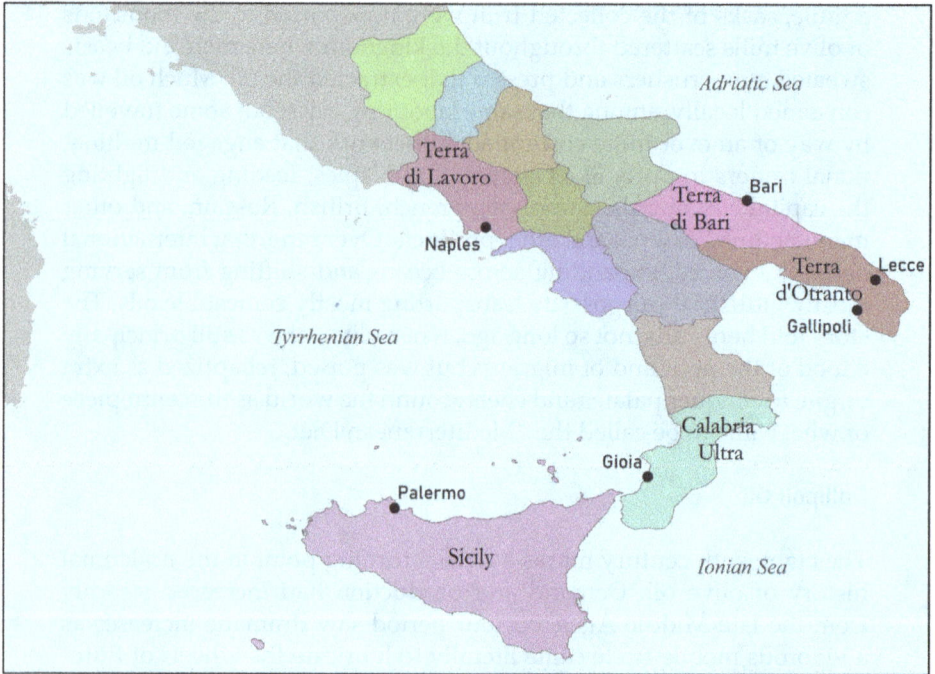

Kingdom of Naples

Figure 6.1 The Kingdom of Naples in the eighteenth century. Jordan Blekking, cartographer.

eighteenth-century "intense and grandiose transformation of the southern agricultural landscape," an expansion that with a notable pause centred on the Napoleonic Wars would continue into the middle of the nineteenth century.[6]

What then was the motor that provoked the movement of thousands of kilograms of Neapolitan oil? The "Cloth" entry from the second edition of the *Encyclopaedia Britannica* (1778–83) provides a clue: "[The wool] is now in a proper condition to be oiled, and carded on large iron cards placed slopewise. *Olive oil* [my emphasis] is esteemed the best for this purpose: one fifth of which would be used for the wool intended for the woof, and a ninth for the warp. After the wool has been well oiled it is given to the spinners who first card it on the knee with small fine cards, and then spin it on the wheel, observing to make the thread of the warp smaller by one third than that of the woof, and much compacter twisted [*sic*]."[7]

And while sheep, of course, thrived in the British countryside, olive oil was necessarily imported and again mostly from Italy. Indeed, a later edition of the *Encyclopaedia* (1910), and other sources as well, specifically identifies "Gallipoli oil" (so from Puglia) as the finest for this purpose.[8]

Meanwhile, the Calabrian-Genoese aristocrat and landowner Domenico Grimaldi (1734–1805) included the following in his 1773 *Instructions on the New Manufacture of Olive Oil Introduced in Calabria*: "Oil is the most precious product of the Kingdom of Naples. The huge consumption of oil in the capital city and in all the Kingdom's provinces for the daily preparation of foods, for lighting, for textile and soap production, and for other uses make this noble extract deserving of governmental protection. [...] The northern nations, that have long needed our oil for the manufacture of wool and of soap, have recently begun to use it for other purposes and as a welcome condiment for various foods."[9] Oil was again a staple of the southern Italian diet and fuelled lamps throughout the kingdom; quantitatively we may never know which was more important. Meanwhile, already in the late eighteenth century, olive oil had begun tentatively to penetrate northern European foodways, a process that would take two more centuries to complete. More significant in the "northern nations" at the time was the use of oil for soap manufacture, to lubricate machinery, and, as described above, for processing wool. It was in eighteenth-century Britain that technological advances and expanding wool production provided the spark for the Industrial Revolution, a process in which the humble Puglian peasant also played a role as the oil he hauled from the Salentine groves to the port of Gallipoli literally greased the wheels of European commerce.[10] Oil then moved not only in space and time but also in purpose.

Oil production can vary dramatically from year to year, and production statistics from the eighteenth century are in any case of questionable reliability. That said, Grimaldi and other sources[11] suggest that oil production from the eighteenth-century Kingdom of Naples amounted to about 100 million kilograms per year. Today, Italy might produce four times that, most coming from the regions that made up the former kingdom, so our historic estimate seems reasonable. Oil was, in fact, the kingdom's most important item of foreign trade, and legal exports, according to those same sources, ranged between 2 and 16 million kilograms per year (with perhaps another 30 per cent in contraband). Two-thirds of those exports came from Puglia and the rest from Calabria (while Sicily, important in the twentieth century, does not really figure in eighteenth-century discussions of olive oil).[12]

The leading oil provinces in the kingdom were the Terra d'Otranto – often referred to as the Salento or the Salentine peninsula – and the Terra di Bari, which together made up two-thirds of what is the present-day region of Puglia, Italy's heel, followed not too far behind by Calabria Ultra, the toe (see figure 6.1). Each of the oil-producing provinces in Puglia occupied 5,000–6,000 square kilometres and, already in early modern times, olives constituted a true monoculture there. According to one eighteenth-century estimate, three-fifths of the arable land on the Salentine peninsula was planted with olives, while another describes two-thirds of the Terra d'Otranto and the Terra di Bari as covered with groves.[13] A nineteenth-century British source further discussed below observes: "All that part of Italy which is known as the heel of the boot is little else than one continuous olive grove. […] Starting from Gallipoli, as I have often done, and travelling to the Cape Santa Maria di Leuca, or to Taranto, or to Lecce […] you literally are scarcely ever ten minutes out of the shade of olive-trees."[14] It is worth recalling that this author was travelling on horseback, so in those ten minutes might have travelled as little as one kilometre. In response to a network of demand that stretched to points scattered across Italy and Europe, olive groves dominated the Puglian landscape as far as the eye could see.[15]

In the pre-Napoleonic decades, the best cloth oil came from the Terra d'Otranto. Indeed 50–70 per cent of the kingdom's oil exports left from the modest Ionian port of Gallipoli, and more than half of those exports went to England. According to a later source, as many as seventy ships at a time might anchor in the bay north of the island city (see figure 6.2). Gallipoli oil was prized as fatter and more expansive than other oils so that a similar quantity could lubricate more wool than that from other locales; it was also clearer and could reportedly resist rancidity – the normal and inevitable deterioration of oil over time – for several years. In a typical year in the eighteenth century, Gallipoli might ship 5 million kilograms of oil abroad (Britain, Holland, northern Germany, Scandinavia, Russia) and a like amount to the city of Naples. So important was this fundamental foodstuff and fuel to the Parthenopean capital that maintenance of social order required a steady supply of inexpensive oil lest the urban masses revolt in protest. Meanwhile, oil from Terra di Bari went mostly northward to Ferrara in the Papal States, Venice, and the Austrian port of Trieste, while oil from Calabria, more turbid and generally considered inferior to Puglian oil, shipped mostly out of the Tyrrhenian port of Gioia (or simply from the beaches) and found buyers in Genoa and Marseille (mostly for soap). These latter two locales were well known for producing some of the best food oil in the world, but the quantities produced were always small compared with Puglia. Just

Figure 6.2 Jakob Phillip Hackert, *Gallipoli* (1790). The painting is part of the collection of the Reggia di Caserta (Royal Palace of Caserta).

as British wool manufacture relied on imported oil, so French *savon de Marseille* would likely not have gained its international reputation had it not been for oil supplied from Italy. The eighteenth-century oil network was vast, and Gallipoli oil travelled well-established Mediterranean and Atlantic trade routes on sea voyages that might exceed 4,000 nautical miles.[16]

Domenico Grimaldi and Giovanni Presta

In terms of domestic consumption, oil was a staple and a necessity: olive oil circulated through the Neapolitan body politic as a sort of life blood, carrying both nutrition and, literally, enlightenment throughout the kingdom. According to the imperfect statistics that we have, domestic oil consumption may have been as high as 10 litres per person per year and perhaps 14 in the city of Naples itself, not too far below where it is today, though the historic figure represents both food and fuel.[17] According to one nineteenth-century source, the *oliondolo* or oil vendor wandered the streets of Naples carrying an oil-filled *otre* or goat-skin bag calling out *"uoglie"* to announce his arrival. With a set of measuring cups and a funnel he distributed oil door to door to the city's inhabitants in small quantities. That source *only* refers to the use of oil for lamps though surely the *oliondolo* was selling food oil as well and most consumers at the time used the same oil interchangeably.[18]

Our best sources for eighteenth-century Neapolitan production, first step in olive oil's complex itinerary, are the already-cited Domenico Grimaldi and Giovanni Presta; Presta was a producer from Gallipoli in the Terra d'Otranto, who published his famous *On Olive Trees, Olives and the Method for Extracting Oil* in 1794.[19] Both men call for improved methods and describe how to make better oils, and both give us a glimpse into what were at the time standard practices that would make the present-day producer shudder and wonder at the reputation of Gallipoli oil. In both regions, rather than harvesting olives at ideal maturity, usually in October or November, Calabrian and Puglian growers waited for the olives to fall naturally from the trees and gathered them off the ground, a process that stretched out to April or May. Gathered olives were then stored in vats (in Terra d'Otranto cut into the earth) where they heated up and naturally fermented for days, weeks, or even months as they awaited processing. They were then crushed on the familiar rotating stone crusher and subjected to multiple pressings; the later pressings employed hot water to extract additional oil (see figure 6.3). Both Grimaldi and Presta called for early harvesting, avoiding fermentation by getting the olives quickly to the press, and the segregation of a first pressing, performed without any hot water, from subsequent ones. That first cold pressing would produce *olio fino*, the best-quality comestible oil consumed by the better classes. Both men claimed to make oils that could compete with the fine oils made in Provence (Aix), Tuscany (especially Lucca), and Genoa, considered the best food oils of the day.[20]

Presta's work also gives us an insight into a term little used at the time but crucial to our story. He describes obtaining a "virgin" oil by taking a wicker basket and pressing it into a bucket of crushed (but not pressed) olives. The basket then functions as a sieve, allowing high quality oil to seep into it: virgin in that it has never been subjected to the olive press. Presta uses the term *olio vergine* on just three different occasions, while Grimaldi never uses the term.[21] *Olio fino* was the appellation generally used for good-quality food oil at the time, though even *olio fino* was a rare commodity. According to Presta, a remarkable four-fifths of oil production at the time was used by the wool and soap industries. The remaining 20 per cent, presumably of marginally better

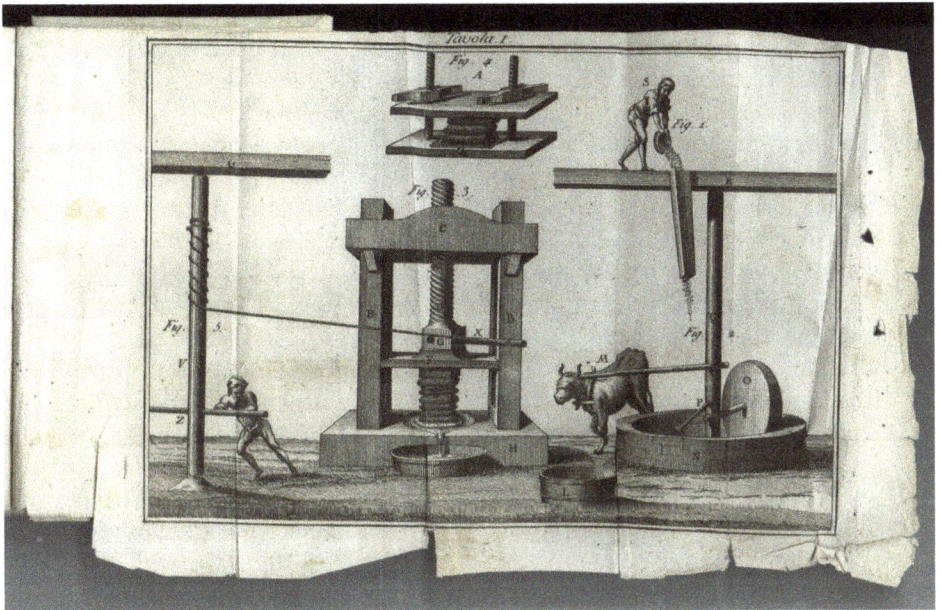

Figure 6.3 Domenico Grimaldi, *Olive Mill* (1773). The illustration comes from a copy of Domenic Grimaldi, *Uliveti, olio ed economia neela storia della Calabria*, 1773 held at the Kenneth Spencer Research Library, University of Kansas.

quality, served as food and as lamp oil. Lamp oil, moreover, was of better quality than soap oil, and *chiaro, giallo, e lampante* was a positive descriptor for oil: clear and yellow but also *lampante*, which might refer to the oil's brilliant quality; today *lampante* is the term used for the lowest-quality oils. Presta adds that perhaps only 1 per cent of production at the time (the late eighteenth century) was devoted to *olio fino*, a more expensive product that graced the tables of the rich.[22] Nor did domestic oil figure as an especially prized fat in the pantry (dare I say larder) of the Neapolitan aristocracy and bourgeoisie. On the king's table, one apparently found oil from Provence or Lucca rather than the homegrown product.[23] And again there is reason to believe that much cooking for the better off at the time was done with animal fats.

The relative scarcity of good quality food oil also owed much to the technological limitations of the day. Based on an as yet unpublished calculation, I estimate that eight men working a standard milling operation (one crusher and two presses, though many were larger) could process three batches of olives (*macinate*) per shift (two groups of four men working twelve hours each). To produce the estimated 100 or so million litres of oil then would require about 700,000 round-the-clock person-days of crushing that to be accomplished in six months would need over 4,000 mills with a workforce of about 32,000, mostly in Puglia and Calabria. That calculation assumes a high level of efficiency, so the numbers are likely higher still. To the men working the mills need also to be added animals, mostly oxen, turning the crushers, and the thousands of women, children, and men who gathered and cleaned the olives and transported them to the presses. A massive undertaking. This calculation is based on a series of informed if shaky assumptions. Still, it may give us some sense of the scale of the operation. The industrial transformation of the olive entailed a significant mobilization of labour. Given that it took many months to crush all the olives grown and harvested, it was moreover impossible at the time to produce significant quantities of *olio fino*; nor is it clear that there was demand for it.

The Salento boasted another feature that distinguished it from other oil-producing regions: many of the presses there were built underground (*frantoi ipogei*), carved out of the soft local stone (*pietra leccese*). This practice offered several advantages. Much oil is produced in the colder months while oil yields increase at higher temperatures, and so the underground presses took advantage of geothermal heating. In addition, carts of olives could simply be dumped into ground-level pits that opened below to the crushers, facilitating the transport from tree to press. At the same time, these underground presses must have constituted an infernal environment. In caverns with little air circulation, perhaps half a dozen men worked around the clock. The olfactory experience must have been intense: human sweat, excrement, and exhalations from oxen used to turn the crusher, oil lamps and fires used to heat water, and fermenting olives all combined to create a heady atmosphere and not one (as Presta notes) ideal for producing *olio fino*.[24]

From these humble, indeed disgusting, origins emerged the golden liquid that lubricated European industry and would eventually conquer palates the world over. Most eighteenth-century oil, whether comestible or industrial, was produced in lurid conditions like those described above and was generously described as "strong" oil. Only a tiny minority of consumers at the time demanded, enjoyed, and appreciated *olio fino*. That minority would grow over the following centuries with the expanding global network of the olive oil trade and olive cultivation. That earlier tension, however, between the *olio forte* of the peasants and the *olio fino* of the wealthy remains in some sense unresolved. Today almost all oil is "extra virgin," but an often-unappreciated chasm exists between the inexpensive oils sold in supermarkets, some fraudulent or blended, and the high-quality oils made by the best producers. As we continue to explore below, throughout this history, oil moved in a complicated space where levels and perceptions of quality were anything but straightforward.

The *Statistica Murattiana*

It was, again, initially industrial demand that linked the toiling peasantry of the kingdom to other parts of the Mediterranean and to northern Europe. So while Sicilian or Balkan wheat might fill Spanish and Dutch bellies, most food oil was still consumed not far from where the trees grew. Oil production and exports nonetheless increased steadily throughout the eighteenth century and enjoyed something of a golden age in the years leading up to 1790–91. After that, multiple forces conspired to buffet the trade. Revolution and war disrupted the usual export channels and poor harvests raised fears among the Neapolitan rulers that Naples itself might run low on oil. Shortages of oil, as much a necessity as bread, raised the spectre of urban uprisings by the poor, and this just a couple of years after the outbreak of the French Revolution. There followed export bans in 1793, 1795, and 1797, and while calm was maintained in the capital, the rural populations in Puglia and Calabria suffered miserably.[25] We might even imagine a period of relative oil immobility imposed by political crises, doubtless creating an incentive in Britain and elsewhere to develop alternative fats, in particular seed oils, that might again serve both industrial and culinary needs.

Naples had its own brief and bloody revolutionary moment in 1799, followed by Napoleonic conquest in 1806. The subsequent French occupation lasted until 1815 and was dominated by Napoleon's brother-in-law, Joachim Murat, crowned King of Naples (meanwhile the Bourbon King Ferdinand retreated to Sicily where he enjoyed British protection). Exports to England were blocked throughout this period, and so Gallipoli lost one of its primary clients. Meanwhile, with the rationalist zeal that characterized Napoleonic rule, Murat's administration sought to better know its territory by the collection of "statistics" and sent out a questionnaire in 1811 to all of the provincial *intendenti* (prefects) that included queries regarding territory, climate, population, foodstuffs, agriculture, hunting and fishing, manufacture, customs, and more. The responses were compiled in the justly famous *Statistica murattiana* (after Murat). Included were questions on oil cultivation and manufacture and about the use of oil as a food, though curiously not about its other applications (wool, soap, lighting).[26]

The first thing that strikes one in the report is that while oil was an essential food for the poor, it was less so for the rich. Predictably, the poor consumed an inferior quality and so less expensive oil. The *redattore* from Abruzzo Citra – *redattori* were the provincial census takers who responded to the survey – reports: "Delicate oil [*olio dolce*], made from selected, freshly harvested olives, is consumed by the well-off populations in the major population centres. Strong oil [*forte* or *piccante*], made from olives that have sat long fermenting in vats, is used by the peasants, artisans, and all those living in small towns. Strong oil has a spicy, disgusting flavour that attacks the throat, but the common people prefer it, either because they are used to it or because with a small amount of oil one can flavour a large amount of food." [I: 229, 264] In Calabria Citra: "The rich use [oil] very little to flavour their foods, while the poor do instead use it." [II: 334] And in Calabria Ultra: "The common people [*popolazzo*] use oil every day to flavour their foods and it is rare that they substitute instead pork fat." [II: 540] In Abruzzo Ultra: "The poor use oil to excess" [I: 67].

Oil consumption was predictably widespread in the major oil-producing provinces, such as Calabria Ultra (cited above) and Terra di Bari: "All classes flavour their foods with oil; the common people (*basso popolo*) and the peasants use it the most, dressing greens and legumes"; wealthy *baresi* predictably paid more to get delicate *olio dolce*. [II: 44] While in Terra d'Otranto: "The peasants know no other condiment." [II: 178] Finally, in Terra di Lavoro (which included the capital city of Naples), "all the classes use [oil] generally, but the poorer classes more than the wealthy. The latter use it on a small number of foods (for frying fish, for dressing cooked or raw greens [insalate], on legumes); the poor on the other hand use it on greens [erbe] polenta and the occasional legume that make up their usual diet." [II, 233] Indeed the popular classes in this period ate meat rarely – perhaps two to three times per year[27] – and so oil served as an essential fat for their vegetarian fare. One reads of oil being used in a wide array of foods: greens, salads, legume soups, green and white soups, boiled or soaked bread, panzanella, polenta, hard lasagna, frascarelli or millefanti (a simple pasta of water and flour finely broken up or sgranellata), pancotto, maccherini. A couple of *redattori* also mention fish. Food oil consumption, both in terms of quantity and quality, would remain a marker of class for decades to come. Oil was the staple fat of those involved in its production: from those production centres oil travelled as food and fuel throughout the kingdom and as fuel and lubricant throughout Europe and then beyond. Only in a later century would it start to conquer foreign palates.

Vegetable Substances

Overlooked in the *Statistica murattiana*, perhaps intentionally, is the long crisis that characterized the oil trade from the 1890s and throughout the French occupation. We get some insight into that period from a remarkable and anonymous British source. In 1833, The Library of Entertaining Knowledge published a volume with this catchy title: *Vegetable Substances: Materials of Manufactures*. It includes a short section on olive oil obviously penned by an Englishman who had spent an extended period in Gallipoli, probably a trader.[28] Regarding the Napoleonic period he remarks:

> The hilarity of the Gallipolitans when I first became acquainted with them might have been heightened by an agreeable contrast, for it was shortly after the fall of Bonaparte, whose system, whatever good parts of it may have done in the rest of Italy, was certainly most ruinous to the provinces of Lecce and Bari. Unable to export or to find other markets for their produce, the proprietors in many parts of those provinces let the olives lie and rot upon the ground. For some years the price of oil hardly paid the price of preparation [...] I have been in no part of Europe where the benefits resulting from the peace were so broad and tangible as here.[29]

Our British observer goes on to offer a vivid portrait of the renewed post-Napoleonic mobility of Puglian oil, from the groves and mills of the countryside to the tiny – less than a square kilometre! – city of Gallipoli, frequented by ships and traders of many nationalities: "The oil is carried to Trani, Barletta, Bari, Mola di Bari, Molfetta, Giovinazzo, Brindisi, Otranto, Taranto, and some other sea-ports, but its great *depôt* for some ages has been the town of Gallipoli, which gives its name to the oil imported in such great quantities by the English, French, Americans."[30] He then describes the oil warehouses that occupy the ground floors of many of the town's residences and include multiple cisterns, each for a different quality of oil, cut into the soft stone that constitutes the island. Even the most turbid *olio mosto*, "dark and black as pitch," would quickly become bright and yellow (*chiaro, giallo e lampante*) in these "excellent cisterns." He also refers to American ships at Gallipoli, a reference not found in earlier sources cited above. That presence corresponds well with the establishment and growth of wool manufacturing in the United States, manufacturing that also required oil.[31] Nor was oil alone among the Italian agricultural products crossing the Atlantic: Sicilian citrus also notably found markets in both northern Europe and the US at about this time. Still predominantly agricultural, nineteenth-century Italy predictably engaged with the global economy and foodways by offering its bountiful produce (and eventually also its labour).

Our trader goes on to describe the intense traffic of the long oil season. Peasants come to Gallipoli from throughout the Terra d'Otranto and even from Terra di Bari, leading mules laden with oil-filled goatskin bags – the roads were generally too poor for wheeled transport – that are emptied into the underground cisterns. On a single afternoon he has counted as many as a hundred mules trekking back homeward from the port. Once clarified and ready for shipping, the oil is again transferred into goatskin bags and porters carry it on their shoulders down to the water's edge where it is poured into wooden barrels that are then sealed up by coopers. The barrels are lashed together with rope and floated out by sailors to the waiting anchored ships. In 1816, our source reports having seen at one time "nine English, two American, two French, and six Genoese vessels (not to mention some small craft from the Adriatic)" waiting to be loaded up with oil.[32] This would have been just the first or second post-Napoleonic harvest: suppressed during the previous years of conflict, the global oil network quickly revived with the return of peace. Thousands of peasants, day labourers, mill operators, porters, oil merchants, tradesmen, and sailors once again followed the oil from the fruit's maturation in the Puglian groves to places as far-flung as Russia and America.

The Nineteenth Century: Fine Oil and Refined Oil

Just as cloth oil continued to circulate globally, so did demand for good-quality food oil grow throughout the nineteenth century, both at home and abroad. Scottish economist John Ramsey Culloch, for example, describes so-called Florence oil being used in Britain for culinary purposes circa 1850.[33] But Florentine production was necessarily limited, and in response to the demand for food oil important strides were made in Terra di Bari (whose industrial oil had always been inferior to Gallipoli oil). Pietro (or Pierre) Ravanas, a trader from Aix-en-Provence, came to Bari in 1826 to purchase oil and remained to try his luck as a producer. Ravanas introduced improved crushers and hydraulic iron presses and insisted on harvesting olives directly from the trees. So, while Terra d'Otranto continued to make the "disgusting" *olio forte* described in the *Statistica murattiana*, Ravanas within a few years was producing an *olio fino* that fetched double the price of the usual oil from Bari (or Gallipoli). Despite local opposition from jealous growers, he expanded his operation with a large (above-ground) olive mill and exported oil to his brother in France where it competed with oils from Genoa, Lucca and even Aix itself. And compared with these other regions, Puglia always enjoyed the advantage of a much greater volume of production (and no danger of destructive winter freezes). Ravanas' business sense eventually failed him and he went bankrupt in 1840, but not before his innovations caught on and other producers in Bari also began to produce fine oils. Within a few decades it was being celebrated as the finest oil in Italy. And there was a lot of it: according to one estimate, by mid-century Bari was producing half the kingdom's oil.[34]

The Kingdom of the Two Sicilies, as the southern kingdom was known after the Bourbon restoration in 1815, did not survive the forces of Italian nationalism that led to its incorporation into a new Kingdom of Italy in 1860–61. In a spirit much like that of the *Statistica murattiana*, the new regime undertook an important agricultural study directed by Stefano Jacini, a Lombard economist and political figure. On the subject of Puglian oil, the *Inchiesta Jacini* (1877–86) relates: "The provinces of Bari and Lecce [which coincided approximately with the Neapolitan provinces of Terra di Bari and Terra d'Otranto] surpass all others for oil production. [...] In the *Barese* alone there are more than 30 steampowered mills; and the superfine oils (*olii sopraffini*) made there rival the best in Italy, including those of Lucca."[35] Another contemporary observer, the Florentine Alessandro Bizzarri, noted in 1879 that "the province of Bari has made great strides in oil production. Its comestible oils now travel around the world, and it can be described as a model southern province. [...] Today the two best oils in Italy are the oil of Lucca and the oil of Bari,"[36] high praise from a Tuscan!

Oil mobility underwent other important changes in the "long" nineteenth century. Previously, Naples and Italy had produced oils of varying qualities for domestic consumption and for export that arrived to consumers more or less in the same state as they left the mills and cisterns. Between 1850 and World War I, technological developments allowed for the processing or refining of oil, while the production of cheaper seed oils encouraged the blending of those with olive oil to increase profit margins. Neither of these developments on the face of it presented particular problems, though as we shall see both processed and blended oil would be advertised as pure or fine (eventually virgin) olive oil and so create the complicated and occasionally duplicitous situation that characterizes the olive oil market up to the present day. Moreover, the successful marketing of processed and blended oils exceeded Italian production capacity so that low-quality olive oil and seed oils in ever greater quantities were *imported* into Italy. Much of that oil was refined and/or blended only to be then re-exported (as comestible Italian oil). Adding new vectors to the mobility map outlined above, Italy as a result became both the world's leading importer and exporter of oil. The former title it retains to this day.

Bizzarri devotes a portion of his 1879 text to chemical methods used to refine olive oil (his term is *depurazione*). These methods led to the establishment of oil refineries, especially in southern France and Liguria (and later in Puglia), that became of major importance in the twentieth century. Refining methods generally lowered acidity and rendered oils that burned cleaner and made better soaps; those oils, however, also achieved increasing importance as food oils. Bizzarri's work also betrays a changing meaning for *olio vergine*, namely oil derived from the first cold pressing of olives and not subjected to chemical treatment, i.e., not refined.[37] The already-cited *Inchiesta Jacini* from this same period also describes the frequent blending of olive oil with cotton seed oil (e.g., in Rome). The Italian government had by then imposed an import tax on seed oils to discourage this practice, but apparently to little avail. The problem was so widespread that a Milanese journalist commented in 1881: "Nowadays it is more difficult to find pure olive oil than to find an honest man." And according to the Sicilian Antonio Aloi in the 1890s, "Today it is a rare bit of luck to find pure olive oil for sale."[38]

Laws and Migration

The late nineteenth century witnessed both the first legislative attempts to guarantee the quality of food oil and a global expansion of the market for that same oil. It was concern about blending and fraud that led to Italy's first olive oil legislation. A law in 1890, reinforced in 1908, decreed that whoever blended olive oil with other oils was obliged to label their blends as such. One ruse had been to simply label the cheaper blends as *olio* or more cleverly something like *olio di Lucca*. A still more extensive law was passed in 1925: it stipulated that only pure olive oil could be labelled as either *olio di oliva* or even simply *olio*. Blended oils were permitted and had to be labelled as such (*miscela*) providing they contained at least 50 per cent olive oil. If the percentage were lower, they had instead to be labelled as seed oil. That law also forbade the sale of *olio di sansa* (oil derived by chemical extraction from the marc left over after pressing) as food oil, but that provision was reversed the following year.[39] As the relative proportion of food oil to industrial oil increased, chemical treatments that seemed reasonable for the production of industrial oil raised public health concerns when that same oil was marketed as comestible.

Following unification, the new Italian state began collecting statistics on agriculture (and much else). Oil production figures generally ranged between 200 and 300 million kilograms per year for the century or so after unification (1860–1960). Exports for the decade and a half before

1914 meanwhile averaged 32 million kg, and while exports to Europe were declining in those years, those to Argentina and the US each accounted for about 20 per cent of the total and were increasing. These were, of course, exactly the years of massive Italian migration to those two destinations, migration that created a market for olive oil and other Italian foodstuffs.[40] It is really only with the Italian diaspora in these very decades that olive oil as food broke out of its Mediterranean homeland, planting the seed for its eventual conquest of foodways in Europe, the Americas, and beyond. As a harbinger of things to come, Italian oil exports encountered growing competition in the early twentieth century from, especially, Spain. The global mobility of oil became more complex with the development of new nodes of consumption and production.

Oil mobility altered within Italy as well. A work from 1940 by the geographer Luchino Franciosa provides a concise snapshot of interwar oil production. Regionally, Puglia accounted for about 25 per cent of Italian oil, and Sicily and Calabria another 13–14 per cent each. The most significant central region was Tuscany at 10 per cent. Meanwhile, Italy imported a large quantity of oil, principally from Spain, which by then had already surpassed Italy as the world's largest producer. Imports served to make up Italian shortfalls in bad years, but as Franciosa observes, 80 per cent of the imported oil, generally of poor quality, was "rectified," i.e., treated chemically to mask defects, in refineries located mostly in Liguria and Puglia, and then re-exported to foreign markets that wanted "Italian" oil. Between 1928 and 1938, annual imports ranged between 10 and 80 million kilograms. Some of that refined oil also went to northern Italy, where consumers preferred an oil lighter in both colour and body (or indeed seed oils).

So, while olive oil by this time had followed southern Italians migrating throughout the world, it had yet to make much progress across the Apennines. Franciosa in fact cites provincial consumption levels that ranged from 3 litres per adult per year in rural Milan to over 25 for peasants in Lecce.[41] Meanwhile, a journalist for the Milanese *Corriere della Sera* paints a telling picture of the oil market in his city in 1929. According to his informants, you can count on one hand the shops in Milan that sell pure oil. That is not too surprising for, as he describes it, olive oil is "a condiment not much cared for in Milanese cuisine which prefers butter or even margarine. One need only mention spaghetti dressed in oil to certain Ambrogian traditionalists [a reference to Milan's patron saint] to see them turn up their noses; at best oil might dress a salad or at the absolute limit be used to fry fish on days of abstinence."[42] The Milanese at the time made little distinction between olive oil and peanut or linseed oils.

Meanwhile, Italian olive oil legislation continued to grapple with the issue of fraudulent and poor-quality oils. A 1926 law imposed an upper limit on acidity (4 per cent) for all comestible oils, meanwhile bowing to industry pressure and allowing for the sale, correctly labelled, of both refined oil and *olio di sansa* as food oils.[43] Laws seeking to protect and promote quality oil came in 1929 and 1936. The first outlawed blending with seed oils altogether, stipulating that seed oils simply be labelled as such,[44] while the second introduced the first legal classification of olive oils. In 1935, Mussolini, who sought to organize the Italian economy along corporatist lines, created an Oil Corporation that proposed a five-part oil classification according to which the best-quality oil was *Olio sopraffino vergine di oliva* (an earlier draft included *extravergine* but that odd term was discarded).[45] Virgin olive oil would be produced only by mechanical means (so not refined) and have a maximum acidity of 1.2 per cent. Similarly, *olio fino di oliva* (maximum acidity 2.5 per cent) and *olio di oliva* (4 per cent) were comestible oils and ostensibly made exclusively by mechanical means (though a loophole allowed some blending of refined olive oil in the lesser grades).[46]

A quintessentially Italian product, olive oil consumption in Italy would seem to fit well with the fascist emphasis on autarchy or self-sufficiency. This alimentary policy was in some sense one of food *immobility* insofar as it encouraged the consumption of homegrown foodstuffs over imports. Yet while wheat, the primary focus of that policy, was a prestige product that the Italian masses had only come to enjoy broadly in the decades leading up to the Great War – wheat bread and pasta instead of preparations made from maize (polenta), chestnuts, potatoes, rye, or lentils – olive oil remained a product often associated with poor southerners. Mussolini himself came from a part of the country (Romagna) that preferred animal fats to olive oil, so it is perhaps little surprise that oil was not yet celebrated in the interwar period as an essential ingredient of the Italian diet in the way that it would be in the late twentieth century.[47]

The 1936 law remained in place for a quarter-century. During that time, unblended first-press *olio sopraffino vergine* and *olio fino* accounted for 20–30 per cent of production, while the rest consisted of blended and refined oils. The oil most in demand as food oil was reportedly a blend of 20 per cent virgin and 80 per cent refined. Although a minority objected to treating refined oil as comestible (especially *olio di sansa*), clearly the quantity of virgin oil produced fell short of satisfying Italian demand (not to mention demand abroad), and oil refineries were at the time an accepted and dominant component of Italian oil production.[48] The weight of public and political opinion awoke to continued reports of oil fraud: in addition to the century-old practice of cutting olive oil with seed oils (and selling it as pure olive oil), a newer process used to neutralize *olio di sansa*, "esterification," could also be used to extract oil from animal parts and from soap; and the resultant products were being marketed by disreputable sorts as comestible olive oil. News reports of those practices, and of massive quantities of imported raw soap that seemed to vanish into thin air,[49] mobilized trade groups and Italian lawmakers, leading to a new olive oil law in 1960 and the creation of the *extra* virgin category.

The Triumph of Extra Virgin Oil

That law marked the beginning of what we might call the modern history of olive oil. By 1960 the transition away from cloth oil was nearly complete: most olive oil was food oil and had come to represent Italy's most important comestible fat.[50] Still, only about 20 per cent of Italian oil at that time was reportedly *vergine*; the rest was refined.[51] According to the landmark 1960 legislation, the best-quality oil – acidity less than 1 per cent and made exclusively by mechanical means – would henceforth be labelled *olio extra vergine di oliva*. The law also specified other less virgin categories.[52] Over the next half-century extra virgin oil found its way to the heights of culinary excellence, yet another phase of oil mobility. However, at the time, olive oil was still hard to find outside the Mediterranean, save among diasporic communities who consumed imported olive oil, much of it Italian (or at least labelled Italian). Whether in Italy or abroad, extra virgin olive oil was a rare product.

The introduction in 1960 of this new category, extra virgin, came at a propitious moment for several reasons. Technological innovations introduced in the early 1960s revolutionized oil production, replacing traditional crushers and presses with a mechanized continuous-cycle process that increased productivity by a factor of 10 or 20, reduced oxidation, and made it possible to increase the overall proportion of virgin and extra virgin oils. This accelerated production process along with increased global wealth and more rapid transportation all combined to create the phenomenon that is present-day EVOO.

Olive oil also achieved extra virginity just as American physiologist Ancel Keys was carrying out his Seven Countries study (1958–1964). That study laid the basis for the so-called Mediterranean Diet, and while Keys' research was flawed in various ways, the Mediterranean Diet – difficult as it has been to define – was a triumph, and all agree that olive oil is an essential ingredient, perhaps the most essential of all. Enthusiasm for an olive oil–based cuisine has been such that UNESCO, while declining to identify any of the specific foods it might include, added the Mediterranean Diet to its *Representative List of the Intangible Cultural Heritage of Humanity* in 2013.[53]

Conclusion

Over two centuries earlier, in the 1790s, Giovanni Presta estimated that 80 per cent of olive oil in the Kingdom of Naples served industrial purposes, and while the remaining 20 per cent was for domestic consumption, only 1 per cent was best-quality *olio fino*. In 1960 a similar proportion of Italian oil, 20 per cent, met the new virgin standards. At that later date, olive oil was still hard to find in Britain and little appreciated, for example, in northern Italy (except by a growing segment of migrants from the south). In the decades since, olive oil, and specifically EVOO, has conquered Milan, Britain, and the world. That history includes European legislation; oil consortia, test panels, and competitions and prizes; the planting of olive groves in far-flung parts of the globe; fraud; television chefs; and the seemingly never-ending struggle of quality producers to get consumers to distinguish between high-quality oil and the sometimes dubious product frequently found on supermarket shelves at impossibly low prices. Today, all oil would seem to be extra virgin.

The mobility of olive oil then has increased dramatically since 1960, with regard to speed of production and transport, geographic scope, and cultural penetration: there is, for example, a growing market for olive oil, and even olive cultivation, in China.[54] That said, olive oil was far from immobile prior to that date, and as we have seen, although production was long restricted to the Mediterranean basin, oil itself travelled far and wide, as food and fuel in the producing regions but also as an industrial product throughout Europe, playing a key role in the Industrial Revolution. It also followed population movements, as a food, across the Atlantic and to the Antipodes, most notably in the late nineteenth and early twentieth centuries. That latter century also saw the gradual conquest of non-Mediterranean palates. By mid-century, Elizabeth David was promoting olive-oil cookery in Britain, paving the way for increased imports of good-quality food oil to places where Gallipoli oil had once supplied thriving wooleries. By the early twenty-first century, one might take as an index of olive oil's mobility the fact that "Everyday EVOO," endorsed by US television celebrity Rachael Ray (and made by Italian producer Colavita), can be purchased online from Walmart, the world's largest retailer. It is a safe bet that few consumers of EVOO today are aware that once upon a time most olive oil was cloth oil.

NOTES

Winner of the 2021 Sophie Coe Prize for Writing in Food History.

1 It is telling that the historical work seemingly most cited in the recent mobilities paradigm literature is Fernand Braudel's study of the Mediterranean in the Age of Philip II, first published in 1949. See e.g., Mimi Sheller and John Urry, "The New Mobilities Paradigm," *Environment and Planning A* 38 (2006): 209.

2 B.R. Mitchell, "Population and Vital Statistics," in *International Historical Statistics Europe 1750–1988* (London: Palgrave Macmillan, 1992), 72–3.

3 Piero Bevilacqua, "Il paesaggio degli alberi nel mezzogiorno d'Italia e in Sicilia (fra XVIII e XX secolo)," *Annali dell'Istituto Alcide Cervi* 10 (1988): 277. Even today, the Italian *mezzogiorno* accounts for about 85 per cent of Italian national production; Italian regional figures can be found here: https://www.ismeamercati.it/flex/cm/pages/ServeBLOB.php/L/IT/IDPagina/3523.

4 Vincenzo Ricchioni, "L'olivicultura meridionale e l'opera di Pietro Ravanas," *Japigia* (1938): 70; Culloch offers that in 1830 of the 2.8 million gallons of oil imported by Britain, 2 million (70 per cent) came from Italy. There is no reason to imagine that the percentage was any smaller in the previous century; indeed, it may have been larger. John Ramsey Culloch, *A Dictionary, Practical, Theoretical, and Historical, of Commerce and Commercial Navigation*, 2 vols. (Philadelphia: A. Hart, 1852), 253.

5 This decree is oft repeated in the existing literature on olive oil history but never so far in my reading with an explicit citation leading to the decree itself. See, e.g., Ludovico Bianchini, *Storia delle finanze del Regno di Napoli*, 3rd ed. (Naples: Stamperia Reale, 1859), 367 (also cited in Ricchioni, "L'olivicultura," 77).

6 Bevilacqua, "Il paesaggio," 279–85.

7 *Encyclopaedia Britannica,* 2nd ed. (Edinburgh: Balfour and Co., 1778–83), vol. 3, 2021–2.

8 *Encyclopædia Britannica* 11th ed. (Cambridge: Cambridge University Press, 1910–11), 810.

9 Domenico Grimaldi, *Uliveti, olio ed economia nella storia della Calabria,* ed. Francesco Tigani Sava (Catanzaro: Millenaria, 2006 [1773], 34); Grimaldi published two important works on olive cultivation and oil production.

The one cited here in 1773 and then another ten years later: Domenico Grimaldi, *Memoria sulla economia olearia antica, e scavamenti di Stabia* (Cosenza: Pellegrini, 2000 [1783]). It is worth noting that he makes no reference in this passage to the export of lamp oil; lighting in northern Europe was fuelled primarily with animal fats and eventually coal derivatives. David DiLaura, "A Brief History of Lighting," *Optics and Photonics News* (September 2008): 22–8.

10 David Landes, in his classic work on the Industrial Revolution, describes the importance of wool in eighteenth-century Britain as an initial phase in British economic expansion and industrialization. During that century, wool production far outstripped cotton and in the period 1740–70, just when Neapolitan oil cultivation was expanding, grew at a rate of 13 to 14 per cent per decade. David Landes, *The Unbound Prometheus* (Cambridge: Cambridge University Press, 2003), 45.

11 There are two fine works on olive oil production and trade in the eighteenth-century Kingdom of Naples, much relied upon in this chapter: Patrick Chorley, *Oil, Silk and Enlightenment, Economic Problems in XVIIIth Century Naples* (Naples: Istituto Italiano per gli Studi Storici in Napoli, 1965) and Aldo Montaudo, *L'olio nel Regno di Napoli nel XVIII secolo. Commercio, Annona e Arrendamenti* (Naples: Edizioni Scientifiche Italiane, 2005).

12 These estimates and that below regarding Gallipoli are based on Grimaldi, *Memoria*, 34 (who suggests a much larger figure for exports); Chorley, *Oil, Silk*, 21–2, 60; and Montaudo, *L'olio nel Regno*, 164–71. The figures in those sources generally cite the traditional oil units of *salme* and *staia*. Conversion figures can be found in Jan Gyllenbok, *Encyclopaedia of Historical Metrology, Weights, and Measures*, vol. 3 (Cham, Switzerland: Birkhäuser, 2018), 1788. The specific gravity of olive oil is about 0.9 so 1 litre = 0.9 kg, though sources, even official statistical ones, tend to use units of mass and volume interchangeably.

13 Giovanni Presta, *Degli ulivi, delle ulive e della maniera di cavar l'olio* (Lecce: Tipografia editrice salentina, 1871 [1794]), 453; Giuseppe Maria Galanti, *Nuova Descrizione Geografica e Politica delle Sicilie*, vol. 3 (Naples: Gabinetto Letterario, 1789), 218.

14 The Library of Entertaining Knowledge, *Vegetable Substances: Materials of Manufactures* (London: Charles Knight, 1833), 198. I suspect that the anonymous author made the not unusual mistake here of switching Taranto for Otranto.

15 Sadly, outbreak of the *Xylella* epidemic starting in 2009 has drastically altered that centuries-old landscape. See, e.g., Carl Ipsen, "*Xylella fastidiosa* and the Olive Oil Crisis in Puglia," *Gastronomica* 20, no. 2 (2020): 55–66.

16 Bartolomeo Ravenna, *Memorie istoriche della città di Gallipoli* (Naples: Miranda, 1836), 105, 114–15; Montaudo, *L'olio nel Regno,* 160–82; Presta, *Degli ulivi,* 366, 369, 412. Presta claims that Salento oil made with ogliarola olives holds up well for two or three years, while the oil from Aix turns rancid after just one.

17 Grimaldi and Chorley give consumption figures for the city of Naples of 5–6 million litres per year. With a population of about 400,000 – estimates for the eighteenth century range from 300,000 to 438,000 – the capital consumed about 14 litres of oil per person per year. As for the rest of the kingdom, given the above figures and a total population of a bit over 5 million people, annual consumption levels would have been about 10 litres per person per year. Grimaldi, *Memoria,* 34 and Chorley, *Oil, Silk,* 60.

18 de Bourcard, Francesco, *Usi e costumi di Napoli e contorni* (Naples: Longanesi, 1866), 743–7.

19 Presta, *Degli ulivi.*

20 Grimaldi, *Uliveti,* 65–127; Presta, *Degli ulivi,* 323–72.

21 Presta, *Degli ulivi* 362, 434, 500; he also refers once to *huile vierge* (462).

22 Presta, *Degli ulivi,* 239, 426, 430.

23 Montaudo, *L'olio del Regno,* 290.

24 Presta, *Degli ulivi,* 330–2; for more on the Salentine *frantoi ipogei,* see Lucia Milizia Fasano, *Il trappeto sotterraneo in Terra d'Otranto* (Manduria: Cappone, 1991), and Antonio Monte, *Frantoi ipogei del Salento* (Lecce: Edizioni del Grifo, 1995).

25 Chorley, *Oil, Silk,* 60–82; Aurelio Lepre, "Una crisi olearia verso la fine del settecento," in *Contadini, borghesi ed operai nel tramonto del feudalismo napoletano* (Milan: Feltrinelli, 1963), 241–68.

26 Domenico Demarco, ed., *La "statistica" del Regno di Napoli nel 1811,* 4 vols. (Rome: Accademia Nazionale dei Lincei, 1988); subsequent references in the text refer to volume and page nos.

27 See, e.g., Hasia R. Diner, *Hungering for America: Italian, Irish, and Jewish Foodways in the Age of Migration* (Cambridge, MA: Harvard University Press, 2003), 32–3.

28 *Vegetable Substances,* 194–204. This work is also cited in Culloch, *A Dictionary,* 254–5, and indirectly in Ricchioni "L'olivicultura," 70, 77.

29 *Vegetable Substances,* 202–3.

30 *Vegetable Substances,* 200–1.

31 L.G. Connor, "A Brief History of the Sheep Industry in the United States," *Agricultural History Society Papers* 1 (1921): 89–197.

32 *Vegetable Substances,* 202.

33 Culloch, *A Dictionary,* 253.

34 Montaudo, *L'olio del Regno,* 24; Angelantonio Spagnoletti, *Storia del Regno delle Due Sicilie* (Bologna: Il Mulino, 1997), 259–61; the claim regarding

Bari's level of production comes from Spagnoletti, who cites a figure of 300,000 *cantaia*. *Cantaia* would seem to be an alternate spelling for *cantari* (= 89 kg); his figure then comes to about 29 million kg (32 million litres), a bit low compared with our eighteenth-century calculation and to post-Unification statistics cited below. On the other hand, Bari may well have been producing half of the kingdom's *olio fino*.

35 Stefano Jacini, *I risultati della inchiesta agraria* (Rome: A. Sommaruga, 1885), xii, 104–6.

36 Alessandro Bizzarri, *L'olio d'oliva: Sulla sua estrazione, chiarificazione e condizionatura per l'esportazione*, 3rd ed. (Florence: Sborgi, 1879), 5–14.

37 Bizzarri, *L'olio*, 22–9.

38 Jacini, *I risultati*, xi, 240; Bizzarri, *L'olio*, 39; *Corriere della Sera*, 28 October 1881, 2; Antonio Aloi, *L'olivo e l'olio*, 4th ed. (Milan: Hoepli, 1898), 329.

39 Legge 3 agosto 1890, n. 7045; Legge 5 aprile 1908, n. 136; Legge 15 ottobre 1925, n. 203.

40 See, e.g., Diner, *Hungering*, 48–83.

41 Luchino Franciosa, *L'Olivo nell'economia italiana* (Rome: Failli, 1940), 73–6, 82–3. The regional percentages are an average calculated for the years 1920–37.

42 *Corriere della Sera*, 3 January 1929, 6.

43 Regio Decreto 1 luglio 1926, n. 1361

44 Legge 30 dicembre 1929, n. 2316.

45 *Corriere della Sera*, 6 July 1935, 2.

46 Legge 27 settembre 1936, n. 1986.

47 On fascist food policy, see Carol Helstosky, *Garlic and Oil: Politics and Food in Italy* (Oxford: Berg, 2004), 63–126.

48 *Corriere della Sera*, 14 August 1951, 4; 16 January 1960, 3; 19 January 1960, 5.

49 *Corriere della Sera*, 7 October 1960, 9; 11 October 1960, 11.

50 Rolando Balducci reports Italian consumption of 5 kg of olive oil per person per year as compared with 2 kg of butter. *Corriere della Sera*, 30 July 1958, 4.

51 *Corriere della Sera*, 19 January 1960, 5.

52 Other categories in the law included: *olio sopraffino vergine di oliva* (<1.5 per cent), *olio fino vergine di oliva* (<2.5 per cent), and *olio vergine di oliva* (<4 per cent). Refined *olio lampante* and *olio di sansa* could still be sold as food; oils obtained by esterification could not. For analysis of the 1960 law (and others), see Mario Pacelli, "C'era una volta," in Mario Pacelli and Giampaolo Sodano, *Il valore dell'olio*, vol. 1 (Rome: Associazione Italiana Frantoiani Oleari, 2015), 59–115.

53 On the problems with Keys' work and the debates over the Mediterranean Diet, see Nina Teicholz, *The Big Fat Surprise: Why Butter, Meat, and Cheese Belong in a Healthy Diet* (New York: Simon & Schuster, 2014), 19–46, 174–224.

For the official UNESCO statement, see https://ich.unesco.org/en/RL/mediterranean-diet-00884.

54 See, e.g., https://daxueconsulting.com/the-olive-oil-industry-in-china/#:~:text=China%20produced%20only%205.000%20tons,%2FConsumption%2FImports%20Reports).&text=The%20domestic%20production%20of%20olive,oil%20consumption%20in%202016%2D2017.

7 The Global Mobilities and Local Immobilities of Tea

JAYEETA SHARMA

Tea is a plant, comestible, and beverage that appears in multiple, mobile guises across human history: a medicinal herb, luxury drink, coffeehouse social, parlour ritual, drug food, street brew, supermarket staple, plantation commodity, craft crop, and connoisseur good. This chapter explores tea as a local food that became regionally, globally mobile, and generated a diversity of cultural artefacts as it did so. It considers how the distinct histories of the *camellia sinensis* and *camellia assamica* species collided and conjoined when modern Euro-American colonialism carried the tea plant into agro-industrial spaces that accelerated the global consumption of its beverages. However, those same historical processes that enhanced tea's global mobility also restricted the mobility of the working classes engaged in its making. Ironically, famed global teas were largely inaccessible in the local spaces and for the Indigenous peoples who pioneered its use as a food and drink.

For centuries, a single plant species, camellia sinensis, dominated plant–human discourses around tea. While there are three major species of camellia tea plant, only sinensis and assamica became widespread. Cultivated in China since the early era of its agrarian history, the culinary, botanical, political, ritual, and cultural enchantments around the camellia sinensis catalysed a steady stream of textual and cultural production. Across the medieval into the early modern eras, its supplies of the beverages circulated across Asia, as the plant's cultivation. By contrast, camellia assamica stayed as a wild plant whose edible parts were foraged, preserved, and consumed by the Indigenous peoples of South east Asia. This was the case until the nineteenth century when it joined sinensis in becoming globally mobile. Over the modern era of colonization and empire, both plant species were transformed into a global commodity. Hundreds of thousands of workers were involved in cultivating, picking, brewing, packing, and marketing their leaves. That production engaged peasant smallholdings and agro-industrial planta-tions. Consumers everywhere benefited from the ready availability of a relatively inexpensive, delicious, and non-alcoholic drink.

However, that mobility benefited only a tiny portion of the people enmeshed with tea production: mostly connected to colonial, metro-politan, and local elite and bourgeois groups. For the vast majority of tea workers, and for the Indigenous groups who were its first inno-vators, the commodity's modern globalization reinforced the systems that limited their livelihoods, dislocated them from their homelands, and appropriated their knowledge. Through the twentieth century, the unjust corporate structures that immobilized Indigenous tea knowl-edge and its proletarianized growers continued to largely control local tea economies and global tea trades. Nonetheless, the chapter ends with an exploration of a few of the twenty-first-century alternative artisanal marketplaces that promise to do better for tea localities, grassroots interlocutors, and custodians of Indigenous tea knowledge.

Early and Imperial Mobilities: *Camellia Sinensis*

Lacking direct evidence as how plant–human tea interactions began, we may start from the premise that such Indigenous knowledge accu-mulated as the people who lived in the plant's vicinity learned to apply basic processing and preserving techniques to its edible parts, in order to preserve their longevity, and accentuate their taste. Fresh plant leaves were likely chewed right after picking. Leaves would have been infused in water. As the Indigenous technologies of preservation advanced, they started to roast, dry, smoke, or ferment leaves, buds, and flowers. Across different times and places across monsoon Asia, these Indige-nous custodians learned to prepare balls, cakes, bricks, or powder from those edible parts of different tea-plant camellias.

There is little or no archival evidence of when and where such first advances in tea processing occurred. Camellia sinensis is the best-known of these tea-plant species. Chinese archaeologists in 2012 iden-tified sinensis plant remains from the Hemudu Neolithic culture of 5,500–3,300 BCE. They took it as proof that Chinese tea's lineal ancestor lay in those fossilized plant remains from more than six million years ago and that tea cultivation began at that point.[1] However, the use of the terms Chinese and China to reference that distant past of this plant in nationalist terms is anachronistic. There is also no indication as to whether those remains came from a cultivated or wild plant. There is a leap of several thousand years from those Indigenous traces to the emer-gence of a documented archive about the mobile journeys of camellia sinensis across the Chinese empire.[2] The jury is still out on how other, recent archaeological findings might alter the tea chronology that food historians currently accept.[3]

The elision of an indigenous wild plant from a monsoon Asian borderland into an unbroken Han Chinese lineage for the cultivation of camellia sinensis is therefore somewhat ahistorical. However, what is incontestable is that from roughly a thousand years ago, imperial China's social elites produced large numbers of poetic, prose, aural, and visual tea texts. Across dynastic eras from the Tang into the Qing periods (the eighth to the nineteenth centuries CE), they discussed its botanical and agrarian aspects, culinary, and symbolic meanings. Such cultural artefacts bring important insights into how the camellia sinensis plant moved over many centuries of history from forest to field and farm, from cake and brick to powder and oolong, from bowl to teapot to samovar, from porter to caravan to ship, from monastery to palace to parlour to street.

The doyen of East Asian food historians, E.N. Anderson, informs us that it was during the Tang dynastic era (618–907 CE), that camellia sinensis became integral to the written canon of China's food plants, albeit a relative newcomer against ancient staples such as rice or cabbage.[4] A significant figure in the generation of such a literary tea canon was Lù Yǔ, author of the oldest known prose treatise of the world, the Chajing (茶經) (ca. 780 CE). In his words, "Tea has a thousand and one faces."[5] He implicitly staked a claim for Sichuan as the authentic homeland of tea when he wrote that its wild trees were an ancient, indigenous species, very different from the peasant's cultivated plant. Until the fifth century, Sichuan had certainly been the locus of tea production and consumption. It was over Lù Yǔ's own era, the Tang, that tea started to circulate across the empire as a beverage for both northerners and southerners.[6] Lù Yǔ had little to say about how the wild plant of Sichuan was harvested. Rather, he focused on how peasants and artisans processed freshly picked leaves from cultivated tea plants into stable and portable forms of the food. They steamed and pounded the processed leaves into powder, then shaped that powder into tea cakes, ready to be brewed, and conveyed to discerning consumers.

Lù Yǔ's text is notable in the history of tea in that it was the first to employ a novel Chinese ideogram, "chá"茶, to denote the camellia sinensis plant and its associated drinks. This ideogram distinguished it from older texts that employed a variety of ideograms to denote other trees whose leaves supplied different infusions. Once that writing innovation appeared in text, it was there to stay in the language. The character and the name "cha" proved almost as mobile as the drink and commodity that they denoted. Beyond China, "cha" entered many world languages. This happened either through a writing system as in the case of Japanese, or through its sound as a name to denote the drink.[7] Historical linguist George Van Driem views the Tang-era spread of such a linguistic device as crucial testimony that the mobile transformation of a previously local drink into a spatially dispersed food commodity was underway.[8] This transformation went hand in hand with changes in form. As Lù Yǔ had shown, tea makers had learned that preserved leaves pounded into cakes and bricks of tea were easily portable and lasted for much longer than fresh leaves. Another early innovation was the production of sturdy tea bricks. On those Himalayan borderlands, camellia sinensis was not just a source of nutrition, but a key currency, used for centuries on the famed tea-horse trading circuits.[9]

Reading and writing about "chá"茶 became an important cultural device to display erudition, taste, intelligence, and creativity.[10] The way was shown by the Huizong emperor of the Sung dynasty (960–1279 CE) who produced a *Treatise on Tea* (大观茶论) (ca. 1107 CE). He noted: "All the nobles under Heaven can afford to revel in the appreciation of exquisite rare tea, seeking its literary gems and pretty bits of golden verse, sipping from its flowers and sucking on its blossoms, weighing the value of its literature, debating the distinctions in its appraisal and judgment, not to mention the innovative designs of their tea-ware collections."[11] Expanding literati interest in the plant's culinary and medicinal properties led Su Song, author of a renowned botanical opus, *Bencao Tujing* (本草 圖 經) (ca. 1062 CE) to include a sketch.[12] This was perhaps the first time that readers outside the tea-growing regions could view the plant. Ming-era (1348–1643 CE) statesman Xu Guangqi acclaimed the drink's versatility in his agricultural treatise, *Nong Zheng Quanshu* 農政全書 (ca. 1313 CE): "Tea is a divine herb. Profits are ample if one plants it. The spirit is purified if one drinks it. It is something esteemed by the noblemen and well-to-do which commoners and déclassé folks cannot do without. Truly it is a necessity in the daily lives of the people, and an asset for the fiscal prosperity of the state."[13]

Already by the ninth and tenth centuries CE, camellia sinensis was a plant food that was being cultivated, produced, consumed, and distributed from Sichuan to Zhejiang to Fujian, assisted by the creation of an elaborate state supervisory system connected to a web of regional monopolies.[14] Tea expert Kevin Gascoyne observes that as the plant moved across China, its botanical forms adapted to changing terroir and climes, to create a wealth of cultivars.[15] He notes that the east-bound plant's cultivated leaves became noticeably smaller in size than its original form in Sichuan.[16] A variety of texts from literati authors – from poetry to gazetteers to medicinal manuals – provide a wide range of testimonies as to how the Fujian and Anhui regions proved especially hospitable for this adaptable camellia sinensis. Such tea-plant mobilities transformed the ecologies and economies of previously marginal regions such as Fujian. That region's uplands, inhospitable to rice, proved ideal for sinensis and gave rise to numerous cultivars.[17] Tea took on multiple roles for the Chinese empire: it was a cultivated food plant, an important nutritional source as a beverage that moved from monasteries and palaces to tea houses and street stalls; a cash crop crucial for state revenues, peasant, artisan, and mercantile incomes; a crucial component for social networks, especially linked to gifting, trading, religious, marital, and tributary connections. Moving outside of China, camellia sinensis continued its influential role as a catalyst for social practices that effectively reshaped religious, commercial, leisure, medicinal, agrarian, botanical, and culinary cultures across a considerable portion of East Asia, especially Japan, Korea, and Vietnam.

One way in which the taste for camellia sinensis circulated beyond China was through the overseas trading and diasporic communities closely linked to regions such as Fujian which acted as nodes for migration.[18] Another key route was through foreign Buddhist monks and visitors to monasteries who developed a passion for the beverage. As in the case of Lù Yǔ', many tea connoisseurs and authors had been devout Chinese Buddhists. Buddhism was an institution that James Benn, a key historian of East Asian religions, views as essential to camellia sinensis's social dissemination into transregional worlds.[19] He analyses numerous poetic and prose texts from China, Japan, and Korea that describe tea's Buddhist voyages and acculturation into those spaces. It moved into medieval Japan and Korea as a food, drink, medicine, and commodity that gradually moved through social spaces and classes, as it was doing in China. The camellia sinensis plant became domesticated in those countries, just as "chá"茶 entered their speech and writing systems.

Possibly the earliest tea mention from Japanese texts comes from the emperor Shōmu (724–749 CE). Apparently, he honoured high-ranking Buddhist monks with a new drink he called in-cha (cloister tea), prepared from a Tang courtly gift of powdered Chinese cakes. However, Tang dynastic decline brought a hiatus to those mobile transactions.[20] But the "chá"茶 ideogram stayed on as an important kanji writing character although the drink became unavailable in Japan for a few centuries. The camellia sinensis plant – and its beverage – became newly mobile through the agency of later generations of Buddhist pilgrims who voyaged back and forth between China and Japan. The most renowned was the twelfth-century Japanese monk Myoan Eisai, who carried back seeds, bowls, and powder after a lengthy stay at Zhejiang monasteries. His medicinal treatise, Kissa Yoji-ki 喫茶養生記, that expounded on the plant's healing properties, received much acclaim when the shogun Minamoto no Sanetomo's (1192–1219) credited its prescription of green tea for his recovery from a serious illness.

Numerous texts from foreign traders, monks, diplomats, and missionaries who encountered tea in China whetted curiosity and desire about this refreshing stimulant and medicinal elixir. Sometimes, this happened long before the beverage became available in their countries. Often, such tea texts circulated for centuries, albeit in translated, anthologized, and abbreviated forms, and across different spaces. The longevity and reach of such transcultural texts, often over centuries, and over several languages, enhanced the historical authenticity that Chinese tea enjoyed. When a Persian merchant Sulayman-el-Tajir visited Guangzhou (ca. 831–851 CE), he remarked that its smell and properties were more impressive than its taste: "Cha is produced from a shrub bushier than the pomegranate tree, and of a more pleasant smell, but having a kind of a bitterish taste. The way of using this herb is to pour boiling water upon the leaves, and the infusion cures all diseases." But this Persian description circulated over centuries worldwide. For example, it appeared in the tenth-century CE in Arabic within a travel compendium called Akhbar al-Sin w-alHind (Information about China and India) edited by Abu Zaid al-Hasan, a merchant who traded around Indian Ocean ports.[21] About five hundred years later, it reached as far as France, when the Arabic text was purchased for the library of Baptiste Colbert, the prime minister of Louis XIV.[22] By that time, those same French social elites who read about the plant were able to access the beverage as a luxury maritime import.

In a parallel journey Persian enthusiast Chaggi Memet's advocacy of the "China herb" was translated from Persian for an early modern Venetian anthology of travel writings. Subsequently, his tea text was retranslated into English, for a wildly popular travel treatise from the noted print entrepreneur Richard Hakluyt (ca. 1552–1616 CE). "All over Cathay, they made use of a herb, or rather its leaves, which these people call the chiai of Cathay. The Chinese people say that if only people knew about this stuff in Persia or France, the merchants here would without a doubt cease to buy ravend Cini, as they call rhubarb (a Chinese medicinal commodity)."[23] Those Italian and English readers too, were now able to lay their hands on tea to drink, thanks to the early modern maritime mobilities between Asia and Europe.

Translating Early Modern Tea Mobilities

Original observations on tea in different European languages originated from the maritime intermediaries – the early modern merchants
and missionaries. They directly encountered tea cultures – and tasted
the drink – at Asian port cities such as Goa, Batavia, Macao, and Nagasaki. Since the Ming dynasty's policies prevented most foreigners
from entering China, most Western observers first encountered camellia sinensis in Japan. While the Japanese shogunate did allow limited
entry to Westerners, it confined them to the Nagasaki area. The camellia
sinensis plant from China had by then become a Japanese cultural artefact, grown widely in the country. Jesuit visitors such as the Portuguese
missionary Luis d'Almeida (1525–1583) wrote of a "powder of a certain
herb called Chia, of which they put as much as a Walnut-shelle may
containe, into a dish of porcelaine cup and drinke it with hot water."[24]
D'Almeida was the first European author to transliterate the Japanese
sound of 茶 into the what became the early modern Portuguese name
for tea, "cha." Originally written in 1564, his tea text was absorbed
into Samuel Purchas's famed travel compendium in English, in 1614,
around when tea shipments arrived at London.

Another Portuguese Jesuit Joao Rodriguez (1561–1634) translated a
local description of tea as grown in Japan into his diary, later published
and translated into different European languages. "Cha itself comes
from a small tea or bush, rather similar to the myrtle bush. Its new
leaves, which are used for the drink, are soft and delicate, and must be
protected from frost."[25] While Rodriguez's writings show that he had
become a tea connoisseur, the Portuguese Jesuit missionary interest
in tea was largely instrumentalist in character. They hoped to use tea
ceremonies to promote social interactions with the elite Japanese figures whom they wished to convert to their faith. Rodriguez even built
a tea hut at his residence. They had some success with this approach,
as when they converted a few devotees of the tea master Sen no Rikyu.
But this proved a pyrrhic victory since those conversions spurred the
shogunate to expel the Portuguese for the crime of proselytization.[26]

In a few decades, the Dutch East India Company, or Vereenigde
Oostindische Compagnie (VOC), usurped the Portuguese Jesuit
place as Japan's chosen Western intermediaries. The word "cha" had
reached the Dutch language in a 1595 book, *Itinerario*, translated into
English in 1598. Its author, a former Jesuit employee, Jan Huyghen van
Linschoten, mainly conveyed Portuguese Asian trading secrets but
included an important tip for European merchants about an exciting
herbal powdered drink of Japan and China.[27] Just a few years later,

Dutch VOC ships started to convey tea: to Holland in 1610, France in 1636, and England in 1645. Tea was already popular in Dutch colonial spaces such as Batavia. Conveyed to Europe on VOC ships, it became Holland's most valuable export commodity.[28] However, during the eighteenth century, the English East India Company received a monopoly over the sale of Chinese tea that enabled it to steal a march on its Dutch rivals for the European trade.

Just as tea bricks and tea powder were well suited for the overland and short seaborne journeys of tea within Asia, the plant's leaves were rendered suitable for distant maritime mobilities with new craft innovations. Chinese and Japanese tea artisanal producers remade harvested leaves into new innovative forms to withstand the lengthy voyages in ship holds. Leaves underwent an oxidation process that kept them green and unfermented, yet durable, after being pan-fried, rolled, and dried. An Italian Jesuit, Matteo Ricci, described how Ming-era tea makers prepared such preserved plant materials into a delicious drink. "The Chinese place some of the dried leaves in a pot of boiling water and when the water has extracted the virtue from the leaves, they strain off the leaves and drink what is left."[29] Such innovations allowed leaves to be oxidized after picking, then wilted, pan-fried, rolled, and dried into oolong forms of tea. After a few voyages between Europe and Asia, Chinese merchants learned that dried black tea leaves withstood lengthy seaborne journeys better than the green kind. Not coincidentally, black tea was to eventually become the modern world's predominant type of globally consumed tea.

By the Ming era, the wide bowls and whisks that Sung China bequeathed to Japan for its powdered tea beverages, had gone out of vogue. They were superseded by the lidded bowls, cups, and teapots suitable for the new, leaf-brewed forms of the beverage. All over early modern Europe, an earlier fashionable habit of consuming exotic Eastern goods such as porcelain tableware that had percolated downward from European aristocrats to mercantile classes, now become linked to tea drinking. Porcelain mobilities thus played an important role in reshaping tea drinking's mobile trajectories from aristocratic privilege to bourgeois ubiquity. Literary scholar Eugenia Jenkins explores how textual and material cultural encounters connected to travelogues, fantasy fiction, landscape design, decorative objects, and domestic rituals systematically incorporated commodities connected to tea into the everyday lives of European subjects.[30] By the eighteenth century, porcelain and tea consumption developed hand in hand, as did a multitude of material objects and social rituals linked to them. Another innovation from Ming China, the hard-paste porcelain teapot became a desirable global artefact that took on diverse forms and different materials, from porcelain to wood. The teapot's mobile journeys, across imperial and colonial spaces as diverse as England, Australia, Canada, Sikkim, and Tibet, gradually adapted it into a huge diversity of local forms connected to specific rituals, spaces, and materials.

Contrary to theories that tea remained a luxury commodity until the era of the Industrial Revolution, we see, instead, that within a hundred years of its maritime mobility, camellia sinensis tea moved from an exotic Oriental luxury food and elite health elixir to a well-accepted social beverage across Europe, and rapidly was carried beyond.[31] After 1707, the English East India Company followed the Dutch lead in adding tea to its existing Asian cargoes of spices and textiles. Soon, a majority of people in Britain and Europe were cognizant that a novel combination of sugar cane and tea leaf, both the result of maritime mobilities, made a refreshing and temperate hot drink. Mobile cargoes of tea would dominate shipping lanes from China to London, and beyond, into colonial and imperial spaces worldwide, for centuries. As governments reduced tea taxes and duties, consumption went up across social classes and regions. In 1757, in the aftermath of a significant duty reduction, no less than 3,000,000 pounds of tea per year landed in Britain from China.[32] Wooden chests of Chinese tea were carried in European ships, moved from Asia to warehouses in Rotterdam and London, then loaded back on ships on their way to port cities across North America, the Caribbean, India, and the Antipodes.

Although the English East India Company enjoyed growing profits from its tea monopoly with China, for the British government and public, that monopoly was less positive in its impact. By the late eighteenth century, 20 million pounds of tea arrived every year in Britain from Asia. That massive scale was a grave economic and political concern. Scientists and political economists considered it a weakness for Britain to depend so much on a foreign plant. Historian Richard Drayton explores what he calls the doctrine of "plant colonialism," which held that important plant commodities such as tea should be available from the lands that flew the British flag, rather than from countries where Britain had no say.[33] Hence the numerous official and unofficial attempts to smuggle out camellia sinensis plant to grow elsewhere. During the 1790s, the Macartney embassy to China risked the Qing court's official censure when it smuggled out camellia sinensis plants to grow in Bengal, where they perished.[34]

The doyen of British botanists, Sir Joseph Banks, encouraged additional efforts to recruit Chinese cultivators who might successfully grow such smuggled tea in British-ruled territories.[35] His protégé Robert Kyd proposed, for his Calcutta botanical garden, "the cultivation of cotton, tobacco, tea etc, to outstrip our rivals in every valuable production."[36] The London-based Society for the Manufacture of Arts, Manufactures, and Commerce offered a lavish sum of money to reward successful tea cultivation anywhere outside of China. However, those plans had little success for the time being. British attempts failed to grow sinensis in Bengal, Penang, Java, and Ceylon. But the urgency for Britain to break the Chinese hold over tea supplies escalated as diplomatic relationships reached a new low by the early nineteenth century, largely due to opium smuggling.

Providentially, a new British solution emerged in the 1820s: an alternative to camellia sinensis. This took the form of the "discovery" of a previously unknown, large-leafed tea plant in a newly acquired British colonial territory, Assam. The plant was called *camellia assamica*, after the region, but it proved to grow wild across the forested peripheries of Thailand, Burma, and Yunnan in China. The Indigenous peoples of the lands had long prepared assamica's wild leaves into medicinal drinks. Now the transformation to global commodity involved the plant's move from forest to plantation, from wild to agro-industrial. This was a newly mobile destiny for camellia assamica, one that forcibly sundered it from its indigenous cultural origins and homelands.

Indigenous Immobilities and Modern Mobilities: *Camellia Assamica*

All the evidence at our disposal indicates that camellia sinensis was the only mobile form of the tea plant, and the sole global source of tea, until the mid-nineteenth century. This mobile character was inextricably tied to its functions and processed forms within the Chinese empire. Through that imperial agency, camellia sinensis made its mobile journeys into medieval East and Central Asia, and into early modern Euro-American spaces. By contrast, the camellia assamica species existed and thrived – through an indeterminate span of time, several centuries or more – solely as a locally available plant. Assamica's plant–human interactions revolved around the food and healing practices of the Indigenous peoples of what are now called Asian borderlands. They gathered its edible plant parts for consuming in fresh form, or applied drying, smoking, and other techniques to preserve those leaves and flowers. The indigenous foods and drinks that resulted from such local actions were known by various local names, such as *laphet* in Burma, or *falap* in Assam. Those forms of tea remained almost entirely immobile within those localities, as did the assamica plant itself, until the nineteenth-century advent of colonialism.

During the 1830s, a colonial Tea Committee from British India announced that a large-leafed tea plant grew wild in forests on the Assam–Burma border. "The tea shrub is beyond all doubt indigenous to Upper Assam … by far the most important and valuable (discovery) that has ever been made on matters connected with the agricultural or commercial resources of this empire."[37] The East India Committee learned from a British military officer how the Indigenous groups living near those forests used it as a beverage. "The Singphos and Kamptees are in the habit of drinking an infusion of the leaves, which I understood they prepare by pulling them into small pieces, taking out stalks and fibres, boiling and squeezing them into a ball, which they dry in the sun and retain for use."[38] The East India Company was, at first, willing to collaborate with those Indigenous custodians and other local interme-diaries. It arranged with the Singpho chief, Ningroola, to collect a thou-sand pounds of wild leaves. The aim was to sell the leaves at auction in London. "A reasonable hope may be entertained that he and other Sing-phos similarly situated, may eventually become valuable auxiliaries to the objects of our Company."[39] Meanwhile, East India Company official Charles Bruce was given charge of an experimental tea-growing initia-tive. It aimed to recruit labourers from China to hybridize and cultivate unique plants – an Assam hybrid – that would unite the two camellia species. The ultimate goal was to "enrich our own Dominions and pull down the haughty pride of China."[40] That initiative employed as its local manager an enterprising aristocrat, Maniram Barbhandar Barua, who had begun to grow tea himself.[41]

However, colonial collaborations in the locality proved short-lived. They came to a quick halt largely due to the vociferous opposition of British scientists. The most prominent was botanist William Griffith, who criticized the proposal to export the wild tea leaves to Europe. Unsurprisingly, he and other imperial scientists had nothing but scorn for Indigenous knowledge and expertise, and for the wild plant associ-ated with them. Instead of the collaborations that the East India Com-pany proposed, Griffith and his peers advocated harsh policies to bring that indigenous tea under British control.[42] The colonial state followed those recommendations. Almost two hundred years later, a chieftain's letter of protest speaks to us of how those Indigenous custodians of camellia assamica protested at their dispossession. "Now it is said that where the tea grows, that is yours, but when we make sacrifices (and) we require tea for our funerals; we therefore perceive that you have taken all the country, and we cannot get tea to drink."[43]

Through the second half of the nineteenth century, British science and capital devised multiple ways to reshape Assam and other suitable territories to produce globally mobile tea. Its chosen plants were an assortment of hybrid and local cultivars bred from a mix of camellia sinensis and camellia assamica, or either species on its own, transplanted into Darjeeling, the Dooars, the Nilgiris, and Ceylon. British capitalists were encouraged with cheap or free grants of so-called waste lands, to start large plantation estates. They were supplied with a captive indentured workforce of migrant men, women, and children, drawn largely from the dislocated Indigenous peoples of regions such as Chotanagpur. A penal regime of indentured labour was transplanted from Caribbean sugar plantations to colonized India and Ceylon's tea plantations. It disciplined workers into agro-industrial proletariats who lacked access to any form of social or economic mobility, since they depended upon plantation employment.[44]

The expansive actions of imperial capitalism became the catalyst for entirely new forms of tea mobilities that reconstituted world markets, consumption cultures, and agrarian systems. The smallholder tea system of China was denigrated as old-fashioned, inefficient, unscientific, and unhygienic. After the 1870s, as Assam, Darjeeling, and Ceylon tea factories and plantations expanded, the world market share for China's smallholder tea began a steady decline. From 1900, Chinese black teas lost major ground to Indian and Ceylonese plantation ones, while green teas from Japan dominated the American market. By contrast, the imperial spaces of Assam, Ceylon, Darjeeling, the Dooars, the Nilgiris, and Kenya were the laboratories that harnessed an agro-industrial proletariat of indentured and migrant workers to produce factory tea for enormous numbers of global consumers. After British India became independent and its tea industry was nationalized, a brown Raj of tea merely replaced the white. Indian teas – and later African, were for a long time, mostly marketed as a modern, low-priced, factory-made alternative to Chinese peasant-made tea.

Global Tea Mobilities, Local Immobilities, and Alternative Mobile Marketplaces

Modern tea, as a food commodity, had steadily moved across the world, adopting protean guises as it did so. Novel names such as Darjeeling, Indian, Assam, Ceylon, English Breakfast, Yorkshire, Twining, Tetley's, Lipton, denoted a diverse, global, mobile marketplace for modern tea. Distinct rituals and institutions developed historically across local and global spaces, in tandem with tea mobilities: the Tibetan monastery; Central Asian chaikhana, English parlour; Indian hawker and roadside stall; Australian bushstation; Hong Kong cha chaan teng; urban tea boutiques. New forms of tea as a food emerged – locally and globally: black tea leaves carried on Dutch ships to which Caribbean sugar was added, then milk; Russian and Kashmiri samovar teas; leaves blended with scented bergamot to produce British Earl Grey; American iced tea, sweet tea, and tea bags; CTC factory-rendered tea-dust blends from which arose the masala chai calorific foods of lower-class British, South Asian, Antipodean, and African streets and homes; chai latte, bubble tea, turmeric lattes, and single estate or small grower or forest craft teas of recent times.

The modern tea plant, as a non-human entity, was subject to an unprecedented series of mobilities, connected to a variety of human agents, including governments, planters, growers, and brokers. The confirmation that at least one local species of tea plant existed outside of China, had been a sign, after all, that the plant could thrive if transplanted elsewhere. By the end of the nineteenth century, both major camellia species were successfully cultivated to provide tea far from their homelands. When the Russian empire selected Georgia as its chosen space for tea production, it employed Chinese manager Lau-Dzhen-Dzhau to plant and nurture sinenis cultivars at Chakva.[45] New regions such as Persia/Iran, Nepal, Turkey, and Kenya steadily acquired shares in the world market for tea.

Within the new globally mobile world of modern tea, it might seem that China had irretrievably lost ground. However, there are important spatial and cultural nuances that modify this picture. Historian Jason Lim points out that twentieth-century Western historians who have regarded recent Chinese tea history as a backdrop to the global success of the British industry, have ignored much of the regional and transregional nuances in its modern trajectories.[46] The camellia sinensis of China retained appeal for transregional cultures where it had historically taken root, such as Singapore, Malaysia, Tibet and Sikkim. In the twenty-first century, while much of the mass-market tea sold in China comes from cheap blended imported leaves, its new forms of artisanal and organic tea, as well as the historically high-end classics, hold sway for local and global connoisseurs, as does the importance of tea as a drink in the national imagination.[47]

It needs to be noted, however, that local people from the vicinity of the tea plant, whether in Assam or Fujian or Darjeeling, typically drink its cheaper forms of tea, the only ones available to them. China is one of the world's top producers of highly desirable organic teas today, but those exist at the high end of the global marketplace. Growing up in a lower middle-class family of Assam, I had never even seen or tasted a single-estate or first or second flush form of tea until I moved to the Global North. My parents drank endless cups of tea all their lives, but knew only its cheaply homogenized, CTC factory form. Ironically, they could not relish the taste of any other, pricier, tea that I might bring them.

Even as we appreciate the vibrant and manifold mobile forms of modern tea, we still need to delineate the troubling aspects of the class, race, and gender hierarchies that enabled its globalization. The upper echelons of world tea drinkers whether in New York or London or Hong Kong, then and now, enjoy expensive, blended teas such as Earl Grey, single-estate varieties from Darjeeling and China, or rare aged Pu-er teas from Yunnan. By contrast, the modern mass-market tea of the lower classes, denotes cheap brews from the lowest grades of leaves, or tea-dust. Both the masala tea and the builder's tea of the British and Indian working classes developed out of the culinary necessity to accentuate the taste of a low-quality raw material. Such delicious forms of tea arose despite, and against, the inequitable immobilities that prevailed for their makers.

Systemic immobilities of labour and land are the dirty, essential, underbelly of our modern global tea mobilities, and continue into the postmodern era. The industrial production of tea was, and remains, intrinsically tied to exploitative forms of employment and existence.[48] Industrial tea was gloriously mobile, but its workers were not. Invisible to most people, the global production and movement of the bulk of the world's tea after the mid-nineteenth century originated from the proletarianized and racialized labour of colonial plantations that were built on expropriated local lands. While the departure of the British colonial state led to some alterations that benefited a portion of the Indian tea industry's unionized employees, those were not systemic changes. Ceaseless demands for accelerated production and profitability wrought an increasing dependence on chemical inputs applied to a monoculture whose everyday violence upon labour, land, the plant, and our planet has long been unregulated. A recent academic study obtained rare, first-hand worker testimonies to show that even ostensibly organic and fair-trade certified plantations did no better than the mainstream ones as regards the immobile and unjust labour conditions that prevailed.[49] Recent investigations by journalists and activists are starting to reveal how post-colonial female descendants of an imperial plantation workforce have been trapped into regional and global trafficking nets due to the poverty and immobility that afflicts their families.[50]

This chapter has explored key historical moments of tea plant and human mobilities across time and space.[51] The textual tea knowledge and tea mobilities of the historical past became inextricably connected to camellia sinensis's interactions with the literate civilizations and connoisseur cultures of China and East Asia, and their burgeoning connections with Euro-American empires. The modern British empire's forcible assimilation of another species, camellia assamica, into a globalizing world of food and commodity mobilities, also produced immobilities around labour, environment, and possibly, homogenized mass-market tastes.

Conclusion

In conclusion, this chapter considers how a re-conceptualization of tea histories in terms of those immobilities and mobilities, might allow us to consider some of the alternative marketplaces that sought to bridge the gap between Global North consumers and Global South producers in the twenty-first century.

Votaries of little-known and previously immobile tea cultivars and craft tea types from South and Southeast Asian borderlands have often desired to bring them to the notice of global experts and discerning consumers. So have small, independent producers of new forms of organic and artisanal tea from Taiwan and China. However, in India, the tea plant has long been immobilized on corporate-owned plantations, manned by forced labour.[52] Only in the late twentieth century did the postcolonial Indian state belatedly overturn colonial regulations that made tea commercially exclusive to the plantation sector, so that independent small growers could legally undertake its making and selling and hold rights over those lands. The tea industry lost no time in opposing this, characterizing such small tea growers as the biggest threat it faced.[53] This was probably justified since, as tea activist-scholar John John points out, in 2017, the contribution of big growers had decreased to 53.17 per cent (from 98.4 per cent in 1991), while 46.83 per cent was from small growers.[54] Many of those small growers are content to sell to the corporate factories, but among them is a small but significant portion of artisanal producers who wished to experiment with culturally nuanced and egalitarian modes of production and organization.

As digital media and technologies allow for new forms of mobile marketplaces, Global North connoisseurs have been able to connect with those new/old local forms of tea from the Global South, and welcome new possibilities for taste, artisanal craft, and sustainability.[55] Such alternative marketplaces appeal in particular to a small yet influential cross-section of self-proclaimed foodies who combine environmental concerns about vanishing biodiversity with a new sensitivity to the intangible cultural heritage and authenticity of local food practices, processes, and products at risk of extinction. It remains to be seen if alternative, mobile marketplaces for craft teas can fulfil their promise to offer a blend of fine tastes equitable work conditions, craft skills, leavened with a dash of culinary tourism, and with due attention to Indigenous histories and traditions.

The Camellia Sinensis tea firm started in 1990s Montreal as a bohemian teahouse where you could quaff shisha and sip tea. By the 2000s, it was a creator of prize-winning coffee-table gourmet books (available in French, English, Russian, and Korean). Most importantly, it had become a marketplace for rare teas, acquired at source, via its proprietors' annual journeys to craft producers across China, Taiwan, India, and Nepal. Such claims of "going to the source" are regularly showcased in their monthly blogposts and "producer of the moment" writings.[56] The grassroots producers with whom they collaborate range from a sencha organic producer from the Ashikubo (Shizuoka) region where tea cultivation started eight centuries ago, or a second-generation farmer from Wei Shan, a tea-making region since Tang China, who turned organic in 2003. Today, the firm often finds that the source is coming to them. Co-proprietor Kevin Gascoyne describes how he is constantly alert to the prospect of a new craft producer from a hitherto unknown locality sending samples to his Montreal desk "from deep forest, rebel growers, and/or a wild tribe."[57] His reaction reveals a blend of respect and excitement, commercial instinct and gourmet indulgence. "Instead of marching in as a critical buyer or technical consultant, I intend to savour the moment for pure pleasure, exploring the situation with an open mind. The hopes of recognition and future trade from these distant tea-folk must also be treated with the utmost respect."[58]

The historical and local immobilities endemic to wild and indigenous tea were accentuated by the distance from the world economy and their micro-artisanal production methods, but those factors also unwittingly protected the uniqueness of those products. It is interesting to see what happens when such teas acquire mobility and end up on the tables of global foodies especially through new types of mobile marketplaces. Often, this process interacts with digital tea texts that propagate tales of taste, terroir, craft, and sustainability, just as printed ones once circulated tales of tea, taste, and empire. When local, immobile forms of tea come into contact with new audiences, new technologies, or new markets, they might acquire mobility and the prospect of building diffused, niched, yet globalized loyalties.

An alternative marketplace that has steadily built such loyalties is Siam Tee. It deals with sustainable whole leaf teas, and is in its second decade of dispatching tea from Asian borderland small growers to consumers all over the world.[59] Importer Thomas Kasper's German office regularly receives modest shipments from eight Asian countries that it repackages to EU standards and mails to customers across the European Union and North America. Kasper's blog recounts how his market took off in the 1990s after he encountered an amazing Shan tea forager-producer in the politically volatile territories between Myanmar and northern Thailand.[60] Kasper acquired 350 kilograms of a rare semi-wild tea, sheng hei cha, the start of a unique digital portfolio of small-batch borderlands teas. Siam Tee's digital market stands out for its unique definitions of borderlands sustainability: "biodiversi teas," which are "health and environment-friendly teas from biodiverse cultivation or wild collection" or "forest- and climate-friendly grown artisan teas by [a] master hand." Such novel categories such as "forest-friendly tea" acknowledge the authenticity of their indigenous plant–human histories while admitting that their making is no longer "wild."[61]

Siam Tee helped bring to world notice a tiny marketplace that unlike many others was based in the Global South. This was Tea Leaf Theory, the rare local marketplace with a global lens that valiantly sought to function from the heart of tea-growing country, Sibsagar, Assam, at the remote peripheries of India.[62] Tea Leaf Theory broke new ground in plantation-dominated India when it dared set strict producer and seller guidelines for a program of organic close-to-nature cultivation, fair prices for its participant micro-producers (across Assam, Arunachal, and Darjeeling), and fair labouring wages.[63] It ambitiously sought to challenge the established rules for a locality where the once wild camellia assamica had become a plantation commodity. British and Indian tea capitalism seemed to have almost entirely erased both assamica's indigenous histories and the potential for artisanal taste innovations. Tea Leaf Theory sought to revive, on one hand, the indigenous tea traditions of the Singpho people's smoked falap. On the other hand, it propagated such novel teas as Latumoni, birthed from a mud hut and a two-acre smallholding to reach 95 on the Tea Epicure's scale.[64] When I visited them in 2019, it was still a moot point if Tea Leaf Theory could make it. I wondered if Tea Leaf Theory's future was best used as an aggregator and mediator between such grassroots micro-producers and Global North alternative markets such as Siam Tea and Camellia Sinensis, given all the infrastructural and other challenges it faced.

We will never know that answer. During 2020, Tea Leaf Theory's slender hold in the global marketplace received a death blow from the economic and social disruptions of the COVID-19 pandemic, their impact undiluted by any form of state assistance. When I learned this melancholy news, I tasted once again in my imagination the falap tea at grower Rajesh Singpho's home. I tasted once again the exquisite craft innovation of grower Sailen Medhi's Latumoni tea made from assamica's buds and flowers. Neither grower spoke any language other than the local vernaculars. Neither had the capacity to directly sell to the global connoisseurs who now will await in vain Tea Leaf Theory's parcel dispatches all the way from Sibsagar. Old and new, new and old, traditional and innovative, such Indigenous and local teamakers of South Asia await once again the mobile marketplaces that will enable them to surmount these global South immobilities and inequities. For the time being, Siam Tee has stepped in to supply small quantities of Latumoni to the world.[65] It remains to be seen on what terms such micro-producers will function in the global marketplace of a post-pandemic world when the terms are set once again, by Global North connoisseur capitalism.

NOTES

1 Shaodong Zhai, "New Discovery at the Tianluoshan Site, Yuyao, Zhejiang Province in 2012," *Chinese Archaeology*, 17 April 2013.

2 Popular and internet sources on tea often cite the Shijing or Book of Song (ca. 1122 BCE) as the first text on tea. It does mention the use of a beverage brewed from leaves, but this cannot be authenticated as camellia sinensis. The text uses an older ideogram that referred to a variety of herbs whose leaves were consumed in this form.

3 Shaodong Zhai, "New Discovery." Also, Houyuan Lu, Jianping Zhang, Yimin Yang, Xiaoyan Yang, Baiqing Xu, Wuzhan Yang, and Tao Tong, "Earliest Tea as Evidence for One Branch of the Silk Road across the Tibetan Plateau," *Scientific Reports* 6, no. 1 (2016): 18955.

4 E.N. Anderson, *The Food of China* (New Haven: Yale University Press: 1988), 55.

5 Lu Yu and Tingcan Lu. Cha Jing. Di 1 ban. Kunming Shi: Yunnan ren min chu ban she, 2006, based on a eighteenth-century Qing-era copy by Lu Tingcan. I relied on English translations, notably a recent online one from the connoisseur website Global Tea Hut, http://archive.globalteahut.org /article/595, and an older text whose translation was commissioned for his book by tea entrepreneur, William Ukers, *All About Tea* (New York: Tea and Coffee Press, 1935).

6 Robert Gardella, *Harvesting Mountains: Fujian and the China Tea Trade, 1757–1937* (Berkeley: University of California Press, 1994), 22–3.

7 Many early modern European "cha" names were supplanted by ones derived from the dialectal sound of Fujian and southern Chinese ports, "tê." The British working-class phrase "char" survived, perhaps through

speech patterns of seamen who encountered Hindustani-speakers from colonial India, with their name, "chai." Many tea experts claim that there is a neat demarcation between the languages whose cultures encountered tea via overland routes, which use names starting with "tea," while the cultures that received tea overland, use names similar to "cha."

8 George Van Driem, *The Tale of Tea* (Leiden: Brill, 2019), 157–62.

9 Morris Rossabi, "The Tea and Horse Trade with Inner Asia during the Ming," *Journal of Asian History* 4, no. 2 (1970): 156.

10 A popular list of historical tea texts from China: http://www.chinaknowledge .de/Literature/Science/nongjia-chalei.html.

11 *Daguan Tea Treatise*, http://archive.globalteahut.org/docs/pdf_articles /2016-04/2016-04-a036.pdf.

12 Jing-nuan Wu, *An Illustrated Chinese Materia Medica* (New York: Oxford University Press, 2005).

13 Xu Guangqi, *Nong Zheng Quanshu* (Beijing: Zhonghua Suzhu, 1956); Joseph Needham, *Science and Civilization in China*, vol. 6: *Biology and Biological Technology, Part 2: Agriculture* (New York: Cambridge University Press, 1994).

14 See Paul L. Smith, *Taxing Heaven's Storehouse: Horses, Bureaucrats, and the Destruction of the Sichuan Tea Industry, 1074–1224* (Cambridge, MA: Harvard University Press, 1991).

15 Kevin Gascoyne, *Tea: History, Terroirs, Varieties* (Richmond Hill, ON: Firefly Books, 2019), 21. A cultivar is a plant species created through hybridization or mutation that has to be reproduced through cuttings, not seeds.

16 Gascoyne, *Tea*, 36.

17 Gascoyne, *Tea*, 44; Gardella, *Harvesting Mountains*, 23.

18 Gardella, *Harvesting Mountains*, 27.

19 James A. Benn, *Tea in China: A Religious and Cultural History* (Honolulu: University of Hawai'i Press, 2016). Benn debunks and historicizes the founding fables that link tea to the divine emperor Shen Nong and legends of other Buddhist savants.

20 Sōshitsu Sen, *The Japanese Way of Tea: from Its Origins in China to Sen Rikyū* (Honolulu: University of Hawai'i Press, 1994), 48.

21 George Fadlo Hourani, *Arab Seafaring in the Indian Ocean in Ancient and Early Medieval Times* (Princeton, NJ: Princeton University Press, 1951), 68.

22 Stewart Saunders, "Public Administration and the Library of Jean-Baptiste Colbert," *Libraries and Culture* 26, no. 2 (1991): 283–300.

23 Van Driem. *The Tale of Tea*, 246–8.

24 Samuel Purchas, *Purchas his Pilgrimage: Or Relations of the World and the Relations observed in all the Ages and Places Discovered, from the Creation into this Present* (London: William Stansby, 1614), 1614, 524.

25 Michael Cooper, "The Early Europeans and Tea," in *Tea in Japan: Essays on the History of Chanoyu*, ed. Paul H. Varley and Kumakura Isao (Honolulu: University of Hawai'i Press, 1989), 122.

26 Cooper, "The Early Europeans and Tea," 118.

27 John Huighen van Linschoten, *His Discours of Voyages into ye Easte [and] West Indies: Deuided into Foure Books* (London: John Wolfe, 1598).

28 Yong Liu, *The Dutch East India Company's Tea Trade with China, 1757–1781* (Leiden, The Netherlands: Brill, 2009), 2.

29 Matteo Ricci, *De Christiana Expeditione apud Sinas Suscepta ab Societate Jesu* (1616), quoted and translated by Jeremy Clarke, "Tea Jesuitica," *China Heritage Quarterly* 29 (2012); Louis J. Gallagher, *China in the Sixteenth Century: The Journals of Matthew Ricci: 1583–1610* (New York: Random House, 1953); Ronnie Po-chia Hsia, *Matteo Ricci and the Catholic Mission to China, 1583–1610: A Short History with Documents* (Indianapolis, IN: Hackett Publishing, 2016).

30 Eugenia Zuroski Jenkins, *A Taste for China: English Subjectivity and the Prehistory of Orientalism* (New York: Oxford University Press, 2013), 18–21.

31 Anne McCants, "Poor Consumers as Global Consumers: The Diffusion of Tea and Coffee Drinking in the Eighteenth Century," *Economic History Review* 61, no. S1 (2008): 172–200.

32 Philip Lawson, *The East India Company: A History* (New York: Routledge, 2014), 44–60.

33 Richard Drayton, *Nature's Government: Science, Imperial Britain and the "Improvement" of the World* (New Haven: Yale University Press, 2000), 58.

34 "William Griffith, Report on the Tea-Plant of Upper Assam," in Great Britain, Parliament: House of Commons, *Parliamentary Papers* Vol. 39, paper 63 (1839).

35 R.C.D. Baldwin, "Sir Joseph Banks and the Cultivation of Tea," *Royal Society of Arts Journal* 141, no. 5444 (1993): 813–17.

36 Kalipada Biswas, *The Original Correspondence of Sir Joseph Banks* (Kolkata, India: Royal Asiatic Society of Bengal, 1950), 185–236.

37 "Extract India Revenue Consultations, 7 January 1835"; "From Tea Committee to Revenue Department, 24 December, 1834," *Parliamentary Papers*.

38 "Letter from Andrew Charlton to Francis Jenkins, 7 November 1834," *Parliamentary Papers*.

39 "Report, Part 2, 1840–1804," in Assam Company, *Reports of the Local Board in Calcutta* (Calcutta: Samuel Smith, 1841), 12–13.

40 "Appendix 3 to Charles Bruce's Report, June 1839," *Parliamentary Papers*.

41 Jayeeta Sharma, *Empire's Garden* (Durham, NC: Duke University Press, 2011), 42–3.

42 "William Griffith, Report on the Tea-Plant of Upper Assam."

43 "Letter from Beesa Gaum Chief, 12 August 1843," *Foreign Consultations and Proceedings* Vol. 96, National Archives of India.

44 Jayeeta Sharma, "'Lazy' Natives, Coolie Labour, and the Assam Tea Industry," *Modern Asian Studies* 43, no. 6 (2009): 1287–1324.

45 Sergey Prokudin-Gorski, "Tea Factory in Chakva: Chinese Foreman Lau-Dzhen-Dzhau," Prokudin-Gorski Photograph Collection, Library of Congress, https://www.loc.gov/pictures/item/2018679751/.

46 Jason Lim, *Linking an Asian Transregional Commerce in Tea* (Leiden: Brill, 2010).

47 Gary Sigley, "Tea and China's Rise: Tea, Nationalism and Culture in the Twenty-First Century," *International Communication of Chinese Culture* 2, no. 3 (2015): 319–41.

48 Oxfam and the Ethical Tea Partnership, *Report 2013.* See also the documentary film *Assam's Modern Slaves: The Real Price of a Cup of Tetley Tea,* https://www.theguardian.com/global-development/video/2014/mar/01/tetley-tea-maids-real-price-cup-tea-video.

49 Genevieve LeBaron, ed., *Researching Forced Labour in the Global Economy: Methodological Challenges and Advances* (New York: Oxford University Press, 2019).

50 "How Poverty Wages for Tea Pickers Fuel India's Trade in Child Slavery," *The Guardian,* 20 July 2013.

51 Eric Tagliacozzo, Helen F. Siu, and Peter C. Perdue, "Introduction: Seekers, Sojourners, and Meaningful Worlds in Motion," in *Asia Inside Out: Itinerant People,* ed. Eric Tagliacozzo, Helen F. Siu, and Peter C. Perdue (Cambridge, MA: Harvard University Press, 2019), 1–28.

52 National Campaign on Labour Rights, *Brewed in the Sweat of Forced Labour: A Fact Finding Report on the Conditions of Tea Plantation Labour in West Bengal and Assam* (New Delhi: NCLR, 2000).

53 Press Trust of India, "Biggest Threat from Small Growers," *Business Standard,* 8 November 2019.

54 John John, "Alienating Commercial Crop or A Re-appropriated Native Crop: The Changing Teascape in Assam," unpublished paper, 2019. Dr John John is an academic-activist change-maker deeply involved with a sustainable network of 250,000 indigenous Bodo, Garo, Karbi, and Khasi small tea growers, organized into the Grassroots Tea Corporation Private Limited, which has begun directly marketing its tea under an Equifarm label, www.grassrootstea.in.

55 Slow Food represents one such confluence. See the handful of entries in its Ark of Taste that document local teas, such as https://www.fondazioneslowfood.com/en/ark-of-taste-slow-food/pingyang-huangtang-tea.

56 https://camellia-sinensis.com/en/blog/producer-of-the-moment-kunihiro-yoshimoto;https://camellia-sinensis.com/en/blog/producer-of-the-moment-m-huang-wen.

57 Gascoyne, "Harnessing the Inherent Charm and Potential of Farm and Forest Tea."
58 Gascoyne, "Harnessing the Inherent Charm and Potential of Farm and Forest Tea."
59 https://www.siam-teas.com/shop/.
60 https://siamteas.com/project-shan-tea/project-shan-tea/.
61 https://www.siam-teas.com/product-tag/forest-friendly-tea/.
62 https://siamteas.com/siam-teabloid-2/siam-teabloid-vol-2019/the-tea-leaf-theory-an-all-india-organic-small-tea-growers-association/.
63 https://www.tealeaftheory.com/tribal-n-traditional-tea/singpho-tea/singpho-falap-4-years-smoked-bamboo-tea-/37/ and https://www.tealeaftheory.com/about-us/: Interviews with Upamanyu Barkataki of Tea Leaf Therory, Reba G., Koliapani micro-producer, and Sailen P. Latumoni micro-producer, November–December 2019, Assam, India.
64 https://teaepicure.com/2019-autumn-exquisite-black-assam-latumoni/. The weblinks are still extant, but since late 2020, the company no longer responds to inquiries.
65 https://www.siam-teas.com/product/latumoni-royal-tippy-assam-first-flush-black-tea/.

PART THREE

Mobilities and Immobilities

8 Street Food and Street Life in Immigrant Enclaves: A Case Study of the Jews of the United States

HASIA R. DINER

Food made the Jewish street in its many diaspora iterations. It did so in certain distinctive ways, but as far as the essential framework, it reflected all immigrant communities regardless of where women and men came from, in which new homes they planted themselves, and when. The linkage between the street, Jewish or not, and American or not, and food pivots around business as a crucial element in immigrant and ethnic life and the reality that particularly among economically marginal people, shopping takes place locally and enclave denizens own and operate the food businesses.

Shopkeepers and customers speak the same language. They share calendars, knowing when holidays and other key moments punctuate ordinary time, and that those special days require special foods. Both partners in this exchange know whether they observe or not the religious taboos and requirements associated with food. The small-scale business of food, the constant exchange of money for edible goods, breathed life into immigrant neighbourhoods, embodying their residents' literal tastes and aspirations, and forging relationships along lines of class, age, and gender. The purchase and purveying of food along with other goods, the extension of credit to those who had to eat, and the social life that went on in food shops, connected immigrants with their co-ethnics, the co-residents of their enclaves.

Mobilities coursed through these activities. As the buyers and sellers had moved from one place to another, they both brought with them ideas about consumption nurtured elsewhere and tastes, attitudes, and opportunities shaped by their new place of residence. Mobility involved as well the scurrying through the streets from home to marketplaces, and additionally, the long history of moving from one neighbourhood to another. In each new place they moved to, they once again both recreated elements from the old enclave to the circumstances of the new one, and opted for new formats in terms of type of food, shopping conditions, and transportation.

These movements came with nostalgia for the familiar and the excitement of novelty. These two at times jarred with each other, yet at other times harmonized. The movements of Jewish foodways, whether from overseas origin to the destination land or from area of first settlement to the second and beyond pivoted around certain details. Jewish consumers and Jewish food entrepreneurs operated and at times conflicted with each other within the web of assumed commonality and shared identities. Some among them owned the markets, whether grocery stores, general or specializing in a particular item, as well as the bakeries, food carts, butcher shops, saloons, and cafes, earning their bread, as it were, from the fact that their neighbours spent money there. Flipping the perspective, the residents of the neighbourhood frequented these commercial food venues and ensured the livelihoods of their neighbour entrepreneurs. Both needed each other, and the system grew out of common roots, shared tastes, and trust between sellers and buyers.

Furthermore, the larger the enclave, the more bakeries, meat markets, pushcarts, cafes, and the like competed with each other for the patronage and hard-earned money of the enclaves' immigrant denizen. The men and women of the immigrant neighbourhood could spell the difference between success and failure of one vendor or another, forcing entrepreneurs to offer the best goods for the best prices with the most helpful service possible. Historically these transactions took place on walking streets, and those streets provided the locus for community interaction. It may not be an exaggeration to say that this took place in all immigrant neighbourhoods, and this simple reality shaped the lives of all migrant populations, at all times, certainly over the course of American history.

Only the amount of attention that scholars have given to this subject and the extent of the documentation available to study this phenomenon differentiated communities from one another. Some immigrant populations have left behind and archived more material than others. While all stories of food, marketing, and the immigrant street would offer rich and detailed histories, some have merely saved more of the words generated by the consumers, merchants, and observers who considered this matter worth recording. Unearthing primary documents would allow for studies of the street food cultures of French Canadians in Manchester, New Hampshire; Syrians in Mexico City; Italians in Buenos Aires; Greeks in Melbourne; Poles in Chicago; Chinese in Cuba; and on and on. Each history would have its particular twists and would reveal idiosyncratic patterns, but all would conform to the basic principle that the ethnic streets, inhabited by immigrants and their immediate offspring, served, among other functions, to feed the enclave and to structure relationships around that basic yet complicated act. The complicated processes involved in the purveying and purchasing of goods within Jewish communities can and ought to be historicized and divided into categories of analysis, yet always linked to ideas about community. The ordinariness of selling and shopping did not make the matter historically irrelevant. Rather, the quotidian commercial concerns of Jewish communities gave them deep social, cultural, and political meanings.[1]

Businesses both large and small, wholesale and retail, served larger communal purposes well beyond the history of Jews in America or anywhere. As one historian of shopping as a factor in English social history noted, "Wherever we live, whoever we are, our shopping is very much a reflection of ourselves."[2] Most of the literature, however, has tended to emphasize the nature of goods up for sale, patterns of consumption, and changing tastes.[3] Few, either focusing on the United States or elsewhere, and whether historically based or concerned with the contemporary, have twinned the idea of community with that of commerce.

Yet shopping streets, wherever and whenever they developed, functioned as common space, places where individuals met, interacted, saw what they shared with each other, and in the process of buying and selling carved out a zone for public life. Immigrants or indeed long-time residents of any country or region engaged in the constant everyday business of getting food, defining streets as places to get something to eat. In the context of American history, we have examples from a number of subfields as to the importance of retail space in the forging of community ties. Studies of small-town life, both the empirical and the nostalgic, have made much about the country store as a gathering place that bound people together. Lewis Atherton in his 1954 homage to the dying small towns of the Midwest, the "middle border," offered an entire chapter to the shopping areas of the towns that served primarily farm families. In particular he pointed to the classic general store, a place where men and women congregated in different areas and where "close to the stove and the conversation" the shopkeeper tallied his ledger and supervised the flow of the shopping. *Main Street on the Middle Border* also made emotionally and historically significant the barbershops, hotels, saloons, and livery stables that lined the village thoroughfares and where men and women met, bought, sold, talked, and made community.[4]

The Reifel store in Four Corners, Iowa, a town analyzed by historian Carol Coburn, provided the men of this rural, heavily German community with "a gathering place at night [...] where they gathered to exchange the latest news." The store, as analyzed by Coburn, served as the least problematic, and most positive, common denominator for the men who otherwise divided over matters of politics, religious doctrine, and the lure of American culture. Only the store functioned as an uncontested community space.[5]

The histories of all minority communities, like the German enclave of Four Corners, could be told from the vantage point of the ethnic marketplace and the multiple functions served by the buying and selling of goods within the community. No immigrant or ethnic community existed without the commercial infrastructure in which group members shopped in stores owned by co-ethnics, and in particular imagined those shops to be key places to fulfil group needs. John Bodnar has elevated the ethnic merchants in *The Transplanted* to their rightful place as community leaders, noting in this broad synthetic book, that "[i]n every settlement a group emerged to pursue entrepreneurial ventures which depended upon the support of the immigrant community." He offered bits and pieces of evidence drawn from numerous histories of various groups that demonstrated how ethnic neighbourhood businesses served "neighbourhood clienteles," although he did not go much further than that in analyzing the role played by those stores in enabling communities to form.[6]

The historical scholarship on nearly every ethnic group has been replete with listings and descriptions of food establishments, bookstores, music stores, taverns, and clothing stores that through commerce made it possible to "be" a participant in the ethnic project. The more sophisticated of these studies, like George Sanchez's *Becoming Mexican American*, put such ethnic businesses squarely into the analytic framework, showing how merchants and consumers mediated between remembered formats from the places they left and American realities, and how the stores functioned as meeting places for Mexicans in Los Angeles, thereby creating sites for the growing community. In Sanchez's Boyle Heights not only did the merchants who owned record shops, clothing stores, and food shops arbitrate between the many musical, dress, and gustatory formats derived from various regions in Mexico and between those defined as Mexican versus American, but also the music emanating from the shops, the dresses on the racks, and the smells wafting out to the streets drew customers in, put them in conversation with the merchants, with each other, and solidified notions of Mexicanness and community membership.[7] Lizabeth Cohen's *Making a New Deal* charted the close relationships that existed in Chicago's immigrant neighbourhoods between shopkeepers and customers, co-ethnics. The former not only provided needed goods to the latter but also offered credit to struggling families, thus becoming brokers in the political and economic life of the communities. In all these places, though, food loomed largest as the item that crossed the counter from seller to buyer.[8]

This is a subject that for the most part has not received its due. Few historians studying ethnic communities in the United States have done more than mention in passing the vast amount of commerce that linked merchants and customers of the various enclaves. Histories of one group or another contain what might be seen as an obligatory paragraph or two on the range of stores that community members favoured and sustained, drawing attention to which goods shoppers preferred, but historians have, by and large, not paused longer to actually study the phenomenon directly, systematically, or thoroughly.

Rather, political scientists and sociologists studying post-1965 immigration have drawn our attention to the analytic gravitas of entrepreneurship (and consumership) in the construction of ethnic communities. Ivan Light and Edna Bonacich, for example, in their study of Korean *Immigrant Entrepreneurs* in Los Angeles have provided a theoretical model that identified an entity they called "the ethnic economy," which, unlike the "ethnic *enclave* economy" did not require "locational clustering of ethnic firms, nor does it require that ethnic firms service members of their ethnic group as customers or buy from coethnic suppliers."[9] Like sociologist Alejandro Portes in his numerous studies of the Cuban enclave economy of Miami, Light and Bonacich saw significant analytic significance in the social, economic, and political implications of the clustering of Korean-owned businesses located in the heart of Los Angeles' "Korean Town," and the almost inexorable draw of those stores for the residents of the neighbourhood.

Jewish Communities as Food Communities

Jewish communities have for millennia served as places where Jews worshipped together, provided charity, protected each other, and fulfilled basic religious needs including marriage, burial, circumcision, and education, where Jews bought food from other Jews, and where Jews sold to their co-religionists.

Indeed, the life of Jewish enclaves, stretching back in time as far back as evidence exists, illustrated in the pages of the Talmud compiled at the turn of the Common Era, hummed around the constant flurry of buying and selling that took place on the Jewish street with no clear line separating the religious, social, and political definitions of Jewish community and the flow of goods among Jews. Rather, commercial transactions and the comings and goings of the Jewish marketplace made the other, presumably loftier, functions possible, at the same time that stores and other kinds of commercial places often did double duty as either formal or informal community centres and as places that sustained religious functions. The particularities of Jewish street life and its relationship to food involved the complex issue of the Jewish dietary laws. For food to be kosher, that is, acceptable, meant that it had to conform to standards inscribed in Jewish law, *halachah*. Jews had to buy their food from those whom they trusted to observe the strictures of the system and for the most part, eschewed buying food from non-Jews.

The world of the Jewish food marketplace also took its particular tempo from the flow of the Jewish calendar. Food in general and certain foods in particular had to be available in greater abundance to greet the Sabbath than at other times in the week. Every holiday had its distinctive foods, and while different foods showed up on Jewish tables around the world, the holidays were same. For Passover, Purim, Shavuot, and other festivals, Jewish consumers expected their food merchants to have available the necessary stuff to make the holiday truly holy. Customers demanded that Jewish entrepreneurs satisfy their yearnings for particular foods, at specified times, and in particular ways. Consumer and entrepreneur depended upon each other to make sacred time, spinning a web of reciprocal relationships that bound them together through the commerce of food.

While conflict sometimes characterized intra-Jewish commercial transactions, the degree to which Jews depended upon each other for basic and special goods invested the entrepreneurial sector with cultural meaning and put food at the centre of their street life. Whether the commercial transactions functioned smoothly and harmoniously or conflict arose as the two groups sparred with each other over such matters as cost versus quality, their continuous interactions created a common business zone, requiring daily intimate connections. Whole histories of Jewish communities could in fact be told from the vantage point of the mundane reality that wherever Jews lived they sold to and bought from each other, and the shopping street, no less than the synagogue, the study house, the ritual bath, cemetery, or community centre forged the bonds of mutuality.

Doubtless neither buyers nor merchants thought about the deeper meaning of what they did when they exchanged a loaf of bread, a bunch of radishes, a hunk of cheese, or any other quotidian goods for money. They likely did not imagine that their transactions constituted historically significant behaviour, probably not thinking at all beyond the shelves and the cash registers in the stores and the larders and cabinets of their homes.

The American Jewish Street and Its Food Stories

Enclave food commerce ran through all of American Jewish history, which points to the intricate links between business and the ways in which American Jews lived in their Jewish communities. Not only did the buying and selling of Jewish "stuff" have long historic roots but also those ordinary, constantly repeated commercial acts lay close to the heart of what it meant for American Jews to live in their Jewish communities. American Jews invested meaning in their marketplaces and defined them as key sites in the construction of both identity and lived life.

In terms of types of Jewish commercial transactions as they lay at the centre of the history of Jewish community life, a number of categories suggest themselves. First, some of the goods that flowed along the Jewish commercial chain fell clearly in the domain of what has commonly been assumed to be essential to the practice of Judaism. As such the commercial sector never stood apart from the religious. Merchants who sold kosher foods, those who marketed particular delicacies associated with Sabbath and holidays, those who enticed customers with new clothing for festivals, as well as the merchants who displayed new pots and pans, crockery and cutlery, in the weeks before Passover provided the material underpinnings that enabled holy time to be marked and lived. Likewise, the sellers of books, almanacs, greeting cards, magazines, candles, and various objects that carried religious or ethnic valence, acted through the medium of their commercial transaction as religious functionaries. Their displaying and selling of particular "things" on a weekly or seasonal basis fostered a Jewish tone and helped infuse the streets with a sense of Jewish time.

For those who purchased these goods, their many and repeated acts of shopping and the range of merchants they depended upon to secure these goods, all made possible such sacred acts as marking the Sabbath, making the holiday, and fulfilling a continuous set of other religious mandates. Indeed, given the degree to which Judaism functioned first and foremost as a home- and family-based religious system, the masses of Jews depended more upon merchants and their stores in order to perform Jewish rituals than they did upon synagogues and rabbis. As such, the commercial life of the Jewish street cannot be distinguished from the performance of religious as it stood at the forefront of getting ready for ritual activities.

The literature as it exists now, despite the fact that few have scholars have devoted much specific attention to the web of relationships that linked Jewish shops to Jewish community life, already offers many examples of how places of Jewish commerce served simultaneously as places that dispensed Jewish news, fostered Jewish interactions, and made possible the provision of Jewish services. Ewa Morawska in her study of the small Jewish enclave in Johnstown, Pennsylvania, for example, described how the kosher butcher shop that opened up in 1903 stood next to the railroad station. In her study, that kosher market "served as a referral service for passengers just off the train. If they were transients, travel assistance was provided by women of the *Hakhnoses Orkhim*, a society constituted to provide aid to wayfarers." The implications of this small detail bear thinking about as we imagine community.[10]

The Jews of Johnstown supported a butcher shop by spending their money there on food that they believed Judaism obliged them to consume, and the women of Johnstown banded together to create a formal society that ministered to the needs of Jews in transit from one place to another. Placing the butcher shop near the railroad station may not have been done specifically to fulfil a communal obligation – *hachnassat orchim* – but rather it may have been just good business act. But its physical location, prominently placed nearby the depot, made possible the intricate fusion of economic, philanthropic, and religious needs, all of which sustained the community of Jews in Johnstown and which by implication made the Jewish community of Johnstown a player in the creation of a larger American Jewish community.

While some kinds of business establishments, like kosher markets, clearly depended upon Judaism and Jewish law, as well as on a network of Jewish religious functionaries, other stores like those that sold household wares, clothing, stationary, and the like also served Jewish functions. Stores that lined the Jewish street did not have to sell specifically Jewish goods in order to play a role in the creation of Jewish community life. Again, a small detail in the scholarship winks at us, pointing out that the entrepreneurial sector intersected with the communal, indeed fostered it.

Food businesses defined Jewish community in the broadest sense of the concept. This same point has emerged as an analytic detail in writing about the other end of the century. Historian Gerald Gamm, in a study subtitled *Why the Jews Left Boston and the Catholics Stayed,* documented the entrepreneurial Jewish infrastructure of the community that its merchants and customers abandoned. After ticking off the number of kosher butcher shops supported by the Jews who shopped along Blue Hill Avenue, as well as the bakeries, groceries, and fruit markets, Gamm put the G&G delicatessen onto historic center stage, as *the* place that "gave the district its special character." Quoting from a local newspaper, Gamm offered an insight into the close connection between the making of Jewish community and the existence of particular commercial establishments. The article deserves here to be quoted at some length. Referring to the delicatessens of the neighbourhood the reporter noted:

> Of all the fortresses only one reached the proportions, could claim palatial amenities that testify to high culture, that immense landmark which any traveller who has passed down Blue Hill avenue will smile in recognition of, the G&G. On the tables of the cafeteria Talmudic jurisprudence sorted out racing results, politics, the stock market, and the student could look up from his "desk" to leer at the young girls sipping cream soda under the immense wings of their mothers; watch the whole world of Blue Hill avenue revolve through the G&G's glass gate.

The dissolution of the Jewish neighbourhood of Dorchester, a dense Jewish residential community by all accounts, according to Gamm, can be marked less by the moving of the synagogues than by the final closing of the "glass gate," the end of the food businesses.[11]

Gamm's reference to this quite mundane eatery did not constitute the first scholarly valorization of it as a dense, powerful, and magnetic Jewish communal institution. Hillel Levine and Lawrence Harmon in their 1992 study of Boston Jewry, aptly entitled *The Death of an American Jewish Community*, also focused on decline following "the glory years" of Blue Hill Avenue. They placed the delicatessen at the centre of the Jewish community's political and social history and went so far as to declare that it "enjoyed the greatest drawing power of any institution in the Jewish community." Politicians, Jewish and non-Jewish, eager to win the Jewish vote made an obligatory pilgrimage to the G&G, for example. Indeed, so central a role did it play in bringing Jews together and providing them with a place to be with other Jews, that, if asked to free-associate about Jewish Boston, former residents invariably utter "the G&G [...] a place to dine, cut deals, and evaluate prospective sons-in-law." Levine and Harmon asserted, suggestively, that the intellectual and religious leadership of the community expressed disdain, and possibly jealousy, for the G&G and resented the fact that it competed with schools, synagogues, and more refined places of Jewish communal life. The authors asserted that "those charged with shaping the community" actually "struggled for ways to get people off the Avenue and into the classroom or clubhouse." To no avail, since, at least in the realm of meaning and memory, while many Boston Jews did attend classes at the Hebrew Teacher's College, "few former residents think first of Hebrew College when reminiscing of the old neighbourhood. That place of honour belonged to the G&G."[12]

While Gamm, and before him Levine and Harmon, identified a few dozen Jewish food establishments alone as key places in the community's self-conception as distinctive and as providing for its own needs, other and larger Jewish enclaves supported even more retail establishments where Jews sold to each other, congregated, and did business in a dense Jewish environment. New York obviously stood in a category by itself, as a mammoth and complicated place for Jewish marketing and Jewish community. An 1899 survey of New York's Eighth Assembly District, which encompassed parts of the immigrant neighbourhood, listed no fewer than 631 food establishments that

> catered to the needs of the inhabitants of this area. Most numerous were the 140 groceries which often sold fruits, vegetables, bread and rolls, as well as the usual provisions. Second in number were the 131 butcher shops which proclaimed their wares in Hebrew letters. The other food vendors included 36 bakeries, 9 bread stands, 14 butter and eggs stores, 24 candy stands, 62 candy stores, 1 cheese store, 7 combination two-cent coffee shops, 10 delicatessens, 9 fish stores, 7 fruit stores, 21 fruit stands, 3 grocery stands, 7 herring stands, 2 meat markets, 16 milk stores, 2 matzo [...] stores, 10 sausage stores, 20 soda water stands, 5 tea shops, [...] 11 vegetable stores, 13 wine shops, 15 grape wine shops, and 10 confectioners.[13]

One of many immigrant era memoirs, Harry Roskolenko's *The Time That Was Then* recalled "flamboyant displays" of food, of "bakeries, with their pushcart adjuncts," that sold the various breads of the world. Russian, Polish, Hungarian, Austrian, German – all heavy, all good, all the breads with or without every variation of kimel, or caraway seed, were there. He went on to remember Orchard Street, "devoted to the enormous barrels of brine containing herring from every part of the world," and his mother with her "big shopping bag. The bag was cavernous, capable of containing fifty pounds of herring, potatoes, huge amounts of black bread, smoked fish, red cabbage for the borscht."[14]

If to every one of these places a steady stream of Jewish women and men came in and out, stopping to talk to the shopkeeper and to the other customers, exchanging news, finding out about each other's fortunes and misfortunes, then we can see how the profusion of retail establishments on the Jewish street created a thick space for making community. The photographic record of that Eighth Assembly District, that is, the Lower East Side, testified to the intensity of the street life and the degree which commercial activities drew Jews out of their apartments and into the public spaces, talking as well as buying, interacting as well as inspecting merchandise, drawn to food, and in the process shaping life on the street.

Likewise, for decades Jews who had once lived on the Lower East Side, but then moved out to newer areas in the Bronx and Brooklyn, trekked back to the "old neighbourhood" to shop. Memoirs told and retold the details of Jews from other parts of New York coming to the Lower East Side before Passover to buy nuts, dried fruit, and wine, returning on Sunday mornings for bargains on clothing as well as for pickles and "appetizing," and finally, in a nearly religious act tantamount to a pilgrimage, fathers brought their pre–bar mitzvah sons to the "sacred space" to purchase a *tallith* in anticipation of their thirteenth birthdays. Each one of these acts of Jewish shopping not only helped make the Lower East Side the crucible of American Jewish memory culture but in the process played a part in creating the key narrative of community in its most authentic form.

The quest for Jewish foods, defined as authentic by those who left the immigrant enclaves hardly limited itself to New York. On the other coast in Los Angeles, by the 1930s Jews, mostly immigrants from eastern Europe who had achieved some economic mobility and left Boyle Heights, the area of first settlement, returned to the city to eat. One writer chronicled the trek of those who arrived in their "'ritzy' cars, from Beverly Hills [...] unloading Jews who would think of 'living in Boyle Heights,' but who are tied to the Ghetto by a bond that is stronger than race or religion – the mouth-watering desire for a good piece of Russian rye bread, a herring [...] and a lox sandwich." The writer labelled these returners, "Gustatorial Jews coming back to give lip and tooth service to their own people."[15]

Jewish commercial life not only sustained ritual practice and provided the spaces where Jewish socializing and community building activities could happen but also the ways in which different groups used those places reveal to historians some of the fissures that divided communities. No issue demonstrates this more sharply than that of gender. Jewish women and men had different, albeit linked, histories of commerce and community. The business sector of the Jewish street, in big cities and in smaller ones, provided a crucial zone for the performance of gender roles, a crucial element in the fabric of community life. For one, street-level businesses brought men and women together as both husbands and wives "manned" the stores, suggesting a host of questions.

To what degree did the small-business sector, the shops along the Jewish main street, employ the labour of all family members rather than function as the sole domain of male or female entrepreneurs? What role did married women play in these stores and how did their entrepreneurial activities enhance their authority within the family? How did Jewish women's involvement in these shops and stores limit their options? A range of first-hand accounts bear witness to the ways in which Jewish women as shopkeepers blurred any kind of line between the public world of selling food and the private one of preparing food for one's family. Countless numbers of Jewish shops doubled as places of residence where families lived above and behind "the store." Mary Antin offered a description in her lyrical autobiography of how her mother tended the store and "in the intervals of slack trade, she did her cooking. [...] Arlington Street customers were used to waiting while the storekeeper [her mother] salted the soup or rescued a loaf from the oven." Hers may be the most famous depiction of a phenomenon that predominated among Jewish entrepreneurial families and existed literally everywhere immigrant Jewish families operated small businesses.[16]

Small business meant family business. Some women actually operated independent businesses of their own, continuing the European tradition of multiple enterprises within a single nuclear family: one belonging to the husband, the other to the wife. However, most Jewish small businesses in America involved husband and wife working together. While both men and women, recalling memories of the past, may have defined their small business as a place in which women "helped" out in the men's stores, a different kind of pattern emerges from the on-the-ground descriptions of how these stores actually functioned, with Mary Antin's as an exemplar. Husbands and wives worked in a symbiotic relationship as they both struggled to make the business profitable.

Men often decided that when they married they could transition from being someone else's employee to being self-employed. Entrepreneurship, particularly small-scale, street-level business, rarely involved single men, and being married meant that they, whether former sweatshop workers, garment factory labourers, or peddlers, now had their lifelong partners behind counters and cash registers. The Jewish men who arrived in America and went out on the road to peddle finally married or brought over their wives only when they had the means to open a shop. In numerous cases, the erstwhile peddlers continued, at times, to sell from the road while their wives operated the in-town stores.[17] For Jewish women, marriage meant leaving behind the garment factories where they laboured as hired hands and becoming "helpers" or better still, unofficial co-owners of grocery stores, bakeries, delicatessens, dress shops, and dry goods emporia.

One story, like the hundreds of thousands that left few archived records, involves Harry Cohen, who came to Baltimore in 1906 from Chernigov, Russia, with his brother. His family had been food purveyors back home, and Cohen hoped to replicate this in America, albeit at a higher level. Realizing this dream, however, had to wait. He first took a job with Schloss Brothers, a garment shop, as a buttonhole maker and presser, living simply and saving his money. In 1913, he took the first step towards fulfilling his aspirations by marrying Sarah Kaplansky, also an immigrant from Russia. He continued working at Schloss Brothers while she took in boarders and laundry, continuing to earn an income after marriage. For six years, Sarah and Harry scrimped and saved, and eventually had enough to invest in a business. By 1919 they had saved enough to buy a building at 1427 East Baltimore Street. Living on the upper floor, they operated a delicatessen on the ground level. Although Sarah continued to take in boarders and do laundry for others over the course of an unrecorded number of years, she also waited on the customers in the restaurant, prepared kugel, latkes, and knishes and baked the challah, while Harry did the work that publicly defined the enterprise as his. He cured and sliced the meat, the "stuff" intrinsically associated with the world of the delicatessen, but she engaged with the customers, presumably using her personal qualities to make them feel welcome and ensure return visits to the business.[18]

Variations of these themes fill American Jewish oral history and reminiscence literature. Although these stories have not been systematically studied heretofore, they point to a rich focus for the study of gender. Women and men came together in the realm of small businesses, and family stores existed because women and men laboured there together. In most cases, at some point or other in the history of these stores, the family lived above or behind the shop, further merging the traditionally male sphere of the marketplace and the culturally sanctioned women's work at home.

So, too, the consumers of the Jewish shopping districts divided and converged along gendered lines, bringing out both Jewish women and men in search of goods. Some sources indicate that they divided their responsibilities as to who bought what. Louis Wirth in the 1927 study *The Ghetto* declared that in the Chicago Maxwell Street market, "Thursday is 'chicken day,' when Jewish customers lay in their supplies for the Friday evening meal. Most of the purchasing is done by the men, who take a much more active part in the conduct of the household and the kitchen than is the case among non-Jewish immigrant groups. The man sees that the chicken is properly killed for if something should go wrong, he, as the responsible head of the household, would have to bear the sin." Buying the fish, however, he observed, fell more squarely in women's domain on this same Jewish street. As such, Wirth suggested that a gendered shopping world existed and this in turn offers us another way of seeing how the world of consumption in Jewish neighbourhoods is rife with analytic possibilities.[19]

Statements like these provide tantalizing hints that indicate that gender and gender relations underlay the commercial life of the Jewish street. They help us see that full-scale histories of Jewish communities as places where Jews bought from and sold to each other have to be refracted through the lens of gender. That Jewish women and men have experienced migration, adaptation, and the process of community building differently, rests at the centre of our historic understanding. That they experienced America as a place of conflict also figures prominently as an accepted element in our understanding of the past.[20]

The commercial zone can provide yet one other place where this gender struggle played itself out. Paula Hyman has certainly shown this in her classic article on the kosher meat boycotts that raged in New York at the turn of the twentieth century. Those food fights pitted Jewish women, the consumers who considered themselves and their families to be entitled to the right to consume meat at a fair price within their means, against Jewish male merchants, the butchers, who had behind them the communal leadership, the slaughterers, and the rabbis. As the women saw it, the merchants, as Jews, had a responsibility to provide kosher meat to them, as custodians of their families' consumption. They demanded that the business of kosher meat be conducted with their sensibilities and pocketbooks in mind. The women's demands underscored the degree to which marketing and community functioned as fused categories. The drama that played out in front of the butcher shops, and in the pages of Hyman's article, demonstrate the degree to which commerce, community, gender, and conflict all need to be considered as pivotal forces in Jewish history.[21]

The size of a community as well as the gendered nature of community life reflected itself in the realm of Jewish shopping. From the early twentieth century onward, Jewish visitors who came to New York from the "hinterlands" commented in awe about the great metropolis as a place to buy Jewish goods. The sheer size of New York's Jewish community made possible a diversity of markets whereby Jewish "things" could be consumed. The ability to buy Jewish goods – books, ritual objects, and pickles – on the Lower East Side added to its sanctity and made it in the process a metaphor for the image of an organic and dense Jewish community.

Likewise, in any number of memoirs or autobiographical fragments American Jews who had grown up and lived outside of New York described, as did art historian Alan Schoener, how a visit to the Lower East Side evoked a sense of Jewish connectedness through what could be bought on its streets. "I found myself," he wrote, "roaming around Delancey Street and Second Avenue, eating food that my mother never cooked."[22] He connected emotionally to a metaphoric sense of Jewish community through those rambles and through those acts of consumption. In order to eat that food, which transported him to a time when the neighbourhood had been a dense Jewish enclave, he had to pay money to a merchant, be it the vendor of a cart, the owner of a restaurant, or the proprietor of a store. Schoener, like so many other Jewish voyagers to the old immigrant enclave reconnected to a mythic community by means of a commercial transaction. (Schoener went on to curate the Jewish Museum's exhibit, "Portal to America," itself a powerful text in the furthering of the idea that the Lower East Side constituted a formative site in the construction of American Jewish communal identity.)[23]

These commercial transactions between Jews, in whichever century they took place, had tremendous impact on the nature of community life and community self-understanding. Although Jews sold to non-Jews historically more often than they sold to other Jews, the close connections that developed between Jewish merchants and local Jewish buying publics helped sustain Jewish space and Jewish community. By patronizing neighbourhood merchants and transforming shopping places into community spaces, Jewish consumers in concert with the merchants whom they may at times have conflicted with over quality and price, nevertheless helped make the personal public, and the private communal. Memoirs, autobiographies, as well as a vast number of journalistic sources, described often in exquisite detail the ways in which Jews in cities and towns in many lands and several continents congregated in Jewish stores and shops. Here they mixed together their buying of fish, meat, wine, bread, hats, and socks with the spreading of community news, the selling of notions with debates over notions of community priorities. The stores and shops provided places to gossip, sites for planning public activities, as well as venues for getting the goods defined as both necessary and desirable.[24]

The literature on American Jewish history, despite its relative silence about small neighbourhood business as something that mattered, does point to a number of crucial eras. The first era, the one which extended into the early decades of the nineteenth century relied on the imposition of a pre-modern European Jewish (and also colonial style) model of high levels of community control in which Jewish merchants who served the Jewish public had to submit to community control.[25] Those goods that Jews saw as crucial to the practice of Judaism – kosher wine, kosher meat, and matzah in particular – rather than flowing to customers through independently owned and operated stores that needed to woo the public to come and buy in competition with others selling the same goods, instead fell into the domain of the congregation – only one per city – which enjoyed a monopoly on the provision of such goods. Those congregations could withhold goods from Jews who deviated from community standards of behaviour, and enterprising entrepreneurs had no chance of setting up their own businesses. That the goods came from the congregations also made for a kind of subterranean Jewish market. We have no evidence that shops with Hebrew letters, marked with words like "kosher" or "Jewish," graced the streets of early America.[26] While the Jewish women and men who inhabited these early communities made a living primarily in commerce, in the selling of various kinds of goods to the general public, Jewish goods came to Jews through the regulated world of the congregations.

Hyman Grinstein in his pathbreaking history of the Jews of New York, the first of the notable community biographies that dominated the scholarship in the mid-twentieth century, introduced the community–commerce nexus as early as the third page of the book. Grinstein asserted in this introduction that the key moment in the history of the community, a moment that presaged later diversification, seen by some as disunity and the decline of authority, came about in 1812 when a brief, unsuccessful breakaway from Shearith Israel, the only congregation in the city, went out and hired its own *shohet*. While the "rift was soon healed" and "Shearith Israel continued to supervise the sealing and sale of kosher food," a powerful trajectory had been set on its course. The universal practice that had prevailed in America since the end of the seventeenth century that the one congregation that existed in each city with an organized Jewish presence maintained total control over the selling of kosher food began to unravel.

Instead, under the "broad concept of liberty which existed in America," commercial individualism flourished and competition between congregations and merchants became the norm. The communities unravelled in the face of the "climate of freedom" and a culture of enterprise infused the Jewish commercial world no less than it came to suffuse nearly all aspects of American life.[27]

With that unravelling there ensued a long period, from the 1820s through possibly the 1960s, in which Jewish community life derived much of its impetus and structure from the vibrant and flamboyant tone of the commercial transactions of the Jewish street. In that extended history, in one city after another, Jewish neighbourhoods became distinctive in large measure because of what got sold and bought on their streets, and how. Jews went out onto streets in the ordinary course of life, making the purchases of necessities and luxuries in company with other Jews, shopping at stores owned by their co-ethnics. Street, store, and living spaces flowed into one another as being Jewish in large measure meant shopping and consuming Jewish. That marketplace culture flowered in every city where Jews lived and existed in its particular way until the age of suburbanization, when the rise of the low-density automobile culture created a set of new realities.

In the years when the streets of Jewish neighbourhoods functioned as Jewish marketplaces, merchants had to court the Jewish buying public. The signs, advertisements, hawking, and pulling-in, all tactics designed to attract customers, gave the Jewish streets their particular appearance, announcing to all that these streets constituted Jewish space. Alfred Kazin describing his Brownsville of the 1920s, remarked looking backward from the late 1940s, how the "electric sign […] lighting up the words Jewish National Delicatessen" made him and the others who used this Brooklyn street, Pitkin Avenue, as their turf, feel "as if we had entered into our rightful heritage."[28]

The needs of ordinary Jewish women and men to buy particular foods and the desire of the Jewish shopkeepers, also quite ordinary Jewish women and men, to win over the consumers meshed. In that meeting place between Jewish consumers and Jewish entrepreneurs, although conflicts between the two groups flared with frequency, the sense of community flourished. Stories embodying this theme can be drawn from nearly every history written about every American Jewish enclave. A few examples will have to suffice.

Thinking back about all that he had seen in his life, Isaac Mayer Wise, in his 1901 *Reminiscences* remembered the Jewish community that had taken shape on the east side of Baltimore in the early 1850s as a place where "there seemed to be many Jews … although everything is very primitive. Women in the small shops carrying children in their arms, or else knitting busily. Young men invited passers-by to enter this or that store to buy […] M'zuzoth, Tzitzith, Talethim, Kosher cheese and Eretz Yisrael earth were on sale."[29] Wise's recollections of family life and entrepreneurship, of the mixed male–female marketplace, the absence of meaningful distinctions between sacred and mundane, between foodstuffs and religious paraphernalia, reflected the ubiquity of food and the overlapping of community and consumption.

In his sociological analysis of Chicago's Jewish community of the late 1920s, Louis Wirth observed the same centrality of food to the Jewish public sphere, played out on the streets. "The description of the ghetto," opined Wirth, "would be incomplete without mention of the great number of other characteristic institutions that give it its own peculiar atmosphere and mark it as a distinct culture area." Here Wirth included,

> the Kosher butcher shops, where fresh meats and a variety of sausages are a specialty [...] the basement fish store to gratify the tastes of the connoisseur with a variety of herrings, pike, and carp, which Jewish housewives purchase on Thursday in order to serve the famous national dish of *gefülte fish* at the sumptuous Friday evening meal. Kosher bakeshops with rye bread, poppy-seed bread, and pumpernickel daily, [...] the bathhouse, which contains facilities for Turkish and Russian, plain and fancy, baths, [...] basement and second-story bookstores, cafes, and restaurants, [...] the cigar stores, and the curtained gambling houses, [...] the offices of the shyster lawyers, the *realestateniks,* and sacramental wine dealers.

Wirth's monograph came adorned with a series of woodcuts by the artist Todros Geller that identified as "ghetto" types the "Horseradish grinder" who sat "on the sidewalks in front of butcher shops and fish stores ... bowed and bearded," selling to the women and men who walked by as well as an artistic rendition of the Maxwell Street Market, streaming with people scurrying around buying goods of various kinds.[30]

In their history of the Jews of Buffalo, Selig Adler and Thomas Connally provided yet another example of how thinking about Jewish community cannot be divorced from considering the role of retail. In charting how "Buffalo's first distinctly Jewish neighbourhood" came into being, the two historians noted that it coincided with the rise of the community's first "shops and business institutions." In particular they noted the centrality of Rosenblatt's Bakery, where at 268 William Street "Jews met as they picked bagel, honey-cake and *hallah* out of the bins in the store windows." The opening up of Rosenblatt's stimulated competition, so Joseph Cohen, "went into the same business." With his purported "secret recipe" brought from Warsaw, Cohen opened up shop on Strauss Street and "here his son, Albert, made "Cohen's rye bread" a household word in Buffalo." The upstate New York city's

Jewish entrepreneurial nerve centre extended beyond just bread, and "by the turn of the century, kosher butcher shops throughout the area had multiplied rapidly. There were Jewish barbershops in the neighbourhood, a bicycle shop operated by Levi Russlander at 136 William Street, and a number of Jewish shoe repair shops." But the food establishments provided the daily draw of women and men to the William Street corridor.[31]

Throughout this long period of time small business meant family business. Some women actually operated independent businesses of their own, continuing in America the European tradition of multiple enterprises within a single nuclear family, with one belonging to the husband, the other to the wife. However, most Jewish small businesses in America meant husband and wife working together.

The Jewish streets of Baltimore, Chicago, New York, and all the other places where Jews settled provided more than just sites for supplying ordinary Jews with necessities. Rather these streets offered Jews informal and organic ways to interact with other Jews. Although the world of Jewish commerce never existed independent of politics and ideology, the reality that some Jews needed these stores to make a living, while others needed them to feed, clothe, and supply themselves with a range of goods, made for reciprocity and connectedness, essential elements of the idea of community. The relatively mundane commercial activities, the making, selling, and buying of foodstuffs, revealed the realities of Jewish community life.

Existing in an intermediate zone between the formal structure of communities – the synagogues, associations, societies with their charters, by-laws, and elections of officers – and the informal, the groups of friends, relatives, neighbours, and even strangers, the food merchants and their customers made possible Jewish public space.

NOTES

1 A quite robust literature on the history of consumption and the significance of shopping has already been developed. A few of the key works of recent years include Susan Porter Benson, *Counter Cultures: Saleswomen, Mangers, and Customers in American Department Stores, 1890–1940* (Urbana: University of Illinois Press, 1986); Gary Cross, *An All-Consuming Century: Why Commercialism Won in Modern America* (New York: Columbia University Press, 2000); and Lisabeth Cohen, *A Consumer's Republic: The Politics of Mass Consumption in Postwar America* (New York: Alfred A. Knopf, 2003).

2 Molly Harrison, *People and Shopping: A Social Background* (London: Ernest Benn, 1975), 5.

3 See Grant McCracken, ed., *Culture and Consumption: New Approaches to the Symbolic Character of Consumer Goods and Activities* (Bloomington: Indiana University Press, 1988).

4 Lewis Atherton, *Main Street on the Middle Border* (Bloomington: Indiana University Press, 1954), 44.

5 Carol Coburn, *Life at Four Corners: Religion, Gender, and Education in a German-Lutheran Community, 1868–1945* (Lawrence: University of Kansas Press, 1992), 22.

6 John Bodnar, *The Transplanted: A History of Immigrants in Urban America* (Bloomington: Indiana University Press, 1985), 131–8.

7 George Sanchez, *Becoming Mexican American: Ethnicity, Culture, and Identity in Chicano Los Angeles, 1900–1945* (New York: Oxford University Press, 1993).

8 Lizabeth Cohen, *Making a New Deal: Industrial Workers in Chicago, 1919–1939* (New York: Cambridge University Press, 1990).

9 Ivan Light and Edna Bonacich, *Immigrant Entrepreneurs: Koreans in Los Angeles, 1965–1982* (Berkeley: University of California Press, 1988), xi.

10 Ewa Morawka, *Insecure Prosperity: Small Town Jews in Industrial America, 1890–1940* (Princeton, NJ: Princeton University Press, 1996), 51.

11 Gerald Gamm, *Urban Exodus: Why the Jews Left Boston and the Catholics Stayed* (Cambridge, MA: Harvard University Press, 1999), 198–9.

12 Hillel Levine and Lawrence Harmon, *The Death of an American Jewish Community: A Tragedy of Good Intentions* (New York: Free Press, 1992), 13.

13 Quoted in Moses Rischin, *The Promised City: New York Jews, 1870–1914* (Cambridge, MA: Harvard University Press, 1962), 56.

14 Harry Roskolenko, *The Time That Was Then: The Lower East Side, 1900–1914: An Intimate Chronicle* (New York: Dial Press, 1972), 93, 99–100.

15 Hasia Diner, *Lower East Side Memories: The Jewish Place in America* (Princeton, NJ: Princeton University Press, 2000), 139, 141; quoted in Hasia Diner, *Hungering for America: Italian, Irish, and Jewish Foodways in the Age of Immigration* (Cambridge, MA: Harvard University Press, 2003), 203; David Weissman "Boyle Heights: A Study in Ghettos," *Reflex* 6 (1935): 32.

16 Mary Antin, *The Promised Land* (New York: Penguin, 1997), 155–6.

17 Hasia Diner, *Roads Taken: The Great Jewish Migration to the New World and the Peddlers Who Led the Way* (New Haven: Yale University Press, 2016).

18 Barry Kessler, "Bedlam with Corned Beef on the Side," *Generations: The Magazine of the Jewish Historical Society of Maryland* (1993): 2–7.

19 Wirth, *The Ghetto*, 237.

20 Riv-Ellen Prell, *Fighting to Become American: Jews, Gender, and the Anxiety of Assimilation* (Boston: Beacon Press, 1999).

21 Paula Hyman, "Immigrant Women and Consumer Protest: The New York City Kosher Meat Boycott of 1902," *American Jewish History* 70, no. 1 (1980): 91–105. See also Dana Frank, "Housewives, Socialists, and the Politics of Food: The 1917 New York Cost-of-Living Protests," *Feminist Studies* 11, no. 2 (1985): 255–85. What is particularly notable in Frank's article was that Jewish women were among the most assertive housewives in New York in demanding that the merchants of their neighbourhoods respond to their consumer needs.

22 Quoted in Diner, *Lower East Side Memories*, 80, 98–9.

23 Quoted in Diner, *Lower East Side Memories*, 80, 98–9.

24 The one work in American Jewish history that has given the marketplace its due as an analytic construct is Andrew Heinze, *Adapting to Abundance: Jewish Immigrants, Mass Consumption, and the Search for American Identity* (New York: Columbia University Press, 1990).

25 The scholarship on the pre-modern period in Jewish history has stressed the degree to which business and commerce within the ghetto operated under the control of and with the strict regulation by the formally sanctioned community. Rabbis and wealthy elites controlled the commercial sector no less than they controlled the religious sector or the relationship between the community and the larger non-Jewish world. See for example, Jacob Katz, *Tradition and Crisis: Jewish Society at the End of the Middle Ages* (Syracuse, NY: Syracuse University Press, 2000), where the power of the elite in the economic activities of the community is a major subject of discussion. Katz, for example, noted that the leadership took upon itself the question of "how to regulate competition among Jews" and to limit the rights of "strangers," even Jewish ones, from settling and doing business in the community. See, for this, p. 49.

26 Eli Faber, *A Time for Planting: The First Migration, 1654–1820* (Baltimore, MD: Johns Hopkins University Press, 1992), 69–70.

27 Hyman Grinstein, *The Rise of the Jewish Community of New York, 1654–1860* (Philadelphia: Jewish Publication Society of America, 1947), 3.

28 Alfred Kazin, *A Walker in the City* (New York: Harcourt Brace, 1952), 33–4.

29 Quoted in Isaac Fein, *The Making of an American Jewish Community: The History of Baltimore Jewry from 1773 to 1920* (Philadelphia: Jewish Publication Society, 1971), 78.

30 Wirth, *The Ghetto*, 224–8.

31 Selig Adler and Thomas E. Connolly, *From Ararat to Suburbia: The History of the Jewish Community of Buffalo* (Philadelphia: Jewish Publication Society of America, 1960), 186–7.

9 Rhythms of Mobility: How (Im)Mobility Shapes Rural Food Retail Practices in South Africa

ELIZABETH HULL

This chapter explores a surprising feature of South Africa's food retail sector. Despite the country's highly formalized economy in comparison with other countries in the region and the dominant role of corporate players in the food market, so-called traditional retailers continue to exist in large numbers. In 2014, as much as 56 per cent of the total food wholesale and retail market was held by this group, which includes small grocers, spaza shops, and street traders – those associated with an "informal" economic periphery.[1] This is significant because as the food systems researcher Stephen Greenberg writes, "while corporate wholesalers and retailers have concentrated market power, exercised in ways that go beyond just direct market share, there is also a wide base of economic activity beyond the corporations."[2]

How do these small retailers continue to exist in such a competitive market environment? The answer has to do in part with issues of mobility. During ethnographic research in a rural area in the province of Kwa-Zulu-Natal, I observed that amid a landscape of dispersed villages and poor road infrastructure – barely improved in the post-apartheid period – small retailers make up the veins and capillaries along which food is distributed. It is precisely the mobile flexibility they offer, alongside the limited ability of consumers to travel frequently to supermarkets in town, that allows traders to manipulate margins of profitability at the edges of a dominant food industry.

In the introduction to this volume, the authors highlight the significance of technology in producing food mobilities. The sociologist and philosopher Georg Simmel argued that technological development "prolong[s] the teleological series for what is close to us and ... shorten[s] the series for what is remote."[3] By this he meant that the link between a person and their basic needs is characterized by increasingly complex chains of actions, while a more differentiated and higher range of wants can be satisfied via ever shorter paths. In a commodified economy, money itself – the quintessential "tool" for Simmel – introduced a link that both separated the individual from their needs while also allowing more direct access to consumption aspirations that would be otherwise unattainable. This raises questions about the kinds of mobilities needed in order for people to satisfy their basic needs as well as more complex wants, and how such mobilities are aided or inhibited by technology. It also implies temporal as well as spatial mobilities.

The shortening and lengthening of series between wants and fulfilment observed by Simmel is evident in the case of food access in South Africa where technology plays a role. In the absence of sufficient jobs or viable farming opportunities, many people rely on the social protection system to meet their basic food needs. At the time of writing, the South African Post Office (SAPO) administered the grants through an electronic card that contains biometric identity verification and is linked to a bank account. This technology condenses the series described by Simmel into a single day, because many recipients access their grants in supermarkets where they buy their monthly supply of food and other necessities at the same time as receiving their grant, without needing to withdraw cash. As well as this shortening of the cycle, the system also introduces a range of links in the chain. It involves the mediation of the state, the corporate sector, and so on, allowing food industry actors such as supermarkets to generate profit. It makes use of people's limited mobility, and therefore their tendency to purchase the bulk of their food requirements on the same day that they collect the grant. Supermarkets advertise aggressively on this day to optimize on sales.

Yet there are other times in the month – especially in the days leading up to grant collection – when food runs out or perishables need replacing. Given the distance that many people live from town, they shop locally to top up these items. This creates opportunities for smaller retailers who offer greater mobility both spatially and in a temporal sense as well, for instance through accepting deferred payments. Households also adopt various strategies to minimize food shortages at home. For instance, women's participation in rotating savings clubs (*stokvels*) allow rural residents to bypass supermarkets altogether and bulk-buy their food from wholesalers. Buying in bulk overcomes the problem of limited mobility because purchases are less frequent. In short, the temporal and spatial limitations imposed by the grant technology create gaps in which other, more mobile actors and activities can emerge.

As I will show in the following sections, these multiple strategies of small retailers and households arise due to both the geographical legacies of apartheid social planning and a present-day political economy of unemployment. These create both physical and economic restrictions on people's mobility. In a context where households' primary food procurement practices are structured around the monthly receipt of pensions and grants, small retailers can make use of the temporal and spatial constraints of the formal sector, providing a flexible mobility unavailable to larger competitors.

In the anthropological literature on mobilities, several authors note the tendency for sedentarism and immobility to be treated as "normal" and therefore not problematized in the way that migration and mobility are.[4] The anthropologist Gunvor Jonsson calls attention to "how people experience and make sense of their existence as non-migrants, and how these aspects relate to a greater socio-cultural matrix of values and expectations informing (im)mobility."[5] Offering an example from the anthropology of food, this chapter shows that integral to an understanding of food mobilities are also the dynamics of immobility. Both are mobilized in contemporary networks of trade and economic gain. This observation was afforded by the ethnographic method, which entailed observing both consumers and retailers and the interactions between them. The immobility of consumers and supermarkets provides a niche for smaller retailers to occupy.

Mobility and Immobility in Northern KwaZulu-Natal

Rural towns in South Africa grew quickly during the 1990s after apartheid-era trade restrictions in the former "homelands" were removed and in tandem with the global expansion of supermarket and fast food chains.[6] Towns in northern KwaZulu-Natal expanded from just a few small shops to larger regional hubs containing between them several large supermarkets, several high-street commercial banks, global fast-food chains such as Kentucky Fried Chicken and Wimpy, chain stores selling furniture, clothes, and cosmetics, and a host of smaller formal and informal retail establishments. In 2011, in the town of Jozini, a shopping mall and two additional large supermarkets opened.[7]

The growth of shopping malls and the expansion of supermarket retail is indicative of the high degree of formalization of the South African economy in comparison with other countries in Sub-Saharan Africa. This has intensified in the post-apartheid period, with supermarkets expanding their operations into rural as well as urban areas,[8] resembling similar processes globally.[9] These dynamics are associated with increasing availability of nutrient-low, energy-dense foods, and are therefore implicated in South Africa's "nutrition transition" to unhealthy diets.[10]

The pace of this process in South Africa is linked to legacies of successive colonial and apartheid policies throughout the twentieth century that drew people into waged work by undermining the agrarian basis of livelihoods and food availability. Small-scale production remains limited while agriculture continues to be dominated by a large agro-industrial sector. South Africans depend heavily on commercially produced foods to meet most of their dietary needs. Yet despite a sector dominated by large corporate players, small and informal providers continue to operate on a wide scale.

Umkhanyakude is a district located in the far north of the province of KwaZulu-Natal, where I have conducted ethnographic research since 2006. It is among the poorest municipalities in South Africa, where roughly nine in ten residents earn less that R1,600 (about $120) per month.[11] About 80 per cent of households receive a government grant or pension, with which they typically purchase most of their food. About 30 per cent of households supplement their diets with vegetables grown in food gardens at or near to their homes (see figure 9.1). Many households experience a high risk of malnutrition because a balanced diet is unaffordable.

Diets are relatively circumscribed given the dominance of commercial food products and the difficulty for many families of affording a wider range of items. Breakfast typically consists of tea with maize porridge or sliced bread and margarine, sometimes with spreads such as jam or peanut butter. The main meal consists of either maize-meal or rice served with a sauce (isishebo) made with onions and several commercially produced ingredients: – soup powder, soup stock, curry powder, salt or Aromat (a seasoning containing salt), and cooking oil. The sauce sometimes also contains chopped vegetables such as green pepper, carrot, potato, or tomato, or beans, meat, or tinned fish. Many people regularly consume broiler chicken meat which is relatively cheap compared with other meats. While supermarkets stock small quantities of vegetables such as broccoli, cauliflower, and aubergine, I have not seen these items cooked or consumed in homes. People say they are too expensive, and instead buy locally produced vegetables and fruits from street vendors, most commonly, tomatoes, onions, cabbages, potatoes, green peppers, oranges, and bananas (see figure 9.2). Street vendors also sell cooked food, including boiled or barbecued maize, barbecued meat, and take-away meals resembling those consumed in the home. Another common meal especially eaten by children is amaasi, which is maize meal (phuthu) mixed with sour milk. Processed foods such as crisps, sweets, biscuits, and yoghurt are widely available. Cooked food prepared outside of the home, either by street vendors or from venues such as Kentucky Fried Chicken, is expensive and people consume it variably depending on economic means.

During several visits I lived in a village of seventy-five households. The village was created in about 1980 as part of a resettlement project during which the government oversaw the removal of residents from the surrounding area and grouped them together in villages to make way for a new irrigation scheme. One legacy of the apartheid resettlement schemes is the spatial layout of homes in relation to towns and the infrastructure that links them. They created scattered villages that, despite being close to agricultural schemes offering the prospect of work, lacked adequate resources. Water, electricity, and road infrastructures remain inadequate, intermittent, or simply absent. The village is situated about thirty minutes' drive from the nearest town along a series of gravel and tarmacked roads. This was a journey made considerably longer by the wait for transport, since only a minority of residents owned a vehicle. To travel to town, there were few buses and people waited for an occasional "taxi" or a lift in a private car, a journey that cost R10 ($0.5) each way.

Poor infrastructure and a political economy of unemployment intersect to restrict people's mobility, limiting their trips to town and requiring food provisioning near to homes. Both consumers and retailers strategize to limit the need for time-consuming and costly trips to town. However, although mobility is constrained in this way, lives are not immobile. On the contrary, migration to and from Durban and Johannesburg has long been an important livelihood strategy for families. We can locate these migration patterns in relation to an earlier period in the country's history when the government used a controlled system of cyclical migration from rural areas to provide labour for industrial production especially in the mining industry, a notorious feature of apartheid social engineering. Today, households are typically "spatially stretched" across rural and urban areas as livelihoods are diversified as much as possible.[12] Over the life course, people are likely to live very mobile lives; many young people view their next trip away as a key marker on their future horizon. Few see their lives as necessarily rooted to the rural, even though almost all retain links to a rural home. Lifestyles exhibit the hallmarks of these

Figure 9.1 Home garden. Credit: Elizabeth Hull.

mobile lives, as clothing, music, and social media all demarcate mobile youth culture.

Yet nested within the longer arch of mobile lives are embedded shorter daily and monthly cycles shaped by restricted mobilities. The temporal and spatial rhythms this creates can be utilized by retailers both large and small. To a great extent, the ultra-mobility of supermarkets is a driving force of the food landscape. Yet it remains the case that people's constrained mobility produces pockets of demand at certain times in the month that cannot be met as easily by supermarkets as by their smaller, informal competitors. In the next section, I describe the dominant practice of food provisioning via the receipt of government grants, before moving on to explore the strategies of smaller retailers and households.

Figure 9.2 Street vendors. Credit: Elizabeth Hull.

Grants, Technology, and Time

In this densely populated rural area of northern KwaZulu-Natal, many families rely predominantly or exclusively on one or more government grants. These are provided via a non-contributory and means-tested system that includes the child support grant, the foster-child grant, the care dependency grant, the older persons grant, the disability grant, grant-in-aid, social relief of distress, and the recently introduced COVID-19 relief grant. The number of social grants has increased exponentially from roughly 4 million in 1994 to over 17 million in 2017 and continues to rise.[13]

The South African Social Security Agency (SASSA) delivers social grants to 30 per cent of the population, via a contract with SAPO, which at the time of writing served as the distribution agent. Grants are paid into the recipient's account once a month. By distributing grants on a monthly basis, the system replicates the durational units of industrial wage labour, extending the rhythms of the formal economy to incorporate those that in other ways occupy spaces beyond it. Child support grants become available on the first day of the month, which means that apart from a minority who can afford to wait a day or two for the rush to subside, most recipients travel to town and queue sometimes for hours at "pay points," as they are known, to receive their grant and stock up on monthly essentials of food and other items at the same time.

In extending its reach to a huge proportion of the population, the grant system is indicative of South Africa's highly formalized economy, in contrast to many other parts of Sub-Saharan Africa. It provides a necessary source of income in a context in which jobs are few and agriculture offers no more than a supplementary source of food or money for most. Grants reduce vulnerability by pegging livelihoods to reliable monthly durations.[14] Supermarkets have positioned themselves as grant pay points, and many people I spoke to said that they felt pressured to make a purchase while collecting their grant. Supermarkets remain popular pay points because people can buy food and other necessities at the same time as receiving the grant, without needing an intermediary step of cash withdrawal. On grant collection day, supermarkets and commercial food brands engage in aggressive advertising by offering promotions, as well as increasing staff and stock.

Accompanying this large program of social protection is a set of narratives reproduced by government and media alike, professing concerns that grants discourage people from seeking work. With the extension of its temporal structures, so too does the logic of wage labour extend, opening a space that is filled by moral discourse, detectable in the cacophony of voices in policy literature and the media about the so-called dependency syndrome or welfare trap. These depict grant recipients as morally dubious and driven by "perverse incentives" to become over-reliant on the state. "Our people are waiting for government," said then president Jacob Zuma in 2013. "Our people are not used to standing up and doing things."[15] The path to well-earned citizenship is constructed in these narratives as an ability both to save money and to use grants "productively," with a view to the future.

This evokes Antonio Negri's observation that "[c]apital not only presents itself as measure and as system, it presents itself as *progress*."[16] Replicating the clockwork regularity of time in industrial production, monthly grant payments also reproduce a capitalist temporal register that implies future-oriented ideas of progress. People are reproduced as consumers through a similar logic. While it is common to hear people blame child hunger on mothers for alleged misspending of the child support grant, the evidence is thin and the cost of a nutritious diet for a child is significantly higher than the amount provided by the grant.[17]

Another narrative relates to the apparent tendency to spend all of one's money at once rather than to plan ahead. In order to reduce the need for cash and promote a "culture of saving," the government introduced a new card system in 2012, the "smart-card," which included more biometric data as well as linking the recipient to a personalized bank account.[18] This is part of a longer history of the South African state using biometric data technology to quantify, classify, track, and control people's movements, rendering them subjects of state surveillance.[19] The role of the new smart-card, which replaced the "citizen card" in 2012, was to improve the smooth and convenient delivery of grants and to reduce fraud as well as to draw a section of largely rural-dwelling people out of a peripheral and obscure cash economy and into the ever-increasing "banked" population. Yet it opened up scope for tracking of grant recipients' purchasing habits as well as for making automatic deductions for financial products such as insurance, leading to a scandal that ended the government's contract with the company Net1, which provided the service prior to SAPO.[20]

The introduction of the smart-card prompted a huge increase of new customers into the formal banking and ATM system. Yet the government remained concerned that financialization and a move away from the cash economy was not occurring as quickly or comprehensively as hoped. On the contrary, the smart-card system may have further entrenched and expanded the reliance on cash. For the first time soon after the new card was released in 2013, spending throughout the country at Boxer outlets – one of South Africa's largest supermarket chains – was bigger on grant payout day on the first of the month than it was on the last Friday of the month when workers received their salary.[21] The peak cash withdrawal day in South Africa moved from payday to grant payout day for the first time.[22]

Social Development Minister Bathabile Dlamini attempted to account for the outcome: "It's not about the banks; it's about the mentality of our people. When it comes to money they want to withdraw the whole amount. They don't trust that the money will still be there [in the bank account] tomorrow."[23] SASSA's Communications Manager, Kelemogile Moseki, encouraged people to use electronic payment facilities such as post offices, banks, and ATMs to access their grant payments, not only to reduce queues at pay points but also to encourage "a culture of saving and ensure that they [grant recipients] move away from temptation because at the bank you can withdraw only the amount you need." He went on to allude to what he saw as the financially irresponsible behaviour of many grant recipients: "At the pay points, they get all the money and end up spending it all on their way home without saving anything, unlike having bank accounts, whereby they will also be able to save the extra money they get elsewhere."[24]

These comments attribute blame for the limits of financialization on the irresponsible financial practices of grant recipients, and are another instance of an ongoing government discourse about the supposed financial illiteracy of the poor.[25] The state is concerned, therefore, not simply with reducing poverty through the distribution of grants, but also with the manner in which recipients spend and save the money they receive, in order that they avoid excessive and unnecessary expenditure. Responsible citizenship is fashioned as a decision to spend money on nutritious foods (a burden especially carried by women), a willingness to save, and a commitment to using money forms other than cash.

These narratives suggest that grant recipients exhibit little regard for costs that may arise at a later point, implying that they lack the capacity to plan ahead and instead engage in reckless spending. Yet contrary to the assumptions of these officials, when people spent a lot on grant day it was generally in the form of a bulk spend on food and other essential items intended to last for the month. Others withdrew the full amount at once because they would need it to spend some of it later in the month, since they lived far from town where smaller shops accepted cash only. Moreover, since fruit and vegetables were prohibitively expensive in supermarkets, people used cash to buy these items from street vendors. People used cash not because of a pathological lack of impulse control, nor because necessarily they lacked trust in the formal banking sector, but rather because cash remained the most suitable money mode despite the widespread use of supermarkets on grant collection day itself. Town is not easy to access for many residents whose homes are scattered throughout the rural hinterland. The smaller retailers that service these areas require cash transactions.

This discussion highlights a strong pull towards economic formalization, characterized by a state–corporate nexus in which the food industry plays a core role by delivering state grants from which it benefits through increased sales every month. Formalization is also evident in efforts by the government to enforce banking practices through the use of biometric technology that supermarkets can integrate into shoppers' purchasing habits. But these systems also produce certain constraints that do not apply to traders and street vendors. In the next section, I discuss how these smaller retailers make use of the gaps this creates, and how households strategize to overcome the limits to their mobility in order to ensure a steady food supply.

Reaching Consumers and Synchronizing Food Needs

The rigid monthly structure imposed by grants does not always synchronize well with people's food needs. While people do buy much of their food in bulk on the same day as grant collection, they must strategize when food runs out towards the end of the month. They also need to buy perishables such as bread more frequently. In this section, I describe practices adopted both by different types of retailers and by households to meet additional food needs such as these. In particular, it is the constraints of mobility – the costly and time-consuming trip to town – that creates demand for locally sourced foods at certain points in the month or for regularly consumed perishables. Small retailers are successful in part because they are flexible and mobile enough to meet these requirements. This produces a countertendency away from formalization and towards the flexible practices of informal retail. It is partly the ways in which these smaller vendors bypass the constraints of the formal sector that accounts for the proliferation of informal retailers even in a context so heavily dominated by supermarkets. In what follows, I describe retailers' strategies followed by the strategies of consumers.

Retail Strategies

The immobility of customers at certain times in the month is central to the strategies of smaller retailers. Due to the difficulty and cost of getting to town, many people make the journey just once a month on the day that they receive their grant or pension. Smaller retailers sell maize meal, bread, and other essentials towards the end of the monthly cycle, a few days before families travel to town to collect their grant instalment and buy their next monthly supply of food.

The corporate retailers do what they can to reach customers in these areas. Supermarkets extend the reach of their marketing strategies using temporary contractual arrangements with local tenders. With a megaphone strapped to the roof of a vehicle, these contractors drive from one village to the next, calling out the items on sale and the savings to be made at the supermarket, while handing out leaflets to passers-by (see figure 9.3). Most food manufacturers rely on informal networks to transport products to disparately located tuck-shops and stores (see figure 9.4). But given the prominent place of sliced bread in most people's diets, the bread company Sasko does not leave it to the local stores to ensure regular supplies. Its delivery trucks can be seen early in the morning, supplying many small stores throughout the region several times weekly. The perishability of an item such as bread ensures the continued importance of local tuck-shops (*spazas*) for its distribution, despite the cheaper prices advertised by super-markets. Food manufacturers have also developed technologies to help cater to rural consumers who do not have the ability to make frequent new purchases. For instance, the company Unilever designed packaging for its margarine brand Rama that preserves the contents and prevents melting in hot weather.[26] This extends the life of the product in a hot climate where many households lack refrigeration. The company has also designed packaging for very small quantities, to cater to people with limited income. Small quantities are also suitable for sale in local shops, where people need only a small amount to tide them over to the end of the month and would rather not pay the mark-up price for a larger quantity that they can buy more cheaply in town.

Throughout this chapter, I have used the terms formal and informal to signify areas of economic activity differentiated by whether or not they fall within the purview of state regulation. Frequently, this distinction is accompanied with an assumption that the two are in competition. Supermarkets use aggressive marketing and pricing tactics to gain an ever-larger market share at the expense of smaller competitors. However, anthropologists have also shown the ways in which these two ostensibly distinct segments of the economic landscape are closely interlinked.[27] This becomes apparent on closer examination of how supply chains operate. For instance, the majority of small-scale producers in South Africa use traders and middlemen to access markets. The anthropologist Ben Cousins describes these as "loose value chains" where formal supply chains integrate with less regulated ones, connected by a range of intermediaries.[28] The delivery of bread to myriad local stores is an example of how supply chains entail cooperation between formal and informal actors. Moreover, elements of the corporate food industry enter into supply chain arrangements with street vendors, in competition with other elements. For instance, street vendors and small retailers purchase stock from wholesalers, bypassing the more expensive supermarkets altogether.

Although food is more expensive than in the larger shops in town, the local establishments attract customers because they make use of gaps, both spatial and temporal, left by the formal retail system. As well as locating close to people's homes, the local tuck-shops also often sell food on credit (*ukukweletha*), to be paid on receipt of the grant. This is one important reason why grant recipients often need to withdraw the full amount in cash on grant collection day, since they will need cash to top up on perishables locally or to repay debt on items previously provided on the basis of an agreed deferral of payment. Shop owners keep detailed accounts of the debts they are owed by their customers and build up trust-based relationships over time, methods that are beyond the reach of supermarkets. Navigating flexibly around the spatial and temporal constraints of the dominant food sector therefore involves negotiating ethical and social relations. Arrangements of deferred payment depend on trust between the retailer and customer. While this involves some risk, the strategy of allowing deferred payment affords marginal gains over time. For the retailer, then, the time delay in payment involves a process of managing promises and building relationships. Over time these relationships become mutually beneficial. *Ukukweletha* assists small retailers to benefit from the time frames imposed by the grant system and assists households to smooth over the end of the monthly cycle, alleviating cyclical food shortage before grant payout day.

These strategies bear similarities with those of the gari chain traders in Ibadan in southwestern Nigeria, described by the anthropologist Mimi Y. Wan.[29] The gari chain is a vast network of producers, traders, transporters and retailers that provide gari to urban markets. Gari is cassava flour that has been fermented, pressed, and roasted, making it amenable for mass consumption. Notably, no formal sector institutions operate or mediate the gari chain. Rather, "the entire complex edifice, with its thousands of operators, has to depend on reliability and trust."[30] As in the case of South Africa's small retailers, financial gains are made on the narrowest of margins. They do not usually allow for expansion, but they are regular, and it is through ensuring this regularity that the traders sustain their livelihoods, providing food in small, consistent quantities. Profits can be made through manipulating certain measuring practices.

Due to being spread out across space and time, coordination of the chain is challenging and involves time lags. These are managed partly by deferral of payments along the chain, both between traders and with the final buyers. Like the local retail practices in South Africa, this system therefore relies on guarantees based on established social relations. Traders keep money from different sources and for different purposes in separate bags or pockets on their money belt, allowing funds to be allocated according to different temporal horizons, for instance, for delayed expenditure, restocking, or for a social event taking place some time away. Many small producers and retailers I spoke to in Umkhanyakude also had systems of accounting, either physical or written, to ensure that they could navigate the complexities of deferred payments or manage money flows from diverse sources.[31] Many shop owners in Wan's example also avoided bank accounts because the spatial and temporal restrictions imposed by banks were impractical, making funds unavailable for pressing expenditures. In the case of the gari chain traders, it is precisely their mobility that precludes the possibility of formal banking.[32]

In both examples, managing temporal lags and physical distances involves skill and coordination, while also presenting opportunities for gain. In Umkhanyakude, informal retailers make use of the immobility both of customers and of the large corporate retailers by offering flexibility, as the anthropologist Maxim Bolt also illustrates among farmworkers in Limpopo.[33] In these examples, it is the degree of mobility – of food and people – that shapes local economies. Consequently, transportation is a key factor. Recently, improved transportation, especially the increased frequency of mini-bus taxis, has created more competition for *spazas* (local tuck-shops) by reducing people's spatial limitations to some extent. Medium-sized stores are also seeking new methods of competing with supermarkets that often have to do with achieving a competitive advantage through overcoming spatial limitations. In one instance, a trader planned to supply goods directly to *spazas* at a 10 per cent mark-up, knowing that the latter would save the same amount by not incurring transport costs to and from town to collect stock.[34] Some small stores introduced informal means of benefiting as pay points. In a small trading store, the owner introduced a system in which a certain amount of the pension pay-out was to be provided in the form of a voucher that had to be spent in store.[35] In all of these strategies, certain times of the month and distances from town afford the possibility of margins of profit, beyond the reach of the larger retailers.

Figure 9.3 Local driver contracted by supermarket to distribute promotional material. Credit: Thami Dlamini.

Figure 9.4 Village tuck shop. Credit: Elizabeth Hull.

Household Strategies

Families use various strategies to mitigate and alleviate food insecurity towards the end of the month. In the previous section, I described the practice of deferring payment in local stores (*ukukweletha*). People also draw on social networks of relatives and neighbours. There are different ways to ask for help, the term *ukunana* signalling acute short-term need. If a child is sent to a neighbouring house to *cela ukunana* (ask to borrow) a certain item, this implies that the family has run out of staple foods. Only maize or other basic items can be requested in this way, with the expectation that the receiving household will return the same quantity of the foodstuff when food is restocked, generally ensured by returning it in the same container. Given that households are used to stocking up basic foods on receipt of a grant, a month would be the longest acceptable period before the item must be returned. Other strategies that families use, as well as rationing and missing meals, include children's distinctive food behaviours. Sometimes young children will go to the house of a neighbour, either encouraged or of their own accord, where they will be fed. This is an important way for children to eat without the need for overt requests between adults. Several other strategies are noted in a study conducted in the same area.[36]

Food is not always obtained for short-term consumption. Nor is money allocated for the purchase of food always spent in the short term. Rotating savings clubs, known as *stokvels*, extend the planning and purchase of food over a longer period of time. Contrary to the assumptions of officials about the financial ignorance of rural dwellers, savings clubs suggest meticulous levels of planning and calculation in order to save and ensure a steady food supply. Returning to the example of the female gari chain traders in southwestern Nigeria, there too, women do not save or bank money. Instead, they quickly invest it: "Food items thus act as a store of wealth as well as a method of accounting."[37] In the context of a fluctuating currency, Wan explains, women use profits to buy a secondary food item such as pepper or okra which acts as a savings bank for a future expense, for instance an upcoming wedding. The gari chain traders also use their earnings to participate in rotating credit associations.[38]

In South Africa, the food bought as part of a *stokvel* is also a form of saving; as well as making food cheaper overall, it consolidates relationships of mutuality between households. The groups generally consist exclusively of women and meet regularly and agree to fixed rules about the conduct and expectations of members. There are different types of *stokvels*, some involving the saving of money alone – sometimes to assist in the purchase of large one-off items such as a home extension or to fund a major event like a funeral – and some involving food purchase. In the case of the latter, members contribute an agreed amount of money each month, and at the end of the year, food is purchased in bulk and distributed between members. Other rotating credit unions substitute cash for food, such that every member contributes a food item each month. The total food collected is then distributed to a different member from one month to the next. In a wider context of financial indebtedness and unstable farming revenue, food has become a type of currency that helps to mitigate the changes time can bring, and such organizations operate like a bank, helping to guard against currency fluctuations and volatility in crop production. Most *stokvels* acquire additional funds throughout the year by becoming *mashonisa* (informal moneylenders), offering loans at high interest rates, typically 30 or 40 per cent each month. These two strategies of buying food in bulk and gaining interest through lending mean individuals receive much more food than they would have been able to buy with the funds they individually contributed during the year.

One member of such a *stokvel* is Busi, a farmer who had a 0.2 hectare "garden" on the nearby irrigation scheme. She paid for monthly food expenses using her disability grant and consumed the vegetables from her garden and those she obtained through exchanging gifts with other garden farmers. She also made additional income from selling vegetables and from selling bottled beer at her home, where men came to socialize and drink together in the yard during the evenings. Membership of the *stokvel* means that she could obtain more purchased food items than she would have been able to otherwise. The group saved money over the course of a year and spent it on food in January, bypassing the supermarkets and buying in bulk from wholesalers. This affected diets not only because it mitigated food shortages of basic items such as rice and maize at certain times in the year, but also because it allowed for a less cautious approach, enabling Busi intermittently to use extra earnings to buy luxuries such as meat.

When the food arrived, the question arose for members as to what to do with all the food that could not be consumed at once, particularly for Busi who lived alone. She explained to me that instead of keeping all the rice in storage, where she feared it would rot over time, she kept what she wanted for her own short-term food needs, distributing the rest to neighbours on a credit basis. When she needed food later in the year, she could go to the person and ask for the equivalent amount of rice in return. In January, therefore, her home was transformed into a kind of food shop where people would come for rice, though no monetary transaction would take place. Higher hunger levels are reported in January, so this practice was particularly valuable to neighbours. Busi emphasized that she did not sell any of the food that she received from the *stokvel*. Rather, this was a strategy for securing food supply over the course of the year, and for overcoming the low durability of foodstuffs while at the same time benefiting from the financial savings incurred by bulk purchase. Like the banking or saving of money, Busi's strategy of "banking" food ensured some continuity and helped to smooth over the vulnerabilities of food supply over the following months.

As a regular commitment that women can justifiably prioritize, membership in a *stokvel* guards against demands made by kin on money and resources. But this raises problems at certain points in the year. In what so far appeared to be a seamlessly profitable practice, there was a problem, one that convinced Busi to relinquish her membership in the *stokvel*, at least temporarily. When I discovered she was no longer participating in the *stokvel* and asked why, she told me with a dismissive hand gesture, "I'm tired. I'm having a rest." She explained that in January, people would arrive and make demands: "I want meat! I want fish!" She continued: "They behave as though I received that food for free. They think we're getting it for free, without realizing that we sweated for it." Busi would feel pressured to give away food in order to allay accusations of stinginess or greed.

This example demonstrates the difficulties of ring-fencing one's wealth, assets, or even food, particularly when accumulation has occurred over a short space of time. In such a case, there may be pressure to provide "gifts" without the necessary obligation to reciprocate. Distributional demands on Busi's food depended on the particular item in question. While no-one would expect to receive a staple such as rice "for free," she explained, meat and fish fell into a luxury food category and could therefore more easily be demanded as legitimate gift items. Such "distributional claims," as the anthropologist James Ferguson calls them, are not simply sporadic incidents but integral features of economies where livelihoods are "starkly disconnected from both agriculture *and* wage labour."[39] The social tensions produced by perceived hoarding ultimately caused Busi to leave the *stokvel*, since her relationship with two male relatives deteriorated.

Conclusion

South Africa's food system is characterized by a corporate-industrial supply chain heavily controlled by large-scale producers, manufacturers, and supermarket retailers. Many South Africans depend on government grants to meet their food needs. Food access relies not only on commercially produced foods but also on incorporation within a formal financial system via the grant technologies. The financial and food industries are knotted together, for instance, by locating supermarkets as grant "pay points." The practical use of the card as well as its limitations also shapes physical mobilities of food access, requiring people to travel to town at particular times of the month.

Yet, despite the aggressive expansion of supermarket retail into rural as well as urban areas, informal retailers continue to play a central role in food distribution. This chapter has addressed the ways in which they are able to do this, making use of both the inflexibility of their large competitors and the partial immobility of residents at certain times of the month, to find marginal opportunities for gain. In order to show this, I have paid close ethnographic attention to the the means by which people procure food when they are not able to travel to town or when their grant money runs out towards the end of the month.

Supermarkets are ultra-mobile in such a way that suggests food will travel automatically to its markets. However, the important role of small and informal traders and vendors in the South African food system suggests that they are capable of reaching consumers in ways inaccessible to the large corporations. At times, this has simply to do with price. Fruit and vegetables grown and sold locally are cheaper than those that one can buy in supermarkets. Questions of mobility offer a lens onto an array of other factors, including how the limits to the mobility of supermarkets and consumers produce gaps that smaller retailers are able to fill. The interlocking factors of geography, infrastructure, and livelihood shape how corporate and informal retailers operate, with the latter affording greater flexibility, allowing them to find marginal gains in the spatial and temporal structures of the formal economy. COVID-19 and the government's responses to it ruptured these practices, but this is beyond the scope of the current chapter.

Mobility arises in another respect, in the circulation of food itself, not only in monetary transactions but also in gifting, lending, borrowing, and exchange between family, neighbours, and small retailers. In this paper I have drawn attention to the ways in which food moves through cultural circuits defined by kinship, friendship, and neighbourly proximity. These circulations based on enduring trust relationships help to smooth over the structured constraints imposed by the formalized economy.

Acknowledgements

I am grateful to Khulekani Dlamini for his assistance during the research for this chapter.

NOTES

1 USDA Foreign Agriculture Service, Global Agricultural Information Network, "South Africa Retail Food Industry" Report, 22 August 2014.
2 Stephen Greenberg, "Corporate Power in the Agro-Food System and the Consumer Food Environment in South Africa," *Journal of Peasant Studies* 44, no. 2 (2017): 480.
3 Georg Simmel, *The Philosophy of Money* (London: Taylor & Francis, 2011), 224.
4 Liisa Malkki, "National Geographic: The Rooting of Peoples and the Territorialization of National Identity among Scholars and Refugees," *Cultural Anthropology* 7, no. 1 (1992): 24–44.
5 Gunvor Jonsson, "Non-Migrant, Sedentary, Immobile, or 'Left Behind'? Reflections on the Absence of Migration," in *Spaces in Movement: New Perspectives on Migration in African Settings*, ed. Mustafa Abdalla, Denise Dias Barros, and Marina Berthet (Köln: Rüdiger Köppe Verlag, 2014), 145–64.
6 The "homelands," or bantustans, were territories set aside by the apartheid government for the purpose of creating ethnically homogeneous, independent states for South Africa's Black ethnic groups. Ten were created altogether, including KwaZulu, within which the area of this study formerly was situated. With the inception of liberal democracy in 1994, the bantustans were dismantled and new borders were created that formed nine national provinces.
7 Spurred on by the growth of the middle class, the pace of change in South Africa is notable in comparison with other countries. South Africa's population of 54 million is served by nearly 2,000 malls whereas in Brazil for instance, a population of 200 million uses 400 malls. "The Magnificent March of SA's Malls," *Mail & Guardian*, 2 October 2014.
8 Elizabeth Hull, "Supermarket Expansion, Informal Retail and Food Acquisition Strategies: An Example from Rural South Africa," in *The Handbook of Food and Anthropology*, ed. Jakob Klein and James L. Watson (London: Bloomsbury, 2016), 370–86.
9 Geoffrey Lawrence and David Burch, "Understanding Supermarkets and Agri-Food Chains," in *Supermarkets and Agri-Food Supply Chains: Transformations in the Production and Consumption of Foods*, ed. David Burch

and Geoffrey Lawrence (Cheltenham: Edward Elgar, 2007), 1–28; Thomas Reardon and C.P. Timmer, "The Rise of Supermarkets in the Global Food System," in *Globalization of Food and Agriculture and the Poor*, ed. Joachim von Braun and Eugenio Díaz-Bonilla (New Delhi: Oxford University Press, 2007), 189–214.

10 Ehimario U. Igumbor et al., "'Big Food,' the Consumer Food Environment, Health, and the Policy Response in South Africa," *PLOS Medicine* 9, no. 7 (2012): e1001253.

11 "The Richest and Poorest Municipalities in South Africa," *BusinessTech*, 19 June 2016.

12 Andrew Spiegel, Vanessa Watson, and Peter Wilkinson, "Domestic Diversity and Fluidity among Some African Households in Greater Cape Town," *Social Dynamics* 22, no. 1 (1996): 7–30.

13 Louise Ferreira, "Factsheet: Social Grants in South Africa: Separating Myth from Reality," *Africa Check*, 28 February 2017.

14 Bureaucratic dysfunctions and mismanagement of the grant distribution system have sometimes disrupted this regularity. The problem increased during the COVID-19 crisis when many people struggled to access grants for which they were eligible.

15 By Sapa, "Our People Are Not Used to Standing Up and Doing Things: Zuma," *Sowetan Live*, 2 October 2014.

16 Antonio Negri, *Time for Revolution* (New York: Bloomsbury Academic, 2013), 110. Italics in the original.

17 Thabo Molelekwa, "World Food Day: The Struggle to Survive on a Child Support Grant," *Health-E News*, 16 October 2019.

18 Pay-point fraud by grant recipients was often spoken about with reference to *isiphokwe* (ghost) – the colloquial term used for a child who has either died or is taken care of by someone other than the grant recipient, but on whose behalf a grant continues to be claimed.

19 Keith Breckenridge, *Biometric State* (Cambridge: Cambridge University Press, 2014).

20 Keith Breckenridge, "The Global Ambitions of the Biometric Anti-Bank: Net1, Lockin and the Technologies of African Financialisation," *International Review of Applied Economics* 33, no. 1 (2019): 93–118.

21 "Stores Score on Pension Payday," *Mail & Guardian*, 3 February 2012.

22 Marc Sternberg, "Social Grant Card Growth Boosts ATM Withdrawals," *Supermarket & Retailer*, 10 September 2013.

23 Lisa Steyn, "Stores Score on Pension Payday," *Mail & Guardian*, 3 February 2012.

24 Gabi Khumalo "Beneficiaries Urged to Use Alternative Payment Methods," *South African Government News Agency*, 24 July 2009.

25 Deborah James, *Money from Nothing: Indebtedness and Aspiration in South Africa* (Stanford, CA: Stanford University Press, 2015).

26 Ethan B. Kapstein, "Measuring Unilever's Economic Footprint: The Case of South Africa," https://www.unilever.com/Images/es_insead-report220208 _tcm244-409736_en.pdf.

27 Elizabeth Hull and Deborah James, "Introduction: Popular Economies in South Africa," *Africa* 82, no. 1 (2012): 1–19; James, *Money from Nothing*; David Neves and Andries du Toit, "Rural Livelihoods in South Africa: Complexity, Vulnerability and Differentiation," *Journal of Agrarian Change* 13, no. 1 (2013): 93–115.

28 Ben Cousins, "Land Reform in South Africa Is Sinking: Can It Be Saved?" https://www.nelsonmandela.org/uploads/files/Land__law_and _leadership_-_paper_2.pdf.

29 Mimi Y. Wan, "Secrets of Success: Uncertainty, Profits and Prosperity in the Gari Economy of Ibadan, 1992–1994," *Africa* 71, no. 2 (2001): 225–52.

30 Wan, "Secrets of Success," 226.

31 Elizabeth Hull, "The Social Dynamics of Labor Shortage in South African Small-Scale Agriculture," *World Development* 59 (2014): 455.

32 Wan, "Secrets of Success," 237.

33 Maxim Bolt, "Waged Entrepreneurs, Policed Informality: Work, The Regulation of Space and the Economy of the Zimbabwean–South African Border," *Africa* 82, no. 1 (2012): 111–30.

34 Deborah Whelan, "Trading Lives: The Commercial, Social and Political Communities of the Zululand Trading Store" (PhD diss., University of London SOAS, 2011), 173.

35 Whelan, "Trading Lives," 165.

36 Mjabuliseni SC Ngidi and Sheryl L. Hendriks, "Coping with Food Insecurity in Rural South Africa: The Case of Jozini, KwaZulu-Natal," *Mediterranean Journal of Social Sciences* 5, no. 25 (2014): 278.

37 Wan, "Secrets of Success," 238.

38 Wan, "Secrets of Success," 236.

39 James Ferguson, *Give a Man a Fish: Reflections on the New Politics of Distribution* (Durham, NC: Duke University Press Books, 2015), 192. Italics in the original.

10 Immobility: Threats to the Livelihoods of the Poor

KRISHNENDU RAY

Once the lockdown was announced, Shibu and five of his friends began walking from Noida, near New Delhi, towards their villages more than a thousand miles away. They bought muri (artisanal puffed rice), cookies, deep-fried savouries, candies, sugar, onions, and chillies to sustain them along the way. By the third day, they were "crippled by their hunger for steamed rice." At this point, they would have given up their quest, Shibu said, in exchange for a bowl of cooked rice. People were distributing food, soap, disinfectants to workers on the road in Odisha, but no cooked rice. So they "began watching videos of rice being cooked on YouTube. No matter what it was that they were eating … they ate while watching rice cooking on a stove somewhere."[1]

Shibu's quest illuminates the fragile threading of labour, mobility, hunger, and desire both in the making of migrant lives and their unravelling in the wake of the pandemic in India. Capitalist systems have always depended on differently regulated flows of people, capital, commodities, and other living things, across and within national boundaries. Capital's general logic has been towards easier circulation of money and commodities. Territorial states in paired contrast have managed the flow of people and other living things, such as plants, seeds, pathogens, etc. built on administrative classifications of use, market value, and risk. The flow of people has been constrained based on their economic function and citizenship rights at least since the end of the nineteenth century, and consolidated by the postwar inter-state system. People with more powerful passports (currently places such as the US, EU, Canada, Japan, Singapore, South Korea, etc.) come from containers strongly correlated with greater concentrations of capital and have easier access to transnational mobility. Furthermore, between and within nations, people with locations higher in the global labour aristocracy – management consultants, development and international aid bureaucrats,

professors, artists, architects, chefs, and sommeliers, all strongly correlated with higher incomes – are allowed greater ease of flow across
national regimes of mobility regulations. In particular, their access to
transnational flows stands in stark contrast to lower-wage construction
workers, farm labourers, street vendors, domestic and care workers.
Connecting class to the current crisis of immobility, a domestic worker
retorted, "*Yeh virus plane vale laye, aur sadak par gareeb aadmi hai cycle par.
Yeh kya insaaf?*" [People on airplanes brought the virus, that elbowed
the poor man on to the bicycle for the long ride home. What kind of
justice is this?].[2] Mobility comes with a citizenship premium, threaded
by class and occupational hierarchy. All people are not created equal in
terms of their access to transnational and intranational mobility. This
chapter seeks to illustrate novel connections between taste, economics,
and inequities in access to mobility as a right and a privilege.

One of the central challenges of the modern world is how to feed the
city and its citizens. Much has been written about the North Atlantic
car-based supermarket system of urban provisioning. British architect
and urban planner Carolyn Steel showed that it was grain transported
over waterways that made the ancient city, while it was meat delivered
along railroads that built the industrial one.[3] William Cronon famously
demonstrated the role of grain, lumber, and meat in the making of Chicago.[4] Andrew Deener's argument in a stimulating recent book *The
Problem of Feeding Cities* (2020) could be summarized as the remaking
of the late-modern city by fresh produce in trailer trucks from suburban distribution hubs. He argues that the strengths and weaknesses
of the system – volume, convenience, variety, waste, and inequality –
are produced during the shift from supplying cities to supplying a
nation, rather than as products of top-down manipulation by a powerful "capitalist hegemonic plot."[5] Furthermore, he shows that the current
infrastructural regime was built by mid- and top-level managers in a
piecemeal, iterative way, producing both the regularities and the cracks
in the system as the unintended consequences of upward aggregation.

What is singularly insightful about this latest volume is that it disag-
gregates the food system, showing how supplying cities with grains
or meats, about which much has been written are quite different from
feeding cities fresh fruits and vegetables. The latter are all biologically
different, with different shapes, rigidity, and give; ripening and rotting
patterns; and requirements for storage, refrigeration temperatures, and
packaging, complicated to streamline in any substantial volume along a
supply chain. In other words, the materiality of produce matters.

Furthermore, the American system of the last century was built to
provide such public goods as electricity and water, while the delivery

process of heterogonous products that we classify as food, was built by a for-profit system. It is this multiplicity of material things and conventions of profit-making that have fatally shaped the supply of fresh produce. It has generated grocery gaps in inner cities that non-profits attempt to fill, trying to re-groove an interstitial system based on moral (access) and aesthetic arguments (good local food).

Taking the case of Philadelphia from c. 1900 to c. 2000, Deener shows us how the urban wholesaler was the linchpin of the city-centred system. By the end of the nineteenth century, as the US was undergoing massive urbanization, there was a growing gap, physical and conceptual, between farmers and consumers. Dry goods, such as flour, sugar, salt, coffee, and tea, were efficiently delivered to overcrowded cities, but perishable goods – fresh fruits and vegetables – were a different matter, as methods of harvesting, packing, refrigerating, and transporting had to be re-jiggered across a wide range of geographic and climatic conditions. Urban produce wholesalers in places such as New York, Philadelphia, Chicago, and St. Louis were trapped in overcrowded city centres built on waterways to supply grain and other bulk commodities. The railroad system had effectively mimicked the system built on waterways on the east coast of the United States. For a moment, in the first half of the twentieth century, it appeared that railroads could open up the supply chain to cities. But by 1949, trucks were delivering more produce to Philadelphia than railroads or ships. Large chain retailers started bypassing wholesale markets, creating vertically integrated distribution hubs in the suburbs based on newly emerging real estate, transportation, and retail regimes.

Most important, for my purpose, Deener shows that supplying cities with fresh fruits and vegetables by the supermarket system has been a persistent challenge, barely mastered by the twenty-first century, even by those cities that have already mastered the supply of potable water, electricity, wifi, dry goods (rice, flour, corn meal, oil, spices, etc.), and meats. Nevertheless, American readers might be surprised to learn that even into the third decade of the twenty-first century, most urban people in the world buy their produce – fresh fruits and vegetables, and often meats and fish – from street vendors and small, informal markets, not supermarkets. Here I illustrate that system under current pandemic conditions.

The car-driven supermarket provisioning system, primed for capital accumulation on a large scale, covers about a billion people worldwide. It is estimated that there were about 1.4 billion cars, trucks, and buses in the world in 2020. That number is expected to double by 2036.[6] In India, which is the locus of this study, it is currently estimated that 22 people out of 1,000 own a four-wheeler.[7] The top quintile accounts for 46 per cent of cars and 22 per cent of two-wheelers. The bottom quintile accounts for most of the bicycles. Most people even in urban India are not provisioning their households via cars from supermarkets. They are mostly doing so by foot, by pedal, and by mass transit system. That system, which feeds most people in the world – in India, vast swathes of Asia and Africa – is under-theorized, in spite of an immense literature on informality some of which will be cited below. This chapter attempts to sketch out a theory of urban provisioning of that other system that depends on foot (human and animal) and pedal for the last mile. The system is built on micro-mobility of immense aggregate scale and scope.

Over the long twentieth century (1880–2020), national boundaries have generally been strengthened while obstacles to intranational mobility between regions have been lowered. In some exceptional cases, such as the European Union, new surrogates have been found to push national boundaries to the perimeters of an economic bloc, now reconstructed as fortress Europe. In other cases, such as China, intranational flows never reached the degree of fluidity and flexibility as in other nation-states or mega-states such as EU. In the context of COVID-19, that would become an asset, but China's internal passport system (*hukou*) – as much as an international passport – determines your fate. Yet 300 million people have left their homes recently to try their luck in a big Chinese city.[8] They are the ones who had to pay the full price of the lockdown. In the following pages we will see how that burden has been borne by the mobile poor in India through the COVID-related health and economic crisis.

Then there is a hierarchy of mobility choices. In an illuminating case, Lin and Yeoh show how the long-established class-based distinction between managerial and contract-labour circuits in Singapore unravelled as the virus spread from tourists to hospitality workers, then to American expatriates and migrant workers in dormitories by the end of March 2020.[9] The attempt to contain, police, and pathologize the migrant poor as an incommensurate category of people in terms of the health of the nation, while continuing to sing the virtues of an open expatriate economy, failed to protect both nationals and wealthy expatriates by the summer of 2020, despite the city's promise to keep the business of East Asian capitalism going. In spite of draconian surveillance limiting the movement and independence of workers that was never tried on either the resident or the citizen population, it was the stacked dormitories of the poor, on the spatial and conceptual margins of the city, that became hotspots of community transmission. Without better housing for migrants, be it in Singapore, New Delhi, New York, or Wuhan, the burdens of the pandemic have been thrust disproportionately onto the poor, who need mobility for access to the labour market.

One of the more striking things about COVID-19, as a once-in-a-century pandemic, is that it has seriously challenged prior presumptions of what can and should flow easily. Who and within what ambit – of building, bloc, street, city, province, region, nation, and globe – must be scrutinized and securitized for greater surveillance? Most nations that have been easing intranational movement and migration have suddenly reversed course. In the rest of the chapter I will look at one of those attempts to dramatically end intranational flows, which was also linked to class assumptions about what kinds of bodies are pathogenic and considered a greater risk to the body politic.

We have learned that states can bring mobility to a grinding halt and that they can do it without much coordination, often led by national and class panic, rather than serious consideration of the lives of the migrant labour force. In the wake of COVID-19, governments in the Global North and South enforced public health measures, from social distancing to full lockdown, that immobilized street vendors, making it difficult for them to make a living, in New Delhi, New York, or Los Angeles. Concurrently, many of the compensatory social welfare measures did not reach the vendors because their place of work was away from their home districts, in the case of India, or because most vendors are non-citizens in the case of Los Angeles and New York City. As a result, an economic calamity ensued that expressed itself primarily as an employment crisis that turned into a food crisis.

Biggest Post-Partition Crisis of Mobility

On 11 May 2020, Atul Yadav's photograph of 38-year old Rampukar Pandit, stranded on the Nizamuddin Bridge in Delhi, India, went viral. Pandit's face, mask pushed down to his chin, a cellphone to his ear, was contorted in agony. He was speaking on the phone and sobbing uncontrollably. "His naked grief shook me," Yadav later said. He couldn't just walk away. So Yadav asked what was troubling Pandit. His infant son, Ramparvesh, was dying in Begusarai, Bihar, almost 1,200 km away, and all he had were his two legs to get there. Pandit's despair knew no bounds when the police stopped him on that bridge on account of the lockdown (Dutt 2020). Pandit's fate was determined by his dependence on mobility, which is linked to his class.

The sudden lockdown imposed on 24 March 2020 by the government of India, paradoxically propelled at least 10 million people to try to return home. What generated mobility here was the attempt to stop it dramatically, too dramatically. It turned into the biggest post-partition crisis of mobility on the subcontinent. The inability to stop the poor from moving back to their home villages, once the lockdown was announced in March 2020 with four hours of notice, helped spread the virus everywhere. The pandemic exposed the central weaknesses of the Indian health-care system in its under-investment in public hospitals, profiteering by private hospitals, and gross inequality of access. In its wake, the formidable Indian journalist P. Sainath wrote with palpable anger, "In our time, even before COVID-19, our 'inclusive' development enshrined the vision of 'smart cities' which would serve 3 to 5 per cent of their existing populations, abandoning the rest to squalor and ill-health."[10] Leading public health scholars underlined that "the concerns of the poor who already bear a disproportionate burden of risk factors and disease must be at the centre of all decisions. Yet a one-size-fits-all approach to COVID-19 has not only been inequitable in its impact but is also likely to increase inequalities in the long-term. A stark example is the inequitable economic impact of lockdowns on people who barely survive on precarious livelihoods,"[11] and that, "In a country with low public spending per capita on healthcare relative to its middle-income peers, the COVID-19 pandemic has further eroded an already fragmented health system."[12] A lockdown may have been necessary as a public health measure but should have been planned with more attention paid to the livelihoods of informal workers.[13]

Without social support, the unplanned lockdowns deepened inequality and accentuated burdens on the poor. Here, I study the phenomenon from close proximity in two cities, Delhi and Bhubaneswar. With the words of street vendors, I will show the specificity of everyday challenges they faced, identify some of the initiatives undertaken by the national and regional governments in terms of income support, and discuss their impact on the last mile of the food system that threaten the future of vendor livelihoods. The point of this piece is to connect system-level understanding to the subjective experience of mobile vendors, especially their sensory-cultural experience of the food system.

Food systems analysis typically considers household consumption forms as a residual black box unnecessary to pry open. On the other hand, those who study cultures of consumption often ignore the rest of the food system. This chapter seeks to pay attention to the meeting point of those two chains of material and social transformation. The processes by which a society provisions, cooks, and eats constitute the last mile of the food system. Local markets and street vendors who supply most Indian kitchens are the penultimate sites of exchange and transformation prior to the consumption of food, connecting the economic process of production to the social reproduction of the body, social group, household, and body politic.

I have been working on a mobility and urban provisioning project with a focus on vendor livelihoods and liveliness of cities for the last few years. As a result, my research assistants and I have been studying migrants – transnational and intranational, rural-to-urban, urban-to-urban migrants – and marketplaces. We have found that wherever there are markets there are migrants, and wherever there are migrants there are markets. These markets and mobile migrants bring the food system to the cusp of consumption and social reproduction sites, which are the household, eatery, school cafeteria, etc. These rural-to-urban, small-town-to-big-city, and transnational migrants are central to feeding cities from New York to New Delhi.

In New York, for instance, just along the last mile of the food system, which includes grocery stores, restaurants, street vendors, and delivery apps, there is a substantial presence of migrant workers. Of the approximately 251,000 workers in the 24,000-or-so restaurants in New York more than 60 per cent are immigrants, about 44 per cent of them Hispanic and 20 per cent Asian.[14] In high-concentration neighbourhoods such as Jackson Heights/North Corona, about 89 per cent of restaurant workers are immigrants. The data are less solid about the number of migrants among the 50,000 or so grocery-store workers in New York City and more than 120,000 or so food delivery workers (the number of food delivery workers doubled through the pandemic).[15] The Coronavirus spread unevenly between the boroughs, spreading most rapidly during the first phase in March and April 2020 through the overcrowded parts of Queens, Brooklyn, and the Bronx, where immigrant populations are packed into sub-standard housing. It is estimated that about 1.5 million people live in over-crowded conditions in New York and almost 65,000 are homeless.[16] Housing, its absence and its quality, would be a persistent theme in every location we have studied.

In India, it is estimated that anywhere between 4 to 10 million people make their living on the streets, selling produce in markets and neighbourhoods and cooked food at major junctions such as bus stands, train stations, traffic roundabouts, parks, and sidewalks. The National Association of Street Vendors (NASVI) estimates that there are about 4 million street vendors; others assert that the real number is more than double that.[17] Much of household provisioning is done by householders and their domestic servants. Estimates of domestic workers who cook and clean in most middle-class and upper-class homes in India range from 4.2 million to 10.6 million (one 2017 ILO study showed that about 56 per cent of housholds in middle-income and upper-income neighbourhoods employed at least one domestic servant).[18] In New Delhi alone it is estimated that there are around 300,000 street vendors (about half of them migrants).[19] There are no good estimates of the total number of domestic workers in Delhi (my guess is that it is probably no less than half a million). The ILO survey in 2017 cited previously showed that almost 80 per cent of domestic workers are female and most are migrants from states such as Jharkhand, Bihar, Bengal, and Orissa (which are more than a thousand kilometres away from Delhi).

We were already interviewing street vendors in Delhi and Bhubaneswar, in India, and working with the Street Vendor Project in New York City when COVID-19 hit vendors hard, so we decided to redeploy our resources to grasp the ongoing challenges of vendor lives and provide aid where possible. I draw on that recent experience to portray the contemporary challenges of segmented mobility.

The Acute Crisis

Millions of migrants rushed home once the lockdown was announced by the government of India with four hours' notice on 24 March 2020.[20] The Union labour ministry informed the Indian Parliament on 14 September 2020 that 10 million immigrants and family members had returned to their home states, but that they did not have data on how many had died trying to do so.[21] More granular reports had to be put together to grasp the scale of this unintended mobility. In a particularly terrible instance, sixteen migrant workers in Maharashtra were run over by a freight train as they dozed on the tracks along their 850 km walk home. Survivors talked about "exhaustion, police harassment driving them to the tracks, the mistaken belief that trains were not running and, above all, the psychological and physical consequences of State abandonment, dulling the awareness of risk."[22] Under severe criticism, the central government started running *Shramik* (Worker) Special trains on 1 May 2020 taking workers back to their home states. But there were repeated complaints about the absence of coordination between states, lack of leadership by the central government, lack of water and food, delays, arcane processes of registration, and black markets for tickets running up to ₹1,500.[23] Executed with little planning and concern, eventually, these very Shramik trains became the carriers of COVID-19 to every corner of the country.[24] Solicitor General Tushar Mehta, appearing before the three-judge panel of the Supreme Court, estimated that by 3 June 2020 the railways had run 4,228 Shramik trains and had taken about 6 million workers home. He estimated that another 4 million had reached home by road, bringing the total number of migrants who had left the largest cities, such as Mumbai, Delhi, and Ahmed-abad, to approximately 10 million within a duration of six months.[25] As the lockdown continued, the number of vendors running through their life savings and taking out predatory loans reached over 50 per cent according to some surveys.[26] In another survey of domestic workers, a quarter were not paid by their employers and more than 44 per cent saw a reduction of wages by 70 per cent.[27]

Street vending also became more competitive in some cities as the unemployed entered the field in an attempt to support their families. Sonu Chhabra, president of the New Fruit and Vegetable Market Welfare Samiti in Rohtak, estimated that the number of street vendors doubled during the lockdown.[28] Jagdeep, an electrician in Rohtak, used to earn ₹15,000 a month but is now selling vegetables and fruits. "I hardly earn ₹100 per day, but it is better than nothing," he said.

The capacity to survive in spite of immobility is a privilege only a few can afford. To give a sense of the scale and scope of it we can start with the 500 million labour force estimated for India in 2020.[29] In the professional and tech world such as Tata Consultancy and IBM the number of employees who can work remotely went up to 40 per cent. Tata Consultancy surprised analysts when it project that by 2025 it expects 70 per cent of its workforce to be remote.[30] Yet all that excitement about the new possibilities of remote work affects a sliver of those employed in India. Overall, formal employment – including government and the private sector – covers less than 10 per cent of the workforce.[31] Most service sector jobs are in personal service that cannot be provided remotely such as domestic work, street vending, garbage collection, etc. Working remotely is a pipedream for most Indian workers.

What Worked in the Crisis

The Public Distribution System (PDS) was one of the few saving graces in the mobility crisis in India. The National Food Security Act of 2013 entitles poor families 5 kg of grains per month. It covers 800 million people, or 62 per cent of the population. But almost 80 million households do not have enough documentary evidence to qualify for the provisions of rice, daal, wheat, and refined oil.[32] Once again we see the importance of paperwork in acquiring support from national passports, residency permits, to ration cards. Part of the problem is that the list of beneficiaries for the National Food Security Act was enumerated between 2013 and 2016 and thus excluded many newly married women and newly born children.[33] Here the illegibility of subjects to the state became a burden on the poor. What generated mobility was the search for the locus of state-sponsored provisioning and the necessary paperwork related to that.

Bhubaneswar, in the state of Odisha, provides a good example of what was working at the local level in the short run. The Odisha State Government declared its lockdown on 22 March 2020 with only essential services open. During the first phase of lockdown, the state government announced three months of ration distribution and ₹1,000 for all Public Distribution System (PDS)–covered families. They subsequently included 85,000 more families, adding to the approximately 9,500,000 already under PDS, to cover nearly 80 per cent of families in the state. In addition, a ₹3,000 cash benefit was disbursed for street vendors that covered about 65,000 residents and ₹1,500 was disbursed to those possessing labour cards. The central government also announced certain benefits: three months' ration (rice, pulses, oil); three gas (propane) cylinders (for those under *Ujwala* scheme); ₹1,000 for those who have *Jan Dhan* Account; and ₹10,000 bank loans, interest-free for one year, to restart businesses (announced the week of 15 May 2020).

We interacted with a number of vendors to learn about their experiences with these initiatives. Manjulata runs a small grocery store in the basti and received 30 kg rice, 3 kg dal and ₹1,000 on her ration card. She and her husband received another ₹1,500 each under their labour cards. Her shop has been doing brisk business and her income has been normal, though she has adjusted the prices of commodities to accommodate for additional transportation costs. Manjulata notes that many of her customers can only purchase their provisions on credit and she is willing to give it to them.

Jayant Kumar, a green coconut seller, received 15 kg rice, 3 kg dal, and ₹1,000 on his ration card. He, however, does not have a gas connection and has not opened a *Jandhan* account so he did not get those additional benefits that Manjulata received. During the first phase of lockdown, he sold off the green coconuts he had stocked. He restarted his sale on 15 April 2020; however sales had been minimal, around ten coconuts per day. Kumar registered for street vendor support, which, when we interviewed him, he was expecting in June.

Kailash, a *gupchup* (a savoury snack) seller, also received 60 kg rice, 3 kg dal, and ₹1,000 on his ration card. Both he and his wife received ₹1,500 each under their labour cards. They also received two gas cylinders and had another one due in June 2020. Many of the students and local business people support him with ration, including oil, flour, semolina, chickpea flour, and potatoes. Kailash has been delivering gupchups to his customers' homes since mid-April and earns, on average, around ₹400 daily.

Minati sells paan, fruits, and the items required for *puja*. She received the standard rations as others. She also received two gas cylinders. Minati's shop has been open since mid-April selling fruits (banana and apple), though she shared that she secretly sold paan, even though it was not allowed. Around 15 May, she restocked her shop with different puja items like bangles, expecting brisk business due to *Sabitri Amavasya*, a ritual observed by married women. Minati was unsure whether she had been listed as a street vendor. However, she did mention that she was going to receive ₹3,000 in her ancestral village under her labour card and her husband's.

Nityananda, a vegetable vendor, received the standard amount of rice, dal, and cash. He also received two gas cylinders. Nityananda was formally listed as a street vendor and received ₹3,000 in June. His son, a vendor, was also listed. As vegetable vending is listed under essential services, many of his friends continued their businesses; however Nityananda could afford to take a break. Immobility appears to be a form of luxury for those who can afford it.

Even in Bhubaneswar, where the PDS, cash transfers, and the cooking gas distribution system worked to provide support, there were those who had fallen through the cracks. Thirty-five-year-old Rama Prusty, ironically a cooking gas vendor of fifteen years, was one of them. "I have seen a substantial reduction in my business. On a normal day I make ₹3,000–4,000. Now I barely make ₹1,000. The rent is ₹3,000," he says. Have you received any government or NGO help, we ask? "No. I have an Aadhar card but no ration card." How much money would help, we asked? "About ₹3,000 per month," he estimated. Alliteratively, he repeats, "khaiba nhai, piba nhai, poisa nhai, potro nhai [No food, no drink, no money, no nothing].

A study in which researchers spoke to seventy-nine female domestic workers living in the cities of Ahmedabad, Bangalore, Delhi, Kolkata, Mumbai, and Pune during the second phase of the lockdown from 24 April to 1 May 2021 painted a dire picture: "Less than half got free ration from the public distribution system or other government sources ... The distress related to food was felt predominantly by those who did not get ration from the PDS. Other surveys also confirm this."[34] They found that some states, like Maharashtra and Odisha, had been comparatively more efficient in making sure rations were distributed. "In Kolkata, Below Poverty Line [BPL] cardholders got rice and wheat for free, whereas Above Poverty Line [APL] cardholders got only rice at a subsidized rate. In Ahmedabad, BPL cardholders got ration, but APL cardholders did not get anything. Some of the workers wanted oil, pulses, and milk so that they could make decent meals for their children."[35] The study also showed that about 1 in 5 received cash transfers. "In Ahmedabad, a participant reported her inability to open a Jan Dhan account because the bank had fulfilled the target of 100 accounts."

The PDS is not the right system to routinely distribute the variety of foods required by a household because it cannot provide the full range and choice of produce as articulated in the first few pages of this chapter, but it plays a crucial role in a crisis, especially for the poor. Jean Dreze, a leading expert on poverty in India, credits the PDS for protecting the bulk of the population from hunger, especially with the doubling of food rations for three months since April 2021.[36] Vendors who were close to home, as in Bhubaneswar, have in fact benefited from the various central and state government schemes such as ration distribution through the PDS system, cash transfers, income subsidies, and interest-free loans. This is in sharp contrast to the fortunes of vendors who are far from home. The paperwork related to the PDS is an important part of the infrastructure where the lessons are simple: enumerate, update registers, and provide benefits that are already written into the law at the locus of residency rather than distant villages. That might explain why there was a desperate rush to get back "home." Priya Deshingkar, a professor of migration and development at the University of Sussex, noted that migrant labourers "will try to go home, because that is where their real social safety net lies."[37] Making ration cards portable and linked to residency rather than natal villages, is one obvious lesson, which will nevertheless face the bureaucratic challenge of cross-state transactions.

In Singapore, for instance, a lesson learned was that migrant workers needed to be provided better accommodation to stem the infection rate that by the end of March 2020 had soared among the dormitory population. Migrant workers were thus moved to public housing estates usually reserved for residents. The government announced that Quick-Build Dormitories in modular form, but with low density, would be rolled out by the end of 2020, and unused state properties, vacant factories, and schools would be converted into temporary migrant housing.[38] These dramatic changes in infrastructural allocations eventually enabled the state to smother the infection rate and keep the deaths to just a single fifty-one-year-old migrant worker. Prime Minister Lee Hsien Loong assured migrant workers and their families in host countries that Singapore would assume responsibility for their welfare and medical care, make sure that their salaries were paid and their treatment covered in full.[39] Advocates for better migrant housing noted that the government had stumbled not because it lacked foresight but because "you can't have foresight for things you refuse to see" – that is, the condition in which migrant workers were living, pre-pandemic. The scale of the problem in Indian cities is different from Singapore and the challenges are many more, but what the latest migration crisis has shown is that the Indian government has to recognize two things: (a) the importance of migrant lives to urban economies; and (b) their lack of accommodation and paperwork at the site of residency. Only when they see that can they develop the necessary foresight for the next crisis.

Even in Bhubaneswar, the capital city of the state of Odisha, which is better organized than the situation in a number of other states, about 10 per cent of street vendors, out of the estimated 22,000, do not have proof of residency.[40] For instance, we talked to a Bengali immigrant, twenty-one-year old Balaram Panda, who used to work at a roadside eatery called Chilika Dhabha. Orphaned at age twelve, he has worked every day since he was a little boy. Now he is laid off from the *dhaba* where he was a cook, as the owners could not afford the rent. For the last four years, he worked seven months of the year in Bhubaneswar before going home to his brother and sister-in-law's in Bankura, in the neighbouring state of West Bengal. Just before the lockdown, he spent ₹15,000 to rent a tiffin stand to sell snacks, fried food, tea, and drinks. It was his life's savings. "This is the first time I managed to save something. Now it is all down the drain." Since the start of lockdown, he has not earned a *paisa*. He eats with another poor family twice a day. Once it is rice and daal and another time it is pakhala (lightly fermented leftover rice in water) which he devours hungrily with a raw onion, a green chilli, salt, and a drizzle of pungent mustard oil. Yet, he is less sanguine about the duration of their generosity. "I am a poor man. They are poor ... Even to use the toilet or take a shower I have to pay ₹10 or ₹5. I do not have a rupee on me. I do not know what I am going to do." He moaned, sobbing into his hands.

Delhi, although the capital city, is a worst-case scenario in terms of vendor support. Among the many vendors we had interviewed, Govind was the most willing to talk to us in August 2020. He had been allowed to resume business in the Vasant Kunj sector four days prior, working four hours a day. The Mehrauli Mandi where he gets his vegetables also opened up the previous week. He was hoping business would resume, saying, "ghar par pade hue the" [For so long I was wasting away at home]. Govind lives in Mehrauli, which had reported cases in several pockets over the three-month period such that sections of the colony were sealed at one time or the other. He says the areas that are sealed keep shifting as new cases of COVID-19 are found and old ones emerge from their quarantine. I ask Govind if he had a regular supply of food. He said his family did not have a ration card. They hadn't needed one previously. I ask him if he had tried to use his Adhaar card instead to obtain rations. He attempted to go to the shop but then decided against it on account of the crowd. "5 kilo gehun ke liye kaun itna karega" [Who'll work this hard for 5 kilos of wheat]. He chose instead to borrow money from a local grocer. He doesn't specify the amount, but the money has seen them through so far. I mention relief measures in other states. He says there were none that he knew of, and, in any case, these would go to whoever was closest to the local political leader. It has been better in his village, he says, because food grains are easier to access and people are allowed greater freedom of movement.

Work as a vendor had been at a standstill for Mehtab. He was very eager to speak but not about his troubles. Instead, he and his wife take turns over the phone giving me social distancing and sanitizing advice. I must stay at home. I must wash all my vegetables and let them dry before I put them in the fridge. Their daughter Noor has been spending her time on YouTube. I ask Mehtab about food and he says they had rations from before the lockdown. This was in the end of March. His son had been to their village in Siwan to attend a wedding and was stuck there. He missed his grandson the most. He has been able to come back now (after borrowing and paying ₹9,000 for a vehicle from Siwan to Delhi) and they are taking turns driving the auto-rickshaw that they share.

He isn't expecting to get to work any time soon. The university campus is deserted and it is the only place he feels comfortable. He is making some money driving the auto-rickshaw. He earned ₹260 the day I spoke to him. I ask him where he has been driving. He says he mostly ferries patients in and around the Patel Chest Hospital in the Delhi University Campus. He laughs that all his debt repayment for the nearly ₹300,000 that he owes will now be pushed further back (and therefore accrue more interest). But so far, they are managing, and the ₹20,000 from us had helped. As we re-interviewed people, we realized we had to provide immediate cash relief to cover rent and groceries for a few months, which we did to everyone we interviewed. But where the threats to their livelihoods are more systemic, that aid is trivial.

System-Level, Longer-Term Consequences

As street vending came to a standstill, policy and development scholars began to predict the consolidation and elimination of micro-entrepreneurs on the last mile as inevitable. The pandemic would have its greatest impact, they argued, on the retail food business. Almost 90 per cent of food purchases in urban India are from labour-intensive, small and medium size enterprises with a high density of workers. Large firms, in contrast, are less dense and perceived to better enforce hygienic practices. As a result, Reardon et al. predicted: "There is likely to be an acceleration in the shift towards e-commerce both for retail and for restaurant delivery ... It is likely that consumers will not fully return to prior buying habits. E-commerce firms and supermarket and fast food chains, and delivery services may see an acceleration of their displacement of the *kiranas* [small shops] and the *dhabas* [popular eateries]."[41] Nevertheless, it is important to remember that 95 per cent of Indian firms have fewer than five paid workers and the average is estimated to be 2.24.[42] As Harris-White puts it, "the informal economy drives growth and livelihoods. It supplies labour-intensive exports. It provides the goods and services that COVID-19 reminds us are essential. Its costs and returns provide the structure of costs and prices for the rest of the economy. India's comparative advantage relies on it. Labelled 'unorganised,' it is far from disorganized ... While it is where poverty is concentrated, it is also the site of considerable wealth."[43]

Since the 1970s, there has been a rich and burgeoning literature on urban informality. We have learned from that literature that informality cannot be easily legislated away unless paired with the generation of strong formal employment, which has only happened in a few places, such as Singapore, Japan, South Korea, and some Chinese cities such as Shanghai..[44] Informality, which is strongly associated with forms of mobility, is by definition what has not been captured by large corporate capital or by the state because it cannot be pinned down easily, things that are neither particularly profitable nor necessary to accumulate substantial territorial power. Capitalism is a particular kind of historical relationship between large capital and large states that have been configured in a particular way for the last few hundred years, as a way to regulate the mobility of people, capital, and commodities, emerging in the Mediterranean and Atlantic worlds, then spreading elsewhere.[45] Ideologues of capitalism constructed markets, including temporary bazaars, as their allies in the course of the Cold War, when Communists, buying into that presumption, destroyed markets and tried to contain mobility with catastrophic consequences in the Soviet Union, China, and Eastern Europe. In reality, competitive markets work against the logic of capital accumulation and state power. We see competitive markets without monopoly corporate control or state bureaucratic domination thriving everywhere in the Global South, as food markets. It is mobile bazaar commercialism that shapes the lives and livelihoods of most of the urban poor and generates the essential face-to-face liveliness that has defined cities since they were born.

Nevertheless, repeated attempts have been made to transform streets into flows of vehicular traffic and erase the traffic in informal markets. A principle of Le Corbusier's new urbanism at the height of modernist planning was "the death of the street," which he tried his best to implement both in Brasilia and in Chandigarh.[46] Analogously, modern Bhubaneswar designed by the German architect Otto H. Konigsberger in 1946 sought to make the streets wide enough to avoid foot and animal traffic from disrupting the flow of automobiles, privileging automobility over foot and pedal mobility. A similar logic is still visible in the extra-wide avenues of Edwin Lutyens's New Delhi, which so starkly separates the two sides that no life is possible in between. The dream of high modernity in urban planning – in western capitalist societies, post-colonial dependent states, and Communist variants – was to get rid of the chaos of streets in their multiplicities; of travel by foot, pedal, animal, machine, and human; and of slums in their sordid weight of the organic human condition. The dream were to reduce bureaucratic disorder in urban living. Cooking and eating were to be driven indoors, turning that which is mobile into something immovable, with the rational management of cities, making the city the bedrock of a transportation hub, office space, and a machine for living.[47] As a result, the logic of development for the last century and a half has been to try and nail people down to a place of work, a place of residence, and a school. The model of residential provisioning has been narrowed down to supermarkets for produce, restaurants for entertainment, and cafeterias for schools and work-a-day lunches. This radical simplification in feeding the city dweller is part of the grand ambition of authoritarian welfare developmentalism – both of the left and right varieties – in the modern world.

Nevertheless, in Delhi and in Bhubaneswar, as in Durban and Bogotá, most people, including the middle and upper-classes, buy their produce from street vendors, often with domestic servants shopping for produce. In those cities, the servant-wife complex of provisioning and cooking is dominant. There is a sharp red line running through Indian society between those who have servants and those who are servants. For those who have servants, cooking is done by them under the supervision of the housewife or the matriarch. For those who are servants, their households depend on their double burden along with the labour of their children, especially daughters, to feed the family. Servants are mobile in the double sense of being migrants to the cities, and moving between multiple households in a workday. As stated earlier, it is estimated that there are over 10 million informal domestic servants in India.[48] Recall that this is in addition to the 10 million or so

street vendors in India. Those two forms of mobile informal employment sustain anywhere between 80–100 million inhabitants in India
(20 million workers x 4 [3 dependents + worker], if you include all
their dependents), that is more than the population of most European
nations. In addition, population growth in India demands another
extra 8–12 million jobs a year (depending on the assumptions of the
model), and even in best years the Indian economy was not producing
enough jobs.[49] That has gotten worse since the pandemic. That deficit
in job creation, which drives informality, is not going to ease anytime
soon. Yet the presumption of professional classes and city managers
has been that informality is a problem of underdevelopment that will
be solved by more capital (big companies investing in supermarkets)
and more state (large welfare states with better surveillance of their
societies).

This is one of the few areas of agreement between Western corporate capitalists and state socialist bureaucrats and their policy planners
at both ends of the political spectrum. Communist urban planners in
Shanghai and corporate developmentalists in Singapore, for instance,
agree that only by driving food off the street can they become First World
Cities. I see that as the error of ideology – statist or capitalist – over history. Instead, theorizing markets against capitalism and communism
is the third corner of conceptualization that awaits fuller elaboration.
This essay is an opening gambit in that reconceptualization building on
the work of social historians, urban geographers, and anthropologists.

Indian cities are at a moment of bifurcation accentuated by the current COVID-related crisis. The delivery method of produce and cooked
food over the last mile is significantly changing in cities such as New
Delhi and Bhubaneswar. Will they move toward provisioning by corporate supermarkets as has happened in the Global North or will they
retain the high-employment-generation prospect of wholesale and local
markets? Will the architecture of the current system be retained with
its rhizomic economy of mobile produce vendors, small store owners,
and municipal ward markets (for instance there are about six wholesale and hundreds of NDMC markets in Delhi)?[50] Predictably there is
much excitement about delivery across the last mile in the big capital
arena.[51] Walmart-Flipkart's online grocery arm, Amazon Pantry, and
the Google-backed Dunzo are some of the big players making their
way into the online grocery segment in India.[52] We are at a moment of
reckoning between the digital delivery age and the street vendor age
in Indian cities. Who wins and who loses will depend on the power of
capital, the regulatory regime instituted by city and national governments, infrastructure and access to it, and the capacity of vendors like

Manjulata, Mehtab, Shibu, Rampukar, and their advocates to intercede between the weight of capital and the power of the state.

The short-term threat to vendor livelihoods is quite acute in many locations. The COVID-19 crisis has the capacity to kill street vending and dry and wet markets, but only in regions where the state is over-developed such as in China, South Korea, and Taiwan. Yet even Chinese cities are finding it difficult to simply legislate street vendors away. On 1 June 2020 the Chinese Premier Li Keqiang noted that street vendors would be welcomed back to alleviate high rates of unemployment in China, which officially stood at 6.2 per cent in February 2021, but unofficially is estimated to be around 20 per cent, which is about 60 to 100 million people. Official statistics show that a city such as Chengdu added 100,000 new street vendors. But the *Beijing Daily*, the mouthpiece of the CCP's Beijing Municipal Committee, published a typical developmentalist commentary embarrassed by the image projected by the "great nation" of China. Jing Ping's retort to Minister Li Kequiang noted acidly, "Beijing is the capital of China. It represents the country, and it has its own way to keep the unemployment rate low" [instead of the suggested method of bringing back street vendors].[53] As *The Economist* noted, "For years, municipal officials pushed out hawkers, trying to tidy up the colourful hubbub that once characterized China's cities. In the name of "civilizing" urban life, they wanted to see steamed dumplings and plastic toys sold inside shopping malls, not from the back of carts."[54] After 1 June 2020, twenty-seven provinces and cities welcomed hawkers back. Although Shanghai city officials still oppose street vendors, they did open a large night market.

In some Southeast Asian cities, such as Bangkok, the balance of forces will keep vendors in play for a little bit longer with no alternatives to formal development models in the short run, although they are under severe threat in the medium to long run. In stark contrast, it will make little difference in parts of South Asia, in places such as Delhi and Bhubaneswar with no prospect of formal employment opportunities improving any time soon or in parts of Latin America and Sub-Saharan Africa where the reach of both capital and state are underdeveloped. So, in the medium run, once the current COVID-19 related crisis is over, there are better prospects for vendors and markets returning with full force in parts of the Global South. But in the long run, dark clouds are gathering on the horizon with changes in the laws that scaffold supermarkets, corporations at the farmgate, and shifting lifestyles of the middle and upper classes.

At the broadest level, this chapter is an attempt, following Fernand Braudel and Karl Polanyi, at rethinking bazaar exchange as socially embedded infrastructure rather than as mere sites of capital accumulation, where mobile people engage across cultural and natural categories, sometimes circumventing the logic of capital.[55] Other bottom-up organic initiatives are emerging in terms of the distribution of cooked food. Homemakers in residential buildings within a small radius are forming WhatsApp groups to offer each other home-cooked meals of rice or roti or daal or subzi for sale, to collate a meal at the end of a long day and commute for working housewives or mothers. Small commercial exchanges around cooked food are animating neighbourhood social relations which I intend to study in their relationship to current networks of vegetable vendors. That study has to await its day when we are allowed to do fieldwork again.

Given the size of the population and the distances people like Shibu and Rampukar have to travel to get home, people with whom I opened this chapter, the lessons are twofold: (a) better planning and longer lead time for a shut-down, from four hours to two weeks; (b) greater infrastructural investment by the state and portable paperwork for the migrant poor. Shibu's hunger for the aroma of steamed rice and Rampukar's desire to hold his dying child in his arms are affective motivators of herculean effort that infrastructure builders must account for in their plans to build things or break up mobilities. The scale and nature of the interventions will have to be different in different places. But in each of the locations – India, China, Singapore – as we have seen, housing and paperwork are linked to feeding, and that is where the strategic vision of the last mile of the food system is essential to plan for a more resilient urban food system. A combination of social investment and information transparency are the best bet to prepare for similar challenges in Shibu's and Rampukar's near future.

NOTES

1 Sumana Roy, "The Smell of Rice: My Existential Fragrance," *Open*, 25 December 2020.

2 @BDUTT. 23 May 2020, https://twitter.com/BDUTT/status /1264170119594487808.

3 Carolyn Steel, *Hungry City. How Food Shapes Our Lives* (New York: Vintage, 2008), 34.

4 William Cronon, *Nature's Metropolis* (New York: W.W. Norton, 1992).

5 Andrew Deener, *The Problem with Feeding Cities: The Social Transformation of Infrastructure, Abundance, and Inequality in America* (Chicago: University of Chicago Press, 2020), 240.

6 Andrew Chesterton, "How Many Cars Are There in the World?," *Cars Guide*, 6 August 2018.

7 Muntazir Abbas, "India Has 22 Cars per 1,000 Individuals: Amitabh Kant," *Economic Times India*, 12 December 2018. https://auto.economictimes .indiatimes.com/news/passenger-vehicle/cars/india-has-22-cars-per-1000 -individuals-amitabh-kant/67059021; Shriya Anand, Keerthana Jagadeesh, Charrlotte Adelina, Jyothi Koduganti, 14 August 2019, "Urban Food Insecurity and Its Determinants: A Baseline Study of Bengaluru," *Environment and Urbanization* 31, no. 2 (2019): 421–42; Pramit Bhattacharya, "One in Three Households in India Owns a Two-Wheeler," *Mint*, 12 December 2016.

8 Xiaowei Wang, *Blockchain Chicken Farm: And Other Stories of Tech in China's Countryside* (New York: FSG Originals, 2020).

9 Weiqiang Lin and Brenda S. A. Yeoh, "Pathological (Im)mobilities: Managing Risk in a Time of Pandemics," *Mobilities* 16, no. 5 (2021): 1–17; on the recent history of street vendors in Singapore see Joanna Tan, "Singapore's Street Food Culture under Threat," *The National*, 20 June 2017; Nicole Tarulevicz, "Hawkerpreneurs: Hawkers, Entrepreneurship, and Reinventing Street Food in Singapore," *RAE: Journal of Business Management* 58, no. 3 (2018): 291–302.

10 P. Sainath, "The Migrant and the Moral Economy of the Elite," *India Today*, 30 May 2020.

11 Richard Cash and Vikram Patel, "Has COVID-19 Subverted Global Health?" *The Lancet* 395, no. 10238 (2020): 1687–8; Sumit Ray and Himadri Barathakur, "The Geography of a Pandemic: What Does It Say about COVID-19," *Fit Connect*, 26 May 2020.

12 Vikram Patel, Kiran Mazumdar-Shaw, Gagandeep Kang, Pamela Das, and Tarun Khanna, "Re-Imagining India Health System: A Lancet Citizens' Commission," *The Lancet*, 10 December 2020.

13 The International Labour Organization (ILO) estimates that over 400 million informal workers in India are at risk of abject poverty due to the nature of the lockdown. The most recent national Time Use Study (1998–9) noted that women spend 4.50 hours per week looking after children, the elderly, the sick and disabled, while they spent only one hour per week. Furthermore, women's burden of domestic work has increased substantially. Dilip Datta, "Women at Work," *The Statesman*, 8 December 2020.

14 Office of the State Deputy Comptroller for the City of New York, September 2020, Report 4–2020, https://www.osc.state.ny.us/files /reports/osdc/pdf/nyc-restaurant-industry-final.pdf; Nicholas Kristof, "Crumbs for the Hungry but Windfalls for the Rich," *New York Times*, 23 May 2020.

15 Kimiko de Freytas-Tamura, "In Pandemic, Driving for Food Apps Has Gone from Bad to Worse," *New York Times*, 30 November 2020, A6.

16 Coalition for the Homeless, *State of the Homeless 2018*, http://www .coalitionforthehomeless.org/wp-content/uploads/2018/03 /CFHStateoftheHomeless2018.pdf; Ameena Walker, "NYC's Housing Crisis Accelerating as Low-Rent Apartment Stock Declines: Report," *Curbed New York*, 26 September 2018.

17 NASVI (National Association of Street Vendors of India), "Statistics and the Street Vendors," 2014, http://nasvinet.org/newsite/statistics-the -street-vendors-2/; Shalini Sinha, "COVID-19 and Challenges of Urban Informality in Delhi, India," interview by Krishnendu Ray, "Meant to Be Eaten," Heritage Radio Network, 16 August 2020. Audio, 32:48, https:// heritageradionetwork.org/podcast/covid-19-and-challenges-of-urban -informality-in-delhi-india.

18 International Labor Organization, "About Domestic Work," https:// www.ilo.org/newdelhi/areasofwork/WCMS_141187/lang-en/index .htm#:~:text=Official%20statistics%20place%20the%20numbers,million%20 to%2080%20million%20workers!; International Labor Organization and Insitute for Human Development, *Persisting Servitude and Gradual Shifts towards Recognition and Dignity of Labour: A Study of Employers of Domestic Workers in Delhi and Mumbai* (Geneva: International Labor Organization, 2017); the 10 million domestic workers figure is from Datta, "Women at Work."

19 SEWA Delhi, https://sewadelhi.org/advocacy-campaigns/street-vendors /#:~:text=There%20are%20close%20to%20300%2C000,which%20around% 2030%25%20are%20women; National Domestic Workers Movement (NDWM) http://ndwm.org/domestic-workers/.

19 Supriya Chaudhuri, "View: The Working Person's Right to Life," *Economic Times*, 12 May 2020; "Lockdown in India Has Impacted 40 Million Internal Migrants: World Bank," *Economic Times*, 23 April 2020; Sruthisagar Yamunan, "As Supreme Court Fails to Protect Migrant Workers' Rights, High Courts Show the Way," *Scroll.in,* 18 May 2020.

20 Chaudhuri, "View: The Working Person's Right to Life"; "Lockdown in India Has Impacted 40 Million Internal Migrants"; Yamunan, "As Supreme Court Fails to Protect Migrant Workers' Rights, High Courts Show the Way."

21 Damini Nath, "Govt. Has No Data of Migrant Workers' Death, Loss of Job," *The Hindu*, 14 September, 2020; Arun Kumar, "How the Lack of Reliable Data Hurts the Most Vulnerable Indians," *Scroll.in,* 16 September 2020.

22 Chaudhuri, "View: The Working Person's Right to Life."

23 Conversion rate = ₹1 = $ 0.014 or $1 = ₹73.54. "About 60 per cent of India's nearly 1.3 billion people [about 780 million people] live on less than $3.10 a

day, the World Bank's median poverty line. And 21 per cent, or more than 250 million people, survive on less than $2 a day." Moni Basu, "Seeing the New India through the Eyes of an Invisible Woman," *CNN India*, October 2017.

24 Jeffrey Gettleman, Suhasini Raj, Sameer Yasir, and Karan Deep Singh, "Rail Spread Virus as Workers Fled India's Cities," *New York Times*, 16 December 2020: A1.

25 Scroll.in Staff, "'No Food, Water for Days': Migrants on Board Special Trains Protest against Delays," *Scroll.in*, 23 May 2020; Supriya Sharma, "Six Reasons Why the Modi Government is Squarely Responsible for India's Worst Migrant Crisis," *Scroll.in*, 18 May 2020; A. Vaidyanathan, "Send Migrants Home within 15 Days, Drop Cases: Supreme Court to States," *NDTV*, 9 June 2020.

26 Poonam Gaur, "57 Per Cent of Female Street Vendors Have Taken on Debt during the Lockdown," *Time Group.Com*, 24 May 2020; Institute of Social Studies Trust (ISST), "Final Impact of Covid-19 on Women Informal Workers," May 2020.

27 Sunaina Goel, Pragya Se, Pritha Dev, and Akshaya Vijayalakshmi, "During Coronavirus Lockdown Women Domestic Workers Have Struggled to Buy Essentials," *Scroll.in*, 4 June 2020.

28 Ravider Saini, "Out of Work, Many Turn Street Vendors," *The Tribune*, 10 May 2020.

29 World Bank, 2020, https://data.worldbank.org/indicator/SL.TLF.TOTL .IN?locations=IN.

30 Shefali Anand, "The Future of Remote Work in India," *SHRM*, 1 July, 2020; Avik Das, "88 per cent of Workers in India Prefer Work from Home," *Times of India*, 29 July, 2020; India Census 2011, https://censusindia.gov.in /census_and_you/economic_activity.aspx#:~:text=Of%20the%20total%20 402%20million,the%20number%20of%20male%20workers.

31 "Formal Jobs on the Up, Stands at 9.98 Per Cent in 2017–18: Economic Survey 2019–20," *Economic Times*, 31 January 2020.

32 Barbara Harris-White, "The Modi Sarkar's Project for India's Informal Economy," *The Wire India*, 20 May 2020.

33 Sayantan Bera, "No Ration Cards, No Food Supplies: Hunger Stalks Rural India," *Mint*, 7 April 2020.

34 Goel, Se, Dev, and Vijayalakshmi, "During Coronavirus."

35 Goel, Se, Dev, and Vijayalakshmi, "During Coronavirus."

36 Jean Dreze, "Averting Hunger during Monsoon Calls for Bold Food Security Measures," *The Indian Express*, 9 June 2020; Laura Alfers, Rachel Moussié, and Jenna Harvey, "The COVID-19 Crisis: Income Support to Informal Workers Is Necessary and Possible," *OECD Development Matters*, 22 April 2020.

37 Jeffrey Gettleman and Suhasini Raj, "'Lionhearted' Girl Bikes Dad across India, Inspiring a Nation," *New York Times*, 22 May 2020; Kunal Dutt, "A Dad Trying to Reach Dying Son," *Telegraph India*, 17 May 2020.

38 Lin and Yeoh, "Pathological (Im)mobilities," 12.

39 Lin and Yeoh, "Pathological (Im)mobilities," 12.

40 Randhir Kumar, "The Regularization of Street Vending in Bhubaneshwar, India: A Policy Model," *WIEGO*, June 2012.

41 Thomas Reardon, Ashok Mishra, Chandra S.R. Nuthalapati, Marc F. Bellemare, and David Zilberman, "COVID-19's Disruption of India's Transformed Food Supply Chains," *Economic and Political Weekly* 4. no. 18 (2020): 18–22.

42 Roshan Kishore, "What's the Average Number of Employees at a Workplace in India?" *Mint*, 9 April 2016.

43 Harris-White, "The Modi Sarkar's Project."

44 Jonathan Shapiro Anjaria, *The Slow Boil: Street Food, Rights and Public Space in Mumbai* (Stanford, CA: Stanford University Press, 2016).

45 Fernand Braudel, *Civilization and Capitalism, 15th–18th Century* (Berkeley: University of California Press, 1992); Francesca Bray, *The Rice Economies: Technology and Development in Asian Societies* (Berkeley: University of California Press, 1994); Karl Polanyi, *The Great Transformation: The Political and Economic Origins of Our Times* (New York: Beacon Press, 2001); Giovanni Arrighi, *Adam Smith in Beijing* (London: Verso, 2008); Ravi Palat, *The Making of an Indian Ocean World-Economy, 1250–1650* (New York: Palgrave Macmillan, 2015).

46 James Holston, *The Modernist City: An Anthropological Critique of Brasilia* (Chicago: University of Chicago Press, 1989).

47 Holston, *The Modernist City*.

48 Sriya Mohan. "Domestic Workforce," *The Hindu*, 15 February 2019.

49 Surjit Bhalla, "India Does Not Need 12 Million Jobs a Year," *Financial Express*, 5 January 2019.

50 Shivam Srivastav, "Unilever Ventures Backed 'Peel-Works' Wants to Bring a Million Kirana Stores under the Digital Umbrella," *Inc42*, 29 April 2019.

51 Bhumika Khatri, "How Retail Giant Walmart Is Modernising Kiranas through B2B E-Commerce Solutions," *Inc42*, 12 October 2018; Bhumika Khatri, "Sachin Bansal Invests $2.86 Mn in Milkbasket Via BAC Acquisitions," *Inc42*, 29 April 2018; W. Mukherjee and S Malviya, "Companies Join Hands to Deliver Groceries to Customers Doors," *Economic Times*, 14 April 2020.

52 Meha Agarwal, "Walmart in Final Stages of Flipkart Deal, Amazon Left Out in the Cold." *Inc42*, 8 May 2018; Khatri, "How Retail Giant Walmart Is Modernising Kiranas."

53 Hannah Zhang, "Shutdown: The Coronavirus – China Resorts to Street Vending to Revive Its Economy," *Pavement Pieces*, 16 June 2020; "China Once Banned Street Vendors: Now It Welcomes Them," *The Economist*, 13 June 2020.

54 "China Once Banned Street Vendors."

55 Braudel, *Civilization and Capitalism*; Polanyi, *The Great Transformation*; David Kuttner, "Karl Polanyi Explains It All," *American Prospect,* 15 April 2014.

PART FOUR

Biodiversity, Taste, and Nation

11 From Cornish Pasties to Mexican Pastes: Mobilities across Time and Space

SANDRA C. MENDIOLA GARCÍA

In December 2019, a young Mexican woman going through customs at the Dallas-Fort Worth International Airport carried a large pizza-like box that read "pastes" on its sides. She and her mother took turns at carefully manoeuvring the box in the narrow line where hundreds of passengers walk up to immigration officials. The woman said that the pastes were from Pachuca and that they were bringing them to their relatives in the United States. The scene is a familiar one: many people bring food from their homelands to their new homes. In this case, the Mexican paste and its predecessor, the Cornish pasty, is a mobile food. As Philip Harben, the British chef and TV host of *Cookery*, wrote about the pasty, "the most important thing about it is that it must travel and that it must be intact when the time comes to eat it." It has to "stand up to the job for which Cornish Pasties were intended."[1]

Harben is referring to how Cornish miners transported the pasties from their homes to the dangerous tin mines of Cornwall. But the pasties travelled longer distances across time and space. Cornish miners introduced their pasties (pastries that are shaped like the letter D and filled with meat, potatoes, turnip, and onions) to the silver mining towns of Real del Monte and Pachuca in central Mexico in the nineteenth century when the British began investing in the region as they expanded their capital globally. British managers and investors brought steam engines to the mines and imposed a new labour force and managerial techniques from 1824 to 1849. Their recipes, however, stayed much longer and Mexicans changed them dramatically. They transformed the pasties into pastes, and filled them with frijoles and the piquancy of their many chiles. The paste mobility, however, does not end there. Almost everything surrounding the paste has been and continues to be mobile: its production, representation, marketing, and consumption. As we know, food does not just move from one place to another and stay the same. This chapter demonstrates that some food, in this case the paste and its predecessor the pasty, continues to move and change according to the local ingredients, taste, traditions, and Mexico's economic conditions.

The consumption and popularity of pastes grew progressively in Real del Monte, Pachuca, and surrounding towns of what is now the state of Hidalgo. But the rapid commercialization of the pastes has only happened recently, coinciding with the drastic decline of the silver mining industry in the region. Like many countries around the world, Mexico embraced neoliberal policies in the early 1980s. In the process, the Mexican state, then owner of the silver mines, sold them in 1989 to Mexican businessmen. The new bosses gradually closed down the mines of Pachuca and Real del Monte, throwing thousands out of work. The neoliberal turn pushed people to find solutions to survive economically.

As the mining industry declined, regional leaders sought to boost tourism and inserted the production and consumption of the paste at the centre of the tourist experience, which targeted Mexican middle-class tourists who have been eager to learn and literally ingest some of the region's history. Several local groups designed projects that selectively display the history of the silver mining industry with a heavy emphasis on the nineteenth century when Mexico began to industrialize. Almost two centuries later, neoliberal tourists who are not content to just lie on the beach, explore Mexico's interior and, in this case, its silver mines. In an ironic twist that showcases the broader meanings of neoliberalism, these tourists literally follow the steps of a few former miners-turned-tour guides inside the mines that have now stopped their centuries-long production and have been transformed into museums. Complementing their guided tours, visitors consume pastes in the many pasterías (paste shops) of the region. Tourists learn that the pastes were brought by the "British" to Mexico and became the quintessential miners' food. The entire tourist experience, which differs much from the working-class experience, is completely mobile and in some ways similar to a time machine. Tourists interactively participate in learning a selective history and are even able to bake their own pastes, imagining and ingesting the past. Visitors move back and forth in time as they tour mining sites, museums, and paste shops and restaurants offering alleged miner-related foods.[2] The working-class experience and history, however, differ much from this neoliberal representation of the paste and the past. Mexican miners did not consume pastes at work. Their wages were low, and they could hardly afford basic food, let alone more expensive items like pastes.

Cornish Miners in Mexico

At the end of Mexico's War of Independence from Spain in 1821, the once profitable silver mines of the towns of Real del Monte and Pachuca stood flooded and unproductive after more than a decade of political and economic turmoil that began with Napoleon's invasion of Spain in 1808.[3] Once Mexico achieved political independence, the silver mines attracted eager British investors who, in their efforts to move their capital globally, sought to put them back into production.[4] In 1824, the British leased mines from the third Count of Regla, the grandson of one of Mexico's wealthiest mine owners in the colonial period, who had made his fortune extracting ore in this region.[5]

British investors formed the Compañía de los Aventureros de las Minas de Real del Monte, which lasted from 1824 until 1849. Capital was not the only one moving. By the mid-1820s, British engineers, administrators, artisans, and Cornish miners and their families began to arrive in the mountainous towns of central Mexico. British companies investing in Latin America recruited workers from Cornwall because they could operate the steam machinery that was sent to Mexico to drain the mines.[6] Captain John Rule, who was the company's first manager, personally recruited Cornish miners from Camborne and Gwennap to go to work in central Mexico.[7] Additionally, British investors and managers distrusted the Mexican labour force.[8] They thought that Mexican miners were inferior and unable to operate steam engines.

The number of Cornish workers was small, but they constantly arrived in Mexico from 1825 to about 1910, when the Mexican Revolution began.[9] Cornish miners continued to work in Real del Monte y Pachuca even after British investors sold the Compañía de los Aventureros to wealthy Mexican entrepreneurs in 1849.[10] In fact, Cornwall witnessed an economic decline in the second half of the nineteenth century that pushed hundreds to migrate to the United States and Latin America. Most of these Cornish migrants were men. According to Sharron Schwartz, only 13.5 per cent of the total Cornish migration to Latin America was female.[11] Some single Cornishmen married Mexican women.[12] Others were joined by their family members who crossed the Atlantic and stayed in the country for decades, or indefinitely.[13] While some remained and worked in the mines voluntarily, others could not afford to go back to Cornwall. This was the case for widowed women and orphaned children, who, despite requesting employers to send them back, received no aid, and presumably stayed in Mexico.[14]

From Pasties to Pastes

Cornish and British men, women, and children brought not only steam engines but also their cultural and culinary artefacts. These immigrants became famous for introducing pasties, soccer, and Methodism to Mexico. In Cornwall, the pasties were consumed by miners and fishermen.[15] Pasties' convenient shape, size, and crust made them mobile and easy to eat without utensils, while the contents stayed warm for some time.[16] Expecting to recreate their food, when the first Cornish families tried to make the pasties in Mexico, they ran into several problems. The silver towns were desolate and poor after Mexico's wars of independence. Mines were flooded and had stopped production. Houses and shacks were scattered in the mountains. People had to wait until their labour and living conditions improved. According to the historian Raquel Barceló, British ovens were made of "tabiques de barro" (bricks), and it was not until the 1850s that the British firm Manning and Mackintosh began to import more goods from England, including ovens.[17] Even then, not everyone could afford them. A Mrs. Carne of Camborne who was born in Pachuca at the turn of the twentieth century remembers that Cornish women "excelled, of course, at cooking saffron cake and pasties [...] in a brick oven, a *brassero* [sic], heated by charcoal, not unlike the cloam oven they had been used to in Cornwall."[18]

Once people began to make pasties in Real del Monte and Pachuca, they went through some transformations. The pasties were Mexicanized. The first change was linguistic and not unusual for foods that are adopted in other places: the pasty became paste, the name that people continue to use to this day. The second transformation was culinary. Paste makers incorporated local foods and ingredients. While the "original" Cornish pasty recipe called for meat, potato, and onions, which are all placed raw inside the pastry to cook, Mexicans filled the paste with refried beans (paste de frijol) and added chopped chiles (i.e., chiles serranos or jalapeños) and sometimes chorizo. Local people now consider the paste de frijol and the paste de papa con carne (meat and potato paste) to be the "original" and "traditional" pastes of this Mexican region. It was perhaps the availability and low cost of beans, plus its protein content, that eventually made the paste de frijol one of the most popular pastes. The paste de papa con carne also gained popularity. After all, the versatile potato, which originated in the Americas, was commonly available, and due to the high cost of meat, people could fill the paste with more potatoes and less meat.

The Popularization of the Paste

There is little evidence that shows any widespread popularity of pastes in the nineteenth century outside of Cornish homes. Due to the precarious labour conditions, it is unlikely that Cornish or Mexican miners brought pastes to their workplaces, at least during the period that they were trying to drain the mines.[19] It is likely that, in addition to making them at home, women, whether Cornish, Anglo-Mexican, or Mexican, began baking pastes in small quantities in Real del Monte (where the Cornish lived) to sell. In 1873, next to the entrance of the Dolores mine, there was a fonda (a modest eatery with few offerings) owned by a "Cornish old lady" where she sold pastes, beer, and bread and butter. It is possible that she sold them primarily to Cornish miners who received higher wages than their Mexican counterparts who did not have disposable income.[20] According to the historian Raquel Barceló, pastes became part of the gastronomy of the region in the twentieth century, not earlier.[21] Those who made the pastes were descendants of the Cornish or people who closely interacted with the Cornish community.[22]

Street vendors, the most mobile of all vendors, popularized the pastes in the twentieth century. Barceló and some of the inhabitants of Pachuca and Real del Monte agree that it was between the 1940s and 1960s when street vendors began to sell pastes. These were usually women from Real del Monte who baked the "original" pastes of meat and potato, as well as pastes de frijol, and sold them in their large baskets in the downtowns of both Real del Monte and Pachuca, especially outside markets in order to attract the attention of passers-by. People still remember these vendors, who sold large pastes that were similar in size to the Cornish pasties, rather than the smaller pastes that are sold at present.[23] By the mid twentieth-century, vendors sold them at the railway and bus stations, at the Coca-Cola plant, in movie theatres, and in public baths.[24] Some of these vendors employed children and teenagers to sell pastes on the streets in small boxes that they carried across their chests. One paste maker mentions that he used to sell pastes on the streets using one of these boxes when he was growing up in the 1990s.[25] Pastes' shape and consistency made them perfect to withstand their transportation, and they did not require refrigeration. While children do not sell pastes in boxes anymore, some street vendors still sell pastes in baskets. Even in the midst of the COVID-19 pandemic and without state resources, paste street vendors put on face masks, hoping to find a few customers on the deserted streets at the height of the 2020 lockdown.

In the second half of the twentieth century, some mom and pop businesses began selling pastes in their already successful shops, helping to popularize the pastes. One of the most famous was a pool hall in Real del Monte. This was a site of recreation for miners in the heart of the town. Men enjoyed drinks and played pool, and the owners began introducing pastes to snack on. This history is proudly displayed by the current owners of Pastes El Billar in posters and photographs on the walls of their establishment. A Pachuca bakery, La Providencia, went through a similar process. Located half a block from a busy bus station (Flecha Roja), the bakery was run by a woman named Carmela, who came from a family of bakers. La Providencia bakery was famous for its bolillos and sweet bread. Her son, Armando, recalls that Carmela was proud of her "British" meat and potato pastes because she used turnip. He claims that Carmela's bakery was one of the first places in Pachuca where people could buy pastes filled with salmon or tuna for Lent. Her well-established clientele welcomed the pastes. Armando estimates that in the late 1970s and early 1980s, the bakery sold between 70–80 pastes per day. Slowly, the pastes became their chief product, replacing the bread that had made them famous.[26]

Mexican Miners' Food

Although the Cornish pasty and the Mexican paste are represented as a working-class food, Mexican miners could not afford making or consuming pastes. The miners of Real del Monte and Pachuca lived in poverty. Employers, whether British or Mexicans, paid them low wages, which meant that miners lived precariously. Their homes were self-built structures located in the mountainous terrains surrounding the mines. Miners' homes became clusters in the twentieth century that were called *barrios mineros* and were characterized by unpaved roads and the lack of running water, electricity, or kitchens. Some had kitchens but no stoves or ovens in which women (men usually did/do not prepare food at home) could bake pastes. Cristina García, a street vendor whose father was a miner, recalls that while she was growing up in the 1970s, her mother had only a modest double burner kerosene stove. García also spent time at her grandmother's house, who only cooked in the *fogón* (hearth).[27]

Most Mexican miners could not afford meat, which was one of the main ingredients of the Cornish pasty filling or the paste de papa con carne. Eating meat was and continues to be a luxury. Former miners recall that when a person brought any sort of white or red meat to the mine, then all miners would fight over it, sometimes depriving co-workers of their own food.[28] Félix Castillo García, a former miner who writes about his experiences in the mines, emphasizes miners' poverty and the modest foods that they brought from home, which did not include pastes.[29]

Photographs, miners' published narratives, and oral interviews indicate that Mexican miners ate tortillas, tacos, tortas, tamales, rice, beans, eggs, local products, and all sorts of leftovers from home.[30] They ate products that either grew seasonally or could be bought for a low price in local markets or from small producers. According to Rosario Villalobos, a former miner, people took advantage of edible native plants. Some ate parts of the maguey, a popular plant in the state of Hidalgo that is best-known for its fermented juice, pulque. In Villalobos's and many others' diets, several products of the maguey were common, such as the gualumbos – the flowers of the maguey. A popular food that miners brought to the mines were tacos de gualumbo with egg. Other miners ate tacos with salsa de chinicuil. Chinicuiles are the red worms of the maguey that are roasted and then mashed with hot peppers to make salsa. People also ate tacos with eggs and regional plants, such as verdolagas (purslane), nopales (cactus pads), and malvas (mallow).[31] However, tourists are not exposed to these local rural dishes because they do not carry the allure of the far-away origin of the paste. Unlike the foods that miners actually consumed, the pastes' appeal rests on their real and imagined mobilities.

Pastes entered the diets of miners and other working-class people as a special treat during political or social events outside the mines. The silver miners in the region belong to one of Mexico's most important unions, the National Union of Mine, Metal, and Allied Workers of the Mexican Republic (SNTMMSRM). The ruling party, the Institutional Revolutionary Party (PRI), co-opted most of the labour organizations, including the SNTMMSRM, appointing union leaders who were subservient to the party and to employers. These leaders were known as *charros*, and they usually did not fight for the rank-and-file members' well-being. Félix Castillo García indicates that during union meetings-turned-parties, *charro* leaders brought pastes, beer, and money to give to the miners in an attempt to buy their compliance with corrupt leaders' decisions, which usually favoured employers. At these events, there was a lot of pulque and aguardiente to get miners drunk and make them vote against their interests.[32] According to one paste maker, politicians often brought pastes to political rallies. On one occasion, during the 1982 presidential campaign of the ruling party's candidate Miguel de la Madrid, this particular baker produced 20,000 pastes for a rally in Hidalgo. All of his employees and family members worked around the clock for four days.[33] All of these pastes were given to the rally attendees. Since miners were members of a *charro* union, they most likely were present at this political event as *acarreados* (literally the dragged ones). In short, politicians and union officials, in addition to having other strategies, also gave pastes away to gain favourable votes from miners or simply get them to attend these events.

Miners and their families also consumed pastes on very special social occasions. Lucía Gama, a native of Pachuca and the former wife of a miner, remembers that the very first time that she and her family ever had a paste was when her eldest daughter got engaged. The fiancé was born in Real del Monte, and his family served pastes to the future in-laws during their first family get-together.[34]

The Pastes and the Neoliberal Turn

The mass commercialization of pastes and the marketing of the food, which emphasizes its connection to miners, the Cornish, and the mining industry in general, happened toward the end of the twentieth century, as the silver mining industry was declining.[35] The famous Compañía de Real del Monte y Pachuca, once owned by the British (under a different name) and later by the Mexican state in 1947, was sold in 1989 to private Mexican businessmen, who slowly ended operations during the next decade. The privatization of the Compañía was part of Mexico's neoliberal restructuring of the economy, during which most state-owned enterprises were privatized, reduced operations, or closed down. As a result of this process, around 3,500 miners at the Compañía lost their jobs, which profoundly hurt the communities of Pachuca and Real del Monte.

Community leaders responded to the economic devastation of mine closures by promoting tourism. Several groups, not always working together, began projects that were intended to showcase the history of the region in order to attract tourists. In the mid-1990s, the government of the state of Hidalgo sought to improve the appearance and infrastructure of the town of Real del Monte, whose economy was sinking. The government paved streets, fixed roads, roofs, and balconies, painted facades, and repaired an iron kiosk and a fountain on the small downtown plaza.[36] In 2004, Real del Monte became a Pueblo Mágico (magical town). The Pueblo Mágico title was part of a 2001 federal government program to increase tourism in small towns across Mexico that fulfilled certain characteristics such as their unique traditions and history. It "aimed to use tourism to elevate standards of living, offer new sources of employment, and provide a model for sustainable local development."[37] Real del Monte earned this title due to the community's connection to the silver mining industry and the British presence.[38]

For instance, Real del Monte houses a British cemetery, where the bodies of more than 600 British and Cornish miners and managers who worked during and after the British tenure of the company, and their family members were buried. Some of the Mexican descendants of these workers are also interred there, and visitors are encouraged to tour the site.[39]

In a multi-year project and with the goal of promoting cultural tourism, a private organization restored and reutilized several mining sites in Real del Monte and Pachuca, which are considered to be industrial heritage. Starting in 1998, the Acosta and the Dificultad mines were restored in Real del Monte and sections of these sites became museums. Visitors tour these spaces guided by former miners, who have a vast knowledge of their former industrial workplaces. At the Acosta Mine, tourists put on helmets and walk inside the mine. At La Dificultad, visitors see traces of Cornish technology. The United States Smelting and Refining Company owned these silver mines from 1906 to 1947 and built a clinic for its employees, which operated until 1982. It has become the Labour Medicine Museum and hosts an impressive collection of orthopaedic instruments, medicines, and hospital furniture that were once financed by American capital.[40]

Tourism is less central to the economy in the nearby city of Pachuca, the capital of the state of Hidalgo. People there make a living working in government offices, higher-education institutions, and formal and informal commercial activities. Pachuca was once an important silver mining town closely associated with Real del Monte. Pachuca had productive mines, ore-processing facilities, and was home to wealthy mine owners. For centuries, the silver of the region was stored in this city before being transported to Mexico City. Recently, Pachuca's tourists are usually people passing through on their way to Real del Monte and other towns in the mountains. Pachuca has a number of attractions related to either the history of mining or the British presence. Architecturally, it features the iconic "Monumental Clock" at the Independence square. Francis Rule, a Cornish miner turned entrepreneur, funded its construction in 1910 to commemorate the centennial of Mexican independence from Spain. His former mansion, the so-called Casa Rule, is now the Municipal Palace.[41] In an effort to preserve the rich history of the region, the same group that converted Real del Monte's industrial sites into museums has also opened the Mining Museum in Pachuca, which among others, houses an impressive historical archive that contains late colonial documents, as well as the mining company's records up to the 1980s.[42]

A third group engaged in boosting tourism consists of local restaurateurs and paste makers. In 2009 they organized the International

Paste Festival, supported by Victor Aladro San Martín, the "Father of the Pasty."[43] Since then, the Consejo Regulador del Patromonio de Real del Monte-Cornwall, has organized it every October. Hotel owners, restaurateurs, paste makers, and other business community members form this committee. During the three-day festival, which takes place in Real del Monte's main downtown square, bakers offer a wide selection of pastes to tourists and the local population and carry out events to engage with community members. Organizers make "the largest paste in the world," which in 2019 weighed 150 kilograms and used 50 kilograms of potatoes, 40 kgs of meat, and 10 kgs of parsley, onion, and hot peppers.[44] Festival promoters claim that the festival was created with the intention of providing an opportunity for tourists to get to know Real del Monte as the cradle of the paste in Mexico.

In Real de Monte, the marketing of the paste emphasizes both its mobility and that of its creators and present-day bakers on both sides of the Atlantic. The Cornish who once went to Mexico as workers now return as festival participants and food experts. But Mexican paste makers also influence the Cornish. For instance, the Paste Festival in Real del Monte inspired people in Cornwall to organize their own one-day Redruth International Mining & Pasty Festival.[45] Redruth used to be an important copper mining town in Cornwall, but in the 1880s, after the decline of mining, it became a "residential and commercial centre." According to Sharron Schwartz, only a minority of Cornish miners who went to Mexico came from this town.[46] However, the connections between these two places have strengthened in recent years as a result of the festivals and a shared mining history, and most likely to increase tourism. Both towns invite guests from Hidalgo and Cornwall to foster these links.

The many mobilities of the pastes are explicitly represented in the publicity surrounding the Mexican festival. Paste Festival organizers have produced posters to promote the yearly event. These posters show the connection between the paste and its Cornish origins and the mining industry. In one, for example, an anthropomorphic paste wears the characteristic miner's helmet and boots and waves a Mexican and a British flag, one in each hand. Other posters prominently feature the flag of Cornwall. Other posters emphasize local elements like hot peppers, or a street vendor carrying a basket full of pastes on a hilly street.

Another of the festival activities also relies on mobilities to encourage people to participate. The children's drawing contest, which in 2019 was opened to fifth graders and middle-school students, consisted of drawing a paste. Participants had to consider the paste's "history, production, relationship to mining, the feelings it provokes, the child's own relationship to the paste, and everything that has to do with the paste." One of the prizes was quite symbolic and evoked the authors' non-corporeal travel. Organizers presented the best twenty drawings at the Redruth International Mining and Pasty Festival in Cornwall.[47] While these students cannot afford a trip to Europe, their drawings representing their feelings and connections to the paste can travel and reach the land of the Cornish pasty.

Boosters also promote the paste throughout the year at the Paste Museum. Here the emphasis rests on the paste's geographical, culinary, and historical mobilities (from Cornwall to the many locations to which the Cornish migrated, and its many fillings and transformations) and on the interactive experience for visitors. In 2012 during the Fourth Paste Festival, the same group of restaurateurs and paste makers also inaugurated the Paste Museum, which is located in one of the main entrances to Real del Monte. Their objective was "to show part of the mining history of the region through gastronomy."[48] A ticket costs 30 pesos (1.5 dollars in 2019), which includes a guided tour and the opportunity to make a paste. Before the guided tour begins, visitors can walk through a couple of exhibit rooms where a series of panels and posters recount the arrival of the British to Real del Monte, as well as the geographical dispersion of Cornish miners around the world. Then visitors move to a large kitchen where they can prepare their own pastes following instructions from one of the guides. Visitors can choose to fill the paste with the "original" potato and meat or the "traditional" beans. While the pastes are in the oven, visitors, which include tourists and local school children on field trips, move to the other exhibition halls, where they learn about the connections between Cornish miners and the introduction of pastes. One of the halls includes a "traditional" kitchen that features an English stove and an oven in which Cornish families are said to have baked their pasties.[49] Unfortunately, museum guides provide no dates or further information. At the end of the visit, tourists go to the cafeteria, where their pastes are ready to be eaten.

The marketing of the paste focuses on representing it as miners' food and emphasizing the pastes' connection to the mining industry, particularly in the nineteenth century. Tourists who consume the pastes during their stay figuratively ingest the history of the mining industry that they have been presented. Through the exhibit halls at the Paste Museum or at the Industrial Heritage sites museums, tourists move across space and time, learning a curated history of the nineteenth-century transfer of capital and technology. Nothing is even remotely mentioned about the history of labour relations, specifically employers' exploitation and miners' resistance and struggles. After touring the sites, visitors often eat pastes at one of the many paste shops and buy dozens to take home as souvenirs. Usually, these paste shops pack them for take-away in small rectangular boxes, or even in pizza-like boxes like one that was carried by the woman at DFW airport whom I mentioned in the introduction.

Museums and industrial heritage sites are not the only ones to market pastes in relation to mining. Most paste shops, whether mom and pops or chains and restaurants where pastes are also served, display images or symbols of the silver industry, regardless of whether or not Mexican miners actually consumed pastes. The mom and pop Pastes El Billar in Real del Monte, for example, displays a large poster in its restaurant in which a miner, a family member of the owners, is working down in the mine. Others name their paste shops in relation to the mining industry: Pastes El Minerito; Pastes La Dificultad (after one of the mines in Real del Monte); and Pastes Real de Plateros. Pastes Kikos, the chain with more than 100 stores throughout Mexico, uses a caricature of a miner to publicize its products. The well-fed miner, in his bright working clothes and a sturdy helmet with a headlamp, faces a paste that he is about to eat. The miner has a big smile, and just by seeing the paste, his tongue sticks out to the side showing the pleasure he is about to experience. This representation cannot be further from reality. The silver miners of the region lacked even the basics. To make this point, miners of Local One of the SNMMSRM organized a unique protest in 1985 in which they showed up naked demanding that their employer provide adequate work clothes, boots, and safety equipment.[50] In contrast, paste makers and restaurateurs have represented a different reality and a sanitized version of the past. What these communities in Real del Monte and Pachuca are experiencing is not much different from what other parts of the world have done with certain products in order to make a living. In the process of "commodifying nostalgia," as Alison Leitch notes for the lardo di Colonnata, people reinvent and repackage local products with "a distinct social history."[51]

All of these marketing strategies and the pastes' flavour have worked well, and bakers make thousands of them per day. As the tourism industry flourished in Real del Monte, a former employee of Pastes El Billar indicated that over a weekend, the shop produces around 4,000 pastes.[52] An employee of Pastes La Dificultad calculated that about 5,100 are sold a day and about 8,000 pastes a day over the weekend. This paste shop's success is related to the quality and flavour of the pastes, as well as to its location. It is situated next to the former mine, La Dificultad, which is now turned into a museum, and is on a main road that goes from Real del Monte to the towns of Omitlán, Huasca, and Atotonilco El Grande.

This paste shop is not unique. The highways that exit Pachuca are filled with paste shops, where travellers and commuters returning home (Mexico City, Puebla, Querétaro, and surrounding Hidalgo towns) buy these treats in boxes. Here, mom and pop shops, as well as large local chains, offer more than a dozen varieties of pastes for people to take with them and to share with family. These pastes are sold for 14 to 16 pesos. Kikos, the large chain of pastes, sells them for 16 pesos in its stores in Hidalgo, for 17 pesos in towns outside of the state, and for 20 pesos (1 US dollar) at Mexico City's International Airport.

The recent commercialization of pastes has led to the availability of many paste fillings.[53] While the "original" Cornish pasty contains meat and potatoes, there is a wide range of pastes available to consumers in Real del Monte and Pachuca. Most vendors, whether chains or mom and pops, divide up their offerings into "salty" and "sweet" pastes. Salty pastes include anything that the mind can imagine, such as the "Hawaiian paste" of ham and pineapple and the paste de salchicha (sausage), a favourite among children. Most of the salty pastes are spicy because the salsas, mole sauce, or the beans contain different chiles, such as the paste of rajas poblanas. Even the "original" paste de papa con carne (potato and meat) is often quite spicy, in contrast with the Cornish pasty.[54] The sweet pastes' fillings include the "traditional" arroz con leche, cajeta, and pineapple or apple jelly. Mom and pop makers of pastes usually offer a smaller selection of pastes, and these producers are proud of their limited selection. Most mom and pop vendors and their customers despise the chains because, in their view, quality has been compromised, and because these chains produced pastes out of puffy paste that crumbles. According to these critics, real pastes should not crumble when eaten. They agree with Harben, who wrote that "any Cornishman will tell you that to be any good a pasty must be so firm that you drop it down the shaft of a tin-mine!"[55]

In the less touristy city of Pachuca, multiple chains of pastes (such as Kikos, Real de Plateros, and El Duque) are located throughout the city, in downtown streets, malls, and in different neighbourhoods. For mom and pop paste shops that have to compete with chains, and whose clients are not tourists, location and quality are important. Small paste shops usually open their businesses close to schools or higher-education institutions, and on busy pedestrian streets. A paste maker, for instance, opened a successful stand at the crowded bus station, where hungry travellers wait patiently for their pastes before boarding. Some take a couple to eat on the bus, while others buy a dozen or so for relatives.

Modest mom and pop paste makers must adjust and adapt to the economic downturns in Mexico. Clemente Castro opened a very small operation on a busy street not too far from downtown Pachuca in 2016. Castro began working at an early age. One of his many jobs was at a popular paste shop in Real del Monte, where he worked for six years and learned to make pastes. He worked a double shift, but without a fair wage. He did everything from washing pots and dishes to preparing the pastes. He left the job and began making pastes at home. He sold them in small towns around Real del Monte on his bike. Later on, he bought a motorcycle to continue selling. Castro constantly got sick after spending hours in front of the stove and oven, and then driving up the cold mountains of Hidalgo. He decided then to open his store front (El Conejo Real) in Pachuca. His clients are neighbours and pedestrians. Until very recently his pastes were of average size and price (14 pesos). In January of 2020, one of the worst months for this kind of business, when people have spent all of their money during the Christmas season, he began making the pastes smaller and selling them for a little bit over half the price (7.50). On a good day, he sells about 250 pastes; on a bad day about half that amount.[56] In the midst of the pandemic, he had two options: close down his business or convince his landlord to lower the shop's rent. He successfully negotiated and continues to sell his pastes, but mentions that sales have never been lower. The streets are empty of his usual clients, as schools and many offices remain closed. Castro and other bakers rely on the fact that all sorts of people in Pachuca consume pastes, not only tourists. And these bakers usually try to keep pastes affordable for their working-class clientele.

For local consumers, pastes are an easy snack to eat during a break and something that people can eat while walking. Vendors usually place the paste in a small paper bag, which allows people not to touch the paste directly with potentially dirty hands. Consumers of pastes in Pachuca are people on the go: street vendors, state employees, parents picking up children from school, and college students. In the words of one street vendor who buys pastes on a regular basis, "this is fast food, but not junk food. It is inexpensive, portable, and I can eat pastes cold, warm, or hot. I say it is not junk food because it has nutritious ingredients; it's like a small meal."[57]

Pastes in the United States

As Mexicans continue to migrate to the United States, pastes have also moved from Pachuca and Real del Monte to the north, bringing Mexican flavours inside the pastes, renaming and reinventing them to adjust to new palates, and expanding the meanings of the Cornish pasty. San José, California, is home to Claudias' Pastes, a mom and pop shop offering the "traditional" and the "original" pasty as well as other half a dozen options, such as Mr. Bean (paste de frijol), El Minero (chicken, vegetables, and jalapeños), and a Breakfast Pasty (bacon or ham, scrambled eggs, potato, and cheddar).[58] In Chicago, home to one of the largest Mexican communities in the US, there is a paste shop called The Golden Tuzo, a clever name that provides several hints to the geographical and cultural origins of this shop that opened its doors in 2010. A tuzo is a kind of mole. These animals inhabit the state of Hidalgo. People born in Pachuca often receive the nickname of "tuzos" given the fact that so many men made their living as miners who, in a sense, do the same kind of work as tuzos. Finally, the mascot of the Pachuca soccer team (the first team ever in Mexico, which was created by the British) is a tuzo. The owners of this paste shop have used the tuzo to name their store. The Chicago-based paste shop offers the same variety of pastes as the large shops in Pachuca and Real del Monte, including ham and cheese pastes. According to Rolando Martínez, owner and paste maker, their most popular pastes are the ones made of puffy pastry, and not the "original" paste dough. Most of their clientele are Mexicans (but not only those from Hidalgo) and other Latinos, who are unfamiliar with pastes and confuse them with the widely known and more familiar empanadas. Martínez, originally from a small town outside of Pachuca, used to get upset about this confusion. For businesses purposes, however, he made peace with it, and has even added the word empanadas to his menu.[59] Like many foods and dishes in Mexico, this reminds us that the paste has remained a regional, even local, food in Mexico, and is only known outside of Hidalgo in a few places where franchises like Kikos or mom-and-pop shops and their owners have settled such as California, New York, or Illinois.[60]

Whether bringing them from Mexico as did the mother and daughter in the introduction, or making them in the host country, Mexican immigrants are expanding the meaning of the pasty in North America that once pertained exclusively to Cornish Americans. The descendants of Cornish miners who arrived in the United States have their own pasties and ways of consuming and marketing them. The Arizona-based Cornish Pasty Co., catering mainly to a non-Mexican clientele, features the "Mexican Pasty," which consists of "Mexican-spiced and simmered steak, potato, egg, hatch chilli, and cheddar with a side of sour cream and salsa." Certainly, this pasty would not be found anywhere in Mexico. This regional chain also serves the "traditional pasty" of steak, potato, onion, and rutabaga with a side of red wine gravy or ketchup.[61] The Cornish pasty in the Upper Peninsula of Michigan contains meat (beef, pork, or venison), potatoes, and carrots or rutabagas.

Some Cornish and Finns in Michigan (who once claimed the pasties as their own invention) also prefer to eat them with ketchup, chowchow pickles, or crisp vegetables. Some cut pasties in half, adding butter or gravy. Some like to drink beer, tomato juice, or tea when consuming them.[62] In recent years, migrants from Hidalgo have catered to Latino communities, make pastes de frijol, red mole with chicken, poblano peppers, tinga and chipotle, and guava with cheese. The pasty and the paste continue to change and move around.

Conclusion

This chapter has focused on the several mobilities of pastes, the Mexicanized version of the Cornish pasties that came to central Mexico in the nineteenth century. Since the mid-1820s, the Cornish miners who were hired to work in the silver mines of Mexico were part of a larger movement of labour, capital, technology, and material objects that circulated globally. More than a century after the Cornish arrival, local bakers and street vendors – the most mobile of all food vendors – popularized the pastes in Real del Monte and Pachuca. By the end of the twentieth century, when the silver mining industry declined and many mines eventually closed down, local boosters promoted tourism. The industrial landscape changed dramatically. Several former mines and industrial facilities became museums. Tourists began to arrive, attracted by the history of the region. Mom and pop paste shops and chains mushroomed and produced thousands of pastes, connecting them with the mining industry in their promotional materials. Since then, visitors tour different industrial heritage sites, museums, and consume pastes. In the neoliberal era, the entire tourist experience allows visitors to move back and forth in time and space as they learn about a selective history of nineteenth-century technological progress and the modernization of Mexican silver mines. Tourists actively interact with that history, walking through the shafts, baking their own pastes, ingesting them, and buying dozens to take back home.

Boosters in these central Mexican towns present a sanitized history that is palatable to middle-class tourists when they publicize the pastes and emphasize technological progress in their exhibit halls. Boosters promote the myth that miners ate pastes regularly at work, implying that workers received decent wages and hiding that miners' homes lacked potable water, electricity, and kitchens. In their menus, restaurateurs and bakers carefully select which foods should be considered miners' dishes. They erase the tacos de gualumbos and the salsa de chinicuiles that miners and their families ate but are unattractive to the

Mexican neoliberal tourist who may disdain peasant dishes associated with poverty and indigeneity. Museum halls simplify the rich labour history of the area. They suppress the struggles of silver miners and the other working-class people who could not afford to make or consume pastes. Sadly, and until this day, working-class people (including former miners) cannot buy pastes unless they get the small ones that Castro sells for 7.50 pesos or the ones from the street vendors selling them for 13 pesos.

After the acute economic crisis of the 1980s and the start of neoliberalism, many people from Hidalgo moved to different locations in search of a better life. Some have found their new home in the United States. Through these migrants, the paste and its predecessor, the Cornish pasty, continue to be a mobile food. In addition to their shape and crust, which were designed to allow people to carry them around easily, the pastes' representations and fillings keep changing and moving geographically. The pastes de frijol and pastes de papa con carne, as well as the mole, rajas poblanas, and the sweet pastes filled with arroz con leche, continue to travel with Hidalgo's communities across the United States.

NOTES

1 Philip Harben, *Traditional Dishes of Britain* (London: The Bodley Head, 1953), 10. For chefs on TV see Harriet Jaine, "Television and Food," in *The Oxford Companion to Food*, ed. Tom Jaine. 3rd ed. (Oxford: Oxford University Press, 2014).

2 In this region restaurants offer common dishes served in many parts of Mexico but the menus add the words "minero/as" such as enchiladas mineras, tacos mineros, and chilaquiles mineros to emphasize the mining history of these towns. These dishes are beyond the scope of this chapter.

3 John Tutino, *Mexico City 1808: Power, Sovereignty, and Silver* (Albuquerque: University of New Mexico Press, 2018).

4 For an analysis of the British in this Mexican region see Robert W. Randall, *Real del Monte: A British Mining Venture in Mexico* (Austin: University of Texas Press, 1972).

5 For a history of Pedro Romero de Terreros, the First Count of Regla, see Edith Couturier, *The Silver King: The Remarkable Life of the Count of Regla in Colonial Mexico* (Albuquerque: University of New Mexico Press, 2003). For the importance of Mexico's silver in the world, see Tutino, *Mexico City 1808*.

6 According to Sharron P. Schwartz, "in the first half of the nineteenth century, Cornwall was a dynamic industrial region in the vanguard of the industrial revolution." See her "Migration Networks and the Transnationalization of Social Capital: Cornish Migration to Latin America, A Case Study," *Cornish Studies* 13 (2005): 267, 272, 274.

7 Schwartz, "Migration Networks," 274. Schwartz mentions that about 66 per cent of the Cornish who went to Mexico arrived from Camborne (265).

8 Randall, *Real del Monte*, 126–7, and Victor Miguel Licona Duarte, "Los mineros 'cornish' en el distrito minero de Pachuca y Real del Monte, una minoría étnica en México, 1849–1906" (BA thesis, Escuela Nacional de Antropología e Historia, 1998), 19.

9 Licona, "Los mineros cornish," 7; A.C. Todd, *The Search for Silver: Cornish Miners in Mexico: 1824–1947* (Exeter, UK: Cornish Hillside Publications, 1977), 163.

10 Licona, "Los mineros cornish," 7; Todd, *The Search for Silver*, 163.

11 Schwartz, "Migration Networks," 262.

12 Raquel Ofelia Barceló Quintana, "Ingleses en Real del Monte: tejiendo identidades, 1824–1910," in *Extraños en tierra ajena: migración, alteridad e identidad, siglos XIX, XX, y XXI*, ed. Raquel Barceló (Mexico: Plaza y Valdés Editores, 2009), 32.

13 Todd, *The Search for Silver*, 158–78.

14 Todd, *The Search for Silver*, 107–9 and postscript 158–78.

15 Harben, *Tradidional Dishes of Britain*, 10–12.

16 Yvonne R. Lockwood and William G. Lockwood, "Pasties in Michigan's Upper Peninsula: Foodways, Interethnic Relations, and Regionalism," in *Creative Ethnicity: Symbols and Strategies of Contemporary Ethnic Life*, ed. J.A. Cicala and S. Stern (Logan: Utah State University Press, 1991), 6, 9.

17 Barceló, "Ingleses en Real del Monte," 38, 42 and Raquel Barceló, "Los pastes llegan a Real del Monte, Hidalgo," *Cuadernos de Nutrición* 28, no. 2 (2005): 59.

18 Todd, *The Search for Silver*, 162.

19 Barceló, "Ingleses en Real del Monte," 38.

20 Barceló, "Los pastes llegan a Real del Monte," 60, and "Ingleses en Real del Monte," 45–6.

21 Barceló, "Ingleses en Real del Monte," 39.

22 Barceló does not always write "Cornish"; she simply says "British."

23 I gathered this information from conversations with taxi drivers, paste makers, street vendors, and archivists in Pachuca and Real del Monte during several research trips in the past three years.

24 Barceló, "Los pastes llegan a Real del Monte," 61.

25 Interview with Clemente Castro, 11 March 2019, Pachuca, Mexico.

26 Interview with Armando Ramírez, 14 March 2019, Pachuca, Mexico.

27 Conversation with Cristina García, 12 March 2020, Pachuca, Mexico.

28 Interview with Felipe Baca, summer 2018, and interview with José Luis Gama, 12 July 2018, Pachuca, Mexico.

29 Félix Castillo García, *Un infierno bonito* (Pachuca, Hidalgo: Consejo Estatal para la Cultura y las Artes, 1994), 64–5.

30 See David Maawad's photographs in *Hablando en plata: Ensayo fotográfico sobre minería en Real del Monte y Pachuca* (Hidalgo: Casa de las Imágenes, 1987); Adolfo Benavides, *El doble nueve: La vida en las minas mexicanas de plata* (Mexico: Iberoamericana de Publicaciones, 1949); Castillo, *Un infierno bonito*, 50, 65. Interviews with Rosario, Crisóforo, Felipe, José Luis, Marcelino. Interestingly, food historian Jeffrey Pilcher writes that the Real del Monte miners "called their explosive charges of gunpowder wrapped in paper 'tacos.'" When they lost their jobs, they migrated to Mexico City, bringing their tacos, which became "tacos mineros." Pilcher, *Planet Taco: A Global History of Mexican Food* (Oxford: Oxford University Press, 2012), 7–8.

31 Interviews with Rosario Villalobos, 12 March 2020, Real del Monte; Guillermo Lazcano, 13 March 2020; and Laureano, 12 March 2020, Pachuca, México.

32 Castillo, *Un infierno bonito*, 235.

33 Interview with Armando Ramírez, 14 March 2019, Pachuca, Mexico.

34 Interview with Lucía Gama, 2019, Pachuca, Mexico.

35 According to Barceló, since 1994, the number of paste shops in Pachuca went up to 97. The first formal paste shop was registered in the city council in 1985 (Pastería Luna); see her "Los pastes llegan a Real del Monte," 62.

36 For an overview of these improvements see Jean-Gérard Sidaner, *Real del Monte, el esplendor de ayer para siempre* (Hidalgo: Gobierno del Estado de Hidalgo, 1997).

37 Lisa Pinley Covert, *San Miguel de Allende: Mexicans, Foreigners, and the Making of a World-Heritage Site* (Lincoln: University of Nebraska Press, 2017), 186.

38 Secretaría de Turismo, "Pueblos Mágicos, Real del Monte, Hidalgo," http://www.sectur.gob.mx/gobmx/pueblos-magicos/real-de-monte -hidalgo/.

39 For a list of family names at the cemetery see https://opc-cornwall.org /Resc/latin_america/real_del_monte.pdf.

40 Belém Oviedo Gámez, "Industrial Heritage in Mexico: 20 Years of Research, Recovery, Reutilization, and Difussion," *Patrimoine de l'industrie: ressources, pratiques, cultures* 13 (2005): 33–7. For a thorough description of its orthopaedic collection see José Luis Gómez de Lara, *Inicios de la ortopedia en México como especialidad médica* (PhD diss., El Colegio de Michoacán, 2017).

41 Sharron P. Schwartz, *Mining a Shared Heritage: Mexico's Little Cornwall* (St Austell, UK: Cornish-Mexican Cultural Society, 2011), unnumbered.

42 Belém Oviedo, "The Heritage of Mexican Mining: The Case of the State of Hidalgo," *Patrimoine de l'industrie: ressources, pratiques, cultures* 29 (2013): 62.

43 Poster in the Paste Museum; Lauren Cocking, "A Piece of Britain Lost in Mexico," *BBC Travel*, 21 May 2018.

44 "Festival Internacional del Paste: no te lo pierdas!" *México Desconocido*, 17 June 2019.

45 Nick Rider, "Cornish Mexico: How the Pasty was Transported to the Sierras," *Independent*, 25 September 2015.

46 Schwartz, "Migration Networks," 268–9.

47 Convocatoria de Dibujo, Festival del Paste, 2019.

48 Placa, Proyecto Comarca Minera, Paste Museum, Real del Monte, Mexico, 2019.

49 In August of 2017, five years after Real del Monte opened its own, Cornwall witnessed the opening of its "pasty museum," the Cornish Pasty Heritage Centre located at Cornucopia, a multi-million-pound indoor hall of "interactive food and drink attraction" situated outside of the town of St. Austell. "Take a Look Inside the UK's First Cornish Pasty Museum," 17 August 2017; "Cornucopia Opens to Public," *Business Cornwall*, 14 August 2017.

50 Sandra C. Mendiola García, "Baring It All for Activism: The 1985 Naked Protest in Mexico," *Bulletin of Latin American History* 40, no. 3 (2021): 337–51.

51 Alison Leitch, "Slow Food and the Politics of Pork Fat: Italian Food and European Identity," *Ethnos* 68, no. 4 (2003): 448.

52 Interview with Clemente Castro, 11 March 2019, Pachuca, Mexico.

53 This is not unique to Mexico. Everywhere pasties are sold there has been a diversification of their fillings. See Lockwood, "Pasties in Michigan's Upper Peninsula," 7, 10.

54 The Cornish pasty received the Protected Geographical Indication in 2011 by the European Union, which "protect[s] the name of a product, which is from a specific region and follows a particular traditional production process." The "PGI emphasizes the relationship between the specific geographic region and the name of the product, where a particular quality, reputation or other characteristic is essentially attributable to its geographical origin." https://ec.europa.eu/info/food-farming-fisheries /food-safety-and-quality/certification/quality-labels/quality-schemes -explained.

55 Harben, *Traditional Dishes of Britain*, 10–11.

56 Interview with Clemente Castro, 11 March 2019. Pachuca, México. In a recent communication, Castro mentioned that during this quarantine, he has sold nothing and has considered closing down.

57 Conversation with Cristina García, 12 March 2020, Pachuca, Mexico.
58 "Claudia's Pastes Menu," https://themenustar3.com/webspace/menus
   .php?code=orderclaudiaspastes.com.
59 Phone interview with Rolando Martínez, June 2020.
60 In Queens, New York, pastes Kikos, one of the largest franchises of pastes
   in several cities in central Mexico (Puebla, Querétaro, and Mexico City),
   ran their business for about three years before closing down in 2016–17.
   Yanin Alfaro, "La revancha del mexicano que conquistó a NY con pastes,"
   Entrepreneur, 7 March 2017.
61 Cornish Pasty Co. Expanded Menu, https://www.cornishpastyco.com
   /wp-content/uploads/2020/06/EXPANDED-MENU-06.01.2020-1.pdf .
   There's also the Carne Adovada [*sic*] pasty.
62 Lockwood, "Pasties in Michigan's Upper Peninsula," 8–9.

12 How the World Eats: Myra Waldo and the Around-the-World Cookbook

DANIEL E. BENDER

"Bon Voyage and Bon Appétit." In 1954, Myra Waldo, the food consultant for Pan American World Airways, compiled recipes from the airline's staff to write *The Complete Round-the-World Cookbook*.[1] A few months later, a Boeing Stratocruiser, the two-storey flagship of the Pan Am fleet, took off to circle around New England – an around-the-world journey in seven courses to promote her cookbook. On board chefs cooked from Waldo's cookbook on the shortest around-the-world trip on record.

The Stratocruiser featured a cocktail lounge on its lower deck. Guests, drawn from the nation's press, from the *New York Times* to *Gourmet* to *Seventeen*, began their trip around the world with Kamano Lomi, Hawaiian salmon. Camarones con Salsa de Almendras – shrimp with almond sauce – came from Ecuador. The salad was Italian, the beef was Flemish, and the Ohn Htamin – coconut rice – was Burmese. The Champagne was French. The cheesecake was "good old American."[2]

On-board, abroad, and in print, Waldo married tourist pleasures to home cooking "on this trip around the world to all those who love travel and fine food." About halfway between the Austrian brennsuppe, the cookbook's first recipe, and Venezuelan arroz coco, the last, Waldo visited Fiji. The ocean was the bluest in the world, the beaches the whitest, and the Natives were "bushy-haired." The food was somewhat "primitive," but there were "several fine native dishes." Fearful of eating anywhere but the "Grand Pacific Hotel, most visitors, though, rarely tasted them. Waldo noted that Fiji's most interesting fruits and vegetables, from breadfruit to soursop to duruka (the Fijian asparagus), were unavailable to home cooks in the United States. Other notable foods just wouldn't appeal to American tastes. The Natives, she wrote, "drink a homemade firewater" called kava, made from water mixed with a pounded or masticated root. The Fijians served the drink at festivals, but visitors "do not find it to their liking." In her cookbook, Waldo included "banana cup," not kava.[3]

Fijian dishes like "Baigan Soup" (which she translated as "Mock Turtle Soup," a decidedly American name) appealed equally to Jet Age travellers and home cooks eager for unfamiliar, but not frightening, tastes. Baigan soup, and thousands of other recipes that flowed from across the globe through cookbooks and into the American home kitchen, added spice to the American diet – literally, a host of spices and, metaphorically, an exotic cultural taste. bell hooks, in bemoaning the commodification of "otherness," writes that "ethnicity becomes spice, seasoning that can liven up the dull dish that is mainstream white culture," or in this case, bland, overpriced, or poorly cooked Continental foods.[4] That oft-cited analysis, though, omits historical chronologies. What was the appeal of unfamiliar, spicy flavours at this particular moment, especially when a previous generation of travellers had so assiduously avoided eating locally?

Waldo's Baigan soup, initially a Fijian dish, became an American appetizer, an exotic treat, a virtual journey to the tropics, and, for some, an edible souvenir. This transmutation helps understand the mobility at stake in how tourists, diners, and home cooks in the Global North (especially the United States) learned to eat foods in the Global South. Cookbooks like Waldo's published for Pan Am were bestsellers, beginning in the 1950s and in the midst of the Cold War. Often in tension with national cuisine cookbooks, around-the-world cookbooks – world cookbooks, we might term them – invited Americans simultaneously to travel and to eat something other than British or continental standards both abroad and at home. Waldo wrote publicly what so many travellers already privately realized: British cooking in England was bland; when prepared in hotels in its former colonies, it was barely edible. French cooking could taste spectacular in France, uneven and overpriced in the United States, and unpalatable in most other places.

If, as Arjun Appadurai writes, national cookbooks were "artifacts of culture in the making," revealing projects of imagining the nation, the world cookbook combined recipes as artefacts that ignored or even denied that "culture in the making." Waldo's cookbook, and myriad others published between the 1950s and early 1970s, introduced diners to foods form the Global South through dishes, not cuisines. The writing of a world cookbook compelled a micro reordering of recipes and their macro editing into categories of meats, seafood, appetizers, main courses, or desserts (or more). Turning a dish like Baigan soup into an American first course demanded a form of global disordering that privileged global tourist itineraries over national cuisines, traditions, or borders. Here, conceptions of commodity mobility that Alberto Arce and Terry Marsden applied to a corporate food system, can also help understand the appeal of the world cookbook.[5] As it gains economic and cultural value, the mobile food commodity generates relationships between consumers, typically in the Global North, and producers, typically in the Global South. In similar fashion, the world cookbook, in valuing world cookery over the homogeneity of continental food, transformed relationships between travellers and "the travelled upon" – to borrow Hal Rothman's phrase.[6] Local cuisines became tourist attractions and local cooks, sources of recipes fascinating to diners leafing through cookbooks far, far away.

Ripped out of national cookery through the experience of travel, individual dishes like Baigan soup were now available to American diners, but devoid of local contexts, meanings, and use. The soup reminded home diners and cooks of Fiji's white beaches and local peoples. Philip Crang's examination of the "displacement" of exotic commodities and foods highlights how "imagined and preformed representations about 'origins,' 'destinations,' and forms of 'travel' entangle diners in flows of both commodities and knowledge." "Take a look at the rest of the world through the kitchen window," suggested Lesley Branch in her 1955 cookbook, "and help yourself." Lunch in Turkey, sup in Lapland, and the next day, breakfast in Portugal and dine in the Congo.[7] World cookbooks reimagined unfamiliar dishes as taste travel. It rendered the cuisines beyond Europe edible, appealing, and accessible, but, paradoxically, through the methods and vocabulary of Euro-American cookery. If you could cook mock turtle soup, Baigan soup was easy.

Central to this displacement – the process of agglomerating dishes from specific locales into world cookbooks – is a process of replacement. Add anchovy paste and canned chicken stock to your Baigan soup. Cookbooks like Waldo's attached a positive value to seeking out, preparing, and eating world cuisines. But, in its appeal to home cooks, they did not valorize either authenticity or regional specificity. Rather, they offered a domestic, gastronomic reproduction of the around-the-world journey, with all the inequalities, demands for service, and presumptions of the tropics as sites for leisure fully intact. The replacement of familiar ingredients for unattainable or frightening ones and of global itineraries for national cuisines helps expound when and how consumers came to attach values to authenticity in restaurants long before in meals at home. In fact, the emergence of the world cookbook during the Cold War suggests that home cooks brought "world foods" into the American diet alongside and often in tension with the "ethnic restaurateur," as described Krishnendu Ray. If the ethnic restaurateur offered authenticity, the world cookbook reassured with replacement. In the end, they produced dishes that combined taste travel with familiarity.[8]

How the World Eats

Waldo turned her job as food consultant to Pan Am into a long career instructing Americans how to travel through eating and how to eat while travelling. She offered a list of "how to's" that together advocated a new, global diet for the postwar generation. She integrated world cuisine into American around-the-world tours, nights out, dinner parties, and daily meals that many wondered were making them fat – an admission that eating Western wasn't necessarily the best way. Was American food worse than palate dulling? Was it also dangerously fattening? In the world cookbook, a spicier diet promised world understanding and, simultaneously, happier, slimmer heteronormative American couples.

Waldo joined a postwar pantheon of cookbook authors who emerged from behind the anonymity of dust jackets to model ideal living in the midst of postwar prosperity. Julia Child explained how to cook French food. Craig Claiborne listed where to dine. James Beard described the right way of entertaining.

Waldo knew that a postwar generation that had learned to travel and was beginning to relearn how to eat, needed advice: where to stay, where to visit, what to eat, and what to avoid. Travelling with her husband in Greece, she met an Athenian family. Aware that Waldo and her husband were American (and surely wary of local foods), the Greek family suggested the nearby "very large, elaborate hotel." Waldo requested local foods, rather than "the sort of international food that could be expected at the fancy hotel." Their hosts were delighted, Waldo claimed. She and her husband ate baked fish at a ramshackle local restaurant and drank a pitcher of retsina. "I don't know when I've enjoyed myself more," said Waldo, just by leaving the hotel.[9]

Waldo was, by profession, a tourist, not a chef. She travelled as a food consultant for Pan American World Airways and, therefore, also for its Intercontinental Hotels subsidiary. She capitalized upon her work for Pan Am to edit the "How the World Eats" column for *This Week*, the popular Sunday magazine inserted into newspapers across the United States. Waldo also developed her own celebrity persona, blending experience as a leisure tourist, expertise as a corporate adviser, and her status as "wife." In travel guides, cookbooks, diet plans, and restaurant ratings, she appealed to an audience that could plan a trip around the word with just one call to Pan American. Child's cookbooks still top bestseller lists. Claiborne's *New York Times* cookbook has gone through numerous editions. Of Waldo's books, only her soufflé cookbook remains in print. She is less remembered, but among the most prolific, of this postwar celebrity-cookbook generation. In fact, today's anonymity represents an entrée into understanding her historical significance in the midst of the Cold War as American diners were tentatively learning to "eat the world."

Waldo and the vast range of her culinary and travel advice offer a chronology in the development of what Josée Johnston and Shyon Bauman have labelled "culinary omnivorousness." They note that, today, in an era when French food has been "de-sacralised," "the culinary omnivore can dabble in a variety of culinary forms picked from ethnic and class cultures around the world."[10] Omnivorousness, however, has its histories rooted in Cold War mobility. If today's culinary omnivores value "authenticity" and "geographic specificity," the postwar world cookbook valorized the exotic attraction of jet travel. Exotic foods represented stops on a tourist trail and Waldo recommended meals that picked freely from the spicy foods, especially from Asia and Latin America.

Spice, for hooks, is metaphor, but as real spices filled American pantries, they did, in fact, assume new meanings. Spices, like world foods in general, evoked travel and adventure. Waldo and other world food cookbook authors reimagined spices – and the foods they favoured – as exciting, exotic, but still accessible. Even the two biggest packaged spice companies that stocked supermarket shelves printed their own world cookbooks. Try "Ging Boortha" ("hot savoury prawns"), recommended Spice Islands. Of the sixteen ingredients, ten were Spice Islands dried spices and herbs. Indian foods were "artfully blended, exquisitely seasoned dishes," not "a one-sided cuisine of palate-paralyzing sameness," the spice company explained. As Lisa Heldke writes, contemporary dining guides "give us a good sense of how to make the exotic familiar." Much the same can be said about world cookbooks. "International dining," advertised Spice Islands, offered "flavours exotic and familiar."[11]

World cookbooks flourished from the early 1950s and until the 1970s when Waldo published her two-volume *The International Encyclopedia of Cooking*.[12] Though a handful were English or French, world cookbooks were especially popular in the United States. These cookbooks dashed across the world and grabbed recipes from as many places as possible. They chose their recipes based on their appeal and accessibility to American home cooks. The foods they promoted were not necessarily notable, traditional, or symbolically important dishes. Rather, they were exotic but unthreatening foods that fit neatly into a lexicon of lunch, dinner, breakfast, snacks, and hors d'oeuvres.

Often world cookbooks were, like Waldo's, published by companies either promoting global travel or possessing global reach. Among travel brands, Hilton, Sheraton, and SAS all published around-the-world cookbooks. ITT, Avon, Tupperware, and magazines from *Good House-keeping* to *Women's Day* also published world cookbooks.[13] In 1968, *Time-Life* began publishing its monumental *Foods of the World* series, blending recipes and accounts of travel adventures.[14]

Typically, Branch promised an adventure "around the world in eighty dishes." A world war and "the increase in international travel" whet the appetites of a "newer generation" for spicy foods, she explained. Waldo was part of that generation. Military mobility shaped tourist mobility and both, ultimately, increased the circulation of ingredients and recipes from the Global South. During the war, "when her husband was in the Navy," Waldo shopped at Army or Navy commissaries and began collecting local recipes.[15] Thousands of American soldiers returned home hungry for "a taste of Oriental and Mediterranean foods." Between 1948 and 1956, the sale of McCormick's dried oregano alone rose 5,200 per cent. "Americans today," the company enthused, "enjoy more interesting, more varied and more satisfying food than any nation has ever known before."[16]

Such curiosity for exotic foods not only appropriated dishes and ingredients but also promoted a particular kind of politics – a dining table liberalism. The taste for spice is not purely, as hooks might have it, a hunger for the "other." Through the popularity of the world cookbook, it reflected, as well, a desire for new global encounters and a liberal belief that the culinary omnivorousness of travel could produce a politics of understanding. The Women's Club of the Army Language School published its own world cookbook in 1953; NATO published its own four years later.[17] And, before either of these, the United States Committee for the United Nations published *Favorite Recipes from the United Nations*, featuring 170 recipes from everywhere from Afghanistan to Yugoslavia.[18] Food, as a reminder of "those fundamental elements common in the life of all of us," was a perfect representation of the liberalism behind support for the United Nations. Optimistic postwar liberalism promoted a sense of shared humanity and universal rights: in effect, an end-run around the legacies of race and racism that had produced not only empire but also fascism.[19]

Such a politics of commonality and friendship, overt in a political cookbook like that of the United Nations Committee and subtle in a branded world cookbook like Waldo's, helped link culinary adventure to tourism and liberalism to pleasure travel, both real and armchair. "Knowledge of another's way of life, and the pleasure derived from that knowledge," wrote the Committee to introduce its recipes, "will help to contribute to that awareness which precedes mutual friendship and respect." The Committee recommended its cookbook for "unusual food bazaars" or "progressive dinner parties." It turned to foreign offices, embassies, and legations in the United States for recipes and then passed those recipes to the American Home Economics Association to translate, test, measure, and frequently replace ingredients. The politics of commonality clashed with the reality that ingredients were hard to find and, even more, with reactions of disgust to some traditional ingredients. "Some ingredients like the one word 'organs' eluded our comprehension but aroused our anxiety," the Committee wrote.[20] Mobilities may have been entwined, but they followed different routes and occurred at different speeds. The knowledge of a recipe might have preceded the ingredients it required or, for that matter, their sensory acceptance. That was the challenge of writing an around-the-world cookbook.

How to Write an Around-the-World Cookbook

Start with an airline.

Postwar airplanes, trading speed for space, offered a different gastronomic experience than pre-war steamships. If steamships advertised multi-course meals in vast dining salons, airlines served trays at seats and drinks from rolling carts. Steamships sheltered timid passengers in the dining salon, even while in port. When Pan Am passengers landed, they disembarked. The complete around-the-world jet journey demanded eating more than broiled meats and boiled vegetables.

The pre-war steamship company printed elaborate menus for passengers to keep; Pan Am, instead, printed Waldo's cookbook and shared its recipes in its in-flight magazines. As a hard-bound brochure for the culinary adventures awaiting Pan Am tourists, the cookbook also offered around-the-world travel to anyone with a kitchen, money to spend on ingredients, and a few Western-style pots and pans. Waldo's "Mahi Biriani," the airline promised in 1969, is "a good dish to whip up at home." Marinate fish (halibut or cod, North American alternatives to local East Pakistani – now, Bangladeshi – fish) with some yogurt, garlic, ginger, and cumin. Add the fish to fried onions and rice. Boil with water, tinted with saffron, for a "taste-tickler" familiar to Americans as fish with rice, but in its spicing and methods, likely unfamiliar to a Bangladeshi home cook. Waldo linked the real experience of travel with the ability to produce dishes plucked from world cuisines in American kitchens for American dinner parties. For the airline, Mahi Biriani tempted to the tourist to travel. "There's more to Pakistan than meets the eye," it introduced the recipe. "Food [. . .] titillates the palate."[21]

Waldo's expertise flowed from travel, not professional cooking. That she travelled more and in the employ of the leading American airline, provided the network she needed to collect recipes and the platform for publishing. An airline promoting around-the-world travel and hotel holidays employed Waldo to promote local foods through domestic home cooking. That gendered blend of domestic homemaking and foreign travel shaped her "persona" as cookbook author, advice author, and travel guide. When she wrote about her travels, she blended her role as a working professional with that of a wife. As she made clear later in her cookbook for newlyweds, world cuisine recipes were meant to be made by women for men and guests.[22] The infrastructure and experience of travel could enliven a domestic (in all its meanings) monotony of meat and two veg.

Add local travel agents.

Waldo, the frequent flyer, wrote asking Pan Am employees across the globe to send recipes and details on local eating and drinking customs. Agents gathered recipes and "other culinary information" from nearby hotels and restaurants and, even, "local gourmet groups."[23] She then tested the recipes, replaced ingredients that were too hard to find and others that were "not in accordance with American taste by reason of excessive sweetness, spiciness, and so forth." Replacement transformed local foods from forbidding dangers to avoid into tourist attractions to taste. Here was travel, not as observation, but as interaction, however limited and guided. "In this atomic age," noted Waldo, "our neighbours *are* the Patagonians, the Zulus, and the people next door." Still neither Patagonian nor Zulu recipes made the list of culinary stops on her around-the-world journey; Pan Am did not (yet) fly to southern Argentina or South Africa.[24]

Recipes evoke place, but displaced and replaced in the world cookbook, they become, in effect, mass-reproducible souvenirs. Souvenirs can sometimes be that kind of overarching view that Mary Louise Pratt describes as the travelling gaze.[25] Just as often, souvenirs, whether postcards focused on a single monument or recipes of a single dish, deliberately decontextualize. As a way of reliving or virtually experiencing world travel, the world cookbook removes recipes from cuisine in all its regional, cultural, historical, or traditional contexts. Their appeal lies in the ability of home cooks to reproduce them, alongside other dishes from elsewhere, as part of a global culinary adventure.

Travel around New York to collect ingredients.

Need ingredients to make "Otak Otak – Fish, Straits Chinese Fashion"? Indonesian and Malay ingredients remained a tough find, but Edward Jurrjens imported a few. Waldo gave his post office box address in Farmingdale, New Jersey. There were, by contrast, plenty of Italian importers and she preferred Manganaro Foods for basic ingredients and Paul A. Urbani for her truffles.[26]

At a time when home cooks needed to contact importers at post office boxes, Waldo, the cookbook author, translated recipes from airline agents abroad for American cooks at home. Home cooks would have struggled to find coconut milk for Otak Otak, the base for her sauce. Without explaining what exactly this exotic ingredient *was*, Waldo provided a substitute. Combine milk with dried coconut, easy enough to find at many postwar supermarkets. Boil, then let sit for a half-hour. Strain and discard the pulp. Then brown some more coconut in butter, an untypical ingredient in Malaysia. Flavour chopped fish – whatever kind you found – with ginger and a pinch of turmeric from a jar purchased at the supermarket.

When Waldo promoted home cooking, she was far less insistent on authenticity than when she later judged ethnic restaurants in New York City. Miso may have been difficult to find and tasted strange, but when she recommended substituting beer, Japanese food became both familiar and exotic. When recipes preceded ingredients to American tables, Waldo selected recipes for her cookbooks based on which flavours she could replace, approximate, and domesticate.

Cook for your husband.

During World War II, Waldo directed, produced, and acted in a training film for the American Women's Voluntary services. She designed modern furniture, helped write a couple of dictionaries, and developed a hobby: "cooking and gathering recipes from all over the world." Pan Am happily promoted Waldo as a hobbyist, not a paid food consultant. Her cookbook was aimed at the "the American housewife" to experiment with new flavours and serve them to her husband. Luckily, the airline explained, Waldo's husband was a "seasoned traveller," a war veteran who didn't mind "tournedos one night and tufoli the next." She tested her recipes on her husband.[27]

Serve exotic food at a dinner party.

Waldo even adapted the Otak Otak preparation for the American dinner party. Place the fish and milky coconut in aluminum foil or parchment. (Few Americans could find banana leaves, the more typical

Malayan wrapper, in the United States at a time when Malaysia was just emerging from its anti-colonial insurrection.) She gave a novel hint to spice up the dinner party: "have each person open his at the table." Or, just as well, smaller servings "may be used as a hot hors d'oeuvre."[28] In the mobility of the recipe encouraged by Jet Age tourism, cultural context didn't travel.

Much was missing in Waldo's recipe, starting with the translation of the dish's name. In the cookbook, Waldo provided the Malay name with a soupçon of authenticity, but her translation was bland: "Fish, Straits Chinese Fashion." Otak, though, in Malay means "brains." The coarse-chopped fish, tinted yellow from the turmeric Waldo required, and from the spices, lemongrass, and chilli powder that she omitted, resembles scrambled brains. She thickened her mixture with ground almonds, easy enough to purchase, rather than the sago starch, so difficult to find that it would have needed explanation. In urban Indonesia, otak otak, wrapped in banana leaves and grilled, was common street food. Waldo turned it into a dinner party exotic starter. What emerged was an around-the-world cuisine, flown metaphorically to the American table on Pan Am jets, and ready for an American dinner party that offered something exotic, yet simple enough to cook and easy to approach. Airline mobility produced a particular kind of food mobility. Thus, in 1969, Pan Am invited its passengers to send the airline a recipe "that you'd like to introduce to the world."[29]

How to Travel

"What a wonderful age we live in!," cheered Waldo.[30] About a decade after she had begun her consultancy with Pan Am, Waldo began writing travel guides that advised travellers on what to eat and what to avoid. "Travel to foreign lands," she celebrated, "has become a way of life for Americans." The hotels were better in Asia and the Pacific than in Europe, she insisted. There were "fresh vistas and pleasures for American sightseers," but "merely seeing the sights" was not enough. Tourists, she advised, needed to get the "feel" of a foreign land. But, could tourists eat the food? Drink the water? What dishes should they eat and, just as important, which should they avoid?[31] In the context of Cold War politics, tourist mobility demanded strategies – and advice – for how to navigate ingredients, recipes, and restaurants.

Visit a Pan American representative, she recommended. She promoted her employer: "it is the one airline that always keeps pressing for lower fares."[32] She filled her guidebook with a list of "hows," including how to pack. Don't forget "two folding *plastic hangers*."[33] Cured meats, fruits, or vegetables "are never worth the trouble involved" in bringing home and "foreign candies" won't be allowed past customs.[34] Her guidebook advised travellers where to stay and, just as important, where to eat. Paid by Pan Am, she preferred Intercontinental to Hilton. "Naturally," she shrugged, "a Hilton hotel is the same all over the world." In Delhi, however, tourists would enjoy the Intercontinental. The Oberoi Intercontinental was 600 rooms of pure opulence – "everything you'd expect in a luxury hotel."[35]

In some Pan Am destinations, even those with Intercontinental branches, she gave her readers a gentle shove, out of the hotel, and into a select few local restaurants. Don't worry about eating raw fish in Japan, she reassured. In Japan, sushi and sashimi were just like "hot dogs of the Americans and fish and chips of the Britishers." They were foods to eat while drinking.[36] In Japan, eat out. If you feel "adventurous" and can overcome your "prejudice against raw fish," then "try *sushi* at Ozasa." She warned: sushi was expensive, so sample the raw fish with just a few bites. "Better try this first," she suggested, "before you attempt a complete meal."[37]

In India, Western-style hotels, where tourists were certain to sleep, served "just average" continental meals. After her visit to the Taj Mahal with her husband, Waldo sat down for lunch in a "British" hotel. The waiters offered roasted leg of lamb and a clear consommé. "My woe-begone expression caused the Indian waiter to ask me if anything was wrong." After some debate, he hesitantly offered the biryani the wait-staff were enjoying as a staff meal. As she appropriated their foods, she decided that the mixture of rice and spicy lamb, cooled with yogurt, was "to *memsahib's* taste, and yours too."[38]

On first bite, Indian foods might "taste strange." Be patient "and give it a try." She promised: "within a day, you'll probably learn to like it." You can't eat this way at home: "the pre-packaged curry powder you buy at home just doesn't exist here. That's why." Still, tourists should try those curries only in "western-style places." Calcutta "jumps at night" and there are "hundreds of Bengali restaurants," but tourists should remain wary. Instead, she recommended the curries at the Western-style Skyroom or Trinca's.[39]

There are travellers for whom "nothing makes them happier on a trip" than chicken soup, roast beef, and baked potatoes – even in Singapore. If you had to eat Western food, dine at your hotel, but the menu was still "British." That meant, Waldo warned, "almost inedible food." "As for me," she said, "I always have at least one Chinese meal a day" in Singapore. "It would seem," she explained, "that part of travelling, part of having an open mind, and part of your sightseeing would consist of dining out and seeing what the world eats." Just avoid the street hawkers and their unclean foods, "no matter how tempting they may seem."[40]

How to Diet Round-the-World

After eighteen trips around the world, Waldo admitted that food at home tasted dull. Even worse, if you were trying to diet, nothing could taste more "boring" than a regimen of cottage cheese, shredded lettuce, and skim milk.

By 1968, Waldo had become a celebrity cookbook author, travel guidebook author, and host of her own radio show on New York's WCBS. That year, her diet cookbook, like her travel guides and more fat-friendly cookbooks, offered vicarious journeys around the world.[41] In this case, they invited readers, home cooks, and dieters to play the role of tourists, trying many flavours in order to lose weight. The world cookbook as a diet guide helps expose not only the place assigned to non-Western foods on the American table but also the relationship of service behind the politics of culinary omnivorousness.

In her diet cookbooks, Waldo questioned the superiority of American diets. Too much food. Too many carbohydrates. Too much fat. Too boring. As a cookbook author – a tour guide across the world's tables – she removed strange ingredients and stranger tastes, extending the process of displacement and replacement. She reimagined world cuisine, not as disgusting or dangerous, but as interesting and slimming. A few (like Korean kimchee), she chided her readers to taste and taste again until the spicy tang became pleasing.

The world's cuisines, with a healthy serving of portion control, margarine, and sugar substitute, would save bloated and bored Americans. Don't be afraid of the food from "exotic, mysterious India," Waldo urged. The food was not quite as spicy as tourists or home cooks assumed. Try the tandoori chicken, the same dish she had recommended to tourists in Delhi, or the "morgee korma," simply chicken and yogurt. "Simply" – she chose the word to render exotic India accessible. For the dieter at home, she recommended Indian curried fish. Plenty was lost or replaced as a South Asian dish became an American diet recipe. Sauté onions and celery in butter or margarine. Add yogurt and 3 teaspoons of curry powder – the home cook shouldn't worry about the secret variations of each proper Indian cook. Pour that mix over strips of sole, flounder, or haddock and bake – just 155 calories a serving.[42]

Continue your diet travelling across the Sea of Bengal from India to Malaysia – "we're definitely in spice country!" To prepare "dondeng," tamarind, garlic, onions, and ginger flavoured "bits of steak." "It's all quite exotic" and "highly spiced," like other "warm climates."[43] Cross the Pacific all the way to Mexico where "one of the high points of the cuisine" is the "mole de guajolote (turkey in mole sauce)." Mole, she explained, even included chocolate. Here was Waldo's lesson for anything so exotic: "Before you reject the thought, taste. Delicious."[44]

How to Cook Spaghetti

Cold War tourist mobility informed the politics behind the omnivorousness that Waldo promoted. "If we are increasingly aware of those fundamental elements common in the life of all of us," the United Nations began its cookbook, "basic similarities and needs can unite human beings around the world far more than their differences divide them."[45] When the politics of world cuisine recapitulated pleasures of travel, emphasized culinary similarities, and, based on those likenesses, freely replaced ingredients to render dishes exotic, yet approachable, authenticity was not a priority for the home cook. As cookbook methods turned dinner-table liberalism into edible meals, Waldo stressed transferable methods, common utensils, and base recipes that tasted suspiciously European. This dinner-table liberalism rejected the supremacy, but not the centrality, of French or other European cuisines. "The joys of the table," argued Spice Islands, "belongs equally to all ages, conditions, countries, and times." That quote, though, was from Jean Anthelme Brillat-Savarin, the French gourmand.[46]

Spice Island's choice of a French aphorism to invite sampling of non-Western foods hints at Waldo's secret to world cooking: there were many recipes, but only a few methods. Any housewife with the loosest knowledge of Western cooking could produce exotic food starting from a base recipe. Waldo, too, quoted Brillat-Savarin: "Chicken is a canvas upon which the cook can paint." A simple sautéed chicken – the vocabulary remained French – was also a passport to the South Pacific and India. A few added pineapple chunks, raisins, and a splash of rum made it Pacific. Chopped onions, canned chickpeas, canned broth, yogurt, and a few teaspoons of pre-ground spices oriented the dish to India. "*Pollo, galinha, huhn, gai, Poulet, hens, kip, kykling, kana* [...] they're all chicken," she wrote.[47]

That was the secret of the world cookbook. Bengal muchlee was just "Ceylon's version of fish rolls." Ise-ebit was Japan's fried lobster. "Strange names," she wrote in a Pan Am in-flight magazine, "conceal homely dishes." The Siamese, for example, "disguise" the cruller under the "unlikely name of khanom saika."[48]

If the French or the Italian chicken could become Indian with just a few canned or packaged ingredients, how different could its peoples be? Rather than de-sacralising European foods for the home cook, the world cookbook author used its ingredients, methods, and utensils to render exotic foods familiar. Spaghetti, Italian noodles, were easy, comprehensible, and comforting. For Waldo, the "art of spaghetti" was, as much, an invitation to Asia.

Entangling pasta strands with Asian noodles, Waldo turned an Italian favourite into a world cuisine. On the inside cover of her *Art of Spaghetti Cookery* (1964), she provided a picture reference for pasta: rigatoni, fusilli, and below that a splayed pile of spaghetti. Between the spaghetti and the long macaroni curled Asian medium egg noodles at home on the same table as Italian pasta. If America loved its macaroni so much, that they added it to a patriotic song, Waldo pointed out that they could also love their Chinese noodles. Or their Vietnamese pho.[49] Spaghetti cookery revealed common bonds, a little gesture of culinary peacemaking in a fractured world. The commonplace nature of Italian food for American diners would help familiarize Chinese, Japanese, or Korean cooking. And, even better, if American cooks couldn't purchase Chinese noodles, Italian products – common enough in supermarkets – could stand in just fine. Even in her basic recipes, Waldo entwined west and east, ingredient evidence for a shared world cuisine. "Pasta al uovo" – egg noodle dough – kneaded together 4 cups of flour with 4 eggs with a teaspoon each of salt and vegetable oil.[50] Roll out the dough and cut into half-inch strips for fettucine or one-quarter-inch strips for tagliatelle. Chinese egg noodles were – with two extra eggs – identical to Italian pasta half a globe away. Add flour and eggs, knead "until smooth and elastic."[51] Once made, the dough – global pasta – could become either Chinese fried dumplings ("Chiao-Tzu") or ravioli.

The dinner-table liberalism practised in the art of spaghetti cookery blended travel and home cooking. Both were activities for couples. World food, in its appeals to mutual understanding and when wed to tourism, primarily added spice to the lives of Americans as tourists, dieters, home cooks, and couples. Waldo wrote as "food consultant to Pan American World Airways" and as one-half of a tourist couple. She assumed the roles of both the travel expert and as an ordinary American wife, as eager to try new tastes as to please her husband. She never actually named her husband in her writing (he was, in fact, Robert J. Schwarz, an attorney). Instead, they were together the travelling unit of "we." "We enjoyed these dishes abroad," she wrote to introduce her *Complete Meals in One Dish* (1965), "and our guests have enjoyed them too."[52]

How to Eat World Cuisine

"I have long been fascinated about what makes a particular person like a certain restaurant," Waldo introduced her diner's guide to New York in 1971. She imagined diners, dieters, wives and home cooks, and tourists constantly in motion around the world. When she advised them where to dine out in New York, she offered a global buffet in which exoticism mattered more than French class. As she complained about the doyens of fine dining and enthused over cheaper, non-Continental places, Waldo politicized the choice of evenings out. Waldo aligned herself with diners who craved nearby, yet exotic dining adventures, and when she awarded her "crowns," prices didn't matter; authenticity did.[53]

A few of New York's French palaces earned four crowns. (She refused to award any restaurant five crowns, holding out hope for improvement.)[54] La Côte Basque, earned its four crowns, but Waldo had her reservations. The service was "competent and professional," but if you weren't known to the restaurant, "distant." For its four crowns, you could only expect "generally quite good food" and a large cheque.[55]

By contrast, she lavished praise on El Parador, a Mexican restaurant. The service was courteous, never distant. She particularly liked the "chilli bean soup." La Caravelle featured an extensive, expensive wine list; El Parador offered Mexican beers, "the perfect accompaniment to this type of fiery food." "I have no hesitation," she decided, "in recommending El Parador as a model restaurant."[56] Humble, but authentic Chinese, Japanese, and other non-Western restaurants bested some of the city's Continental bastions. Màharlika earned its three crowns. Its Philippine cuisine was interesting, the service was welcoming, and the atmosphere was "delightful." Try the lechon (crispy, roasted pig) as an example of Chinese culinary influence.[57]

Le Cirque, however "handsome," earned only two crowns. The food could be excellent, but unless you were a regular, you were likely to be "ignored" by hassled, forgetful waiters. Choose wines from a comprehensive, but "wildly overpriced" list.[58] Or, you could save money and head cross-town to Tandoor, which served two-crown Indian delicacies like samosas, "unsweetened pastries stuffed with meat or potatoes." The namesake tandoor chicken was excellent, even if the curries were "toned down a bit for American tastes." At Tandoor, you didn't need to be a celebrity.[59]

But celebrity status would help at Trader Vic's to improve the food and the service. On weekend nights especially, this Polynesian pioneer was crowded, but Waldo wondered why. Maybe it was the "wildly expensive drinks." She used the word "Polynesian with considerable caution" to describe the chain. Trader Vic's food was "imitation Chinese" with "imitation Malayan, imitation Hawaiian South Pacific, and so on." The restaurant altered the dishes so dramatically that they no longer even resembled the authentic versions she had tasted on her own travels. Replacement was a necessity for the homemaker, but a sin in a restaurant. Not even worth a single crown, you can have a "much better and much cheaper Chinese meal" in Chinatown.[60] Why not try my own family's favourite: Say Eng Look? Just like Waldo, we always ordered and enjoyed their green fish, "strange looking but delicious," and the lion's head, "meatballs with cabbage, arranged to resemble a lion's mane."

Waldo agreed with my parents: she gave it two crowns.[61]

Conclusion

"Miss Waldo," admired the *Los Angeles Times*, "literally travels as the Army does – on her stomach." In 1967, Waldo was on the road again, travelling this time to promote her masterpiece: *The International Encyclopedia of Cooking*.[62]

At each stop in her publicity tour, Waldo, the home cook, wife, culinary tourist, and "food consultant for a globe-circling airline," prepared a banquet from her book. The menu listed the courses and the page number in her *Encyclopedia*. In San Francisco, she cooked Chinese foods. A guest in Phoenix wondered about the hearts-of-palm in the salad.[63] Check the page number. The first volume offered 4,000 recipes and the second, the glossary, included 20,000 terms.

"Why go abroad to eat steak," asked Waldo, more than a decade after helping popularize the world cookbook? The core of the encyclopedia remained the "*haut* [sic] *cuisine* of France, and the tasty, homelike dishes of Italy." The dishes and vocabulary from "eighty foreign countries" were, by contrast, souvenirs from her "years of travel" and from the tours of her readers. "Americans have thrown off their gastronomic inhibitions," she explained, "chiefly as a result of foreign travel." It would be easy to categorize her cookbooks as cultural appropriation and leave them in the dustbin of failed Cold War liberalism. Such a dismissal, though, ignores the way her encyclopaedia, her cookbooks, and many other popular world cookery books valorized encounters, however unequal, between Western, especially American, tourists and servers, cooks, and diners outside of the places of accepted and prestigious dining.

Cuisines are grounded in place, but, in the world cookbook and in the context of tourist mobilities, they became souvenirs. Waldo's two-volume encyclopedia prioritized the knowledge she gathered through the experience of travel over the intricacies of cuisine – at least, in the context of non-European foods. Ultimately, her encyclopedia represented a one-way introduction, offering Western readers insights about non-Western foods (but hardly, the other way around). Like a guidebook, this was a resource only for curious visitors. The recipes she included were "only those which are prepared with ingredients easily obtainable in our country." The ability of the American home cook to prepare a dish at home was Waldo's primary concern, as one news-paper noted: "She writes her recipes first for practicality, second for authenticity." For that reviewer, such an observation was praise.[64]

Sifting through a career's worth of recipes and food notes, Waldo recognized those foods travellers might encounter because of their local importance, but still guided them to what they should taste and what they should avoid. Cook, taste, and, then, travel. "A try-out at home is a help to the prospective tourist," suggested Waldo. Be wary, though, of the durian. The melonlike fruit had a "repellant odor"; the local appre-ciation was, therefore, inconsequential.[65]

The Jet Age, of course, didn't last. By the time Waldo published her encyclopedia, the outlook for world travel had passed from giddy to gloomy. Amid the 1970s oil crisis and economic downturn, Pan Am announced losses and trimmed its schedule. Waldo, though, announced the 22nd edition of *The Complete Around the World Cook-book*. As oil shocks rattled the optimism of the postwar enthusiasm for mass tourism, food promised virtual travel for couples at home when their real mobility confronted the 1970s economic downturn. For those who could still afford to travel, her advice remained the same: "Eat as much like the natives as possible." For everyone else "in these times of higher-than-ever food prices," she offered new meanings for exotic foods. "Because they're ethnic," she explained in Pan Am's in-flight magazine in 1973, "many of these recipes are moneysavers."[66]

NOTES

1 Myra Waldo, *The Complete Round-the-World Cookbook* (New York: Doubleday, 1954).
2 "For Release to Publications," 21 October 1954, Pan American World Airways, Inc. records, University of Miami Special Collections, Box 213, Folder 14.
3 Waldo, *The Complete Round-the-World Cookbook*, 283–4.

4 bell hooks, *Black Looks: Race and Representation* (Boston: South End Press, 1992), 21–39.

5 Arjun Appadurai, "How to Make a National Cuisine: Cookbooks in Contemporary India," *Comparative Studies in Society and History* 30, no. 1 (1988): 3–24; Alberto Arce and Terry Marsden, "The Social Construction of International Food: A New Research Agenda," *Economic Geography* 69, no. 3 (1993): 304; David Bell and Gill Valentine, *Consuming Geographies: We Are Where We Eat* (New York: Routledge, 1997), 192; Philip Crang, "Displacement, Consumption, and Identity," *Environment and Planning A* 28, no. 1 (1996): 47–67; Philip Crang and Ian Cook, "The World on a Plate," *Journal of Material Culture* 1, no. 2 (1996): 131–53.

6 Hal Rothman, *Devil's Bargains: Tourism in the Twentieth-Century American West* (Lawrence: University Press of Kansas, 1998).

7 Lesley Blanch, *Around the World in Eighty Dishes: The World through the Kitchen Window, Good Food from Other Lands and How to Cook It, Told to Young America* (New York: Harper, 1955), vii–viii.

8 Krishnendu Ray, *The Ethnic Restaurateur* (New York: Bloomsbury, 2016).

9 Myra Waldo, *Complete Meals in One Dish* (Garden City, NY: Doubleday, 1965), 36.

10 Josée Johnston and Shyon Baumann, "Democracy vs. Distinction: A Study of Omnivorousness in Gourmet Food Writing," *American Journal of Sociology* 113, no. 1 (2007): 165–204.

11 Spice Islands Home Economics Staff, *International Dining with Spice Islands* (San Francisco: Spice Islands, 1963), 25–31; Mary Collins (pseud.), *The McCormick Spices of the World Cookbook* (New York: McGraw-Hill, 1964), 1; Lisa M. Heldke, *Exotic Appetites: Ruminations of a Food Adventurer* (New York: Routledge, 2003), 70.

12 See, e.g.: Henry Smith, *Classical Recipes of the World, with Occasions for Their Use, and Master Culinary Guide* (New York: Macmillan,1954); Cyril Von Baumann and Beulah Phelps Harris, *The Four Winds Cookbook* (New York: Crowell, 1954); Dorothy A. Stevens, *Table Talk and Tidbits: Stories and Recipes from around the World* (Philadelphia: Judson Press, 1953); Frank Dorn, *The Dorn Cookbook, A Treasury of Fine Recipes from All around the World* (Chicago: H. Regnery, 1953); Ambrose Heath, *The International Cookery Book* (London: F. Muller, 1953).

13 *Food for Thought: An International Cookbook* (New York: International Telephone and Telegraph Corp., 1967); Mary Ann Zimmerman, *The Tupperware Book of Picnics, Parties & Snacks around the World* (New York: Simon & Schuster, 1967); Hilton Chefs, *Hilton International Cookbook* (Englewood Cliffs, NJ: Prentice-Hall, 1960); Myra Waldo, *Inter-continental Gourmet Cookbook* (New York: Macmillan, 1967); Charlotte Adams, *The SAS World-Wide Restaurant Cookbook* (New York: Random House, 1960);

Good Housekeeping: Around the World Cook Book (Chicago: Consolidated Book Publishers, 1958); *Woman's Day International Collector's Cook Book* (Greenwich, CT: Fawcett, 1967); Dorothy B. Marsh, ed., *The Good Housekeeping International Cookbook. Official World's Fair ed.* (New York: Harcourt, Brace & World, 1964); Dorothy Krell, *Adventures in Food, by the Editorial Staffs of Sunset Books and Sunset Magazine* (Menlo Park, CA: Lane, 1964); Wendy Buehr, *The Horizon Cookbook: A Treasury of 600 Recipes from Many Centuries and Many Lands, by the Editors of Horizon Magazine* (New York: American Heritage Press, 1971).

14 William Irving Kaufman, *The Wonderful World of Cooking* (New York: Dell, 1964); Ruth Gilmour, *International Food Flair: The Gourmet Cook's Tour* (New York: Pageant, 1967); Eileen Weppner, *The International Grandmothers' Cookbook: Favorite Recipes of Grandmothers from around the World* (Boulder, CO: Blue Mountain Arts, 1974).

15 "Try Some Bengal Muchlee," n.d., c. 1954, Pan Am Papers, Box 213, Folder 14.

16 Collins, *The McCormick Spices of the World Cookbook*, 1–6.

17 NATO Cookbook Committee, *The Best of Taste: The Finest Food of Fifteen Nations* (Annapolis, MD: U.S. Naval Institute, 1957); Army Language School Women's Club, *What's Cooking around the World* (Monterey, CA, 1953).

18 United States Committee for the United Nations, *Favorite Recipes from the United Nations: 170 Authentic Dishes. Edited and Kitchen-Tested by the American Home Economics Association* (Washington, 1951).

19 Carol A. Horton, *Race and the Making of American Liberalism* (New York: Oxford University Press, 2005); Michelle Brattain, "Race, Racism, and Antiracism: UNESCO and the Politics of Presenting Science to the Postwar Public," *American Historical Review* 112, no. 5 (2007): 1386–1413.

20 United States Committee for the United Nations, *Favorite Recipes from the United Nations*, 3–4.

21 "Gourmet Recipes," *Pan Am Clipper* 29 (1969): 4.

22 Myra Waldo, *1001 Ways to Please a Husband* (New York: D. Van Nostrand, 1958).

23 Waldo, *The Complete Round-the-World Cookbook*, 6.

24 Waldo, *The Complete Round-the-World Cookbook*, 6, 219–24.

25 Mary Louise Pratt, *Imperial Eyes: Travel Writing and Transculturation* (London: Routledge, 1992).

26 Waldo, *The Complete Round-the-World Cookbook*, 270–1, 466.

27 "Press release: Doubleday," n.d., c. 1954, Pan Am Papers, Box 213, Folder 14.

28 Waldo, *The Complete Round-the-World Cookbook*, 270–1.

29 "Gourmet Recipes," 4.

30 John C. Caldwell, *South Asia Travel Guide* (New York: John Day, 1960), 24.
31 Myra Waldo, *Myra Waldo's Travel Guide to the Orient and the Pacific* (New York: Macmillan, 1965), xxi–xxii, 21.
32 Waldo, *Myra Waldo's Travel Guide to the Orient and the Pacific*, 3–4, 22.
33 Waldo, *Myra Waldo's Travel Guide to the Orient and the Pacific*, 47.
34 Waldo, *Myra Waldo's Travel Guide to the Orient and the Pacific*, 68.
35 Waldo, *Myra Waldo's Travel Guide to the Orient and the Pacific*, 112, 403.
36 Waldo, *Myra Waldo's Travel Guide to the Orient and the Pacific*, 89.
37 Waldo, *Myra Waldo's Travel Guide to the Orient and the Pacific*, 118–22.
38 Myra Waldo, *Complete Meals in One Dish* (Garden City, NY: Doubleday, 1965), 178–9.
39 Waldo, *Myra Waldo's Travel Guide to the Orient and the Pacific*, 368–86, 394–5.
40 Waldo, *Myra Waldo's Travel Guide to the Orient and the Pacific*, 445, 452–3.
41 Myra Waldo, *Myra Waldo's Round-the-World Diet Cookbook* (New York: Macmillan, 1968).
42 Waldo, *Myra Waldo's Round-the-World Diet Cookbook*, 43.
43 Waldo, *Myra Waldo's Round-the-World Diet Cookbook*, 44.
44 Waldo, *Myra Waldo's Round-the-World Diet Cookbook*, 56.
45 United States Committee for the United Nations, *Favorite Recipes from the United Nations*, 1–5.
46 *International Dining with Spice Islands*, frontispiece.
47 Myra Waldo, "How the World Cooks: A Basic Recipe – Plus Four Exotic Variations," *Baltimore Sun*, 23 March 1969, 336; Myra Waldo, "How the World Cooks: Cooking for the Nixons," *Baltimore Sun*, 3 November 1968, TW12.
48 "Try Some Bengal Muchlee."
49 Myra Waldo, *The Art of Spaghetti Cookery* (London: W.H. Allen, 1965 [1964]).
50 Waldo, *The Art of Spaghetti Cookery*, 57.
51 Waldo, *The Art of Spaghetti Cookery*, 72–3.
52 Waldo, *Complete Meals in One Dish*, 1–3.
53 Myra Waldo, *Myra Waldo's Restaurant Guide to New York City and Vicinity* (New York: Collier Books, 1976), v–vi.
54 Waldo, *Myra Waldo's Restaurant Guide*, vii–ix.
55 Waldo, *Myra Waldo's Restaurant Guide*, 96–7.
56 Waldo, *Myra Waldo's Restaurant Guide*, 124.
57 Waldo, *Myra Waldo's Restaurant Guide*, 242.
58 Waldo, *Myra Waldo's Restaurant Guide*, 87–8.
59 Waldo, *Myra Waldo's Restaurant Guide*, 391–2.
60 Waldo, *Myra Waldo's Restaurant Guide*, 404.
61 Waldo, *Myra Waldo's Restaurant Guide*, 357.

62 Myra Waldo, *The International Encyclopedia of Cooking*. 2 vols. (New York: Macmillan, 1967); "More Adventure in Eating," *Los Angeles Times*, 16 November 1967, G24.

63 "An Atlas of Recipes from Aal to Zythum," *Arizona Republic*, 15 November 1967, 22D.

64 "More Adventure in Eating."

65 Waldo, *The International Encyclopedia of Cooking*, vol. 2, 193.

66 "Books That Make You Soar," *Pan Am*, December 1973, 38.

13 Hop Movements: The Global Invention of Craft Beer

JEFFREY M. PILCHER

In 1840, a German brewer named John Wagner carefully wrapped a sample of Bavarian, bottom-fermenting yeast and migrated with it across the Atlantic to Philadelphia, where he established the first lager brewery in the United States.[1] The Bavarian-style beer, with its mild, clean taste, proved enormously popular with Americans and by century's end, it had largely displaced the stronger flavours of English-style, top-fermented ales. Then in 2016, a California brewer named Greg Koch, an exponent of the West Coast-style of intensely bitter India Pale Ale (IPA), opened an outpost of his Stone Brewery in Berlin, daring German beer drinkers with the motto "You Are Not Worthy!" The irony of a descendant of German migrants returning to the ancestral homeland with an American version of an English ale was not lost on the *Berliner Kurier*, which dubbed Koch "Der Bier-Jesus aus Amerika" (The Beer Jesus from America).[2] This circular migration seemingly encapsulated the global history of beer, from the nineteenth-century spread of industrial lager beer out of Germany to the twenty-first-century revolution by post-industrial craft beer from the United States, although just three years later Koch closed the Berlin brewery. But contrary to the established narrative of heroic American entrepreneurs challenging global, corporate "Big Beer," as it has been called, this chapter examines the craft movement as a product of knowledge networks and circuits of mobility that blurred the boundaries between global and local, producer and consumer, and corporate and communal.

The desire to construct genealogies that nationalize foods and venerate founding fathers has been common in food history, and craft beer is no exception. The sociologist J. Nikol Beckham explained that such origin stories served to orient society by naturalizing the accomplishments of exceptional individuals and conferring authority and legitimacy on them. According to this narrative, early American microbrewers Fritz

Maytag, Jack McAuliffe, Jim Koch, and Ken Grossman shared a passion for good beer and a dissatisfaction with bland corporate products. Except for the cantankerous McAuliffe, all were rewarded with enormous wealth. Beckham concluded: "Though the microbrew revolution is frequently heralded as anticorporate, it did (and continues, through retelling, to do) much to reinforce the logics of the dominant capitalist regime by asserting that the most estimable form of leisure activity is that which generates a profit – that rebelliousness does not resist the corporate imperative, but rather extends it by making money at play."[3]

As a tale of American exceptionalism, the founding-father narrative of countercultural rebels also obscured the global nature of the craft movement. First, although the homebrewers who pioneered the industry traced their lineage to Prohibition-era outlaws, the hobby would have remained a fringe pursuit without international supply chains of high-quality malt, hops, and especially yeast, which became available after the UK legalized homebrewing in 1963. Second, this narrative depicted the brewer as mad scientist, tinkering with chemistry sets and assembling breweries out of junkyard surplus, when entrepreneurs depended on a technological infrastructure constructed by Big Beer. Much of the surplus equipment that ran early microbreweries came from regional firms that had been bankrupted by industrial consolidation in Europe and North America. For this reason, Jim Koch and other so-called contract brewers, whose business model employed the industry's skilled personnel and excess capacity, elicited scorn from rivals within the movement. Third, the rugged individualist narrative concealed the professional organizations and knowledge networks of beer writers and internet forums in circulating technical advice and running the beer festivals that served to educate consumers and to promote brands – an essential service for firms without large advertising budgets. These organizations and networks also devised and disseminated a shared vocabulary of taste that enabled aficionados to assert their rugged individual preferences for big, flavourful beers. And all of these supply chains, technical infrastructure, professional organizations, and knowledge networks were quickly globalized; while craft breweries languished in the US and UK for a decade around the turn of the millennium, they spread from Italy to Indonesia and from Brazil to Japan.

By examining supply, infrastructure, organizations, and knowledge, this essay applies a mobility studies perspective to the field of food studies. Despite their diverse methodological approaches, mobility studies scholars focus on three fundamental concepts: mode, scale, and exception. Mode implies the connections between movements of goods, people, and ideas, thereby unifying what are too often compartmentalized approaches to the commodity chains underlying food systems, the human mobilities that create culinary cultures, and the knowledge networks of shared taste communities. Scale draws attention to the connections between global, national, and local movements, helping to understand the concurrent processes of globalization, nationalization, and localization. Exception recognizes the power of nations and empires to regulate mobility, allowing some things and people to move while others are held in place. Taken together, these perspectives illustrate that the taste preferences and cultural practices of the craft beer movement arose literally through movement rather than as a product of a particular milieu, the West Coast counterculture.

Craft beer developed through three periods, each exemplified by a particular beer style. The story began in the 1960s, centred not on California but rather on the English Channel, as British and Belgian brewers and consumers sought to revive regional ales, whose full, sweet flavours were being displaced by light, dry lagers. In the 1970s and 1980s, craft beer spread through the British Commonwealth as well as the United States, although it was in the latter country that a revivalist movement anchored on the communal pub took a more individualist and innovation-driven direction. During the second period, from about 1990 to 2010, the microbrewing industry consolidated in its original Anglo-Belgian homelands while enthusiasts introduced homebrewing and niche brewpubs to new markets around the world. India Pale Ale, the iconic beer of this period, constituted less than 8 per cent of US craft sales as late as 2008, but its intensely bitter hop profile influenced the taste of beers across the craft market. Mobile print cultures of the internet promoted this preference through "imagined communities" of taste, to adapt Benedict Anderson's theory of nationalism to transnational beer connoisseurship.[4] A final period, beginning about 2010 and running at least through 2020, established microbrewing as a stable, mature industry, not just in Anglo-Belgian countries, but in non-traditional markets as well. Although some brewers continued to unleash ever more bitter beers, others increasingly followed a Zen path of spontaneous fermentation and barrel-aging in pursuit of mellow, sour beers. In seeking to expand beyond a niche market, brewers had to confront the movement's reputation for white, male exclusivity, a process of reconciliation that may have left a sour taste for some who had cultivated craft beer for its aura of individuality and status. In short, we can trace the global evolution of the craft beer movement through its shifting flavour profile, from sweet to bitter to sour.

The Sweet

On 5 March 1976, a rumpled British journalist named Michael Jackson called on the Liefmans Brewery in the town of Oudenaarde and met with the elegant brewmaster, Rose Blanquaert-Merckx. In his letter of introduction, Jackson had declared himself eager "to learn something about the traditional beers of Belgium!"[5] They toured the "sparkling copper kettles and well-racked cellars," then tasted the beers, including Gouden Band (Golden Band) Special, "a medium-strength brown ale, with a dry palate and a slightly sweet aftertaste."[6] A photographer followed later to portray Blanquaert, who smartly coordinated a tartan skirt and a Jeroboam of Kriek with the green Flemish landscape. The tasting notes and portrait appeared prominently in Jackson's *World Guide to Beer* (1977). This meeting constituted one link in a larger consumer movement spreading on both sides of the English Channel dedicated to the revival of sweet, regional ales. Their commercial and educational efforts inspired and facilitated the founding fathers of home- and microbrewing in the United States and the British Commonwealth.

Publication of the *World Guide to Beer* established Jackson as the prophet of craft brewing, a dialectical synthesis of Marxist organic intellectual and capitalist entrepreneur. Born in 1942 to a working-class, Jewish family in Huddersfield, West Yorkshire, he loved modern English literature and Samuel Smith's beer, which led naturally to a career in journalism.[7] Unlike the Oxbridge-educated Hugh Johnson, whose *World Atlas of Wine* (1971) was lavishly produced by the firm of George Philip, Britain's leading mapmaker, Jackson researched his beer guide on a shoestring. With journalistic inventiveness, he sent a mass mailing to the publicity departments of breweries around the world requesting information on beer types, flavour profiles, and most importantly, labels. The volume focused heavily on Europe; for Czech breweries, which did not have publicity departments under communism, he commissioned the journalist Jaroslav Kořán to compose the text and gather illustrations.[8] Elsewhere, he may have raised hackles with an Orientalist vision of the "romance of the East" and a request to South African Breweries for publicity materials from regional competitors.[9] He met resistance with equanimity, explaining in the preface: "Some of the brewers whose products I most admire have been recalcitrant to the point of discourtesy. I have made every effort, nonetheless, to do justice to their beers."[10]

Jackson's volume received a clamorous reception from a growing consumer movement in Britain. In 1971, four journalists and public relations consultants founded the Campaign for Real Ale (CAMRA), which challenged a tightening oligopoly of national breweries. The Big Six had cut costs in their chains of brewery-owned pubs or tied houses by replacing hand-pumped cask ales with the sterile fizz of carbon dioxide. One of the six, Carlsberg Tetley, dismissed the group as "bearded, be-sandaled, and with a generous girth from sampling a 'tad' too much fine ale."[11] Nevertheless, they attracted 40,000 visitors to the Covent Garden Beer Exhibition in September 1975 and published a *Good Beer Guide* listing pubs with flavourful ales.[12] The nostalgic appeal of traditional ales cut across political divides that shook the United Kingdom in the 1970s. Britain also had a lively homebrewing movement, having legalized the activity a decade earlier. The drugstore chain Boots marketed kits that dramatically raised the quality of amateur brewing, and they soon faced competition from the malting firms Edme and Munton & Fison. Homebrew accounted for an estimated 10 per cent of all British beer by the late 1970s, and the Amateur Winemaker's Conference added a beer section of the National Guild of Wine Judges.[13]

Consumer demand also inspired a renaissance of small breweries on both sides of the Channel. Many family or local breweries that had fallen on hard times were revived as the next generation took up the trade. In 1972, Martin Sykes relaunched the Selby Brewery of Middleborough, North Yorkshire, which had opened in 1894 and closed in 1954. Others started anew with skills acquired in the industry; David Bruce, a former brewer for Courage, built the Firkin chain of brewpubs starting in London in 1979 with the Elephant and Castle. In Oudenaarde, Rose Blanquaert began as a secretary at Liefmans after World War II and learned to brew as the company struggled with falling demand in the 1950s. She convinced her boss, Paul van Geluwe, to adjust the recipes to meet changing tastes, and when he died unexpectedly in 1972, she took over the operation. Meanwhile, in Hoegaarden, a milkman named Pierre Celis started homebrewing the distinctive local white beer (*witbier*) when the town's last brewery closed in 1957. He began selling to the public in 1965 and over two decades built a thriving regional market.[14]

Homebrewing played an even more important role in launching the US craft movement than it had across the Atlantic. Technically illegal since Prohibition, the bootlegging and back-to-the-land image was undercut by the terrible reputation of beer fermented in garbage cans with Fleischmann's yeast, Pabst Blue Ribbon malt, and granulated sugar. The quality of homebrew began to improve only in the late 1960s with the introduction of English brewing kits through mail-order catalogues and wine supply stores in immigrant neighbourhoods. Homebrewing clubs formed in countercultural enclaves from Los Angeles, California (Maltose Falcons), to Burlington, Vermont (Vermont Homebrewers

Association).[15] Charlie Papazian, the charismatic impresario who drew these networks together, began homebrewing around 1970 as a University of Virginia student, then taught night classes on brewing in Boulder, Colorado. He founded the American Homebrewers Association and published its first newsletter, *Zymurgy*, in 1978, even before legalization went into effect. His self-published class notes grew into *The Complete Joy of Homebrewing* (1984), the movement's bible. In 1981, CAMRA invited him to serve as a guest judge at the Great British Beer Festival, and upon meeting Michael Jackson, Papazian suggested an American festival. Jackson replied: "Yes of course, it would be a great start, but where would you find interesting beer?"[16] The Great American Beer Festival premiered the following year with just twenty beers, but it grew quickly in tandem with the Brewers' Association, a trade group for microbrewers established by Papazian.

The eccentric, outlaw spirit of homebrewing also animated the nascent American microbrewing industry. Fritz Maytag, heir to the washing machine fortune, purchased the failing Anchor Brewing Company of San Francisco in 1965 while kicking around after college. He brought to the business an appreciation for strong flavours inherited from his father's Amish-style, cheese-making hobby, and after a decade learning to brew and modernizing the factory, he broke into the nascent market for premium, imported beers such as Heineken. Meanwhile, Jack McAuliffe showed it was possible to open a small brewery without a family fortune. He had learned to homebrew while stationed as a navy technician in Scotland, then returned to California and earned an engineering degree. Unable to afford San Francisco real estate or even proper machinery, he moved to Sonoma and scavenged junk yards for dairy tanks. Despite his gruff manner, McAuliffe acquired a business partner – Suzanne Stern, a divorced and widowed Vassar graduate who, like many women of that era, moved to California for a new start – and an intern – Don Barkley, who was willing to work for beer to learn the business. They opened the New Albion Brewery in 1976 and gained a cult following in the Bay area but had trouble with distribution and could not finance needed expansion. Although the brewery failed, McAuliffe became craft's culture hero, a rugged individualist and mad scientist who brewed flavourful beer using junkyard scrap before being laid low by evil distributors and bankers. His founding-father narrative also set an industry pattern of erasing the female business partner and unpaid intern whose labour and financial support underwrote the business.[17]

Nevertheless, a more communitarian branch of the craft movement was already spreading across the British Commonwealth through

CAMRA's growing network of real ale aficionados. In 1982, John Mitchell founded North America's first brewpub in Horseshoe Bay, British Columbia, after a tour of English pubs. Another early CAMRA outpost opened at the Wellington County Brewery in Guelph, Ontario. Canadians preferred the term "cottage brewer" to the tech-inspired "microbrewer." Meanwhile, Lex Mitchell left his position at South African Breweries to make all-malt draft lager and cask-conditioned seasonal ales at an eponymous brewpub near Durban in 1983. A year later, an employee at Swan, Phil Sexton, converted to the Real Ale religion and opened Australia's first brewpub, Matilda Bay. Real ale even acquired a following in India among those whose affiliations lay more with the Commonwealth than with the country's two prohibitionist religions, Hinduism and Islam.[18]

Transnational business networks also facilitated the growth of craft brewing. Fritz Maytag first built a sustainable business by carving a niche in the premium, import market, and importers continued to drive an interest in Anglo-Belgian beers. Charles and Rose Ann Finkel, of Merchant du Vin in Seattle, began distributing Samuel Smith and other specialty beers in 1978 after reading Jackson's *World Guide to Beer*. Liefmans likewise entered the US market in the 1980s as Belgian wholesalers expanded their portfolio of exports. Europe also provided an important source for modern equipment, a choke point in the growth of microbreweries; Jack McAuliffe had failed when he could not expand beyond the original Rube Goldberg brewery. Pioneering microbrewers Ken Grossman of Sierra Nevada Brewing Co. in Chico, California, and Mark Stutrud of Summit Brewery in St. Paul, Minnesota, purchased second-hand German equipment in the 1980s to replace their original homebrew kit. American manufacturers and consultants also began to perceive this new market for small-scale producers. Harvard MBA and management consultant Jim Koch leveraged the industry most effectively with the Boston Beer Company. By hiring excess capacity from a regional brewer and marketing Samuel Adams lager himself, Koch bypassed the growing pains of earlier craft breweries to sell 700,000 barrels of beer a year by 1995.[19]

Defining beer styles and creating a language of taste was another transnational undertaking. Industry scientists had long sought to define precise sensory terms for quality control purposes, and a University of Copenhagen flavour chemist working at the Strohs Brewing Company, Morton Meilgaard, published a beer flavour wheel in 1979. Unlike Anne Noble's wine aroma wheel, which followed five years later, Meilgaard's goal was to identify possible flaws.[20] As I have shown elsewhere, Michael Jackson and other beer competition judges depended at first on this industrial approach to evaluation, even as they sought to articulate a more poetic language for appreciating beer's sensory qualities.[21] Critics also sought to define regional beer styles, noting the divergence between Old and New World brewers. In 1982, Jackson described New Albion beer, shortly before the brewery closed, as "what might be regarded as the English style."[22] His hesitation lay in the use of American hops, particularly the Cascade, released in 1972, which had been rejected by Coors as "too rank, pungent, and strong."[23] Fritz Maytag and Ken Grossman also used Cascade in their Anchor Liberty Ale and Sierra Nevada Pale Ale.

From the 1960s to the 1980s, craft brewers throughout the Anglo-Belgian world envisioned a new approach to brewing focused not on stripping out any possible imperfection but rather, as Michael Jackson put it, "getting flavour into the beer."[24] Yet sensory taste was only part of a craft ideal that opposed corporate control and sought to foster communities centred on local pubs. Already in the 1980s, craft's revolutionary spirit was threatened by Jim Koch's contract brewing model as well as by the inroads of Big Beer. Coors and Miller introduced craft-lookalike brands Killian Red and Blue Moon, while movement pioneers lost control of their breweries. A 1985 fire in Hoegaarden forced Pierre Celis to sell his underinsured brewery to the Belgian giant Interbrew, and five years later, the Australian firm CUB, maker of Foster's Lager, bought out Matilda Bay. The industry consultant Robert S. Weinberg observed: "Craft brewers have a wonderful thing because they're having their inefficiencies subsidized by a public that regards the higher price as a valid testimony of the superiority of the product."[25] It remained to be seen if consumers would demand social commitment or if superior flavour alone would justify the premium.

The Bitter

Bert Grant, a flamboyant Scots-Canadian who opened the first post-Prohibition brewpub in the United States, is often credited with the contemporary revival of India Pale Ale. The bracingly bitter beer resulted from a near tragedy in 1983, when Grant lost a large part of his olfactory nerve during brain surgery. "I can still sense a lot of the flavour of beer, but the subtler tastes and smells, especially in the hops, escape me now," he explained in his autobiography, *The Ale Master*. "Some say that's why my beers are 'over-the-top' hoppy – I add hops to the level where I can smell them!"[26] With his deep knowledge of brewing history, he named the beer after the British colonial trade in heavily hopped ale to India. Grant himself qualified his claim for reviving the style by recalling that the Ballantine Brewery of New Jersey had long marketed an IPA, and both Maytag and McAuliffe had experimented with the Cascade hops that gave American IPAs their distinctive citrus aroma, if not with the same intensity as Grant's IPA. "It was full of both the resiny flavour and bitterness of the hops." Michael Jackson declared: "nothing could match the shock of that first encounter."[27] IPAs grew ever stronger as a new generation of brewers, including Greg Koch of Stone, pushed the boundaries of taste. But bitterness was not limited to the beer, as industrial consolidation in the 1990s and 2000s led many to feel the craft beer movement had lost its early idealism.

After promising early growth in its largest markets, craft brewing hit a wall in the mid-1990s and stagnated for a full decade. Microbreweries and brewpubs in the United States peaked at 1,625 in 1998, fell to 1,469 in 2000, and recovered only by 2009. Craft brewers complained with some justice that distributors refused to carry their products on orders from domestic giants, although the real competition for the high-end market came from imports like Heineken. Perhaps the biggest problem was simply undercapitalization in a difficult business environment. Meanwhile, the British government sought to promote competition with the Beer Orders of 1989, which required large breweries to divest their tied houses and to offer "guest ale" in each establishment. But rather than providing outlets for independent brewers, the newly freed pubs were bought up by so-called Pubcos, hospitality conglomerates that allocated their guest taps to mass-market beers.[28]

Nevertheless, craft beer found new adherents in both traditional and new beer markets as an artisanal reaction against the spread of mass consumer culture. After the Iron Curtain fell, Czechs replaced antiquated, Soviet-era machinery with small-scale production, opening 220 craft breweries in two decades. Meanwhile, many young French and Italians embraced craft beer as a rebellion against wine-drinking elders; Teo Musso even played rock'n'roll music to encourage fermentation at the Baladin Brewery, which he founded in 1996 in the Langhe region of Italy, home to the Slow Food movement. Latin American craft beer began as a hobby of wealthy young "juniors" such as the aptly named Eduardo Bier, who opened Brazil's first brewpub in Porto Alegre in 1996. By contrast, Japan's craft beer took off with government assistance, beginning with the 1994 repeal of minimum production requirements and the legalization of homebrewing. Japanese traditions of craftsmanship encouraged an interest in microbreweries, and the giant firms Sapporo and Asahi were also supportive. Some 310 microbreweries opened in just four years, but the resulting overcapacity led to a decade of stagnation.[29] By 2010, craft beer had gained a global foothold among cosmopolitan elites, providing social mobility to the formerly proletarian image of beer, although small producers still offered little competition to mass-market lagers.

Both in the North Atlantic and around the world, the growth of craft beer depended on a transnational infrastructure of finance, education, and engineering. The success of Boston Beer and Sierra Nevada convinced bankers to lend money to entrepreneurs whose only experience was homebrewing. When these novices ran into trouble, they consulted experts such as Keith Thomas at London Polytechnic and Michael Lewis at the University of California, Davis, who provided technical support to craft brewers as university extension services. Berlin's venerable Brewing Institute (VLB) and the Siebel Institute in Chicago, formerly corporate training programs and consultants, began to enrol aspiring craft brewers. Specialist labs such as Wyeast of Mt. Hood, Oregon, assembled portfolios of high-quality, top-fermenting varieties beyond the basic "beer yeast" for mass-market lager. Technological innovation meanwhile allowed engineering firms such as DME Solutions, established in 1991 in Prince Edward Island, Canada, to provide complete kits for opening craft breweries. The storied Kiuchi sake brewery of Japan purchased an early model in 1994 when they began making a Western beer called Hitachino Nest. But even so-called turnkey breweries required installation support from local engineers. Another DME customer, Mazen Hajjar, who founded Lebanon's first microbrewery in the chaos of the 2006 war, recalled: "The brewery arrived in these big containers. I opened them and searched in vain for an instruction book."[30]

Professional organizations also sought to transform a rather anarchic social movement into a coherent industry. Both CAMRA and the Brewers Association replaced volunteers with professional staff, while comparable organizations formed elsewhere, including the Dutch homebrewers of PINT and the Small Brewery Collective (KBC). The proliferation of festivals, from Britain and the United States to the Osaka International Beer Summit, served to educate consumers but also required common standards for judging. In 1985, the United States Brewers Association created the Beer Judge Certification Programme to facilitate the evaluation of beer styles, and three years later, CAMRA began conducting a series of tasting trials under the direction of Mark Dorber at the White Horse Pub in London. Attempts to define beer styles generated confrontations between traditionalists seeking to preserve historic beers and innovators keen to personalize their products. Already in a 1994 seminar, Michael Jackson complained that India Pale Ale was "widely used, but beers no longer fit [the] description."[31]

Although unsuccessful in preserving traditional usages, Jackson's lifestyle journalism helped to forge a global community of beer connoisseurs. In 1989, he filmed a six-part television series with Britain's Channel 4 entitled "The Beer Hunter," which became Jackson's trademark. The series attracted a devoted following of viewers such as Andrew Lennox, who wrote from Australia to describe his father's plans to take him for his twenty-first birthday on a "Beer Hunter" trip to the Pilsener Urquell brewery. Jackson lectured widely and published tasting notes and brewery updates in a series of volumes, countless articles, and eventually a popular website, Beerhunter.com. Brewers around the world sought favourable reviews; importer Deh-Ta Hsiung offered to organize a tasting of Chinese beers at a popular London restaurant. Jackson could not fit the dinner into his hectic travel and writing schedule but did accept samples, which he tasted with his partner, Paddy Gunningham, perhaps over Chinese takeout. He recorded on a paper towel: "Five Star Beijing. At home 92. Clean taste, says Paddy, sherberty finish. I thought sweet, corn taste. Yes, definitely sweet, slight 'brown paper – gum arabic' tastes."[32] Working with industry required negotiations, as Jackson sought to remain impartial while still promoting underdogs, including small Belgian and Czech breweries and the craft movement generally. He insisted that advertisements list tasting notes as such, always attributed to "Michael Jackson – The Beer Hunter TM."[33]

But the imagined community of beer connoisseurship and tourism reached far beyond professional critics. Homebrewing clubs circulated newsletters already in the 1970s, and they often took a cosmopolitan perspective. A Kentucky club celebrated the 1995 defeat of Anheuser Busch's attempted takeover of the original Budweiser brewery in the Czech Republic. Beer tasting went online in 1992 with the Oxford Bottled Beer Database, an aggregate of supermarket listings maintained as a hobby by Tom Fryer. With no income and a flood of spam, the site withered, but in 1996, Todd and Jason Alström founded the *Beer Advocate* website as a venue for reviews. Ratebeer.com launched in 2000, at the peak of the dot-com bubble, but unlike so many startups, these beer sites attracted a devoted following. More than 6,000 individuals published nearly 300,000 reviews in Ratebeer's first four years.[34]

The IPA exerted a gravitational pull toward bitterness, although the global spread of craft increasingly diversified beer styles. California produced some of the best-known IPAs, and West Coast brewers launched a "hop arms race," a predictably military metaphor for the escalation of rankings on the International Bitterness Unit (IBU) scale. The Lagunitas Brewery, founded by Tony Magee in 1993, released an IPA with 51 IBUs, far above the 38 of Sierra Nevada Pale Ale. An old hippie, Magee embraced the northern California pot culture, while to the south, in Escondido, former recording studio entrepreneur Greg Koch's Stone IPA cranked up the IBUs to 71. Koch and his partner Steve Wagner reportedly stumbled on the original, punk-inspired Arrogant Bastard Ale with a recipe miscalculation that doubled the intended hop load. Surfer Sam Calagione, who established an East Coast out-post at Dogfish Head Brewery in Delaware, created a continuous hop-ping system for its 90-Minute IPA, which clocked in at 90 IBUs. But not all IPA brewers pursued hop megatonnage; a New England style of hazy IPAs aimed to bring out hop flavour and mouthfeel in place of sheer bitterness. Meanwhile, English brewers alluded to the beer's historical origins by adding Earl Grey tea to the brew kettle. Brewers Down Under used Tasmanian Cascade and other aromatic local hops to infuse a terroir character to their International Style Pale Ale. Terroir also inspired Fal Allen's brown ale with galangal and gula melaka at Archipelago Brewery in Singapore and Àlex Padró's Catalan winter ale with honey and rosemary at Llúpols i Llevats in Barcelona. Historical revivalism continued with the Dead Brewers Society, which collected pre–World War I regional British ales, and a Haarlem brewery made a historic Jopen beer to commemorate the town's 750th anniversary in 1995.[35]

Despite its global success, many of the social ideals that motivated the craft beer movement had turned bitter with industrial consolida-tion. The movement also lost a voice for moderation in 2007 with the passing of Michael Jackson from Parkinson's disease. Many early pioneers resented the growing corporatization, particularly among contract brewers, dismissed by Bert Grant as "just a bunch of pro-moters who are jumping on the bandwagon."[36] Yet other aspiring craft brewers, such as Dave Bonighton and Cam Hines, used con-tracts as a step to opening their acclaimed Mountain Goat Brew-ery in Melbourne, Australia. Oregon homebrewers actually joined Anheuser Busch in a lawsuit intended to force contract brewers to disclose their methods; the St. Louis giant was seeking to head off microbrewing ventures by Coors and Miller, although AB hedged its bets with stakes in the Redhook and Widmer breweries. Even darker shadows loomed as Inbev, the product of a 2004 merger between Belgium's Interbrew and Brazil's Ambev, proceeded to take over breweries large and small to fulfil its self-proclaimed destiny as the "World's Local Brewer."[37]

The Sour

In 2009, Annick De Splenter opened the Gruut City Brewery in Ghent, Belgium, with a plan to turn back the clock on brewing with hops, not just two decades, to pre-IPA levels, but more than five centuries, to the unhopped, medieval "gruit" beers of domestic brewsters. This was no amateur hobby project; she came from a long line of brewers – the family firm, Riva, was founded in 1896 and had purchased Liefmans in the 1990s after Rose Blanquaert retired. Having been told by her professors at the Ghent School of Brewing that making beer without hops was impossible, De Splenter set out to prove them wrong, experimenting with botanicals, herbs, fruits, and spices. She explained: "It's soft beer, not aggressive as some hopped beers can be. My beers are not sweet – they're drinkable."[38] Some aggressive brewers continued to push the boundaries of taste with so-called extreme beer, but others explored the mysteries of barrel aging and spontaneous fermentation, which restored global brewing to local roots. As the craft market reached a level of maturity, the community continued to diversify.

Before the introduction of pure yeast in the 1880s, all beers were more or less sour due to wild yeast strains like Brettanomyces and acetic and lactic acid bacteria. Belgian breweries that continued to brew in the old styles, such as Liefmans and the Brussels lambic brewery Cantillon, became pilgrimage destinations for craft brewers. Early experiments with sour beers in the United States received a boost in 1996, when the New Belgium Brewing Company recruited Rodenbach's brewmaster, Peter Bouckaert, to create a local version of the fabled Flemish brewery's barrel-aging system. Likewise, in Germany, top fermentation began to challenge the hegemony of lager. The sour Berliner Weisse, once a favourite of the bourgeoisie, ironically survived in socialist East Germany. Craft brewers later replaced the traditional red and green shots of raspberry syrup and woodruff essence with exotic tropical fruits. In the 1980s, even before the Wall fell, a Leipzig publican named Lothar Goldhahn contracted Berliner Weisse breweries to revive a local sour beer favoured with salt called *gose*. Homebrewers also braved wild yeast; a military officer named Joe returned to New York from a NATO posting in Brussels eager to make his own Belgian beers. After spritzing a diluted lambic sediment, he made an "exquisite" beer but disrupted the yeast ecology of his wife Sara's award-winning sourdough bread – clearly their home was only big enough for one microbiota.[39]

The revival of sour beer coincided with the return of stable growth in the craft brewing market. In the United States, the sector expanded more than fourfold in the 2010s from 1,756 to more than 8,000 breweries selling 13 per cent of the nation's beer by volume. Belgium achieved an even more remarkable revival of regional beers, as pilsner collapsed from 80 per cent market share in the 1970s to 30 per cent by the 2010s. Craft proliferated around the world, and although pilsner retained its overall dominance, breweries opened even in remote locations of Sub-Saharan Africa, Central Asia, and South America. Small firms benefited from continued innovation that lowered the minimum efficient volume of production. The Calgary firm Cask Brewery Systems designed canning equipment for limited runs with improved lining to preserve the delicate – or not so delicate – flavours of craft beer. Distribution remained a problem for many micros, but global consolidation actually increased outlets in countries such as Mexico, where local entrepreneurs could effectively protest unfair practices by foreign-owned goliaths.[40]

With continued growth came new opportunities for collaborations, fostering communities both imagined and real. An early exponent of collaborative brewing, Garrett Oliver of the Brooklyn Brewery, travelled widely, from traditional brewing capitals of England and Belgium to emerging craft hubs of Japan and Brazil. By the 2000s, the Danish brothers Mikkel and Jeppe Bjergso led a new tribe of so-called "gypsy" brewers who created recipes expressly for production by far-flung contract brewers. But international collaboration was not limited to globe-trotting celebrities; Jim and Jason Ebel of Two Brothers Brewing in Warrenville, Illinois, contacted Hildegard van Ostaden, brewmaster of the Urthel Brewery in Belgium, for assistance in brewing a Flemish red ale. They created the recipe by email, and then van Ostaden travelled for the actual brew and again for the release. Nor were these joint ventures always long distance; the development scholar Ignazio Cabras observed a "collaborative competition" among neighbouring microbrewers in Britain who shared equipment, expertise, and even exchanged kegs to increase the novelty for customers.[41]

The craft movement gradually began to afford new opportunities for women and minorities, who had been widely excluded from brewing since industrialization. In 1991, Teri Fahrendorf opened the Steelhead Brewpub in Eugene, Oregon, with the backing of a local restaurateur, because she was unable to find a brewmaster who would hire a woman assistant. On a 2007 road trip, she met many other women brewers who had experienced discrimination and formed a support group called the Pink Boots Society, which now counts more than 2,000 members in sixteen countries. The Queen of Craft group, sponsored by the Wellington Brewery of Ontario, sought to call out sexism in craft beer advertisements. Garrett Oliver, who is African American, declined to blame the craft beer industry for the lack of diversity, pointing instead to racism within the wider society. Taking a cue from disability activists, progressive brewers introduced mechanical systems to replace heavy lifting, which took a toll on male as well as female workers. Women and minority brewers also opposed the climate of exclusivity within the craft movement and beyond. A pioneering Latino-owned brewery in Chicago, 5 Rabbit, cancelled a lucrative contract to supply a blond ale to the Trump Hotel in 2015 when Donald Trump launched his presidential candidacy with a racist attack on Mexicans. The brewery sold the remaining stock with a caricature of Trump's hair on a label reading: "¡Chinga tu pelo!" (Fuck your hair).[42]

Even as craft grew more diverse, the collective profile of brewers and consumers changed relatively little since the movement's early days. Industry leaders in the United States admitted that the community was still "very, very white."[43] Globally, craft pioneers retained connections of travel, education, or diaspora to northern Europe and North America. Homebrewing hobbyists remained the essential wellspring of the movement as both consumers and entrepreneurs. The counterculture was another hotbed of craft brewing; old hippies established breweries from the beaches of El Salvador to the highlands of Bolivia, even as young Latin Americans learned to drink and brew craft beer while studying abroad. The information technology industry likewise maintained an affinity with microbrewing. Software engineers Bryan Do and Mark Hamon founded breweries in Korea after leaving Microsoft and Apple, respectively. Many so-called cyber desis and IT wallahs of Bangalore, India, acquired a taste for American-style craft beer on business trips to Seattle or Silicon Valley. Elsewhere in the British Commonwealth, connections back to England and CAMRA inspired a taste for real ale.[44]

The profile of craft beers changed faster than that of brewers, as a radical clique pushed an extreme beer agenda while localization continued around the world. Extreme brewers pursued ever higher numerical ratings, with Double Imperial IPAs reportedly weighing in at 1,000 or even 2,000 IBUs. Meanwhile, the Scottish firm Brewdog made news in 2010 with a 32 per cent alcohol beer called "Tactical Nuclear Penguin." The trade journal *Modern Brewery Age* reported: "The amazing thing is that it actually tastes like a beer."[45] When a German rival brewed an even higher alcohol beer, Brewdog escalated further by producing a dozen bottles of 55 per cent alcohol "End of History" beer, wrapped in taxidermied squirrels and stoats. Garrett Oliver declared: "The whole idea of extreme beer is bad for craft brewing. It doesn't expand the tent – it shrinks it."[46] But beyond the radical headlines, a growing rank of global brewers applied their own taste sensibilities to expand the range

of beers. Brazilian craft brewers, commanding a sophisticated repertoire of sweet and sour flavours, infused beers with *jabuticaba* (Brazilian
grapetree), *pimenta rosa* (Brazilian peppertree), and *erva mate* (mate tea).
The South African microbrewery Triggerfish added *buchu*, a medicinal
herb with peppermint and orange aromas, to a Belgian blonde ale. A
Midwestern American version of terroir emerged as Chicago brewers
aged beer in Kentucky Bourbon barrels.[47]

But with maturity the craft industry had to confront other problems
that had been largely ignored in the early decades of growth. In addition to the lack of diversity, workers remained poorly paid with few
benefits, under a business model that relied on temporary interns hoping to open their own breweries. In a 2014 search, journalist Don McIntosh found precisely one unionized microbrewery in the entire United
States.[48] Studies have shown that consumers continue to devalue the
products of female brewers, and indeed, some of the most prominent
women in craft beer, including Teri Fahrendorf, have given up day-to-
day brewing for better working conditions and healthcare benefits in
allied industries.[49] Climate change posed another formidable challenge
to creating a sustainable industry.[50] All this came on top of continued
threats from Big Beer; the 2015 purchase of the stoner brewery Lagunitas by Heineken illustrated the convergence of craft and tech, as beer
brands like apps were founded with the goal of selling out. Nevertheless, the efficiencies of small-scale production made craft brewing an
accessible form of entrepreneurship, rather like the family restaurant,
as long as consumers were still willing to pay more. Thus, after half
a century of change, craft brewing continued to depend on a sense of
purpose and community.

Conclusion

The craft movement arose in an age of globalization, and the global
pandemic of COVID-19 posed a mortal threat to small breweries in the
spring of 2020. Between border closures and nationwide lockdowns,
countless kegs of craft beer swirled down the drain for want of pubs
to serve them. Nevertheless, a sense of community came to the rescue
of many micros, such as the Attic Brewing Company of Philadelphia,
which delivered their Be Free or Die pilsner with its Harriet Tubman
label to customers isolated at home. At the height of the pandemic,
small groups of socially distanced people lingered by the makeshift
take-out window of my downtown Toronto local, Bar Volo. Brewers
took hope knowing that craft had revived from its decade of millennial stagnation during the Great Recession beginning in 2008, when fine

beer provided an affordable luxury in hard times, like lipstick during the Great Depression of the 1930s.

Craft beer has been enshrined with a revolutionary mythology, particularly in the United States, but like so many past revolutions, tales of founding fathers have obscured the contributions of broader networks of people. The Enlightenment ideals of liberty and equality that circulated through the Atlantic world and inspired revolutions two centuries ago have echoes in today's do-it-yourself rebellions against global corporations and mass consumption. Nevertheless, the tools that have enabled the craft movement – efficient, small-scale brewing technology and supply chains for malt, hops, and yeast – are themselves offshoots of the global brewing industry that craft partisans denounce. Like other foods discussed in this book, modern craft beer would not have arisen without the entwined mobility of people (brewers and consumers), goods (ingredients and beers), and ideas (recipes and reviews). Whether those transnational circulations and cosmopolitan communities will survive the contemporary rejection of globalism remains to be seen. The socially distanced anti-racism protests filling the streets in 2020 remind us of the continued struggle needed to achieve the Enlightenment ideals of liberty and equality. Craft brewers can contribute to that broader struggle by working for inclusion within their own communities.

NOTES

1 *One Hundred Years of Brewing* (Chicago: H.S. Rich, 1903), 207.
2 Alix Faßmann, "In Mariendorf braut sich was zusammen: Der Bier-Jesus aus Amerika," *Berliner Kurier,* 24 July 2014.
3 J. Nikol Beckham, "Entrepreneurial Leisure and the Microbrew Revolution: The Neoliberal Origins of the Craft Beer Movement," in *Untapped: Exploring the Cultural Dimensions of Craft Beer,* ed. Nathaniel G. Chapman, J. Slade Lellock, and Cameron D. Lippard (Morgantown: West Virginia University Press, 2017), 99–100.
4 Benedict Anderson, *Imagined Communities: Reflections on the Origins and Spread of Nationalism,* rev. ed (London: Verso, 1991); Michael A. Elliott, "The Rationalization of Craft Beer from Medieval Monks to Modern Microbrewers: A Weberian Analysis," in *Untapped,* 62.
5 Michael Jackson Collection, Special Collections, Oxford Brookes University, Oxford, UK (hereafter MJ), 4/21/81, Jackson to Rose Blanquaert, 24 February 1976.
6 Michael Jackson, *The World Guide to Beer* (Philadelphia: Running Press, 1997), 123.

7 Carolyn Smagalski, "Quintessentially Michael," in *Beer Hunter, Whiskey Chaser*, ed. Ian Buxton (London: Neil Wilson Publishing, 2009), 6–7.

8 MJ, 4/25/3, Jaroslav Kořán to Jackson, 5 August 1976.

9 MJ, 4/40/7, Jackson to Nicky Careem, 24 September 1976; 4/40/17/2, M.E. Robertson to Susan Van Tijn, 28 June 1976.

10 Jackson, *World Guide to Beer*, 4.

11 Quoted in C.M. Mason, and K.N. McNally, "Market Change, Distribution, and New Firm Formation and Growth: The Case of Real-Ale Breweries in the United Kingdom," *Environment and Planning A* 29, no. 2 (1997): 408.

12 Roger Protz and Tony Millns, eds., *Called to the Bar: An Account of the First 21 Years of the Campaign for Real Ale* (St. Albans, UK: CAMRA, 1992).

13 William Mares, *Making Beer* (New York: Alfred A. Knopf, 1984), 21, 105; "Guild History," *National Guild of Wine and Judges*, 27 December 2018.

14 Brian Glover, "The Growth of the Microbreweries," in *Called to the Bar*, 101–7; Kimberly Craven, "Brewery Calls Boss 'Madame,'" *The Oregonian*, September 1986; Raymond Billen, *Pierre Celis: My Life* (Antwerp, Belgium: Media Market Communications, 2005).

15 Stephen Morris, *The Great Beer Trek* (New York: Penguin, 1984), 206.

16 Charlie Papazian, *Microbrewed Adventures: A Lupulin-Filled Journey to the Heart and Flavor of the World's Great Craft Beers* (New York: HarperCollins, 2005), 17.

17 There are many accounts of craft beer's American founding fathers; a convenient starting place is Maureen Ogle, *Ambitious Brew: The Story of American Beer* (Orlando, FL: Harcourt, 2006), 258–65, 291–9. On the forgotten founding mother, see Frank Prial, "In California Wine Country, a Rare Beer," *New York Times*, 12 June 1979.

18 Vincent Cottone, "Craft Brewing Comes of Age," *The New Brewer* 1, no. 5 (1984): 3; Jackson, *Pocket Guide to Beer* (New York: Simon and Schuster, 1991), 166–71.

19 MJ, 4/40/11, Hans Gunther Schultze-Berndt, "Old Beers Revitalized," VLB lecture, 25 March 1987; Stuart Harris, "Expanding at the Seams," *The New Brewer*, unnumbered (November 1983): 4; Ogle, *Ambitious Brew*, 313.

20 Morton C. Meilgaard, C.E. Dalgliesh, and J.L. Clapperton, "Beer Flavour Terminology," *Journal of the Institute of Brewing* 85 (1979): 41.

21 Jeffrey M. Pilcher and Valeria Mantilla-Morales, "Is That Grapefruit in My Beer? The Rise of a Global Taste Community for Craft Beer," foodmobilities.net, 20 August 2020.

22 Jackson, *Pocket Guide to Beer* (New York: Putnam, 1982), 110.

23 Peter A. Kopp, *Hoptopia: A World of Agriculture and Beer in Oregon's Willamette Valley* (Oakland: University of California Press, 2016), 166.

24 Jackson, "Harmonic Convergence," *The New Brewer* 4, no. 6 (1987): 33.

25 Virginia Thomas, "Here's Looking at You," *The New Brewer* 13, no. 1 (1996): 21.

26 Bert Grant, *The Ale Master* (Seattle: Sasquatch Books, 1998), 97.

27 Jackson, *Michael Jackson's Beer Companion* (Philadelphia: Running Press, 1993), 85.

28 Kenneth G. Elzinga, Carol Horton Tremblay, and Victor J. Tremblay, "Craft Beer in the USA: Strategic Connections to Macro- and European Brewers," in *Economic Perspectives on Craft Beer: A Revolution in the Global Beer Industry*, ed. Christian Garavaglia and Johan Swinnen (New York: Palgrave Macmillan, 2018), 55–88; Ignazio Cabras, "Beer On! The Evolution of Micro- and Craft Brewing in the UK," in *Economic Perspectives on Craft Beer*, 373–96.

29 Charles W. Bamforth and Ignazio Cabras, "Interesting Times: Changes for Brewing," in *Brewing, Beer and Pubs: A Global Perspective*, ed. Cabras, David Higgins, and David Preece (London: Palgrave Macmillan, 2016), 18; MJ, 4/40/12/1, Charlie Papazian to Jackson, 31 March 1997; "Craft Beer Market in Japan," http://beertaster.org/index-e.html.

30 Quoted in Steve Hindy, "Building a Beer Culture in Lebanon," *The New Brewer* 29, no. 4 (2012): 86.

31 MJ, 4/17/104/2, Jackson to Henrietta [?], 14 February 1994. See also Charlie Papazian, "Introducing: Beer Style Guidelines," *The New Brewer* 9, no. 1 (1992): 10–16.

32 MJ, 4/40/8, Deh-Ta Hsiung to Jackson, 30 September 1992; tasting notes, 1992; 4/25/3, Andrew Lennox to Jackson, 9 July 1992.

33 MJ, 4/25/20, David Porteous to Frances Kelly, 20 September 2006.

34 Jessica Boak and Ray Bailey, "A Lost Decade of Beer Writing," *Boak and Bailey*, 19 October 2015; Eric K. Clemons, Guodong "Gordon" Gao, and Lorin M. Hitt, "When Online Reviews Meet Hyperdifferentiation: A Study of the Craft Beer Industry," *Journal of Management Information Systems* 23, no. 2 (2006): 158.

35 IBU ratings are taken from brewery websites; Neil Fisher, "Embracing the Haze: The Rise of New England IPAs," *The New Brewer* 35 no. 4 (2018): 56; Roger Protz, *IPA: A Legend in Our Time* (London: Pavillion, 2017), 7; Brad Rogers, "Australian Pale Ale," *The New Brewer* 25, no. 1 (2008): 21; Cara Parks, "Brewed Free in Catalonia," *Roads and Kingdoms*, 15 November 2013; Michiel van Dijk, Jochem Kroezen, and Bart Slob, "From Pilsner Desert to Craft Beer Oasis: The Rise of Craft Brewing in the Netherlands," in *Economic Perspectives on Craft Beer*, 239–93.

36 Grant, *The Ale Master*, 140.

37 Ogle, *Ambitious Brew*, 328–33; André Sammartino, "Craft Brewing in Australia: 1979–2015," in *Economic Perspectives on Craft Beer*, 397–423.

38 Quoted in Roger Protz, "Annick's Gruut Beer is the Spice of Life," *Protz on Beer* 31 January 2016.

39 MJ, 4/21/76, Hasung "Sara" Lee to Jackson, 4 April 1991. See also Fal
    Allen, *Gose: Brewing a Classic German Beer for the Modern Era* (Boulder, CO:
    Brewers Publications, 2018), 25–6.

40 Brewers Association, "Brewers Association Releases Annual Growth
    Report for 2019," 14 April 2020; Eline Poelmans and Johan Swinnen,
    "Belgium: Craft Beer Nation?" in *Economic Perspectives on Craft Beer: A
    Revolution in the Global Beer Industry*, ed. Christian Garavaglia and Johan
    Swinnen (New York: Palgrave Macmillan, 2018), 137–60; Greg Kitsock,
    "The Beer Can's Rebirth," *The New Brewer* 22, no. 4 (2005): 35–7.

41 Ignazio Cabras, "A Pint of Success: How Beer Is Revitalizing Cities and
    Local Economies in the United Kingdom," in *Untapped*, 46; Jim Clarke,
    "Beer Collaborations," *Imbibe*, 10 February 2010.

42 Courtney Iseman, "According to History, We Can Thank Women for Beer,"
    Huffington Post, 14 September 2018; Bill Simpson, "Driving for Diversity,"
    The New Brewer 13, no. 6 (1996): 69–71.

43 Mike Kallenberger, "Crafting Diversity," *The New Brewer* 27, no. 1
    (2010): 40.

44 "Interview: Brew Revolution Co-Founder Andy Newbom," *Food GPS*, 3
    January 2013; Kyle Navis, "Bolivian Beer," *All About Beer* 31 August 2015;
    Noah Lederman, "Suds Korea," *Slate*, 13 September 2015; Sudesh Mishra,
    "News from the Crypt: India, Modernity, and the West," *New Literary
    History* 40, no. 2 (2009): 315–44.

45 "Tactical Nuclear Penguin Brewdog," *Modern Brewery Age*, 3 January 2011.

46 Quoted in Burkhard Bilger, "A Better Brew: The Rise of Extreme Brewing,"
    The New Yorker, 24 November 2008.

47 Alessandro de Sá Mello de Costa, Rafael Cuba Mancebo, and Luís
    Alexandre Grubits De Paola Pessoa, "Museus Corporativos Estratégicos:
    Uma Analise do Espaço de Memória de Cervejaria Bohemia," *Sociedade,
    Contabilidade e Gestão* 11, no. 2 (2016): 100–17, 111.

48 Don McIntosh, "A Quest to Find Union Beer," *Northwest Labor Press*, 29
    July 2014. See also Dave Infante, "Craft Beer's Moral High Ground Doesn't
    Apply to its Workers," *Splinter*, 17 May 2018.

49 Elise Tak, Shelley J. Correll, and Sarah A. Soule, "Gender Inequality in
    Product Markets: When and How Status Beliefs Transfer to Products,"
    Social Forces 98, no. 2 (2019): 548–77.

50 Jenn Orgolini, "The Sustainable Craft Brewery," *The New Brewer* 28, no. 2
    (2011): 50–6.

14 Transnational Journeys and Biocultural Heritage: The Caribbean Food–Medicine Nexus

INA VANDEBROEK

Caribbean co-mobility of humans and plants spans multiple continents (the Americas, Africa, Europe, Asia), cultural groups, and periods of time, encompassing forced and voluntary historical and contemporary human migrations, native Caribbean plants, as well as deliberate and unintentional plant introductions. These geographic trajectories and cultural relationships are still visible today in the rich diversity of plants used across Caribbean islands and by their diaspora communities in New York City.

Caribbean Plant Knowledge Is Shaped by the Mobility of Humans and Plants

Characteristic of Caribbean plant use is the fluid functional bound-ary, whereby the same plant species can simultaneously function as a food and medicine, which is the case for several aromatics, seasonings, spices, and condiments. Thus, many plants that are well known for their food or culinary applications play a double role as medicines (hereafter called food medicines), representing a functional mobility whereby the part used medicinally and as a food is often different, and thus effective use is made of the whole biological organism.

Throughout this chapter, I use ethnobotany, the scientific study of plants, traditional knowledge about plants, and plant–human rela-tionships, as a lens through which I analyze the dynamic nature of Caribbean food medicines. The central question I pose is: What uni-fies and distinguishes Caribbean island nations in terms of their plant foods and medicines? To answer this question, I use results from field research in the anglophone and Spanish-speaking Caribbean (Jamaica and the Dominican Republic), and in New York City with the Carib-bean diaspora (Dominicans, Puerto Ricans, and Jamaicans), as well as secondary research through a review of the Caribbean ethnobotanical literature.

Delving into the dynamics of Caribbean knowledge systems requires a deeper look at the plants that move these systems. I will first discuss three examples of popular food medicines that are widely known and used across the Caribbean: soursop (*Annona muricata* L.), bitter orange (*Citrus* x *aurantium* L.), and ginger (*Zingiber officinale* Roscoe). These three aromatics feature popularly as Caribbean foodstuffs and in beverages, whereas their medicinal uses as a sedative (soursop), to relieve respiratory problems (bitter orange), or to treat digestive complaints (ginger) are also shared Caribbean-wide. Next, I will highlight three popular food medicines that have a narrower geographic impact and are emblematic of specific islands. These food medicines have a unique taste and flavour profile that instil a national heritage appeal, including orégano chiquito (*Lippia micromera* Schauer) in the Dominican Republic, recao (*Eryngium foetidum* L.) in Puerto Rico, and bissy (*Cola acuminata* P.Beauv. Schott & Endl.) in Jamaica.

The geographic origin of the food medicines discussed here is as diverse as the demographic profile of the Caribbean itself: soursop originates in Central and South America, bitter orange and ginger hail from Asia, orégano chiquito and recao are native to the Caribbean, and bissy was brought over from West Africa through the transatlantic slave trade. The cultural preferences for these food medicines can be traced back through space and time, and reflect distinct heritage contributions from different ancestral populations.

It is important to emphasize that the mobility of Caribbean plant knowledge is not confined to the past. The Caribbean diaspora in New York City continues to use these plants, underscoring their cultural importance, although the plants themselves may acquire new transnational medicinal uses, indicating a spatial mobility.

The central argument in this chapter is that the dynamics of traditional plant knowledge and plant use in the Caribbean islands can be explained by five characteristics of spatial, temporal, functional, and emotional mobility: (1) the exchange, blending, and recreation of multicultural knowledge systems; (2) the dual (opposing) role of aromatic plants as a unifying element in Caribbean cuisines and as a marker of specific national foodways and identities; (3) the multifunctionality of plants as foods and medicines; (4) the cross-cultural diversity of plant use; and (5) the cultural fluidity of plant use across historical and transnational boundaries.

In this chapter, I argue that the rich and dynamic traditional plant knowledge of Afrodescendant communities is moulded on the one hand by the co-mobility of plants and people, but on the other hand it is firmly rooted within the immobile geography of the Caribbean, and therefore merits to be recognized as inherently indigenous to these islands.

Caribbean Plant Knowledge Involves the Exchange, Experimentation with, and Reinvention of Cognitive and Biological Elements from Diverse Cultural Heritage Systems and Ecosystems

The Caribbean islands cover approximately 270,000 km^2 and represent one of the thirty-six hotspots in the world of biological diversity (in short, biodiversity), harbouring an estimated 11,200 native seed plant species, of which 72 per cent are endemics that occur only in the Caribbean.[1] This high degree of biodiversity is a consequence of the highly variable geography of these islands that promotes a variety of habitats and micro-climates. At the same time, Caribbean biodiversity is at serious risk of species extinction, due to deforestation and other human development activities. Most Caribbean islands have only about 21 to 30 per cent of forests left in their territory, and these percentages include natural forests, secondary forests affected by human activity, and forest-like plantations.[2]

European colonization of the Caribbean five centuries ago resulted in the introduction of many new crops and weeds, while Europeans also observed which plants that the Amerindian peoples native to this region used that could be of benefit to the colonial empire. Subsequently, they took and sent many economically useful Caribbean plants and weeds back to the Old World. This process, then called the "Columbian exchange," today would be firmly denounced as "biopiracy."

The history of Caribbean ethnobotany (i.e., the knowledge, use, and perception of plants by Caribbean communities) is one of mixing, blending, experimenting with, and reinventing plant knowledge from different ethnic groups and cultural traditions, resulting in the creation of a uniquely Caribbean biocultural heritage. This process is often referred to as "creolization," although some scholars have argued that this term should not be considered synonymous with either a polarized Eurocentric or Afrocentric hybridity. Others, such as Caribbean linguist Mervyn Alleyne, considered the meaning of the term unclear and abandoned its use altogether.

During the colonization of the Caribbean, between 1492 and 1886 (the date of the last abolishment of slavery in Cuba), Europeans forcefully transported almost five million African people belonging to different ethnic groups – mostly from West and Central Africa – through the transatlantic slave trade.[3] These Africans were obliged to work on plantations under gruesome conditions. Their survival strategy under these hostile living conditions was to grow their own food on provision grounds (if they were allowed to), and to seek out plants as remedies for healing and spiritual protection, and as an act of resistance against their European oppressors. In doing so, Africans in the Caribbean redefined the reciprocal relationships between plants as foods, medicines, and spiritual agents, blurring the boundaries between nutrition, healing, and spiritual well-being (see figure 14.1).[4]

Plantations represented colonial spaces of cross-cultural knowledge exchange between Africans, Europeans, and Indigenous Caribbean (Amerindian) people, even though the extent of this exchange is unclear, and Europeans and their diseases have decimated Amerindians.[5,6] Notwithstanding these multicultural influences, the manipulation of plants on plantations was undeniably in the hands of Africans.

Apart from these colonial spaces, Maroon communities represented independent environments where cross-cultural knowledge transmission took place. These communities were formed in mountainous areas by Africans who escaped from plantations, free Africans, Amerindians (including presumably Arawaks, Caribs, and Ciboney), and other minorities. Although Maroon communities were undeniably "African" in character, it is not possible to trace their African roots back to specific ethnic groups. Being a diverse group of people, Maroon communities in the Caribbean islands formed a shared cultural identity, based on their successful establishment in isolated and inaccessible mountain forests, and their successful guerrilla warfare against Europeans, especially the British.

After emancipation, knowledge exchange about plants continued in Native settlements of free Afro-Caribbean people, with other cultural groups who arrived later adding to, and amplifying, the cross-cultural Caribbean plant knowledge base, such as Asians who came to the Caribbean as indentured workers. Unfortunately, the contributions of these groups remain underexplored today.

Figure 14.1 represents a schematic overview of the non-hierarchical elements that have influenced contemporary Caribbean plant knowledge and plant use. Throughout history, different ethnic groups of Amerindian, African, European, Asian, and Middle Eastern ancestries brought their cultural knowledge, beliefs, world views, and plants to the Caribbean, and exchanged and transmitted their heritage verbally and through practice. In the Caribbean, these multicultural knowledge systems interacted with the existing (native) Caribbean plant diversity,

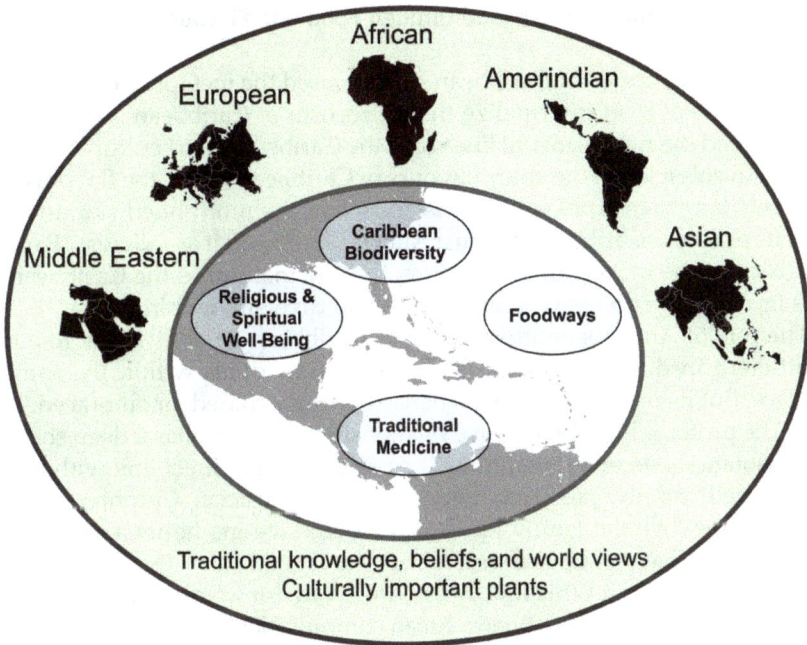

Figure 14.1 Non-hierarchical pillars of Caribbean traditional knowledge as a system of innovation based on the co-mobility of humans and plants, and the interaction with native Caribbean biodiversity. Drawing courtesy of Brian Hockaday.

whereby the multifunctionality of plants as foods, as traditional medicines, and for spiritual well-being took on a central role.

The dynamic process visualized in figure 14.1, and characterized by the multicultural reshaping of traditional plant knowledge, has continued into the twenty-first century due to the transnational mobility of Caribbean communities to the United States, Canada, the United Kingdom, and Europe. Given their multicultural history, innovation has always been at the core of Caribbean knowledge systems. Therefore, in new transnational environments, these systems readily recreate themselves through the incorporation of new cultural uses for already-known plants (e.g., the recent use of thyme to prevent COVID-19 infection),[7] even though the recognition and valuation of this body of knowledge as "Caribbean" remains central at the community level.[8]

Caribbean Culture Is Expressed through Food and Flavour

Higman, a historian of Caribbean studies, used the metaphor of a Caribbean plate of food to visualize the microcosm of Caribbean society. He described the rich historical lineage of the Caribbean as a "cultural stew" that reveals itself in the spicy flavours of Caribbean foods, the flavourful Creole languages spoken in the islands, and the multi-hued skin tones of its peoples.[9] Caribbean linguist Alleyne expressed it as follows: "Paradoxically, the most common feature, the one that unites the Caribbean, is its diversity; diversity among units, and diversity within a unit." [...] The role of Africa is another aspect of Caribbean diversity. This role is different in different places, in different individuals within the same place. But its presence is everywhere – denied, avoided, or embraced."[10]

The profound Caribbean love relationship with food has a deep social connotation and emotional mobility, representing a direct link with (the extended) family. Jamaican Reggae revival musician Chronixx sings "cause me love me family like a cook food/Late ina hours a night we cook food/Every plate haffi full up a rice and good stew" (lyrics from the song "Clean Like a Whistle"). Again, the word "stew" pops up, this time meaning a dish. Among Puerto Rican communities in the United States, those who are "island-born" are often the ones who prepare typical Puerto Rican "soul food" dishes to keep the memory of their distant homeland alive, and transmit that heritage to their children and grandchildren.[11]

The desire to endow dishes with taste, aroma, and colour has been recognized as a unifying basis of Caribbean cooking.[12] Even though a specific "Caribbean cuisine" did not emerge in cookbooks until the 1970s, spice appeared as the distinguishing feature of this common creole cuisine. "Creole," here, Higman specified, "is used to indicate mixture as well as local [Caribbean] origin." Other Caribbean historians have used the word "bricolage" when referring to Caribbean seasonings, emphasizing again the diverse plant ingredients that are native not only to the Caribbean but to different geographic world regions, and that represent the cultural memories and survival strategies of diverse populations that have left their imprint on Caribbean cooking.

Spices, condiments, seasonings, and other aromatics are thus central to Caribbean cooking and considered a daily culinary necessity, although different islands use different blends of plants with varying degrees of spiciness.[13] The process of sautéing herbs, (hot or sweet) chilli peppers, and adding condiments are daily preparatory steps to season meat and prepare legume-based stews that accompany rice. Over time, island-specific seasoning recipes, known as "sofrito" in Puerto Rico, "sazón" in the Dominican Republic, "jerk seasoning" in Jamaica, and "epis" in

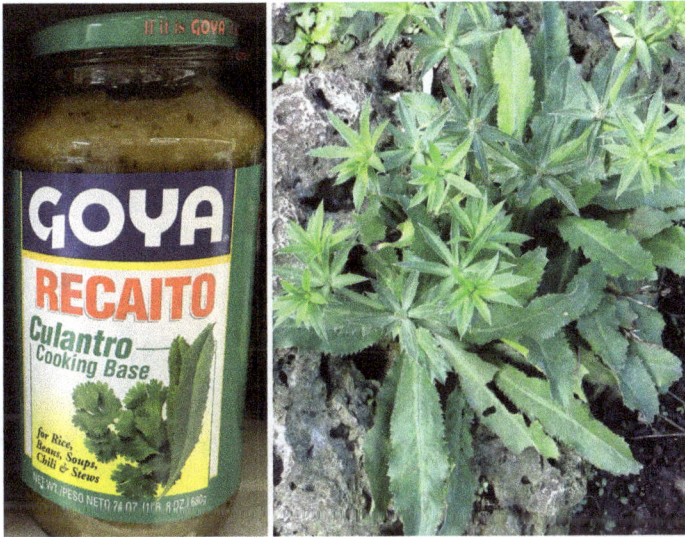

Figure 14.2 The plant species *Eryngium foetidum* is known in Puerto Rico by its common name recao (diminutive recaito), in the Dominican Republic as cilantro sabanero, and in Jamaica as fit(s) weed or spirit weed. In New York City, several brands offer sofrito seasoning featuring this aromatic herb. Photo by the author.

Haiti have become iconic to their national cuisines. These seasonings are so important that they are patiently explained by enthusiastic home cooks in many YouTube tutorials, and exchanged in recipes by members of Facebook groups dedicated to Caribbean cooking.

With the cultural bricolage as a model, the ingredients of Caribbean seasonings came together over time. For Puerto Rican sofrito, these ingredients included "recao" or wild coriander (*Eryngium foetidum* L.), sweet and green peppers (*Capsicum* spp.), annatto (*Bixa orellana* L.), or tomato (*Solanum lycopersicum* L.) (figure 14.2). With the exception of tomatoes, these species were already a part of the flora of the Caribbean before the arrival of Europeans and Africans, and the Native Caribbean Arawak people knew and used them. According to Ortiz Cuadra, the remaining ingredients in Puerto Rican sofrito were "adopted" from Europeans and Africans. These included onions (*Allium cepa* L.), capers (*Capparis spinosa* L.), garlic (*Allium sativum* L.), cumin (*Cuminum cyminum* L.), and cilantro or coriander (*Coriandrum sativum* L.). Non-plant ingredients in sofrito were vinegar, lard, or oil. Onion and garlic were important in the Spanish cuisines of Castile, Extremadura, and Andalusia, and the latter had incorporated the use of cumin and coriander from North Africa.

Figure 14.3 The plant *Lippia micromera* is known in the Dominican Republic and Puerto Rico as orégano chiquito or orégano de cocinar, and as thym or diten in the French-speaking Caribbean. It is a different species than Mediterranean oregano or thyme, although it bears the same name. In New York City, dry orégano labelled as "authentic from your land" featuring the flag of the Dominican Republic is offered in shops and supermarkets catering to Dominican customers. Photo by the author.

In the Dominican Republic, Roersch explained that *Lippia micromera*, the oregano that instils its taste in Dominican seasoning, is not the same plant species as the oregano used in Europe, the latter being *Origanum vulgare* L. *Lippia micromera* belongs to the Verbenaceae (vervain or verbena family), and has a native range that includes the Caribbean and Central America to Guyana. *Origanum vulgare* on the other hand, belongs to the Lamiaceae (mint family), and its native distribution includes temperate western and southwestern Eurasia and the Mediterranean region.[14] Although both spices have similar smell and taste profiles, their aromas are also different enough to instil profound cultural meanings for Dominicans, with *Lippia micromera* receiving the honorary denomination of "óregano del pais" ("oregano from the Dominican Republic" or "our oregano") (figure 14.3).

The meaning of seasoning in the Caribbean extends well beyond embodying "Caribbean flavours" through key spices and condiments. For inhabitants of the Dominican Republic, knowing how to make *sazón*, the Spanish word for seasoning, means to master a certain skill, and to demonstrate creativity, experience, as well as a personalized style of cooking. Puerto Rico and the mainland United States are important export destinations for *Lippia micromera* from the Dominican Republic, because these countries have sizeable populations of Dominicans, and the taste of this particular orégano is seen as "inseparable" from Dominican seasoning.

In her study, Marte elaborated on how Dominican immigrants "season their foods and lives" in New York City, navigating the many hurdles immigrants have to overcome, and how they are "seasoned into new sociocultural relationships in receiving societies."[15] However, she also discussed that the term "seasoning" has some very traumatic historical connotations, in that it "referred to the practice of forceful enculturation or 'breaking' of African enslaved people in the Caribbean and also alludes to the more ideological and representational practices of racialization during colonial times." Hans Sloane, in his nineteenth-century Caribbean work with a special focus on Jamaica, also mentioned seasoning as a process of hardship for European colonizers, stating that "a great many were of opinion that this Fever was what is call'd the Seasoning, that is to say, that every Newcomer before they be accustomed to the Climate and Constitution of the Air in Jamaica, are to have an acute Disease, which is thought to be very dangerous, and that after this is over, their Bodies are made more fit to live there, with less hazard than before; and this is not only thought so in that Island, but in Guinea, and all over the remote Eastern parts of the World."[16]

The Food–Medicine Link Embodies a Functional Caribbean Mobility

In her book on Puerto Rican home remedies, writer Maria Benedetti recalls that while growing up in the United States, her Puerto Rican roots remained obscure until adulthood, when she began recognizing and celebrating them. Her maternal grandmother played a pivotal role in this process, as the person who prepared traditional Puerto Rican "soul food" dishes. At the same time, her grandmother was the family nurse, preparing herbal teas when her grandchildren got sick, thereby personifying and maintaining the close relationship that exists in the Caribbean between family, food, and health.

Some authors have revisited the role of spices and seasonings, not only stating that they add flavour and colour to cooking but also linking their use directly to health in a dual role as medicines. According to Ortiz Cuadra, cultural knowledge of Caribbean islanders about the healing properties of wild herbs, peppers, garlic, and onions probably contributed to the development of a common sofrito recipe in Puerto Rico. The gradual historical development of these seasonings, and their central role in cooking, may reflect countless creative attempts to preserve meat in a tropical climate at times when refrigerators were not available, because they act as inhibitors for the growth of dangerous bacteria. By ranking countries according to their mean annual temperature on the one hand, and by the average number of spices used in meat recipes from traditional cookbooks on the other hand, other authors have shown that hotter countries used more spices (more spices in total, a higher average number of spices per recipe, and a higher proportion of recipes with at least one spice). Furthermore, according to food microbiology studies, popular spices in recipes from these countries exhibited the most potent antibacterial and antifungal properties.[17]

Survey research in 2006 by myself and colleagues in the Dominican Republic showed that spices and condiments were popularly used for gastrointestinal complaints, the flu, and regulation of blood pressure. Orégano (*Lippia micromera*) and garlic (*Allium sativum*) were commonly mentioned by people as a remedy for diarrhea, and garlic also for hypertension. Ginger (*Zingiber officinale*) was a favourite to treat arthritis, labour pain, flu, and hypotension. The main medicinal use of cinnamon (*Cinnamomum* spp.) was to treat the flu.[18]

Fruits are another type of Caribbean food that demonstrate a strong relationship with health and health care. Interestingly, interviews showed that Dominicans used several plant parts for medicinal purposes. Thus, the aromatic leaves of lime (*Citrus* x *aurantiifolia* (Christm. Swingle), bitter orange (*Citrus* x *aurantium*), and soursop (*Annona muricata*) were much appreciated as a tea. These plants and other, non-aromatic species (including guava, *Psidium guajava* L.; coconut, *Cocos nucifera* L.; avocado, *Persea americana* Mill.), again using a variety of plant parts, were also drunk as a tea, applied in rituals, prepared as a steam bath, or soaked in alcohol, for treating a variety of diseases.

Spatial Mobility (Continuity and Transformation) of Caribbean Plant Knowledge and Use

In the transnational urban environment, food plants become even more important as medicines, especially among the Dominican diaspora. In our ethnobotanical research, this quickly became evident when tallying reports whereby Dominicans in New York City mentioned food medicines significantly more often than their peers in the Dominican Republic.

The increased popularity of food medicines after migration became especially relevant for treating non-communicable diseases, which represent the leading cause of death globally and are the consequence of unhealthy diets, physical inactivity, and other risk factors. We observed that the Dominican community dynamically adapted its medicinal plant pharmacopoeia. In New York City, there were significantly more reports of lime to treat asthma and chest congestion, of bitter orange to treat sinusitis and diabetes, and of garlic to treat hypertension, than in the Dominican Republic. In contrast, the medicinal uses of food medicines for health problems that were prevalent in the Caribbean (but not in New York City) decreased in popularity in the latter location, including the use of lime for bruises, bitter orange for shingles and wounds, cinnamon for cough, and garlic for intestinal parasites.

We hypothesized that there were several reasons why the perceived medicinal value of foods increased after migration: (1) common foods are easily accessible and available in commerce in the urban environment; (2) knowledge about foods as medicines does not belong to the domain of plant specialists (healers), and is therefore not proprietary or secret knowledge, which promotes its sharing among laypeople; (3) food medicines are GRAS (Generally Recommended as Safe), and thus concerns about toxicity may be less of an issue than with other plant remedies, which in turn may boost their use; (4) foods continue to be widely promoted by influencers on audiovisual and social media as "healthy" and "medicinal." For Caribbean foods that are important in the diaspora, this will only enhance their status as ambassadors of Caribbean identity.

The Ethnobotany of Caribbean Food Medicines

One cannot fully appreciate the culinary and medicinal plant heritage of the Caribbean, and its continuous path of rediscovery and innovation, without understanding the botany and ethnobotany of the region from a historical and contemporary perspective.

Readers who are not plant scientists may wonder why it is relevant to learn about the botany and ethnobotany of the Caribbean food medicines discussed in this chapter. To answer this question, we have to go back to the fifteenth century, when Florentine physician Paolo da Pozzi Toscanelli told Christopher Columbus that if he sailed westward to the East he would find interesting spices. However, when Columbus reached the Caribbean, it caused him great grief that he was unable to identify the spices and medicinal plants he found there.[19] In October 1492, Columbus wrote in his diary: "There are trees of a thousand types, all with their various fruits and all scented. I am the saddest man in the world because I do not recognize them, for I am sure they are

of great value in Spain for dyes and as medicinal spices. I am bringing specimens of them to Your Highnesses."[20] However, the plants that
Columbus brought back to Europe from the Caribbean were not the
ones he thought they were; they were not mastic, aloes, nutmeg, cinnamon, pepper, gum arabic, sandalwood, incense, or rhubarb. That was
because he had misidentified all these plant species.

It was not until botany emerged as an independent science, and botanists carefully described the distinguishing characteristics of each plant
species in floristic works ("floras"), that plants could be properly recognized and compared with each other. A flora is a treatise of the plants of
a particular region. The botanical descriptions of plants in these floras
are linked to field collections of dried specimens carefully prepared by
botanists, deposited in herbaria, and stored there as permanent records.
A herbarium can be considered a sort of library that is filled with dried
plants instead of books, each plant telling the story of the locality where
it grew at a particular moment in time. These dried specimens support
the plant descriptions in floras, and serve as physical evidence for the
scientific plant name.

A scientific plant name (or botanical Latin name) contains important
information about a plant's identity. Common (local) names of plants
are often insufficient to figure out their identity, because these names
tend to vary across countries, and even within the same country. The
scientific name of a plant unites its various common names under a
single botanical name. For example, the common name of soursop differs in the Caribbean according to country, region, and language, but
all these common names correspond with the scientific name *Annona
muricata* L., which is the accepted scientific name known by every plant
scientist. The abbreviation "L." here represents the family name of the
person who first described the species, in this case the Swedish botanist,
zoologist, taxonomist, and physician Carl Linnaeus The standardization of this naming process is a way for scientists to ascertain which
species they are communicating about. Imagine when a cherry is not
the cherry you know, nor is an apple, or a pear? Imagine that you go to a
market in a foreign country and you want to buy these three fruits, only
to find out that they are not what you asked for? In order to communi-
cate within (and across) disciplines about a plant species, the first step
is to ascertain its proper identity. Botany represents the tool to do that.

Apart from being a hotspot of plant diversity, the Caribbean is also
a diverse hub of cultural knowledge about plants. Different Caribbean
countries share plant species to varying degrees. For example, Jamaica
and the Dominican Republic share about a quarter (23 per cent) of the
plants growing in both countries. However, even though a particular

species is growing in several Caribbean islands, this does not necessarily mean that the inhabitants of these islands also use that plant as a food, or as a medicine. And even if they do use it as a medicine, they might be using it for different medicinal purposes. This is where the complex interactions between the environment, plants, and culture come into play. In the same way that the common names of plant species vary, their human uses vary as well. In order to better understand the ethnobotanical richness of a region, it is thus important to compare ethnobotanical uses across geographic boundaries and time. Here is where (ethno)botany intersects with other disciplines, including geography, anthropology, ecology, and history.

The exact number of medicinal plants in the Caribbean region, or in specific Caribbean islands, remains unknown, but site-restricted surveys in individual islands have yielded inventories that ranged between 100 to 200 plant species.[21] Since these numbers represent only one (or a few) study site(s) per island, it is likely that the actual numbers for entire islands are much higher. This chapter focuses on foods that have a dual role as medicines, and within this category, there exist culturally important food plants that are associated with specific islands and/or play a key role there as spices, condiments, or aromatics.

Given the complex socio-cultural history of the Caribbean, and its global ramifications in terms of plant exchanges with several continents, it is also important to consider the area of origin of plant species that are growing in the Caribbean today. Here, I distinguish between plants that are native to the Caribbean and "mobile plants," those that were brought in from elsewhere. "Native," in this chapter, refers to plants that occur in the Caribbean and have evolved there naturally, and thus were not introduced by humans. In contrast, "exotic" species are those that were introduced by humans, including those brought in by Amerindian groups well before the arrival of European colonizers in the fifteenth century.

Within this dichotomy of native and exotic plants, it seems appropriate to designate a special category, perhaps appropriately called "cultural heritage plants," to species that were introduced by Amerindians (Arawaks and Caribs). These species existed in the Caribbean before Columbus set foot in the region in the late fifteenth century. Examples of such plants include soursop (*Annona muricata*), annatto (*Bixa orellana*), papaya (*Carica papaya* L.), and star apple (*Chrysophyllum cainito* L.).[22] Although these species are technically situated somewhere in between the native/exotic dichotomy, their long-standing use renders them more native than exotic from a cultural point of view.

In the following paragraphs, I will further illustrate the complexity of Caribbean biocultural diversity and its mobility by highlighting three plant species that are geographically shared across several Caribbean islands and are popular as foods and medicines on all of these islands. These are: soursop (*Annona muricata*), bitter orange (*Citrus* x *aurantium*), and ginger (*Zingiber officinale*). In contrast to these three widely used species, there exist plants with uses that are restricted in geographic range to one Caribbean island, or to closely neighbouring islands, and of particular cultural importance there. I will illustrate this using the examples of recao (*Eryngium foetidum*) in Puerto Rico, orégano de cocinar (*Lippia micromera*) in the Dominican Republic, and bissy (*Cola acuminata*) in Jamaica. These plant species, and their uses, are still popular in the Caribbean today.

Three Food Medicines That Have Moved Geographically across the Caribbean

The following three plant species show a commonality in their medicinal uses across the Caribbean island region. Of these species, soursop is a well-known sedative to treat nervousness, bitter orange is commonly used for respiratory problems, and ginger is popular for digestive complaints.

For each species, I provide an overview of its scientific name (in bold), followed by some key identifying morphological characteristics, the plant family it belongs to, its mobility (where the plant originates from), and its popular common names by Caribbean language region. I then trace literature data about the plant's use as a food and/or medicine from history to today, within the Caribbean island region, and in the Caribbean diaspora. These ethnobotanical trajectories offer an often-overlooked opportunity to visualize how human-plant relationships either change or remain the same over space and time, and to better understand their cultural context and diverse meanings.

Annona muricata **L.** is a small to medium-sized fruit tree with aromatic leaves that belongs to the plant family Annonaceae and has a native geographic range from South Mexico to Tropical America. Popular common names for this species include soursop, guanábana, and corossol/corossolier in the English-, Spanish-, and French-speaking Caribbean, respectively. *A. muricata* deserves status as a cultural heritage species in the Caribbean, because it already existed there before the arrival of the Spanish.[22] Reportedly, in Dominica, one of the islands in the eastern Caribbean, the Amerindian Caribs used the fruit to induce lactation.[23] In the eighteenth century, Wright wrote in Jamaica about the soursop: "When pulled off before maturity, and boiled, it is served at the table the same as pompions [pumpkins]; and if roasted or baked, is similar to yams. When ripe it is soft, sweet and detersive: hence good in fevers where the mouth is furred."[24]

Today, consumption of soursop fruit, or its juice as a beverage, remains popular across the Caribbean. In Jamaica, soursop leaf tea is also appreciated as a hot beverage in the morning and evening.[25] Medicinally, Jamaicans boil the leaves (and other parts, including branches, bark, and the fruit skin) of soursop and drink this decoction to "settle the nerves"; they eat the fruit for this purpose as well.[26] The sedative effects of soursop are also known in the French-speaking Caribbean. Other Caribbean uses include drinking a tea of the leaves for hypertension in Trinidad and Tobago, and for bronchitis in Martinique. In addition, the leaves are also applied as a bath for skin ailments in Guadeloupe and Martinique. It remains to be studied how prevalent these various uses in the different islands are.

The most popular use of the leaves among Dominicans living in New York City and in the Dominican Republic according to our ethnobotanical survey was to treat upper-respiratory problems, including the flu, common cold, cough, bronchitis, asthma, and chest congestion. To a lesser extent, transnational Dominicans also knew soursop as a sedative.

Citrus x aurantium L. is a fruit tree with thorny branches and aromatic leaves that belongs to the plant family Rutaceae and is a native of China. From China, it was taken to India, then to Egypt and Africa. The Arabs introduced it to Europe in the eleventh century, and the Spanish brought it to the Caribbean in the sixteenth century. The species is known by the common names bitter, sour or Seville orange, naranja agria, and oranger amer/orange sûre/zoranj si in the English-, Spanish-, and French-speaking Caribbean, respectively. In the eighteenth century, Wright wrote in Jamaica: "The whole of the genus [*Citrus*] are natives of Asia, and the southern parts of Europe, from whence they have been carried to and planted in the warmer parts of America and the sugar islands [the Caribbean]. At present, they are so common as to be formed into hedges."

Today, the Caribbean pharmacopoeia compiled by TRAMIL, an inter-Caribbean collaborative network and program of applied research in popular plant medicines in the Caribbean, recommends the fruit juice of bitter orange or alternatively a decoction or infusion of the leaves for digestive health (colic, flatulence, diarrhea), respiratory problems (cough, common cold, flu, fever), conjunctivitis, headache, and intestinal parasites.[27] Jamaicans drink the fruit juice as a refreshing beverage, while the leaves (and occasionally the fruit skin) are boiled and drunk as a regular tea. As a medicinal plant, they roast the fruit in the fire, and then eat the pulp, or prepare the juice of the roasted fruit with honey or salt, to treat fever, the common cold, and cough. A leaf tea can also be prepared for these conditions, whereas the fruit juice also makes a good cooling bath for fever.

It is common practice for Dominicans living in the Dominican Republic and in New York City to use the fruit juice of bitter orange to rinse chicken meat in preparation for cooking. There also exists transnational commonality in the use of the leaves or fruit to treat respiratory problems (sinusitis, flu, the common cold), and for hypertension. In New York City, we observed that the medicinal use of bitter orange to treat diabetes and sinusitis became more important as compared with the Dominican Republic, which shows how plant remedies are mobilized to actively respond to the increasing prevalence of non-communicable "lifestyle" diseases.

Zingiber officinale **Roscoe** is an herb with linear leaves, aromatic underground stems (called rhizomes or root), and lateral shoots, belonging to the plant family Zingiberaceae. The species is probably native to India and not known in a wild state. Its common names are ginger, jengibre, and jenjanm in the English-, Spanish-, and French-speaking Caribbean, respectively. Cultivation of ginger in the Caribbean dates from the Spanish colonization. Historically, on plantations in the French Caribbean, a piece of crushed ginger was applied to wounds, to prevent tetanus.

Today, the Caribbean pharmacopoeia compiled by TRAMIL recommends drinking decoctions of the root for respiratory problems (including asthma, common cold, cough, fever, flu), and digestive health (including vomiting, diarrhea, stomach ache, flatulence, and indigestion). Jamaican ginger has a specific flavour profile with a unique pungency, and is recognized as an exceptional culinary spice.[28] Jamaicans highly value the ginger rhizome as a preservative, and it is a daily kitchen ingredient to prepare meat, bake, and to use in other dishes. As a medicine, Jamaicans use ginger raw or boiled, and drink the juice or decoction for bellyache caused by colic, gas, or "a cold state [of the abdomen]." Other popular uses of ginger in Jamaica consisted of recipes to improve blood circulation, lower blood pressure, alleviate headache, ease a sore throat, or treat the common cold or flu.

In New York City, the use of ginger for stomach problems, including nausea, gas, stomach ache, and indigestion, remains prevalent among Jamaicans. In addition, Jamaicans also use ginger to treat the common cold and arthritis (unpublished results). Among Dominicans in the

Dominican Republic and in New York City, the top three health reasons for using ginger were flu, labour pain, and arthritis.

Three Caribbean Food Medicines That Are Emblematic of Specific Islands

Several food medicines are of particular cultural importance to specific Caribbean communities. Here, I provide three examples: (1) *Eryngium foetidum* as a key seasoning ingredient for Puerto Ricans, and as an important medicinal plant with spiritual uses for Jamaicans; (2) *Lippia micromera* as an essential ingredient of Dominican seasoning and a remedy for gastrointestinal complaints; and (3) *Cola acuminata* as a traditional hot beverage in Jamaica, especially for those living in rural areas, and a popular remedy to counteract any type of poisoning.

Eryngium foetidum L. is an aromatic, prickly, wild (meaning non-cultivated) evergreen herb with leaves that grow in a basal rosette. The species belongs to the Apiaceae, the family of carrots, celery, and parsley. Its native geographic range extends from Mexico to tropical America, including the Caribbean. Common names for *Eryngium foetidum* include fit(s) weed or spirit weed in Jamaica, recao or culantro del monte in Puerto Rico, cilantro ancho or cilantro sabanero in the Dominican Republic, and shado(n) beni (and other spelling variants) in the Eastern Caribbean islands.

This plant is a central ingredient in Puerto Rican sofrito and also a common ingredient in green seasoning in Trinidad.[29] Barrett described it as "a very common seasoning herb occurring in fields and roadsides [in Puerto Rico].[30] The leaves, preferably used fresh, give a flavor much relished by many to stews, soups and even pastries." Sofrito is so entwined with Puerto Rican cooking that it has followed the migration of Puerto Ricans to New York City, where it is readily available in processed form in supermarkets in Latino neighbourhoods, such as the Bronx (figure 14.2).

Historically, as a medicine, Amerindians in the Caribbean considered the plant a "cure all." Today, popular uses in the islands of Dominica and the Dominican Republic include an infusion or decoction of the whole plant (or leaf) for fever, flu, flatulence, and vomiting. Jamaicans consider the plant a medicine and a powerful spiritual remedy, but not a culinary plant, although occasionally in rural Jamaica some people use it in the kitchen as a seasoning herb. Its medicinal use for "fits," the colloquial Jamaican Patois word to describe seizures, consists of boiling the whole plant (or root) and drinking the decoction. Jamaicans also consider it a good medicine for a teething baby. In addition, its spiritual use for good luck and protection dates from long ago. According to legend, Nanny, the famous female Maroon freedom fighter who was living in the Jamaican mountains in the eighteenth century and who successfully defended her people against the British, allegedly used the plant to become invisible.

Lippia micromera **Schauer** is an aromatic shrub that grows up to two metres tall and has small leaves with a strong aroma reminiscent of thyme. The species belongs to the plant family Verbenaceae and is considered native to the Caribbean, Central America, and Guyana, although it is not listed in the reference work "Flowering Plants of Jamaica," and has not been observed in use in Jamaica.[31] Its common names include orégano chiquito, orégano de cocinar, and orégano del país in the Dominican Republic and Puerto Rico, and thym or diten in the French-speaking Caribbean.

The species is emblematic of the cuisine of the Dominican Republic (figure 14.3). In the northeastern Dominican province of Montecristi, goats are renowned for their exquisite taste ("sabor"), because they are fed on a diet of this orégano and their meat becomes naturally "infused" with the plant's aroma. *Lippia micromera* has followed the migration of Dominicans to New York City, and is readily available as a seasoning herb in Dominican eateries and supermarkets in Latino neighbour-hoods such as the Bronx. A variety of Dominican rice and meat dishes and stews are seasoned to suit a cook's taste by adding orégano and salt ("orégano y sal al gusto).[32]

As a medicine, Dominicans living in New York City and the Dominican Republic commonly use the plant for gastrointestinal complaints, such as diarrhea, stomach ache, and "empacho" (a folk illness that can be described as "gastrointestinal blockade").

Cola acuminata **(P.Beauv.) Schott & Endl**. is an evergreen tree with leathery leaves and star-shaped clusters of fruit pods that contain pink seeds covered in a white seed coat. When the fruits are harvested, the seeds are removed from their pods, and the seed coat is stripped away. The species belongs to the Malvaceae and is native to West Africa. It was introduced to Jamaica in the eighteenth century. According to Asprey and Thornton, the plant was "brought to Jamaica from the Guinea Coast [in Africa] and planted out near [the location of] Guanaboa by one Mr. Goffe."[33] Its common names include bissy in Jamaica, (noix de) cola or kola in the French Caribbean, and obie seed in Trinidad and Tobago.

In Jamaica, the pink bissy seeds are grated and boiled to prepare a hot beverage in the morning as a stimulant in lieu of coffee (figure 14.4). The boiling process emits a particular aroma with earthy notes.

Figure 14.4. The naked pink seeds of *Cola acuminata*, known as bissy in Jamaica, and the processed product (tea bags) with the Jamaican flag. Photo by the author.

Coconut milk (or a soy substitute with the brand name Lasco), sugar, a pinch of salt and other flavourings (almond or vanilla extract) are added before drinking. A little grated bissy added to "country chocolate" is allegedly good "to alleviate hunger." Bissy seeds contain more caffeine than coffee, and also theobromine, which counteract fatigue and thirst. Cola seeds were an original flavouring ingredient and source of caffeine in Coca-Cola, but have since been removed from the recipe.

As a medicine, the use of bissy by rural Jamaicans has been recorded for stomach ache and poisoning[33]. During fieldwork, I noticed that Jamaicans who have never used bissy, especially people in urban areas or those who have migrated overseas, will sometimes say it is a poison. In the French Caribbean, the dry seeds of a closely related species, *Cola nitida*, are reputed as a tonic and aphrodisiac. In Martinique, it is considered an emmenagogue that stimulates menstrual flow, and a treatment for fungal infections. In Trinidad, the seeds are used for infertility.[34]

Conclusion

The rich details that are revealed in the ethnobotanical trajectories of aromatic plants, seasonings, spices, and condiments that grow in the Caribbean today show that the region is an evolving hotspot of plant diversity (biodiversity) and traditional plant knowledge (cultural diversity). An ethnobotanical focus on Caribbean cuisines offers a window onto the mobile cultural meanings (continuing as well as changing) and cultural importance of different plants used in these cuisines over space and time. This focus allows a fuller appreciation of how the geographies and complex mobilities of peoples, plants, and traditional knowledge have shaped, and continue to shape, each other.

The interplay between history, culture, and botany in the Caribbean, and the associated processes of fusion, creation, and recreation of traditional knowledge within the region's geographic boundaries, have resulted in a uniquely Caribbean biocultural heritage involving foodways and plants, with a multifunctional food–medicine nexus. These plants, thus, are not merely restricted to food and cuisine, but are functionally mobile elements of a food–medicine continuum that directly links cuisines and health, and even beyond those, to spiritual (and religious) well-being.

A fitting way to characterize this biocultural heritage is through its seemingly opposing elements of commonality and diversity, expressed by the use of either Caribbean-wide or island-specific seasonings, spices, condiments, and aromatic plant species, which reference either a Pan-Caribbean or an island nation-based cultural identity. It is pertinent to make a compelling argument for considering this biocultural heritage an indigenous Caribbean food system, with the denomination "indigenous" meaning "local to the Caribbean." Having evolved over centuries as a system greater than the sum of its multicultural parts and with a uniquely Caribbean "flavour," the words "fusion," "bricolage," or "creole" do not adequately capture the innovation inherent to this food system that has originated within the geographic boundaries of the Caribbean.

Currently, Afrodescendant communities in the Americas are not taking part in the ongoing international dialogue on indigenous food systems because of their forced historical mobility, in spite of what these communities can bring to this dialogue in terms of innovation and uniqueness that is context-dependent and place-specific, based on their traditional knowledge systems. The Food and Agricultural Organization (FAO) of the United Nations has begun analyzing indigenous food systems from several socio-economic regions around the world and convened in November 2018 the first high-level expert seminar on this topic. Afrodescendant communities in the Americas were notably absent from this seminar. This is because their status as communities, and their food systems in the Americas, have yet to be accepted as indigenous. Further research into these intriguingly diverse food systems that are part of a larger complex that includes medicine and religion, together with a deeper reflection on their roots within the Caribbean, will hopefully bring the recognition that these systems merit.

NOTES

1 Eugenio Santiago-Valentín and Javier Francisco-Ortega, "Plant Evolution and Biodiversity in the Caribbean Islands: Perspectives from Molecular Markers," *Botanical Review* 74 (2008): 1–4.
2 Pedro Acevedo-Rodriguez and Mark T. Strong, "Catalogue of Seed Plants of the West Indies," Smithsonian National Museum of Natural History, https://naturalhistory2.si.edu/botany/WestIndies/.
3 "Trans-Atlantic Slave Trade: Essays," Slave Voyages, http://www.slavevoyages.org/assessment/essays.
4 David Picking, Rupika Delgoda, and Ina Vandebroek, "Traditional Knowledge Systems and the Role of Traditional Medicine in Jamaica," *CAB Reviews* 14, no. 45 (2019): 1–13.
5 Arvilla Payne-Jackson and Mervyn C. Alleyne, *Jamaican Folk Medicine: A Source of Healing* (Kingston, Jamaica: University of the West Indies Press, 2004), 143; Michel Laguerre, *Afro-Caribbean Folk Medicine* (Granby, MA: Bergin & Garvey, 1987).
6 Michel Laguerre, *Afro-Caribbean Folk Medicine* (South Hadley, MA: Bergin & Garvey, 1987).
7 Andrea Pieroni et al., "Taming the Pandemic? The Importance of Homemade Plant-Based Foods and Beverages as Community Responses to COVID-19," *Journal of Ethnobiology and Ethnomedicine* 16, no. 1 (2020): 75.
8 Ina Vandebroek and Michael J. Balick, "Globalization and Loss of Plant Knowledge: Challenging the Paradigm," *PLoS One* 7, no. 5 (2012): e37643.
9 Barry W. Higman, "Cookbooks and Caribbean Cultural Identity: An English-Language Hors d'oeuvre," *New West Indian Guide/Nieuwe West-Indische Gids* 72, no. 1/2 (1998): 77–95.
10 Norma Rosas Mayén, "El impacto de África occidental en la cocina de las Américas," *Delaware Review of Latin American Studies* 15, no. 1 (2014): 5.
11 Maria Benedetti, *Hasta los baños te curan! Plantas medicinales, remedios caseros y sanación espiritual en Puerto Rico* (Cayey, Puerto Rico: Verde Luz, 2001), xii.
12 Cruz Miguel Ortiz-Cuadra, *Eating Puerto Rico: A History of Food, Culture, and Identity* (Chapel Hill: University of North Carolina Press, 2013).

13 Carles Roersch, "The Marketing of Medicinal, Aromatic Plants and Essential Oils in the Dominican Republic," *Acta Horticulturae* 503 (1997): 197–219.

14 Royal Botanic Gardens Kew, "Plants of the World Online," http://plantsoftheworldonline.org/.

15 Lidia Marte, "Afro-Diasporic Seasonings: Food Routes and Dominican Place-Making in New York City," *Food, Culture, and Society* 14, no. 2 (2011): 181–204.

16 Hans Sloane, "A voyage to the islands Madera, Barbados, Nieves, S. Christophers and Jamaica with the natural history of the herbs and trees, four-footed beasts, fishes, birds, insects, reptiles, &c. of the last of those islands; to which is prefix'd an intro., wherein is an account of the inhabitants, air, waters, diseases, trade, &c. of that place, with some relations concerning the neighbouring continent, and islands of America" (1707–1725).

17 Paul W. Sherman and Jennifer Billing, "Darwinian Gastronomy: Why We Use Spices," *BioScience* 49, no. 6 (1999): 453–63.

18 Ina Vandebroek and Michael J. Balick, "Lime for Chest Congestion, Bitter Orange for Diabetes: Foods as Medicines in the Dominican Community in New York City," *Economic Botany* 68, no. 2 (2014): 177–89.

19 J. Worth Estes, "The European Reception of the First Drugs from the New World," *Pharmacy in History* 37, no. 1 (1995): 3–23.

20 George B. Griffenhagen, "The Materia Medica of Christopher Columbus," *Pharmacy in History* 34, no. 3 (1992): 131–45.

21 Wendy Torres-Avilez et al., "Medicinal Plant Knowledge in Caribbean Basin: A Comparative Study of Afrocaribbean, Amerindian and Mestizo Communities," *Journal of Ethnobiology and Ethnomedicine* 11, no. 1 (2015).

22 Bernardo Vega, *Las frutas de los Taínos* (Santo Domingo, Dominican Republic: Fundación Cultural, 1996).

23 Jean-Louis Longuefosse, *100 Plantes Medicinales de la Caraibe* (Martinique: Gondwana Editions, 1995).

24 William Wright, "An Account of the Medicinal Plants Growing in Jamaica," *London Medical Journal* 8, no. 3 (1787): 217–95.

25 Ina Vandebroek and David Picking, *Popular Medicinal Plants in Portland and Kingston, Jamaica* (New York: Springer, 2020).

26 G.F. Asprey and Phyllis Thornton, "Medicinal Plants of Jamaica: Part III," *West Indian Medical Journal* 4, no. 2 (1955): 69–82.

27 Lionel Germosén-Robineau, *Farmacopea vegetal Caribeña* (Yucatán, Mexico: Centro de Investigación Científica de Yucatán, 2014).

28 P.A. Vasala, "Ginger," in *Handbook of Herbs and Spices. Vol. 1* (Cambridge, UK: Woodhead Publishing, 2012), 195–206.

29 Amy Forsberg, "Christmas Herbs of Trinidad, Part II," *The Herb Society of America Blog*, 21 December 2020.

30 O.W. Barrett, "The Food Plants of Porto Rico," *Journal of the Department of Agriculture of Porto Rico* 9, no. 2 (1925): 61–208.

31 C.D. Adams, *Flowering Plants of Jamaica* (Mona, Jamaica: University of West Indies, 1972).

32 Estela Aristy, *Cocina criolla Dominicana* (Santo Domingo, República Dominicana: Editorial Letragráfica, 2007).

33 G.F. Asprey and Phyllis Thornton, "Medicinal Plants of Jamaica: Part II," *West Indian Medical Journal* 3, no. 1 (1954): 17–41.

34 Jean-Louis Longuefosse, *Plantes médicinales Caribéennes, Tome 2* (Saint-Denis, Réunion: Orphie, 2012).

CODA
Food Mobilities in the
Time of COVID-19

Locked Down: Writing about Food Mobility while Sheltering in Place

DANIEL E. BENDER AND SIMONE CINOTTO

We began this book in an era of mobility. We ended it in lockdown. It will be published after a worldwide vaccination campaign that promised a return to normality. And, normality, for many, means unfettered mobility.

Even our collaborative process demanded mobility. In July 2019, most of us gathered for a few days at the University of Gastronomic Sciences. During the day, we commented on drafts of chapters, and at the weekend, we visited Turin's famed Porta Palazzo marketplace.[1] Like the world's best food markets, Porto Palazzo has a comforting feel that blends the hustle of buying and selling with the delicious promise of future meals. Centred around market pavilions and cast-iron canopies that date to 1916, the market sprawls into the surrounding neighbourhood in concentric circles of food shops and cafés. On Sunday weekends, the narrow streets are lined with vendors hawking used … everything, from Fascist-era helmets to furniture to ancient bottles of wine meant for decor, not drinking. By mid-summer, dozens of farmers cram the market selling locally grown vegetables, fruit, meat, cheese, and salumi, and even more resellers hawk foods from across Piemonte, Italy, Europe, and beyond. Inside the market pavilions and in surrounding shops, migrant food vendors and local farmers sell ethno-specific foods alongside the iconic tastes of Italian cookery – Parmigiano and halal meats. In the best of times, the marketplace offers emotionally grabbing evidence of how world cuisines could thrive in mobility and offer gastronomic pleasure and livelihoods to generations of migrants, some from across Italy, others from abroad. Crowds highlight the marketplace as a site of liveliness and cultural encounter. A stand selling cheese so local that the vendor simply shrugs when asked the name of a particularly attractive cheese. "Capra (goat)," he says. Next to the cheese stand, a farmer offers locally raised vegetables like bitter melon, botanically rooted in East Asia.

"Taste unifies the myriad means humans have devised to make food so much more than what makes us able to move, to survive as a species," writes Amy Trubek.[2] Porta Palazzo offers more than food for sale; it thrives for its sociability and its mobility. Moreover, in blending tastes of many places – to borrow Trubek's phrasing – the marketplace unites the pleasures of food mobility and its utopian promises. It offers an opportunity to sample, to develop personal identities and mutual engagement through mobility. By March 2020, it threatened public health. We returned to our homes (via the standard routes of international tourism) and at the same time as drafts became chapters, a virus emerged in a marketplace in Wuhan, China, and spread around the world.

COVID-19 hit Italy and Piemonte early and hard. UNISG, where we first gathered, sent its students home, and health officials shuttered Porta Palazzo. When the market reopened in March, health officials reduced the number of vendors. Bustle gave way to social distance. Shopping became more about sustenance than sociability.

Soon, COVID-19 locked us all in place. In the various locales this book addresses – Canada, the United States, Italy, Ethiopia, India, Jamaica, Egypt, South Africa, China – many residents experienced quarantine as food insecurity. "A high level of commodity-export and commodity-import dependence is another factor that makes several countries and regions more vulnerable to external shocks," noted the United Nations Food and Agricultural Organization (FAO) in its 2020 report on "Food Security and Nutrition around the World."[3] COVID-19 was, indeed, a shock. If Porta Palazzo in summer 2019 represented the promises of food mobilities, summer 2020 elsewhere demonstrated the vulnerabilities of a globally mobile culinary infrastructure. By global standards, the lucky few noted only shortages, disruptions, and transformations. Delivery replaced the drive to the supermarket or restaurant. Meal kits replaced menus. Certain vegetables shipped, for example, from Mexico to Canada disappeared for a while from supermarket shelves.

Levels of hunger and malnourishment steadily rose, even in the most prosperous of countries. In countries like the United States, images of endless lines of cars outside food banks will be some of the most enduring signs of the pandemic. As chronic and acute hunger spiked during the COVID-19 crisis, the FAO estimated that about 8.9 per cent of the world's population face undernourishment. Lockdown, virtually the only epidemiological tool to restrict the spread of the virus, threatened food supplies. "Efforts to contain the COVID-19 pandemic have resulted in unprecedented restrictions on mobility," the United Nations World Food Programme (WFP) reported. As a result, an additional

150 million people could face extreme poverty by 2021. In the midst of the crisis, the WFP for the first time published its annual report in coordination with the International Organization for Migration (IOM). That decision recognized one of the key insights of this book: the entwining of world hunger with migration and the mobility of people, commodities, and ingredients. Together, the WFP and the IOM noted the wide-ranging impacts of the restrictions on mobility. Closed borders, suspended airline flights, and cancelled container ship sailings challenged nations and communities dependent on food exports and imports for both livelihoods and diets. Many countries demanded the repatriation of migrant workers, with disastrous consequences. Crucial monetary and food remittances plummeted. The virus-catalyzed health and food crisis had an outsized impact on migrant and refugee populations. They faced anti-pandemic policies without the aid of family supports and social nets. Refugee camps in 2019 were humanitarian tragedies. By 2020, they were medical and food tragedies as well.

A global pandemic in 2020 meant a global food crisis. The mobility of a virus – its ability to infect – affected the mobile food system. Notably, restrictions on travel meant to curtail the spread of the virus, aimed at business and pleasure travel, also swept up migrant food workers. In Germany, noted Sebile Yapici, such restrictions threatened the asparagus crop. "There is no spring in Germany without asparagus," Yapici explains, but that most traditionally German of foods relies "almost entirely on the labour of seasonal workers from Poland and Romania." As the asparagus spears poked above the early spring soil, the government relented and admitted 40,000 migrant workers to preserve national gastronomic traditions.[4]

Amid the closing of national borders, quarantines, lockdowns, and curfews, the virus produced a frenzy of mobility, especially among migrant workers. Many were forced to repatriate to their home countries. Others who had migrated to work in cities struggled to return home as pandemic restrictions proliferated. In India, the government urged people to "stay home" and cancelled trains and blocked road transit. Hundreds of thousands of migrant workers were left with no option but to walk to their home states and villages. "Social distancing was a privilege that the poor could little afford," explained Saumya Gupta, as the migrant and working poor reluctantly joined crowds around food charities. Ironically, Gupta notes, these were the same working poor who before the pandemic fed Delhi, pushing carts with street foods, vegetables, and fruits.[5]

Such cases demand activists and academics to measure the human costs of our mobile culinary infrastructure. In India, against the backdrop of desperate migrations, the far-right government of Narendra Modi and the Bharatiya Janata Party actually pushed a set of laws that strongly favour large multinational corporations in food retail and farming sectors. The laws remove protections for farmers, price supports for consumers, and restrictions against the hoarding of basic food commodities, such as pulses and cereals. Future devastation is heaped upon current crisis. By December, tens of thousands of farmers gathered to protest in Delhi. Many arrived from the neighbouring state of Punjab. As we write this coda in January 2021, women are on the front lines of the protests. "After all, we are the ones who toil the most in the farms and feed the country," said the Punjabi protester Ramandeep Kaur. Nearly 75 per cent of rural Indian women work full time as farmers. In an already stressed agricultural economy, mobility has already been utilized as a family strategy to cope. Men have migrated to cities, for example, in search of construction work while women farm.[6]

The case of Punjabi farmers and the gendered division of protest labour highlights how, on a larger scale, the immobility of this moment will ultimately generate new forms of mobility. "Food insecurity," notes the WFP, "can be a powerful driver for people to move." Yet mobility is a household strategy to confront food insecurity. Poor households often send one or more family members into cities or to other countries. Seasonal migrants send home food and monetary remittances. In 2017, the International Labour Organization reported that there were about 164 million migrant workers globally. The loss of their remittances worldwide represents acute local crises. The price of forced immobility today is greater involuntary mobility in the near future. The WFP and IMO wrote: "While the pandemic mobility restriction measures have initially reduced international migration flows and caused mass returns in certain locations, in the medium to longer-term, reduced food security and well-being caused by COVID-19 could increase people's need to search for livelihoods elsewhere."[7]

Like many countries, Canada rapidly restricted human mobility in the harsh early spring 2020. Farmers raised the alarm: who would pick the crops? Typically, through the Seasonal Agricultural Workers Programme, about 50,000 agricultural workers arrive in Canada for the short growing season. As Canadian Prime Minister Justin Trudeau recognized, "We require support from people from around the world to grow our food, to harvest our food, to get food on Canadians' plates."[8] With the spring harvest approaching (including Canada's asparagus crop), the government relaxed prohibitions against the arrival of migrant farmworkers. Government regulations, in effect, attempted to disentangle different forms of human and food mobility, in the face of viral mobility. Circulations of capital, tourism, migrants, commodities, and labour entwine in a global culinary infrastructure held together by webs of ships, planes, and trucks. A single airplane might carry tourists, refugees, business people, commodities, fresh foods, and migrant workers. In the midst of the pandemic, Canada only wanted migrant farmworkers and food imports. Regulations on travel to China disrupted food imports and exports. Despite a new free trade agreement with the European Union, food and wine imports to Canada slowed to a trickle in the summer amid a port strike in Montreal and the cancellation of most airplane flights. For food migrants who arrived in Canada after the government realized that its initial restrictions would plough under a year's crops, the summer proved deadly. Outbreaks spread quickly in the cramped housing allotted to migrant workers. Migrant workers were not covered under provincial health insurance programs.[9]

Once the crops were picked, some migrants confronted a new reality: their home countries were happy to let them travel, recognizing that families depended on financial remittances throughout the working season. Yet the same countries, fearful of the spread of the virus, were less willing for them to return. As winter set in across the country, migrant workers now faced unpaid, uninsured, and cold winters – the human cost of where our gastronomic dependence on mobility clashes with the medical imperative for lockdown. "We don't have winter clothes or boots. It's chilly in the house. There's wind coming through the doors and windows," said one worker.[10]

Infection is a cost of human mobility. Environmental devastation, including deforestation and human encroachment on wildlife, increases the risk of zoonotic diseases like COVID-19. From a marketplace, the virus spread along the routes of human mobility. As we write, a vaccination campaign is beginning, albeit only in the world's wealthiest countries. The fitful start of the vaccine rollout, with thousands of doses expiring long before they go into arms, demonstrates how vaccine distribution is an acutely challenging version of a food cold chain.

Thus, we conclude this project amid lockdowns. For much of the year, the global and local restriction on human mobility seemed the only defence against the spread of the virus. A lockdown, it becomes clear, is not complete restriction of movement but rather a shift in the burden of mobility onto a few. Like many countries, South Africa imposed strict lockdowns and curfews and, simultaneously, outlined a long list of "essential services," including agricultural, grocery, and delivery workers.[11] In economically disadvantaged parts of cities, in the Global North and South, data harvested from cellphones pinging from towers and public transit ridership, revealed social and economic status largely determines the impact of the lockdown on mobility. Poorer neighbourhoods, especially with a larger percentage of those who identify as non-white and/or Hispanic/Latinx, "are not afforded the same reductions in mobility as their richer counterparts," reports one study of ridership of New York City's subway.[12] *Immobility* in times of lockdown is a question of race, class, and gender privilege.

The privilege of immobility speaks to the paradox of food in the midst of a lockdown. Lockdowns aim to "flatten the curve of infection" by reducing the R rate, that is, the rate at which one infected person infects others. (Over the course of the year, we all became couch-epidemiologists.) That R rate is, in fact, a measure of the contagiousness of a virus alongside human mobility. Flattening the curve through lockdown, thus, demands restricting mobility for some while demanding it of others in order to maintain the circulation of foods. Thus, supermarket workers became essential and, early on, the large Canadian supermarket chains paid employees a small premium for their role in maintaining the flow of food. In the context of the vast inequalities that define our food system, they were also expendable. As soon as case numbers decreased and despite the clear reality that they would rise again in colder months, the chains, led by Loblaws, took away that CA$2 premium – despite record profits. "Retail workers have always been essential," responded Jerry Dias, president of Unifor, the grocery workers' union. "The fact is, the pandemic did not make these workers essential and did not create the inequities in retail, it simply exposed them."[13]

The political declaration of food workers as essential, alongside the visual evidence of omnipresent food deliverers on bicycles and in cars highlights the reality that lockdowns aim to curb the spread of germs while maintaining the mobility of food.

"Mobility has the status of a fact of life," writes geographer Tim Cresswell. "To be human, indeed, to be animal, is to have some kind of capacity for mobility. We experience the world as we move through it." Its very omnipresence, its banality, suggests why mobility is so implicated in the modern politics of rights and citizenship. Mobility, the chapters in this book highlight, is experienced differently by different people and communities; the pandemic highlights how immobility is also experienced differently.[14]

Mobility may be banal; it is also cast as a fundamental freedom. Constitutions, or similar declarations, in countries as diverse as Canada, Mexico, and Ghana, all enshrine the right to mobility. In the years after World War II, liberal discourse associated with the rise of American global power enshrined a new set of rights and freedoms. By 1948, the Universal Declaration of Human Rights enshrined the "freedom of movement" as Article 13. During the Cold War, the unfettered mobility (especially for pleasure) gained status as a measure of national freedom. Yet this liberal (and anti-communist) articulation of mobility as a *human* right ignored the conditions under which humans move – or are forced to move. As well, it imagined movement as a human condition, disconnected from capital, commodities, and – as the last year demonstrated – viruses.

Ending with this brief history of mobility as a right feels especially relevant at a time when immobility emerges as a privilege and when the need to maintain culinary infrastructure places the perils of mobility onto a few. As we begin to imagine food mobilities *after* lockdown through books like this one, we also begin to recognize limits of a rights-based conception of mobility. Some travel for pleasure. Others for survival. Some by choice. Others by force. Our own human movement is just part of a larger circulation of the non-human. Sheltering in place while writing a book about the circulations of food reveals both the pleasures of world cuisines and their inequalities.

We began, thus, in mobility. We wrote in lockdown. And we hope that the ever-present histories that we've documented provide some logics for the mobility to come.

NOTES

1 Rachel Black, *Porta Palazzo: The Anthropology of an Italian Market* (Philadelphia: University of Pennsylvania Press, 2012).
2 Amy B. Trubek, *The Taste of Place: A Cultural Journey into Terroir* (Berkeley: University of California Press, 2008).
3 FAO, IFAD, UNICEF, WFP, WHO, "Food Security and Nutrition around the World in 2020," https://www.fao.org/3/ca9692en/online/ca9692en.html#chapter-1_1.
4 Sebile Yapici, "Labor and the Love of Asparagus: A German Panic," *Gastronomica* 20, no. 3 (2020): 97.
5 Saumya Gupta, "Lockdown Destitution: Delhi, March 2020," *Gastronomica* 20, no. 3 (2020): 68–9.
6 Sheikh Saaliq, "Month on, Women Hold the Fort at India Farmer Protests," *AP News*, 30 December 2020.
7 International Organization for Migration and World Food Programme, *Populations at Risk: Implications of COVID-19 for Hunger, Migration and Displacement* (2020), 13.
8 Shelley Ayres, "Pandemic in the Fields: The Harsh Realities Temporary Foreign Workers Face in Canada," *CTV News*, 26 September 2020.

9 Sara Mojtehedzadeh, "'The Situation Is Very Sad and Painful': Relative of Migrant Worker Who Died of COVID-19 Speaks of 'Overwhelming' Grief," *Toronto Star*, 13 October 2020.

10 Nicholas Keung, "'We Don't Have Winter Clothes or Boots': These Migrant Farm Workers Toiled through the Pandemic, Now They're Stuck in Canada," *Toronto Star*, 9 December 2020.

11 South African Government, "Essential Services: Coronavirus COVID-19," https://www.gov.za/covid-19/companies-and-employees/essential-services-coronavirus-covid-19.

12 Karla Therese L. Sy, Micaela E. Martinez, Benjamin Rader, and Laura F. White, "Socioeconomic Disparities in Subway Use and COVID-19 Outcomes in New York City," *MedRxiv: The Preprint Server for Health Sciences*, 30 May 2020.

13 "Loblaw, Metro End COVID-19 Wage Premium for Front-Line Workers," *Toronto Star*, 11 June 2020.

14 Tim Cresswell, "The Right to Mobility: The Production of Mobility in the Courtroom," *Antipode* 38, no. 4 (2006): 735–54.

Contributors

Daniel E. Bender is the Canada Research Chair in Food and Culture and Professor of Food Studies and History at the University of Toronto. He is an Editorial Collective Member of *Gastronomica: The Journal of Food Studies*. He is the author or editor of many books, including most recently *The Food Adventurers: How Around-the-World Travel Changed the Way We Eat* (2023).

Simone Cinotto teaches Modern History at the University of Gastronomic Sciences in Pollenzo, Italy. He is the author of *Gastrofascismo e Impero: Il cibo nell'Africa Orientale Italiana, 1935–1941* (2022), *The Italian American Table: Food, Family, and Community in New York City* (2013), and *Soft Soil, Black Grapes: The Birth of Italian Winemaking in California* (2012); the editor of *Making Italian America: Consumer Culture and the Production of Ethnic Identities* (2014); and the co-editor of *Global Jewish Foodways: A History* (2018).

Hasia Diner is Professor Emerita in History at New York University and Director of the Goldstein-Goren Center for American Jewish History. A Guggenheim Fellow, she is the author of numerous books on American immigration and American Jewish history, including *Hungering for America: Italian, Irish, and Jewish Foodways in the Age of Migration* (2001).

Sara El-Sayed is Co-Director of the Biomimicry Center and an Assistant Research Professor at the Swette Center for Sustainable Food Systems at Arizona State University. Her research focuses on regenerative food systems in arid regions. She is co-founder of several enterprises in Egypt, including Nawaya and Dayma, and is an active member in the Slow Food movement.

Sarah Elton researches the human–ecosystems–health nexus in the city. She is an Assistant Professor in the Department of Sociology at Toronto Metropolitan University and the author of several books including *Consumed: Food for a Finite Planet* (2013).

Donna R. Gabaccia is Professor Emerita in History at the University of Toronto. She has written on global Italian migrations, gender and migration, American foodways, and interdisciplinarity in migration and mobility studies. She is the general editor of the forthcoming *Cambridge History of Global Migrations*.

Elizabeth Hull is a senior lecturer in anthropology at SOAS, University of London. She is the Chair of the SOAS Food Studies Centre. She is author of *Contingent Citizens: Professional Aspiration in a South African Hospital* (2017). Her current work focuses on food, livelihoods, and the politics of food systems in South Africa.

Carl Ipsen teaches History and Food Studies at Indiana University. He is the author of *Dictating Demography: The Problem of Population in Fascist Italy* (1996); *Italy in the Age of Pinocchio: Children and Danger in the Liberal Era* (2006); and *Fumo: Italy's Love Affair with the Cigarette* (2016).

Sandra C. Mendiola García is Associate Professor of Latin American History at the University of North Texas. She is the author of *Street Democracy: Vendors, Violence, and Public Space in Late Twentieth-Century Mexico* (2017). She is currently writing her second monograph about two silver mining communities in central Mexico where she explores questions of labour, food, and tourism.

Jeffrey M. Pilcher is Professor of History and Food Studies at the University of Toronto. He is the author of *¡Que vivan los tamales! Food and the Making of Mexican Identity* (1998); *Planet Taco: A Global History of Mexican Food* (2012); and *Food in World History*, 3rd ed. (2023). He co-edits the peer-reviewed journal *Global Food History*. His forthcoming book is titled *Hopped Up: How Travel, Trade, and Taste Made Beer a Global Commodity*.

Krishnendu Ray is a Professor of Food Studies at New York University. He is the author of *The Migrant's Table* (2004), *The Ethnic Restaurateur* (2016), and the co-editor of *Curried Cultures: Globalization, Food and South Asia* (2012). He is an Editorial Collective Member of *Gastronomica: The Journal of Food Studies*.

Signe Rousseau teaches critical literacy and professional communication at the University of Cape Town. She is the author of *Food Media: Celebrity Chefs and the Politics of Everyday Interference* (2012) and *Food and Social Media: You Are What You Tweet* (2012). She also co-chairs the Editorial Collective of *Gastronomica: The Journal for Food Studies*.

Jayeeta (Jo) Sharma is an Associate Professor of Food Studies and History at the University of Toronto, and a member of its Culinaria Research Centre. She leads the Feeding City Lab, which conducts interdisciplinary local–global food- and community-engaged sustainability research. She is the author of *Empire's Garden: Assam and the Making of India* (2011). She is currently writing a book on street foods across historical city soundscapes, and another book on how the Himalayas became a space for global encounters around race, indigeneity, commodity capitalism, and cultural circulation.

Christy Spackman is Assistant Professor of Art/Science, jointly appointed in the School for the Future of Innovation in Society and the School of Arts, Media, and Engineering at Arizona State University. Her research focuses on the intersection between technological and regulatory management of the sensory experiences of smelling and tasting. She directs the Sensory Labor(atory), an art/science research collective focused on disrupting everyday sensory experiences.

Ina Vandebroek is an ethnobotanist and a Senior Lecturer at the University of the West Indies, Mona, Jamaica. Her research is co-created with local communities and centred around the interconnectedness of Caribbean biological and cultural diversity. She has authored and co-authored forty-nine articles in peer-reviewed journals, six books and edited volumes, and twelve book chapters. She is editor-in-chief of the journal *Economic Botany*.

Elizabeth Zanoni is Associate Professor of History at Old Dominion University. She is the author of *Migrant Marketplaces: Food and Italians in North and South America* (2018) and co-editor of *The Bloomsbury Handbook of Food and Material Cultures* (2023).

Index

Note: Page numbers in *italics* indicate a map, illustration, or photograph.